# ENGAGING INDIA

# ENGAGING INDIA

## US Strategic Relations
## with the World's Largest Democracy

EDITED BY

Gary K. Bertsch, Seema Gahlaut,
and Anupam Srivastava

Routledge ✦ New York ✦ London

Published in 1999 by
Routledge
29 West 35th Street
New York, NY 10001

Published in Great Britain by
Routledge
11 New Fetter Lane
London EC4P 4EE

LIBRARY OF CONGRESS CATALOGING-IN-PUBLICATION DATA
Engaging India : U.S. strategic relations with the world's largest democracy / edited by Gary K. Bertsch, Seema Gahlaut, and Anupam Srivastava.
    p.    cm.
Includes bibliographical references.
    ISBN 0-415-92282-8
    ISBN 0-415-92283-6 (pbk.)
    1. United States—Relations—India. 2. India—Relations—United States. 3. India—Strategic aspects. 4. National security—United States. 5. National security—India. I. Bertsch, Gary K. II. Gahlaut, Seema. III. Srivastava, Anupam.
    E183.8.I4 E54 1999
    327.73054—dc21                                    99-20771
                                                       CIP

*Interior designed by Cynthia Dunne.*

# Contents

**PART III: THE REGIONAL CONTEXT**

**CONCLUSION: SUMMARIZING THE NEXT STEPS**

# List of Acronyms

| | |
|---|---|
| AAM | air-to-air missiles |
| ACW | advanced conventional weapons |
| AEC | Atomic Energy Commission |
| AG | Australia Group |
| APEC | Asia-Pacific Economic Cooperation |
| ARF | Asian Regional Forum |
| ASEAN | Association of South East Asian Nations |
| AWACS | Airborne Warning and Control System |
| BJP | Bharatiya Janata Party |
| BTWC | Biological and Toxic Weapons Convention |
| CAVCTS | Combined Acceleration Vibration Climatic Test System |
| CANDU | Canadian Deuterium Uranium Reactor |
| CBM | confidence-building measure |
| CD | Conference on Disarmament |
| CENTO | Central Treaty Organization |
| CEP | Circular Error Probable |
| CIA | Central Intelligence Agency |
| COCOM | Coordinating Committee for Multilateral Export Controls |
| CTBT | Comprehensive Test Ban Treaty |
| CWC | Chemical Weapons Convention |
| DAE | Department of Atomic Energy (India) |
| DOS | Department of State |
| DST | Department of Science and Technology |
| DPG | Defense Policy Group |
| DRDO | Defense Research and Development Organization |
| EAA | Export Administration Act (US) |
| EAR | Export Administration Regulations (US) |
| EAW | early airborne warning |
| ESG | Executive Steering Group |
| EW | electronic warfare |
| FDI | Foreign Direct Investment |
| FMCT | Fissile Material Cut-off Treaty |
| GOI | Government of India |
| GOSMIA | General Security of Military Information Agreement |
| HMG | heavy military guns |
| HAL | Hindustan Aeronautics Limited |
| IAEA | International Atomic Energy Association |
| IAF | Indian Air Force |

| | |
|---|---|
| ICIA | Import Certificate Issuing Authorities (India) |
| IMF | International Monetary Fund |
| JSC | Joint Steering Committee |
| JTG | Joint Technology Group |
| JWG | Joint Working Group |
| LAC | line of actual control |
| LCA | light combat aircraft |
| LIC | low-intensity conflict |
| LICO | low-intensity conflict operations |
| MOU | memorandum of understanding |
| MTCR | Missile Technology Control Regime |
| NMD | National Missile Defense (US) |
| NNPA | Nuclear Non-Proliferation Act (US) |
| NPT | Nuclear Non-proliferation Treaty |
| NSC | National Security Council |
| NSG | Nuclear Suppliers Group |
| ODCI | Office of Defense Cooperation in India |
| OECD | Organization for Economic Cooperation & Development |
| OPCW | Organization on the Prohibition of Chemical Weapons |
| OSCE | Organization for Security and Cooperation in Europe |
| PGM | precision guided munitions |
| PNE | peaceful nuclear explosion |
| PTA | pilotless target aircraft |
| SAARC | South Asian Association for Regional Cooperation |
| SEATO | South East Asian Treaty Organization |
| SNEP | subterranean nuclear explosion project |
| START | Strategic Arms Reduction Treaty |
| UAV | unmanned aerial vehicle |
| UNGA | United Nations General Assembly |
| WA | Wassenaar Arrangement |
| WEU | West European Union |
| WMD | weapons of mass destruction |

# Foreword

## Harry Barnes

The reverberations of the May 1998 nuclear tests in South Asia were felt around the globe, and the initial reaction was a mix of condemnation and consternation. Since then, though, interest has been revived in rejuvenating the moribund global nuclear disarmament, and a sustained effort undertaken by the United States and India to address a range of serious issues.

Though it is common knowledge, it is worth recalling for America that India is home to nearly a billion people in one of the poorest regions of the world, with bewildering variety along ethnic, religious, linguistic and cultural lines. Yet it has managed to weave an intricate seam of unity through its diverse national milieu to create an ornate socio-political fabric that is as elusive to define as it is captivating to observe. In the half century since this ancient civilization was emancipated from British colonial occupation, its vibrant polity has emerged and sustained itself as the world's largest democracy. In the current decade, significant efforts have been made to integrate the country into the global economic matrix. Increasingly, this new sense of pragmatism that pervades its economic sector animates the national security discourse as well. As this modern India searches for its changing place in the community of nations, it presents unique challenges as well as opportunities to the world's greatest democracy, the United States.

The history of US-Indian relations has always been at least lively. The two countries share the over-arching vision of a world order that is free from the scourge of weapons of mass destruction and their means of delivery. Their differences stem from their divergent approaches toward the common goal of comprehensive global disarmament. The United States perceives arms control and non-proliferation as still the most reliable paving stones in the path toward disarmament. India, on the other hand, contends the leading possessors of the weapons of mass destruction need to demonstrate a greater commitment toward rapid realization of disarmament. From the Indian standpoint then, technology control regimes and initiatives are seen as attempts by the five nuclear powers to safeguard and perpetuate their advantage.

As one of the leaders of the developing world, particularly under the aegis of the Non-Aligned Movement, India also long spearheaded the demand to redress the inequities obtaining along the North-South axis. With its tradition of non-violence, it consistently argued for peaceful settlement of international disputes. Yet, it has fiercely defended its right to maintain the option to produce and deploy nuclear weapons and their means of delivery for national security purposes. The search for this "golden mean," between the vision of an eventual peaceful world and possession of the wherewithal to defend itself in the interim, has troubled its conscience for decades. Most recently, domestic opinion began to polarize with the debate leading up to the NPT Review and Extension Conference of March 1995. The situation crystallized further during the CTBT debate in the summer of 1996 even though India had been the earliest champion of the idea. And matters finally came to a head in May 1998 when India conducted five nuclear tests, ending its self-imposed moratorium on further testing after the lone test of May 1974.

The new strategic alignments taking shape at the end of the Cold War are of particular significance to the United States. As the sole surviving superpower, it has the onus of setting an example in leading the world into the next millennium. The long Cold War, despite the bitter ideological struggle, and the attendant risks of total annihilation from the vast arsenals of war, had still become a familiar abode for the policy makers and the analysts. The brave new world, whose contours are still at an inchoate stage, is far more challenging to contend with because it is so much more complex. To paraphrase the title of John Milton's "Paradise Lost," the searchers for the new world order are venturing into the future with only a "Paradigm Lost."

The whole concept of national security is undergoing a metamorphosis in many countries. State sovereignty over national resources, both human and physical, is being undercut by the exponential growth in the complexity and fungibility of *haute finance* and advanced technology. The trade and financial malaise that gripped one economy after another in East and South East Asia, has invaded Russia, Latin America, and seems even to threaten the shores of the United States. Technological growth and diffusion, sustained at a dizzying pace, offer an ever larger pool of countries more choices of using technology as an instrument of prosperity or a weapon of war. State autonomy over national decision-making is being challenged by the very agents of social change that the state helped nurture.

In a sense, the Indian (and Pakistani) nuclear tests have imparted a fresh urgency to the agenda of nuclear disarmament. The Conference on Disarmament in Geneva is seized of the urgency to conclude a Fissile Material Cut-off Treaty, amid growing demands for an expeditious ratification of the CTBT. The United States, for its part, is actively engaged in seeking a comprehensive resolution of the South Asian imbroglio. While the results of the deliberations will probably be slow to materialize, it is fairly certain that "imposed" solutions will not endure. At the same time, given the pragmatism that recent Indian governments appear willing to bring to the negotiating table, patient diplomacy might usher an era of strategic stability and peace to the conflict-prone region.

In this context, the role of the larger security community in each country becomes increasingly important. Whatever the specifics of the framework that American and Indian policy makers agree to, its implementation would be contingent upon generating and sustaining national consensus on the relevant issue areas. Scholars and analysts in the Track II domain need to become synergistic partners of the official dialogue. The contributors to this volume, under the able stewardship of Professor Gary Bertsch at the University of Georgia, perform precisely such a function. The chapters in this book, albeit informed of the historical context, are forward-looking. They provide practical recommendations that address specific policy issues of the kind mentioned above. The analyses reflect the larger strategic landscape of Asia, with specific chapters discussing the influence of Russia, China and Pakistan on the process.

The University of Georgia's Center for International Trade and Security has been a pioneer in research on non-proliferation export controls. It lends this expertise to evaluate Indian export controls. Individual chapters exploring the possibilities of Indo-US cooperation in the areas of chemical and biological weapons, missiles and space technology, as well as advanced conventional weapons, are of particular relevance.

As a former official of the US government with service in the subcontinent, I have long been interested in efforts to optimize and enhance Indo-US cooperation across a range of issues. I continue to believe in the substantial benefits that could come from a persistent deepening and widening of this cooperation. I believe this book to be a valuable contribution to such efforts and recommend it to a wide readership in both countries.

**Harry Barnes** is the former US Ambassador to India (1981-85). He is currently Director of the Program in Conflict Resolution and Chair of the Human Rights Committee at the Carter Center in Atlanta, Georgia.

# Indo-US Strategic Dialogue:
## Rethinking the Agenda

### Gary Bertsch

Why are the world's two largest democracies—the United States and India—so often at odds? The United States has been the leader of the free world since the end of World War II. Throughout the same period, India has maintained a democratic political system despite myriad economic challenges and an adverse regional security environment. These two democracies have never fought each other. Yet they have not been able to work closely together to address a number of important, common concerns that would serve their joint and individual interests. The world of international politics is filled with ironies. The past and present state of Indo-US relations may be one of the most ironical.

## LEARNING FROM THE PAST

One might have expected the United States to embrace the new and independent India finally freed from its colonial status in the 1940s. It might have been so had it not been for President Eisenhower's embrace of Pakistan in 1954, the US dispatch of a carrier group to the region in 1971, and the debilitating distractions of the Cold War, where the driving force of American policy was anti-Communism. Because of India's emphasis on nonalignment and good relations with the Soviet Union, the United States was suspicious of India and insensitive to its distrust of American motives and power.

When the Cold War ended in the 1990s, the two largest democracies had the opportunity to start anew. The United States saw India as a big emerging market. It was, in fact, both India's largest foreign investor and its largest trading partner. In 1991 the United States expanded its military contacts with India. The United States was also eager to bring Russia into the democratic fold. How could it frown upon India's good relations with the new democratizing forces in Russia? With the Cold War over, there were a number of developments and forces pushing the United States and India to cooperate. While some diverging interests continued to trouble the Indo-US relationship, one heard more and more references to "cooperative engagement," "strategic cooperation," and other promising developments coming out of both Washington and New Delhi in the 1990s. By early 1998 it appeared that the two largest democracies were indeed starting over and were prepared to construct a new set of closer, more cooperative relations.

In May 1998 this mutual intent received a major challenge. On May 11 India conducted three subterranean nuclear explosions at the Pokharan test site. On May 13 it conducted two more tests nearby. The official Indian statement said that "the tests . . . provided a valuable database for the design of nuclear weapons of different yields for different applications and different delivery systems."

The US response was harsh. The US Nuclear Proliferation Prevention Act of 1994 automatically invoked a number and variety of punitive responses. The Clinton administration spearheaded a multilateral effort to impose a range of costly sanctions against India. Indo-US relations suffered another downturn.

## LOOKING TO THE FUTURE

Will the missed opportunities and difficult relations between India and the United States reach beyond the Cold War and on into the new millennium? Or will new realities in the twenty-first century and the enlightened self-interests of the world's largest democracies propel these important states into a new, more beneficial state of strategic dialogue and relations?

This book addresses some of the critical issues likely to influence future Indo-US strategic relations. By "strategic relations," we refer to Indo-US cooperation on the fundamental issues of war and peace. Each of the chapters in the book has attempted to redefine the issues, reframe the questions, and assess the costs and benefits of alternative policy choices for each of the two countries in the coming decade.

The first section provides overviews on the perspectives of India and the United States on non-proliferation, regional security and stability in Asia, and the regional dynamics in South Asia that are bound to influence Indo-US relations in the future. P. R. Chari, Raja Mohan, and Virginia Foran address some of the ways in which the two countries can adopt a constructive problem-solving approach and attempt to reformulate their respective security concerns.

P. R. Chari calls attention to the criticality of the non-proliferation issue in this relationship. He notes that although the present is mired in controversy, important opportunities exist for Indo-US nuclear cooperation. These would include exchange of information to enhance the protection of fissile materials and counter nuclear smuggling, processes for placing fissile materials and nuclear facilities under international safeguards, cooperation on nuclear safety and waste disposal, and sustained dialogue on the technological and strategic implications of eliminating nuclear weapons.

In view of the fact that India and the United States are signatories to chemical and biological weapons conventions and have cooperated in the establishment and administration of the obligations assumed thereunder, Chari believes constructive engagement could carry over into the nuclear and missile areas as well. In his opinion, the United States and India have much to gain by engaging in broad-ranging dialogue about their respective strategic outlooks relating to the regional theater in the twenty-first century.

C. Raja Mohan examines common Indo-US concerns and interests within the larger strategic landscape of Central Asia, the Caucasus, and southern Asia. He submits that in the post–Cold War period, India's new "look east" policy presents fresh opportunities to the United States for energy cooperation, involving Bangladesh and Nepal. Further, improved relations with India could complement the overall US strategy of managing China's role in the emerging Asian balance of power.

Raja Mohan contends that both the United States and India have important stakes in maintaining the politico-economic viability of Pakistan. A "failed" Pakistan could seriously complicate the delicate regional stability in western Asia and the Caucasus, in addition to fueling Islamic fundamentalism. Now that the nuclear tests have ended the ambiguity surrounding Indo-Pak nuclear policies, the United States should move forward purposefully to assist them in institutionalizing confidence-building measures (CBMs) and force stability. Overall, Raja Mohan contends that the United States should take advantage of India's aspirations and capabilities to play a larger role in regional affairs, and build a qualitatively superior relationship.

Virginia Foran considers the utility of sanctions and incentives in determining the direction and scope of Indo-US cooperation. A historical examination of US sanctions reveals their limited effectiveness in modifying policies in target countries. This has been particularly true in the case of India, which has resolutely defended its sovereign right to pursue policies to meet national-security threats. In the post–Cold War period, as India seeks to enhance its role in regional and global affairs, access to advanced technology and capital becomes paramount. After the recent nuclear tests, both India and the US are engaged in efforts to rethink the bases of their strategic interaction. Foran contends that regardless of the viability of US non-proliferation objectives in South Asia, a finely calibrated approach of incentives and engagement has better prospects of proving successful.

The second section attempts to deal head on with some of the thorniest issues in Indo-US relations. Although there is much more to Indo-US relations than security and non-proliferation issues, progress on this front is necessary for the future of the broader strategic relationship. The current trends in global technology diffusion indicate that both sides will have to balance their national security and developmental objectives with the urgent need to cooperate and collaborate in international peace and development efforts. Nuclear safety and energy, space, defense, chemical and biological weapons, and export controls are issues that will require pragmatic reappraisal from both sides, and will provide the nuts and bolts of any future bilateral cooperation.

Anupam Srivastava addresses the issues surrounding missile control and space cooperation, and examines prospects for collaboration in both the civilian and military sectors. His analysis indicates that the productive linkages between India's civilian space and military missile programs make it an aerospace power to be reckoned with in the twenty-first century. The deployment of a nuclear-capable Prithvi, further improvements in the range and payload of Agni, and the development of ICBM capability will be the issues that will cause problems in any efforts toward Indo-US cooperation in space technology.

Srivastava considers the costs and benefits confronting India as it assesses international missile non-proliferation efforts, and the costs and benefits to the United States and the Missile Technology Control Regime (MTCR) as they seek to engage India. He draws upon this analysis to propose a number of recommendations to India and the United States in the civilian and military sectors. These recommendations lay the groundwork for Indo-US engagement, and economic and security cooperation, in the space and missile issue area.

Seema Gahlaut examines the debate on Indo-US nuclear issues. In the past, the political rhetoric hardened positions on both sides. However, Gahlaut finds the present period ripe for initiating nonrhetorical public dialogue in both countries, where, with the end of the Cold War, some new factors deserve consideration in the policy environment. These include the changing priorities of the postindependence generation in India, the recent successes of economic liberalization in India, and the increasing emphasis on nuclear energy, not only in India, but throughout Asia.

Gahlaut suggests a two-step model of interaction for enhancing future cooperation. Step one involves measures to overcome past and present misperceptions. She suggests national dialogues, the dissemination of detailed and positive information about each other, and bilateral dialogue on outstanding issues of concern. Step two involves changes in national legislation to allow limited nuclear cooperation between the countries. Using examples of US bilateral cooperation with China, Russia, and North Korea, Gahlaut calls attention to the value of incremental cooperation and incentives to engender institutional trust and foster habits of cooperation.

Aabha Dixit examines the current status of Indo-US cooperation on chemical and biological weapons non-proliferation. India's membership in the Chemical Weapons Convention (CWC) and active participation in the Organization for the Prohibition of Chemical Weapons (OPCW) indicate its willingness to cooperate in non-discriminatory international agreements. She believes that this will present welcome opportunities for India and the United States to work together in a vital area of non-proliferation, and thus generate familiarity, transparency, and understanding about each other's institutional attitudes and processes.

The May 1998 Indian nuclear tests have brought a new sense of realism to Indo-US strategic relations. This, in Dixit's opinion, creates a basis for a stronger, more vibrant, and meaningful strategic dialogue. In the new environment, she argues, Indian negotiators will pay less attention to the moralistic dimension and focus more on the trade-offs that directly affect Indian security interests.

Jyotika Saksena and Suzette Grillot apply the theoretical framework of reciprocity as a means for determining and achieving cooperation among nations. They use the framework to determine how and why defense cooperation might develop between India and the United States. In the pre-1980 period, concerns about ulterior motives, relative gains, and related issues constrained positive developments in Indo-US defense cooperation. Using the 1984 memorandum of understanding (MOU) and the Lindstrom Report as examples, Saksena and Grillot suggest that the 1980s witnessed a growing desire on both sides to improve defense relations. India wanted it in order to reduce its dependence on the Soviet Union and diversify its source of weapons supply. The United States wanted it to secure a share of the Indian weapons market and to reduce Soviet influence in the region.

Although Indo-US relations confronted numerous challenges in the 1990s (including missile and nuclear testing by India), Saksena and Grillot discern a pattern of cooperation that became more sequential than simultaneous (i.e., diffuse rather than specific). Interaction occurred more regularly, creating a foundation of trust upon which future cooperation and exchange could be built. The authors, therefore, recommend that specific, reciprocal exchange based on self-interest may generate trust as a result of recurrent and expanding exchange in Indo-US defense relations.

Richard Cupitt and Seema Gahlaut examine US and Indian perspectives and behavior on a set of non-proliferation export control issues. The past has shown far more debate and disagreement than cooperation between the two countries on these issues. The United States has placed numerous Indian organizations on its list of proliferation concerns. India has been a vocal opponent of the four major US-led non-proliferation export control arrangements.

Cupitt and Gahlaut explore the nature of bilateral interaction on export controls and consider what India and the United States might do to improve cooperation in the future. They suggest that India should make its policy regarding non-proliferation more explicit and its export control policy more transparent, and it should reduce its reluctance to engage with US export control officials. The United States can certainly aid this process by increasing security and economic incentives for Indian cooperation on non-proliferation export control. For the rest, the authors believe that as India's commitment to economic liberalization becomes firmer, openness to transnational networks will become inevitable.

The third section of the book highlights how the changing power relationships in Asia will provide both opportunities and constraints for any serious attempts at Indo-US engagement. Third parties such as China, Russia, and Pakistan will remain important factors that would require a delicate balancing act by both India and the United States.

Kanti Bajpai argues that with the certainties of the Cold War gone, neither the Indians nor the Americans know quite how to approach and deal with each other. Bajpai argues that common geopolitical, economic, and sociopolitical interests are expanding the likelihood of Indo-US cooperation. Non-proliferation is a common goal, and the two countries have an interest in narrowing their differences and expanding their cooperation toward this end. The key difficulties are likely to result from the powerful domestic politics of these large democracies, as well as their relationships to third parties (e.g., China, Pakistan, and Russia).

Amitabh Mattoo examines the current and the future significance of the "China factor" in Indo-US cooperation. He submits that elements within the Chinese strategic culture could make Beijing more assertive in its foreign and economic policies once it perceives the international balance of power to have shifted in its favor. On the other hand, China's recent entry into several multilateral institutions prompts a more benign projection of its foreign-policy trajectory. Mattoo proposes that efforts should be made to increase China's stake in the stability of the international system. This would effectively curtail its latitude for policy adventurism, regardless of which elements of its strategic culture were more powerful within the domestic policy formulation.

Milind Thakar addresses the complex and difficult questions regarding the "Pakistan factor" in the Indo-US relationship. Territorial disputes and ideological and religious differences are among the troublesome issues locking India and Pakistan in one of the most acrimonious relationships of the contemporary period. US relations with either India or Pakistan continue to raise concern and questions for the other. Certainly, US engagement with India will have repercussions that have to be understood and addressed in the coming millennium. Thakar's chapter examines possible Pakistani responses to increased Indo-US dialogue in light of the historical record.

Russia is likely to remain a key variable in any Indo-US strategic equation in the future. The Soviet support for anti-colonialist aspirations of the Indian people, and its good relations with India throughout the Cold War, provide the basis for an Indo-Russian relationship of considerable trust, respect, and mutual self-interest. Igor Khripunov and Anupam Srivastava examine both constant and changing elements of Indo-Russian relations. They conclude that this relationship would not only affect the future of Indo-US strategic cooperation, but also critically influence the Asian balance of power in the foreseeable future.

## THE UNIVERSITY OF GEORGIA PROJECT

The Center for International Trade and Security at the University of Georgia has undertaken a project to explore Indo-US strategic relations as we move into the twenty-first century. The project addresses critical issues of war and peace, including political, military, and economic cooperation between the world's largest democracies. The May 1998 nuclear tests by India and Pakistan brought many of these issues into sharper focus. The tests once again strained US relations with both India and Pakistan. The differing responses to the tests in India, Pakistan, and the United

States, both public and official, indicate that the public and the elite in the three countries appear to have very different perspectives on what the tests represent for regional and international security. This calls attention to the need for more research and better dissemination of information on these issues.

We are, therefore, interested in understanding and exploring the common and divergent ground between the United States and India on economic, military, and technology transfer issues. What domestic factors influence their foreign and security policies? What is the level of understanding and appreciation in each country of the interplay of these factors in the other country? What will be the future role of nuclear weapons and missiles in their respective security policies? How do they perceive the proliferation of nuclear, chemical, biological, and conventional weapons? What are their policies on acquiring and controlling the technologies and materials related to weapons of mass destruction? What are their policies relating to strategic trade and transfer of dual-use advanced technology? These are among the major issues being considered by the University of Georgia project.

This book is a result of a year-long project on Indo-US cooperation that culminated in a workshop held at the University of Georgia in spring 1998. The project was guided by the conviction that in order to develop solutions to these challenges, better information, new thinking, and expanded dialogue are needed. We continue to believe that feasible solutions to the current imbroglio will be most likely to emerge from sustained, policy-relevant dialogue. In that spirit, we hope that this book will facilitate further dialogue and contribute to solutions that can help promote better relations between the United States and India.

Finally, we take this opportunity to thank the Rockefeller Foundation, the US Institute of Peace, and the University of Georgia for their assistance in making this project and book possible.

# Part I

---

## BROAD STROKES
## ON THE STRATEGIC CANVAS

---

# 1

# Indo-US Relations:
# Non-proliferation Concerns

## P. R. Chari

S everal hackneyed phrases have described the essence of Indo-US relations. First, it exhibits a roller-coaster quality marked by alternating periods of normalcy and hostility. The high-water mark in this relationship was reached when the United States pledged arms aid to India after the Sino-Indian border conflict in 1962; this led to "an unparalleled deepening of the Indo-US involvement." [1] The nadir was reached in 1971 when a USS Enterprise–led task force entered the Bay of Bengal during the Indo-Pak conflict. This demonstration of nuclear gunboat diplomacy still rankles in India.

Second, the United States treats Indo-Pak relations as a zero-sum game. Pakistan served American geostrategic objectives faithfully during the Cold War. It was the conduit to arm, train, and finance the mujahideen fighting the Soviets in Afghanistan. In marked contrast, India deepened its relations with the Soviet Union. Its nonaligned foreign policy enabled India to ensure its security with the political and military support of the Soviet Union whilst nourishing Indo-US link-ages in the economic, cultural, and educational spheres. Simultaneously, India dei-fied self-reliance and self-sufficiency in high-technology spheres such as atomic energy, space, and defense as concomitants of its nonaligned foreign policy.

Third, Indo-US relations reveal a pattern of tensions and hostilities despite the two countries' common pursuit of democratic values such as freedom of speech, independence of the judiciary, and so on. "The root cause can be found in the clash over national security issues of major importance to each country. For India, the principal stumbling block has been the US-Pakistan relationship. . . . For the United

3

States, the decisive problem has been India's attitude towards the Soviet Union." [2] A failure to understand each other's political, economic, and geostrategic compulsions has deepened these asymmetries.

Fourth, non-proliferation concerns are most relevant to Indo-US relations. Whether they should be addressed head on or as part of a broader Indo-US engagement can be endlessly debated. But selectivity marks these US concerns. It has treated Pakistan's single-minded search for nuclear and missile technology, chiefly from China, with great circumspection, in contrast to its harsh attitude toward India. This reflects a basic tension between the United States' commitment to global non-proliferation objectives and pursuit of regional foreign policy goals. The empirical evidence suggests that US foreign-policy interests ultimately prevail. There was some intimation earlier that American concerns with non-proliferation would be interspersed with other security priorities. For instance, President Clinton declared on September 27, 1993, before the UN General Assembly (UNGA), "I have made non-proliferation [of weapons of mass destruction (WMD)] one of our nation's highest priorities. We intend to weave it more deeply into the fabric of our relationships with the world's nations and institutions. We seek to build a world of increasing pressure for non-proliferation." In an address to the UNGA in 1995 Clinton listed the major challenges confronting the international system as arising from terrorism, drug trafficking, organized crime, and the proliferation of WMD.[3] And two years later, the First Committee of the UNGA was informed by the director of the US Arms Control and Disarmament Agency that "Security is an increasingly broad concept, involving not only defense but such issues as economics and the environment, science and information, combating drugs and terrorism, and education and human rights. But arms control, non-proliferation and disarmament remain vital components." [4] Therefore, the US preoccupation with WMD proliferation continues, and it has become more acute after the nuclear tests conducted by India and Pakistan in May 1998.

The end of the Cold War has radically transformed the contours of Indo-US relations. India has lost its chief strategic ally following the Soviet Union's disintegration, though Indo-Russian military cooperation continues for unavoidable reasons. US interests in Pakistan have waned following the Soviet withdrawal from Afghanistan and the United States' realization that India's prominent position in the Subcontinent can no longer be ignored. Indeed, the Council on Foreign Relations proposed a "closer strategic relationship with India, which has the potential to emerge as a full-fledged major power," while endorsing the American need to expand relations with both India and Pakistan.[5]

Indo-US non-proliferation interactions need to be examined against a historical backdrop to uncover their underlying tensions. Clearly, India's perceptions of nuclear threat arise from Pakistan. What about China? What about internal factors? These have gained salience after the Bharatiya Janata Party (BJP) came to power in 1998 in New Delhi, announced its revisionist nuclear agenda, and went ahead with its nuclear tests. What are India's future nuclear choices now? What are the areas of Indo-US convergence and cooperation still possible? These issues are discussed in this chapter.

## THE HISTORICAL LEGACY

Indo-US relations in the non-proliferation area can be divided into five phases.

• A first phase began in October 1964 with India's countermeasures to deal with China's first nuclear test and continued till the first Pokharan test in May 1974.

• The second phase coincides with the US "technology denials" policy initiated against India, symbolized by parsimoniously doling out and ultimately stopping the supply of low-enriched uranium fuel to the Tarapur atomic power plant in 1980.

• The third phase, lasting through the eighties, is distinguished by Pakistan's steady progress toward developing nuclear capabilities. India's missile program also developed rapidly. The United States was unable to slow or halt these countries' march toward the acquisition of larger nuclear and missile capabilities.

• The fourth phase corresponds to the first Clinton administration's considerable diplomatic activism armed at reversing the nuclear programs of India and Pakistan.

• A fifth phase started with the second Clinton administration's objective to freeze the nuclear programs of the two South Asian adversaries. This policy has failed dramatically, as evidenced by the 1998 nuclear tests conducted by India and Pakistan. Indo-US relations are currently in a conflictual state, but their future evolution can be speculated upon in the context of India's perceptions of nuclear threat and the policy choices available to it.

Brief details are provided below of Indo-US contentions during these five phases.

**First Phase**
China's first nuclear test sparked off an intense public debate about whether India should go nuclear. The issue was informed by India's humiliating defeat in the Sino-Indian border conflict of 1962. A two-pronged strategy was then pursued, in which India sought multilateral guarantees from the nuclear powers and/or a joint American-Soviet guarantee, and launched a subterranean nuclear explosion project (SNEP) in 1965; it was the technological precursor of the Pokharan device. Later, India refused to enter the Nuclear Non-proliferation Treaty (NPT) on several grounds that need not detain us, but this ensured that India's nuclear option was preserved.

Two technical developments were significant here. First, India established an unsafeguarded plutonium-reprocessing plant in Trombay in 1964. It had earlier established an autonomously controlled 40-megawatt research reactor (Cirus). With this, India acquired the technical ability to manufacture plutonium for nuclear explosives. Second, the Purnima research reactor attained criticality in May 1972. It provided the basic data on neutron multiplication factors, effectiveness of reflectors, critical mass assembly, and so on for manufacturing the Pokharan device.[6] A strategic rationale for the nuclear test in 1974 was provided by the developments following the civil war in East Bengal in 1971. The strategic relationship developing between Pakistan, China, and the United States induced India to actively consider the nuclear option.

Although India's technical capabilities were known, the explosion itself came as a surprise to the United States. It led to an angry reaction from the American (largely Democratic) antinuclear lobby; they were especially irked by India's designation of the test as being for peaceful purposes. But the bitterest criticism came from the liberal Democrats (traditionally supporters of India) who "turned their wrath on New Delhi for breaching the nuclear barrier."[7] This negative image informed the second phase of Indo-US non-proliferation relations.

### Second Phase

The nuclear test was not an infraction of any international treaties or agreements reached by India for supply of the Cirus research reactor from Canada or the heavy water used therein from the United States, since the explosion was meant for "peaceful purposes." Indeed, Indira Gandhi had informed the Indian Parliament earlier that "the Atomic Energy Commission is studying conditions under which peaceful nuclear explosions carried out underground could be of economic benefit to India without causing environmental hazards."[8] Despite this position, the conviction in the United States and international community was that India had violated the spirit of its international agreements. The punitive measures taken thereafter by external suppliers included:

- suspension, followed by cancellation, of Canadian assistance for the Rajasthan atomic power plants

- opposition to the supply of heavy water to the Rajasthan reactors by the Soviet Union under "perpetuity" and "pursuit" clauses

- cessation of enriched uranium supplies by France for start-up of the experimental fast breeder reactor in Kalpakkam

- reduction of the amount of enriched uranium fuel supplied by the United States for the Tarapur atomic power plants despite its contractual obligation to ensure their uninterrupted supply

The Pokharan test also inspired the passage in the United States of the Nuclear Non-Proliferation Act (NNPA) in 1978 to prevent the transfer of sensitive nuclear technology, equipment, and materials to countries without nuclear weapons, except under safeguards. Washington was persuaded that a technology-denial policy would coerce India into joining the non-proliferation regime. The price of continued supplies was India's acceptance of fullscope safeguards upon its entire atomic energy program. This was wholly unacceptable to India, which held the NNPA to be municipal legislation that could not negate the specific provisions of the Tarapur Agreement retrospectively.[9] In any event, the United States finally stopped supplying uranium fuel to the Tarapur plant. This controversy was finally resolved when the United States arranged that France would be the alternative supplier of uranium fuel to Tarapur in 1982 without imposing any extraneous conditions. (In 1995 China stepped into this breach, which was grudgingly accepted by the United States.)[10]

## Third Phase

This period spans the 1980s. The Soviet invasion of Afghanistan in 1979 made Pakistan highly prized as a conduit through which the United States would arm and equip the mujahideen to harass the Soviet forces. Pakistan's single-minded quest to acquire nuclear capabilities was thereafter determinedly ignored. Instead, the US president certified Pakistan's non-nuclear status annually from 1987 to 1989, as mandated by the Pressler Amendment. This certification was finally refused in 1990 after the Soviet withdrawal from Afghanistan. Pakistan was also able to secure presidential waivers of the provisions of the Symington Amendment in 1981, 1987, and 1988, the Glenn Amendment in 1982, and the Solarz Amendment in 1988. They prohibited American aid being provided to countries importing sensitive nuclear technologies to further a nuclear weapons program.[11] Consequently, these certifications imbued Pakistan's steady quest for nuclear status with a certain credibility and legitimacy.

For its part, India laid stress on the acquisition of nuclear delivery capabilities. It had Jaguar, MiG-23BN, and MiG-27 aircraft in its air force inventory that could be converted for this purpose. The Integrated Guided Missile Development program was begun in 1983 to manufacture, among others, the 150–250-km-range Prithvi and 1,500–2,500-km-range Agni surface-to-surface missiles. Several developmental trials of the Prithvi and the first flight test of the Agni were undertaken in the eighties. Pakistan received the 300-km-range M-11 missile from China. It has also tested its Hatf-III missile (600-km range/500-kg payload), resembling the Chinese M-9, and the Ghauri or Hatf-V missiles (1,500-km range/700-kg payload). The militarist view holds that the deployment of missiles would enhance Indo-Pak stability by providing more certain patterns of deterrence, since missiles are cheap and can assuredly penetrate the air defenses available in South Asia.

The United States believes that deployment of these missiles, especially with nuclear warheads, would definitely trigger an arms race in the Subcontinent and enhance present instabilities. These perceptions have influenced its transfer of defense technologies to India, despite an Indo-US memorandum of understanding (MOU) negotiated in December 1984 and an implementation agreement signed in May 1985. This led to India establishing an import-export licensing system that addressed US concerns regarding the possible diversion of technology to other parties. However, approval rates remained low, which influenced the number of approvals being requested. Prominently, the Indian request for a Cray XMP-24 supercomputer was refused on the grounds that it could be used to manufacture nuclear explosives. A license to export the Combined Acceleration Vibration Climatic Test System (CAVCTS) was canceled on the grounds that it could be used to develop nuclear missiles. The Pentagon's reluctance to transfer defense technologies in this period increased after the Agni's first test flight in 1989.[12]

Two serious Indo-Pak crises during the eighties, associated with the Brasstacks exercise in early 1987 and serious internal disturbances in Kashmir in early 1990, heightened US concerns regarding strategic stability in South Asia.[13] The United States had made conscious efforts to resolve these crises. There is no clear evidence that either of these crises had a nuclear dimension, but this likelihood has constantly informed later American analyses of South Asian security.

**Fourth Phase**

Indicative of these concerns is the Central Intelligence Agency's (CIA) conviction that a nuclear arms race proceeds in South Asia, which raises "the most probable prospect for future use of weapons of mass destruction, including nuclear weapons." [14] This belief also informed US perceptions that "if a nuclear weapon is to be detonated in anger in the next five years or so . . . the most likely place would be South Asia. . . . I see countries that are contiguous, both able in the near term to deploy nuclear weapons if they so chose, both with some delivery capability and both moving in the direction of ballistic missile capability that could be applied to nuclear weapons. These are countries that have fought before and that have a near-term crisis that could erupt at any moment in Kashmir." [15] The security situation in South Asia was highly dramatized in this manner.

Consequent US policy to contain nuclear proliferation in South Asia was encapsulated in this formulation: "Our objective is first to cap, then over time reduce, and finally eliminate the possession of weapons of mass destruction and their means of delivery." [16] The tactics identified to achieve these objectives were "urging the two countries to commit: (1) to a no-first-deployment pledge for ballistic missiles; (2) not to produce fissile materials for nuclear weapons as a step towards the global Fissile Material Cutoff Convention; and (3) not to test a nuclear device in advance of a CTBT." [17] India was specifically urged to refrain from deploying ballistic missiles, to join an international agreement to ban the manufacture of fissile materials for military purposes, and to enter a comprehensive prohibition on conducting nuclear tests.[18]

An activist phase in Indo-US non-proliferation relations followed. It was guided by US fears that a nuclear arms race, but more imminently a missile arms race, lay dormant in South Asia. Considerable pressure was mounted upon India to enter negotiations with the United States, Russia, China, and Pakistan to discuss these issues. Largely to deflect American pressures to join these negotiations, India joined two US-sponsored UN resolutions in September 1993 proposing a cutoff in the manufacture of fissile materials for military purposes (under the FMCT) and negotiation of the Comprehensive Test Ban Treaty (CTBT). These resolutions accorded with India's long-held disarmament positions. India's entry into the FMCT, however, would have limited its weapons inventory to existing weapons-grade stocks. More seriously, practically its entire nuclear program would have come under international safeguards. India's entry into the CTBT would similarly have capped its nuclear option by limiting it to an ability to manufacture untested, first-generation fission devices. The delivery of nuclear weapons would also have been restricted to suitably modified aircraft, since a nuclear test series was unavoidably required to miniaturize the nuclear warheads for equipping missiles or to manufacture advanced fission and thermonuclear weapons. [19]

India's decision thereafter to refrain from supporting the FMCT and oppose the CTBT has become a major irritant in Indo-US relations. The FMCT is nowhere in sight. But India radically altered its position on the CTBT after the NPT was indefinitely extended and it discovered that the nuclear weapon powers were serious about comprehensively banning nuclear testing; it had miscalculated on both these counts. India's major objection to the CTBT is that the treaty lays down no time-bound framework to eliminate nuclear weapons. The CTBT also envisages that all countries possessing nuclear power/research reactors would ratify this treaty before the putative date when it would come into force. This includes India, which perceives this provision to be an affront to its national sovereignty. An officially sponsored internal debate was sparked off to consolidate domestic support for India's decision to block passage of the CTBT in the Conference on Disarmament (CD) and UNGA. An exacerbation of the tensions in Indo-US relations was inevitable, and this set the stage for Indo-US non-proliferation relations in the second Clinton administration.

## Fifth Phase

Paradoxically, Indian obduracy in not entering the NPT or CTBT did not generate any domestic debate on weaponizing its nuclear option. A posture premised on "keeping the nuclear option open" was deemed viable. One theoretical construct suggests that there are several reasons nations have slowed down, stopped, or reversed their nuclear capabilities: changes in the international system after the Cold War, and their influence on "new thinking" about the value of nuclear weapons; a new kind of "dollar diplomacy"; US non-proliferation efforts; the quality of political leadership; and the global non-proliferation regime.[20] However, the Indian leadership had consistently maintained the policy of ambiguity because they sought a balance between the deterrent value of nuclear weapons and national commitment to disarmament. The same reason accounts for why it refused to give up the nuclear option despite US pressure. It would be argued below that domestic political imperatives informed the BJP's decision to change the nuclear status-quo. However, it has still to translate the newly demonstrated capability into a nuclear doctrine of relevance to India's total security perspectives.

Several studies by influential Americans have advised the United States to recognize India's nuclear restraint. A study group sponsored by the Asia Society advised "the desirability of a US policy that neither concedes the inevitability of the overt deployment of nuclear weapons [in South Asia] nor fails to address it should it occur. . . . *But for now it should concentrate on efforts to contain these programs in anticipation of the day when regional leaders agree that eliminating them is in their interest. Doing so requires a broad band of strategic, economic, and technological policies*" [emphasis in original].[21] Most recently, a task force sponsored by the Council on Foreign Relations noted that "reversing these countries' de facto nuclear weapons status is currently extremely unlikely. In the non-proliferation arena, US policy should focus instead on establishing a more stable and sustainable plateau for Indian and Pakistani nuclear relations. This would involve concentrating on persuading both countries to refrain from testing nuclear explosives, deploying nuclear weapons, and exporting nuclear weapon- or missile-related technology, or expertise. The United States should also urge both countries to refrain from missile deployments and cease unsafeguarded production of fissile material." [22]

The Council on Foreign Relations Report also propounded the thesis—anathema to non-proliferation purists—that India, Pakistan, and Israel should be separately categorised in appreciation of their nuclear capabilities. It also recommended that the United States seek a "closer strategic relationship with India, and adopt a declaratory policy that acknowledges India's growing power and importance; maintain high-level attention including regular reciprocal visits of cabinet members and senior officials; loosen unilateral US constraints upon the transfer of dual-use technologies; increase military-to-military cooperation; cooperate on elements of India's civilian nuclear power program and other energy-related issues; and undertake limited conventional arms sales." [23] These areas of possible Indo-US cooperation have been disrupted by the nuclear tests but could be profitably pursued whenever Indo-US relations normalize.

The underlying theses in these reports is that a state of "nonweaponized" or "existential" deterrence obtains in South Asia and has contributed to the Subcontinent's stability. As the US National Academy of Sciences noted, "Even the existence of the idea of nuclear weapons—more specifically, the ability of many states to make them—is enough to create an existential deterrent effect against large-scale conflicts of all kinds." [24] This state of existential deterrence was strengthened after the May 1998 nuclear tests made explicit India and Pakistan's nuclear capabilities. Deterrence based on the availability of nuclear capabilities can provide security only against nuclear or large-scale conventional attacks, not against support for ethnopolitical or religious-communal conflicts, or terrorism or militancy by the adversary. Threats of this genre constitute the present danger in South Asia; this fact needs greater appreciation in the United States.

Based on its global non-proliferation concerns, the United States has prioritized its arms control agenda to include securing the ratification of CTBT; beginning negotiations on a Strategic Arms Reduction Treaty (START III) after the Duma ratifies START II; strengthening the Biological and Toxic Weapons Convention (BTWC); finalizing negotiations to ban manufacture of fissile materials for nuclear weapons; and addressing the humanitarian threat posed by antipersonnel land mines scattered around the world.[25] Except for START II ratification, Indo-US cooperation can proceed in all these areas.

## INDIA'S THREAT PERCEPTIONS

An evaluation can be made now of the nuclear security scenario in South Asia as it is adjudged by the United States and India. A US State Department analysis holds that "current political forces combined with threat perceptions . . . drive both countries [India and Pakistan] to continue to develop weapons of mass destruction and ballistic missiles. For Pakistan, nuclear weapons represent the ultimate deterrent. . . . Indians see their most immediate threat coming from Pakistan."[26] In truth, India's nuclear posture is largely derived from the intertwined nuclear threat from Pakistan and China. The latest annual report of India's Ministry of Defence (1997–98), published after the nuclear tests, notes that "China's assistance to Pakistan's nuclear weapons programme and the sale of missiles and missile technology to Pakistan also directly affect India's security. . . . There are credible and well-documented reports of outside assistance to Pakistan in these fields despite the existence of multilateral export control regimes, unilateral declarations of restraint and supply restrictions in producer countries."[27]

This conclusion echoes US analyses of Sino-Pak cooperation in these areas. For instance, James Woolsey, a former CIA director, had testified before the US Senate that "Beijing has consistently regarded a nuclear-armed Pakistan as a crucial regional ally and as a vital counterweight to India's growing military capabilities. . . . Beijing prior to joining the Non-Proliferation Treaty in 1992 probably provided some nuclear weapons-related assistance to Islamabad that may have included training, may have included equipment."[28] In February 1998 the House Committee on International Relations was again informed that "In the 1980s, it [China] provided critical assistance to Pakistan's nuclear weapons program, assistance that clearly would have constituted a violation of the Nonproliferation Treaty had China been a party to the NPT at the time. Moreover, China or Chinese entities have sold missile equipment and technology, dual-use chemicals and production equipment, and advanced conventional arms to recipients in regions of tension and instability, primarily Iran and Pakistan."[29] China's aberrant behavior did not change after entering the NPT in 1992: "While no longer selling complete MTCR-class missiles, China continues to transfer missile components and technology, especially to Pakistan and Iran."[30]

Following the 1998 nuclear tests, an official Indian statement noted that "the Government is deeply concerned, as were previous Governments, about the nuclear environment in India's neighbourhood." [31] This threat from the "nuclear environment in India's neighbourhood" found clearer expression in a letter written by the Indian prime minister to President Clinton, which was leaked to the press, causing immense embarrassment to the Indian government. The letter plainly argues:

> We have an overt nuclear weapon state on our borders, a state that committed armed aggression against India in 1962. Although our relations with that country have improved in the last decade or so, an atmosphere of distrust persists mainly due to the unresolved border problem. To add to the distrust that country has materially helped another neighbour of ours to become a covert nuclear weapon state. At the hands of this bitter neighbour we have suffered three aggressions in the last 50 years. And for the last 10 years we have been the victim of unremitting terrorism and militancy sponsored by it in several parts of our country, especially Punjab and Jammu and Kashmir. [32]

Still, the popular view persists in the United States that India raises the bogey of a Chinese nuclear threat to justify its own nuclear ambitions. This is partly explicable due to past Indian reticence in clearly expressing its disapprobation of Chinese collusion in assisting Pakistan's nuclear and missile programs. Indian references to the nuclear threat from China have consequently been castigated as "not only cynical but inconsistent with the history of Indian defence planning ... Nuclear weapons are hardly relevant to minor border disputes like the one between the two Asian giants." [33]

On the contrary, the history of Indian defense planning shows that the three major events that firmly positioned the nuclear threat in India's consciousness were China-related: India's traumatic defeat in the Sino-Indian border conflict (1962), China's explosion of its first nuclear device (1964), and China's threat to India during the second Indo-Pak war (1965). Further, the technological steps taken by India prior to the May 1998 tests, such as initiating its SNEP (1965), commissioning the Purnima reactor (1972), conducting its first Pokharan test (1974), and initiating its integrated guided missile development program (1984), were China-oriented. Indeed, its intermediate-range and extended-range Agni missiles are designed to be used against China. Later claims that the Indian tests highlight the inequities of the international nuclear regime and dramatize the need to eliminate nuclear weapons only torture the logic informing these tests.

Were domestic compulsions underlying India's retention and, later, expression of its nuclear option? Contrary to prevailing beliefs, the Indian armed forces are acutely conscious that a condition of nuclear asymmetry, in which one nation has nuclear arms and the other is conventionally armed, degrades conventional deterrence. A nuclear deterrent is therefore necessary to defend against a nuclear adversary. In fact, a former Indian Army chief has confessed that "the advocacy of the services that India should go nuclear is as old as 1964. In every forum we have said that you should go nuclear." [34]

Besides, the scientists in the Indian Atomic Energy Commission (AEC) have been strong protagonists of nuclear weaponry. One example will suffice. An account of the crucial meeting where it was decided to proceed with the first Pokharan test (1974) recounts that "the final meeting on Pokharan was one, which involved heated discussions. P. N. Dhar was vehemently opposed to the explosion as he felt it would damage our economy; Haksar took the view that the time was not ripe and gave his reasons; my own view was that it was now impossible to postpone the date given the expense, time and the critical state the experiment has reached. Fortunately for my [Ramanna] team Mrs. Gandhi decreed that the experiment should be carried out on schedule." [35] The influence of the scientific bureaucracy is apparent from this account.

The AEC had obviously secured the necessary clearances from the previous non-BJP governments to proceed with developing these nuclear devices. This enabled the BJP government to order the nuclear tests at will. But the pressure from the nuclear and defense scientists strengthened the BJP government's resolve to proceed with them. This is not surprising. It mirrors the situation in the United States. The weapons laboratories, the armed forces and the Pentagon have favored the continuance of nuclear tests to further sophisticate their nuclear weaponry. But the State Department has opposed such activism because of arms control considerations. In India the Ministry of External Affairs, not the Ministry of Defense, has traditionally dealt with policy issues regarding India's nuclear posture. It has now been revealed that the Defence Research and Development Organization (DRDO) was deeply involved in the nuclear explosives program. Significantly, the leaders of the AEC and the DRDO jointly addressed a press conference to provide technical details of these nuclear tests.[36]

But domestic political imperatives largely occasioned the BJP government's decision to undertake these tests. Its election manifesto had clearly mentioned that it would reevaluate the country's nuclear policy and exercise the option to induct nuclear weapons, and expedite the development of the Agni series of ballistic missiles with a view to increasing their range and accuracy.[37]

Further, the National Agenda for Governance, issued by the BJP-led coalition, stated that "we will re-evaluate the nuclear policy and exercise the option to induct nuclear weapons." [38] Despite these clear postulates, the expedition and deception involved in conducting these tests soon after the BJP came to power suggests that it was domestic compulsions rather than external threats that informed its decision. These compulsions included appearing consistent with its election promises, deflecting public attention from serious contradictions within the coalition, hoping that the euphoria generated would garner votes in the next elections, and so on. Security concerns were the ostensible reason given, and the pressure of the scientific bureaucracy is evident.

## INDIA'S NUCLEAR CHOICES

The foregoing shows that powerful domestic constituencies in India favor the overt weaponization and deployment of nuclear weapons. The other choice available to India is maintaining the status quo in its current state, and not proceeding to weaponize and deploy nuclear weapons and the missiles to deliver them.

The overt weaponization and deployment option must be evaluated within the internal and external context in which India would frame that decision. In the domestic arena, the major institutional pressures for exercising this choice have been discussed above. The intertwined external threats from Pakistan and China are also a factor; they have indubitably been exacerbated by Pakistan's nuclear tests and China's animosity against India. Despite these pressures on India to proceed further toward explicit weaponization and deployment, any such action will increase international opprobrium and heighten the financial and technological sanctions already imposed upon India. No doubt the emotional argument could be used that national-security needs are supreme and merit any sacrifice. But it is increasingly evident that, apart from the direct effect of the sanctions, investor confidence has been affected and the cost of capital borrowing has gone up at a stage when India is liberalizing and globalizing its economy, expanding its infrastructure, and accelerating its economic growth. The direct costs of a diversified triad of nuclear forces would also add to these national and individual sacrifices.

In this milieu the steps taken by the United States to address the aberrant behavior of Pakistan and China will have an important influence on the BJP's future nuclear weaponization and missile deployment agenda. Presently the United States seems anxious to avoid any confrontation with China despite its blatant proliferation activities. The United States would also like to bail Pakistan out of its current financial embarrassment, which is wholly of its own making but has worsened after its nuclear tests and the consequent imposition of sanctions. It would be excessive to suggest that US inaction vis-à-vis China and Pakistan encouraged the BJP government's decision to proceed with its nuclear tests. But continued US inaction could encourage the BJP government to go ahead with its agenda to weaponize and deploy nuclear weapons.

A brief digression is necessary now to discuss the status of India's nuclear weapons program after its current nuclear test series. They included a fission device (yield 12 kilotons), a thermonuclear device (yield 43 kilotons), and three subkiloton devices (yields ranging between 0.2 and 0.6 kiloton). These tests established India's technological ability to develop the full panoply of nuclear weapons, ranging from thermonuclear (hydrogen bomb) to tactical (battlefield) devices. These tests also "provided critical data for the validation of our capability in the design of nuclear weapons of different yields for different applications and different delivery systems. These tests have significantly enhanced our capability in computer simulation of new designs and taken us to the stage of sub-critical experiments in the future, if considered necessary." [39] These measured statements indicate that India can undertake further nuclear designs through computer simulation and laboratory tests, and that they could undertake subcritical (hydronuclear) tests. It could be further surmised that India could now equip its aircraft with nuclear weapons. But it remains unclear if its nuclear devices have been suitably miniaturized for delivery by surface-to-surface missiles, such as the Prithvi (150–250 km), the Agni (1,500–2,500 km), or the extended-range Agni that is being contemplated. The Prithvi is currently in series production, and a number are in storage in the Punjab. The Agni program, however, was terminated after three "technology demonstrations."

Proceeding further, two serious military limitations of the Prithvi missile (150–250-km range) have been noticed. First, the highly volatile oxidizer-fuel combination used requires the missile to be fueled just prior to launch. The time required to fuel and transport the missile to its operational location would constrain its quick deployment and mobility in an operational situation. More significant is that the missiles and their attendant crew would be vulnerable to preemptive attack during the fueling and transportation phases.

Second, the Prithvi can be used in a mobile mode with interchangeable warheads to deliver high explosives, prefragmented or cluster bombs with submunitions such as antipersonnel and antitank mines, and possibly fuel-air explosives. Thus, the longer 250-km (air force) version could interdict fixed targets such as enemy airfields and disrupt the "air based logistical chain," besides attacking railway marshaling yards, oil terminals, and troops in dug-in positions. [40]

However, apart from the problems of prelaunch/postlaunch survivability and reliability, the accuracy achievable by short-range missiles of the Prithvi genre suggests that it could be of only limited use against even unhardened fixed targets such as airfields unless the missiles are used in large numbers, which are just not available. [41] This leads to the conclusion that deployment of the Prithvi missile by India would not make operational sense unless it is equipped with nuclear warheads. This is even truer of the Agni, which costs around Rs. 55–60 crores ($1 = Rs. 40) apiece at current prices. This makes it cost-ineffective for use with conventional warheads. But an extended test series is definitely required to establish the Agni's reliability, since it has been flight-tested only three times—twice successfully. However, the political factor that inheres in the Agni's testing and deployment is that its strategic direction could be only against China. India is currently seeking to repair its relations with China, but this is proving difficult because the latter has taken umbrage at being identified as India's major security threat. China has officially charged that "the so-called China's threat to India security is baseless. Fictitious charges against China have greatly hurt the feelings of the Chinese people and harmed the Sino-Indian relations." [42] China has hinted that India should make some public disclaimer of these accusations. This would prove difficult for the BJP government, which made these accusations deliberately and with calculated intent to justify its tests. Further, India has always perceived China's basic policy toward South Asia as being founded on containing India within its regional confines by assisting Pakistan to counter Indian "hegemonism."

India was dismayed by the joint Sino-American statement following President Clinton's visit to China in June 1998; this stated, in part, that both countries had "agreed to continue to work closely together, within the P-5, the Security Council and with others, to prevent an accelerating nuclear and missile arms race in South Asia, strengthen international non-proliferation efforts, and promote reconciliation and the peaceful resolution of differences between India and Pakistan." [43] This condominium over South Asia sought by the two countries is wholly unacceptable to India, which regards China as part of the nuclear proliferation problem in the region. A decision by India to test and deploy the Agni in this vitiated atmosphere would perforce mean a further deterioration in Sino-Indian relations and that China would definitely take countermeasures to target India with its nuclear missiles. It could also continue to assist Pakistan's nuclear and missile programs through North Korea.

The other remaining choice available to India is continuing in its present state of imperfect deterrence, despite the precipitous deterioration of Indo-Pak relations and the slow improvement of Sino-Indian relations after a severe setback. China and Pakistan, in that order, had been identified as the security threats justifying the nuclear tests in May 1998. Concurrently, Indo-US relations have reached their nadir. A firebreak is still recognizable between India's present state of nuclearization and progress in weaponizing/deploying its nuclear weapons and missiles. A formalization of this position may yet be possible if some agreement in this regard could be reached with Pakistan.

The difficulties in normalizing Indo-Pak relations cannot be minimized. Pakistan has firmly linked its nuclear deterrent with a prior resolution of the Kashmir issue; indeed, it has made the "core issue" of Kashmir the touchstone of its relations with India, and insists that it must be settled before other negotiations can proceed. Pakistan hopes to elicit US sympathy for its position on holding a plebiscite in the state to resolve the Kashmir issue. But this solution is completely unacceptable to India, which holds that because objective conditions in Kashmir have changed, the plebiscite solution is obsolete. On the other hand, India wishes to broaden its negotiations with Pakistan to include all the issues in contention between the two countries. The resulting impasse underlines the dangers of Indo-Pak relations—now more certainly nuclearized—if they remain tense and crisis-prone in the future. Pakistan, incidentally, has not evinced any interest in an Indo-Pak bilateral no-first-use declaration being made, on the grounds that the nuclear deterrent is vital for its security. This parlous situation has led the United States and other developed countries to urge India and Pakistan to "resume without delay a direct dialogue that addresses the root causes of the tensions, including Kashmir." [44]

The need for greater Indo-Pak, Sino-Indian, and Indo-US dialogue to manage these uneasy relationships is apparent, despite the current reality that all these interactions have been disrupted following the Indo-Pak nuclear tests. It is unlikely that

India would abjure its right to weaponize and deploy nuclear weapons should that become necessary. Could India, however, freeze its nuclear weaponization program in its present state? A broader Indo-US dialogue has begun with this purpose, to which attention can now be turned.

## INDO-US COOPERATION

Future Indo-US non-proliferation relations need to be examined against the backdrop of India's nuclear tests; they challenge the power structure established by the international nuclear regime based on the monopoly of the "nuclear five." India's refusal to sign the NPT or CTBT has ruffled US sensitivities. India, however, considers its nuclear option to be an expression of national sovereignty. A cooperative Indo-US relationship must be sought, therefore, within an overarching bargain wherein India retains its current nuclear capabilities but does not proceed to overt weaponization and deployment: in return, the United States would further reduce its nuclear weapons, refrain from their qualitative improvement, and de-emphasize nuclear weapons in its defense posture.

Both countries have a professed interest in halting horizontal and vertical proliferation. But the major US objection to eliminating nuclear weapons is that it finds "it necessary to continue to rely on the core function of nuclear deterrence as long as nuclear weapons continue to exist in the possession of states that might consider using them against this country or its allies." [45] Declarations of this genre reemphasize the role of nuclear weapons in national security, and equate their possession with the accrual of power and influence. However, the NPT, CTBT, and other legal and moral commitments accepted by the United States have enshrined nuclear disarmament as their ultimate goal. The logic is also inescapable that if deploying nuclear weapons will destabilize South Asia, then "the only realistic way to head off this danger is for the United States to take the lead in a global process of nuclear arms reduction, with the declared goal of eliminating nuclear weapons altogether within a period of 20 to 30 years in parallel with non-proliferation efforts. In the final analysis, global and regional nuclear arms control are inseparable." [46] Pursuing regional non-proliferation without addressing the larger problem of global non-proliferation is illogical, especially if the nuclear weapon powers are unable even to express a commitment to eliminating nuclear weapons.

India has made the elimination of nuclear weapons in a specified time frame an article of faith; it has linked its cooperation in other arms control negotiations with progress toward this objective. The United States opposes this "linkage disease" as "a proposal in effect to stall the proven step-by-step approach by the United States and Russia that is in fact bringing nuclear disarmament closer, and then to drag all possible progress on other issues into the same morass." [47] A constructive Indo-US dialogue is necessary to discuss how this "grand bargain" might be negotiated whereby both countries proceed in tandem to achieve their common goal of nuclear disarmament.

Following its nuclear tests, India has been targeted by diverse sanctions. A dual-track policy appears to have commended itself to the United States. At one level, Indo-US negotiations have been intensified between designated emissaries of the two countries to seek a modus vivendi. Simultaneously, the sanctions mandated under US laws against nations undertaking nuclear tests are being implemented. These sanctions envisage that US assistance in some areas, such as defense, will be terminated; government credits to the Indian government will be denied; extension of loans by international financial institutions will be opposed; exports of specified goods and technology will not be permitted; and credits and guarantees by Ex-Im Bank of the United States and by OPIC (Overseas Private Investment Corporation) will not be provided.[48]

However, humanitarian assistance, comprising the education and public health areas, has been exempted from the sanctions' purview. The US administration has also sought and obtained "waiver authority" from Congress for applying these sanctions with "greater flexibility than the law currently allows to tailor our approach, influence events and respond to developments."[49] This reflects US interest in seeking a modus vivendi with India and Pakistan, rather than further escalating existing tensions. There is little doubt that the sanctions will hurt the Indian economy in its present vulnerable state of sluggish industrial and infrastructural growth, given the lack of political will to either reduce subsidies or garner additional resources for budgetary/developmental purposes. The noticeable decline in investor confidence will only accentuate these negative trends.

More concretely, the measures that India and Pakistan must take before these sanctions could be lifted have been spelled out in communiqués issued by the P-5 countries in Geneva, put forth by the G-8 nations in London, and included in UN Security Council Resolution 1172. They require India and Pakistan to "conduct no further nuclear tests; sign and ratify the Comprehensive Test Ban Treaty immediately and without conditions; refrain from deploying nuclear weapons or missile systems; halt the production of fissile material for nuclear weapons; participate constructively in negotiations towards a fissile material cut-off treaty; formalise existing policies not to export weapons of mass destruction and missile technology or equipment; and resume a direct dialogue to address the root causes of tension between them, including Kashmir."[50]

Immediately after the nuclear tests India declared that it was "prepared to consider being an adherent to some of the undertakings in the Comprehensive Test Ban Treaty . . . will continue to exercise the most stringent control on the export of sensitive technologies, equipment and commodities especially those related to weapons of mass destruction . . . [and] participate in the negotiations for the conclusion of a fissile material cut-off treaty in the Geneva based Conference on Disarmament."[51] The U.S. State Department expressed its reservations on this vague phraseology as falling "far short of indicating any meaningful commitment to either accord."[52] This persuaded the Indian prime minister to affirm in Parliament that "India will now observe a voluntary moratorium and refrain from conducting underground nuclear test explosions. We have also indicated willingness to move towards a de jure formalisation of this declaration." [53] In another Parliament statement he added that India was committed to a nuclear dialogue "to arrive at a decision regarding adherence to the CTBT," would not be the first to use nuclear weapons against other nuclear-weapon states, and would never use nuclear weapons against non-nuclear countries.[54]

Proceeding further, the charter of demands laid down by the international community can be divided into five broad clusters. The feasibility of their acceptance is discussed below in increasing order of difficulty.

• First, India's past restraint in exporting sensitive technologies has been noteworthy, despite the receipt of several discreet requests. There should be no difficulty in strengthening existing laws and procedures to formalize this restraint to address the export of materials, technology, and equipment that could be used in the production of nuclear weapons and missiles more specifically.

• Second, India could easily halt the further proliferation of fissile materials for weapon purposes, since its existing stocks are sufficient to establish a credible deterrent force. Usable plutonium in India's inventory of weapons was estimated at 350 kg (plus or minus 30 percent) on December 31, 1993; this quantity suffices to manufacture between thirty and fifty-eight nuclear weapons at the most conservative computation.[55] India has joined the negotiations on the fissile materials cutoff treaty. At present, these negotiations are dominated by the debate on whether the treaty should control future production or should control existing stockpiles as well.

• Third, a direct dialogue with Pakistan was formally initiated in July 1998 with the Vajpayee–Nawaz Sharif meeting in Colombo during the SAARC summit. It was decided to resume the interrupted foreign-secretary-level talks. But it would be fair to note that the basic issue, whether Kashmir should be discussed separately or as another item in the agenda, remains unresolved at the present juncture. Pakistan seems determined to take advantage of American anxieties that an escalation of Indo-Pak tensions focusing on Kashmir could presage an Indo-Pak conflict and trigger a nuclear exchange. Consequently, a direct dialogue between India and Pakistan to address their mutual differences, including Kashmir, could reduce itself to talks about talks.

• Fourth, a decision to refrain from deploying nuclear weapons and missiles would be inconsistent with India's expressed logic justifying these tests on the basis of security considerations. This suggests that credible steps are being taken to meet such security needs with nuclear weapons. A decision to weaponize and deploy nuclear weapons, however, would entail further political and economic costs, and worsen India's strategic situation.

•   Fifth, the question of ceasing nuclear tests and entering the CTBT may appear deceptively simple. India has already agreed to a moratorium on further testing. And India's earlier objections to joining the CTBT may not be valid after its tests. It had drawn attention, for instance, to the CTBT's not being a true disarmament measure since it did not provide for the elimination of nuclear weapons. But this objection loses much of its force after India's nuclear tests and its claim to having become a nuclear-weapon state. In other words, it has now entered the international nuclear regime that it was seeking to reform. It had also objected to the CTBT's not being truly comprehensive, since it permitted subcritical tests. India has now established this capability and could employ it to further refine its nuclear arsenal. Finally, India had objected to the "entry-into-force" clause in the CTBT, which mandated that India must enter this treaty before it could become operative, as affronting its sovereignty. That objection, too, would not remain valid if India voluntarily joins the CTBT.

Consequently, it would seem that there is no difficulty in India's now entering the CTBT. The major problem that persists is internal and linked to domestic politics. The Gujral government had manufactured a "national consensus" by whipping up patriotic sentiments in the country that security would be endangered and sovereignty compromised if India entered the CTBT. The BJP was in the forefront of this campaign. It would be extremely difficult for its government to completely reverse its stand now and establish another "national consensus" in favor of joining the CTBT. These are compelling political realities that cannot be ignored.

## CONCLUSIONS

The foregoing has shown that Indo-US relations are hopelessly mired in controversy at the present juncture, and their difficulties stem from differences in the nonproliferation area. Assuming, however, that a modus vivendi evolves with the passage of time, some possible avenues of Indo-US cooperation in the nuclear area would include the exchange of information to enhance the protection of fissile materials and counter nuclear smuggling; the identification of processes for placement of fissile materials and nuclear facilities under international safeguards; discussions on the safety of power plants and waste disposal techniques; joint studies on the technological and strategic implications of eliminating nuclear weapons; and so on.

The question of transferring nuclear equipment, especially safety and life-extension equipment, is also worth exploring. US policy currently prohibits their export to India, although there appears to be no *legal* impediment to the export of "minor" equipment. Section 109 of the US Atomic Energy Act permits such minor equipment exports provided that IAEA safeguards are applicable, that the equipment would not be used to make explosive devices, and that it would not be transferred to other nations without prior US consent. These are conditions that India can accept in regard to, for instance, safety equipment required for the Tarapur reactors.[56] Specific areas of technology transfers and cooperation have been made possible in the past by "islanding," as with the light combat aircraft (LCA) project. Of course, all such cooperation is currently on hold following the imposition of US sanctions on India.

Incidentally, the United States and India are signatories to several non-proliferation regimes, such as the chemical and biological weapons conventions, and have cooperated in their establishment and administration. In fact, India is playing an active role in negotiations to strengthen the verification provisions of the BWC. Extending this cooperation to the nuclear and space areas is therefore feasible, provided appropriate political decisions are taken in order to have a constructive engagement in these areas. Again, it would be realistic to accept that this would not be possible so long as the sanctions against India remain in place.

Furthermore, there are basic issues of general applicability to Indo-US relations that need inclusion in their strategic dialogue. An important issue for discussion would be their worldview and estimation of the strategic threats they foresee in the next century, notably how they assess China's future role in the international system. Patterns of cooperation and contention are presently discernible in Sino-US relations. What they portend for future Indo-US relations is a question of perennial significance, as they would frame the choices available to India for progressing in its relations with the United States and China. A rich agenda therefore awaits joint consideration by India and the United States after they reconcile their present differences. This could take place sooner rather than later, given the interest in both countries to contain the repercussions of India's nuclear tests conducted in defiance of the international nuclear regime.

## NOTES

1   Surjit Man Singh, "India and the United States," in B. R. Nanda, ed., *Indian Foreign Policy: The Nehru Years* (New Delhi: Radiant, 1976), p. 167.

2   Dennis Kux, *Estranged Democracies: India and the United States, 1941–1991* (New Delhi: Sage Publications, 1993), pp. 447–48.

3   "Clinton Proposes New UN Agenda for the 21st Century," *USIS Wireless File,* October 24, 1995.

4   "ACDA Director John Holum on Global Arms Control," *USIS Official Text,* October 18, 1997, p. 1.

5   *A New US Policy Towards India and Pakistan: Report of an Independent Task Force* (New York: Council on Foreign Relations, 1997), p. 3.

6   *Science Today* (Bombay), September 1974, p. 12.

7   Kux, *Estranged Democracies,* p. 317.

8   *Lok Sabha Debates, Fifth Series,* vol. XX, no. 3, November 15, 1972, col. 125.

9   These arguments are elaborated in P. R. Chari, "An Indian Reaction to US Non-proliferation Policy," *International Security,* Fall 1978, vol. 3, no. 2, pp. 57–66.

10  India Abroad News Service, "UK Okays Chinese Uranium Sale for Tarapur," *Business Standard* (New Delhi), January 14, 1995.

11   Cf. Mitchell Reiss, "The Illusion of Influence," *The RUSI Journal*, Summer 1991.The text of these amendments to the US Foreign Assistance Act of 1961 may be seen in Appendixes 2 and 3 of the Council on Foreign Relations report *A New US Policy*, pp. 66–74.

12   For an insider view of how bureaucratic delays in the United States have derailed the purposes of the Indo-US MOU, see K. Santhanam and Rahul Singh, "Confidence Restoring Measures for Indo-US Commerce in Controlled Commodities," in Francine R. Frankel, ed., *Bridging the Non-proliferation Divide: The United States and India* (New Delhi: Konark, 1995), pp. 334–39.

13   Cf. Kanti Bajpai et al., *Brasstacks and Beyond: Perception and Management of Crisis in South Asia*, (New Delhi: Manohar, 1996). The spring 1990 crisis is the subject of a forthcoming study by P. R. Chari, Stephen P. Cohen, and Pervaiz Iqbal Cheema.

14   "Progress Toward Regional Non-proliferation in South Asia," *USIS Official Text*, May 7, 1993, p. 2.

15   Robert L. Gallucci, "Non-proliferation and National Security," *Arms Control Today*, April 1994, p. 14.

16   "Progress Toward Regional Non-proliferation in South Asia," p. 3.

17   "Davis Outlines US Non-proliferation Policy," *USIS Official Text*, December 10, 1994. Lynn Davis was then the under-secretary of state for arms control and international security affairs.

18   These policy directions were reiterated by the then secretary of defense, William J. Perry, during his visit to New Delhi. Cf. "Remarks by William J. Perry, Secretary of Defense at the United Services Institution," *USIS Official Text*, January 12, 1995. Also "Conference of Defense Secretary William J. Perry," *USIS Backgrounder*, January 13, 1995.

19   These arguments are elaborated in P. R.Chari, *Indo-Pak Nuclear Standoff: The Role of the United States* (New Delhi: Manohar, 1995). See especially the chapter entitled "The Limits of Nuclear Ambiguity."

20   Mitchell Reiss, *Bridled Ambitions: Why Countries Constrain their Nuclear Capabilities* (Baltimore: Johns Hopkins University Press, 1995), p. 321.

21   *Preventing Nuclear Proliferation in South Asia* (New York: Asia Society, 1995), p. 33.

22   *A New US Policy*, p. 2.

23   Ibid., p. 3.

24   National Academy of Sciences, *The Future of US Nuclear Weapons Policy* (Washington, D.C.: National Academy Press, 1997), p. 4.

25   "ACDA Director," pp. 3–4.

26   "Tension Between India, Pakistan Remains US Concern," *USIS Official Text*, December 7, 1995. Robin Raphael, assistant secretary of state, mentioned this in testimony before the House International Relations Committee [Sub-Committee on Asia and the Pacific].

27   Government of India, Ministry of Defence, *Annual Report*, 1997–98, pp. 2–3.

28   Hearing before the Committee on Governmental Affairs, United States Senate, 103rd Congress, First Session, February 24, 1994. Witnesses: R. James Woolsey, director of Central Intelligence, accompanied by Gordon Oehler and Larry Gershwin, p. 18.

29   "Einhorn Statement on Nuclear Cooperation with China," *USIS Official Text*, February 5, 1998, p. 2. Robert J. Einhorn might be identified as the deputy assistant secretary of state for non-proliferation in the State Department.

30   Ibid., p. 7.

31   Text may be seen in *The Hindu*, May 12, 1998.

32   Text may be seen in *The Hindu*, May 14, 1998.

33  Eric Arnett, "Nuclear Weapons and Arms Control in South Asia After the Test Ban," in Eric Arnett, ed., *Nuclear Weapons and Arms Control in South Asia After the Test Ban,* SIPRI Research Report no. 14 (Oxford: Oxford University Press, 1998), p. 11.

34  Interview with General V. N. Sharma, "It's All Bluff and Bluster," *The Economic Times,* May 18, 1998. General Sharma is a former chief of the Army staff.

35  Raja Ramanna, *Years of Pilgrimage: An Autobiography* (New Delhi: Viking, 1991), p. 89. P. N. Dhar might be identified as the secretary to Prime Minister Indira Gandhi. P. N. Haksar was her advisor at that time (1974).

36  Cf. "Joint Statement by the Chairman of the Atomic Energy Commission & the Scientific Adviser to the Defence Minister," *The Hindu,* May 19, 1998.

37  The BJP's election manifesto may be seen at http://www.bjp.org/manifes/chap8.htm

38  The BJP-led coalition's National Agenda for Governance may be seen at http://www.hinduonline.com

39  "Joint Statement by the Chairman of the Atomic Energy Commission."

40  "Development of Prithvi Complete," *The Hindu,* May 9, 1998.

41  Z. Mian, A. H. Nayyar, and M. V. Ramana, "Bringing Prithvi Down to Earth: The Capabilities and Potential Effectiveness of India's Prithvi Missile," *Science and Global Security* (forthcoming).

42  Cf. speech delivered by Zhou Gang, Chinese ambassador to India, in New Delhi on July 25, 1998, at the India International Centre, reported in *The Hindu,* July 26, 1998.

43  Text of the joint statement relating to South Asia may be seen in *The Hindu,* June 28, 1998.

44  This formulation finds mention in the statement issued by the G-8 foreign ministers on June 12, 1998, following their meeting in the United Kingdom to discuss international action after the nuclear tests conducted by India and Pakistan. Cf. Foreign and Commonwealth Office, *Survey of Current Affairs,* June 1998, p. 237.

45  National Academy of Science, *Future of US Nuclear Weapons Policy,* p. 3.

46  *A New US Policy,* p. 57. Selig Harisson expressed these dissenting views.

47  "ACDA Director," p. 5.

48  Inderfurth statement on "Situation in India," *USIS Wireless File,* May 13, 1998.

49  "Inderfurth 7/13 Senate Statement on India, Pakistan," *USIS Official Text,* July 14, 1998, p. 5.

50  Ibid.

51  The text of the official statement on the nuclear tests may be seen in *The Hindu,* May 12, 1998.

52  Inderfurth statement, "Situation in India."

53  Text of the prime minister's *suo motu* statement in Parliament may be seen *in The Hindu,* May 28, 1998.

54  Raja Mohan, "India Offers Nuclear 'no-first use,'" *The Hindu,* August 5, 1998.

55  David Albright et al., *SIPRI Yearbook 1995: Armaments, Disarmament and International Security* (Oxford: Oxford University Press, 1996), table 9.2, p. 320.

56  G. Balachandran, "Indo-US Relations: The Nuclear Hurdle," *The Economic Times,* April 10, 1998.

# 2

## Fostering Strategic Stability
## and Promoting Regional Cooperation

### C. Raja Mohan

Throughout the Cold War, there never was a direct clash of interests between the United States and India. The relations between the two countries at the level of ordinary people have been reasonably warm and have steadily intensified over the years. India and the United States have shared the virtues of political pluralism at home and liberal internationalism abroad. The English language has provided another important bond. Yet the world's two largest democracies find it difficult to build a serious political partnership.

Unlike India, China fought a war with the United States in the Korean peninsula in the early 1950s. On the banks of the Yalu River, the Chinese and American military forces butchered each other. The United States had refused to recognize the existence of the People's Republic of China for more than two decades, and China poured ideological venom on the United States in the 1950s and 1960s and actively undermined its interests in Asia. Yet by the early 1970s the United States and Beijing allied against Moscow and eventually defeated the Soviet Union.

While Sino-US relations have swung between violent extremes, Indo-US ties have stagnated. Indian and American troops have never had an occasion to exchange fire. But their diplomats never missed a chance for a verbal duel. The Cold War saw a steady accumulation of distrust, and permanent irritation resulted in the utter inability of the two governments to conduct their relations in a reasonable manner.

The paradox of Indo-US relations can be understood only in terms of the American approach toward India's periphery and the consequences for Indian security. While there was no direct conflict of interest between India and the United

States, the latter's relations with Pakistan and China and India's ties with the Soviet Union created a political dynamic that was impossible to reverse.

However, US policy toward India's neighbors in the Cold War era was not rooted in an inherent American hostility toward India. It was driven by the imperative of the American global geopolitical competition with the Soviet Union. Nor was India's policy built around an ideological premise that the United States was the fountainhead of all evil. The deepening of America's strategic nexus with India's two major neighbors accentuated India's security problems. To compensate for this, India drew closer to the Soviet Union, and the political distance between India and the United States steadily widened. An occasional effort by the United States to break this vicious circle by engaging India and limiting the spillover from the Cold War never really succeeded.

The broader forces impinging on India's periphery are no longer similar to those that defined it during the Cold War. First, the US-Soviet confrontation provided the principal political overlay for the politics of the region then. Now the Sino-American relationship, although not as dominant as the US-Soviet one, is at the top of the many factors that shape the geopolitics of India's periphery.

Second, the weight of the local actors has gone up manyfold in the last fifty years. Iran, Pakistan, and the Southeast Asian nations were relatively passive actors during the Cold War. Now they will be more active in shaping the destiny of the region. Third, the Indian periphery itself has expanded. The collapse of the Soviet Union has introduced Central Asia and the Caucasus into the equation. Myanmar, which turned inward in the Cold War period and turned its back to the world, is now back in the reckoning.

Fourth, domestic political instability has always been a factor in the geopolitics of the region, though the US-Soviet competition provided some room for the nation-states in the region to manage their internal conflict. But now ethnicity and identity politics have become powerful tools in the mobilization of various nationalities whose grievances were swept under the carpet during the Cold War. As a consequence, the internal conflicts in Afghanistan, Kashmir, the Indian northeast, Tibet, and Xinjiang are among the many that have been established as factors in the regional power play.

The stakes for both the United States and India have gone up significantly in this region. In the past, when the United States focused its energies on defeating the Soviet Union, it could afford to concentrate on a few key areas on India's periphery—the Persian Gulf, Pakistan, and Southeast Asia—and leave the rest alone. Now it is recasting its policies in the priority areas and paying more attention to the nations it has long neglected.

One should note, for example, President Clinton's decision to visit Bangladesh during his projected visit to the Subcontinent in 1998 or early 1999, indicating the growing American interest in that nation. In short, the presence and diplomatic activism of the United States, the only superpower, is likely to intensify on India's periphery. India's own interest in its periphery has dramatically increased after the Cold War. In the past, its attention oscillated from an excessive focus on Pakistan, within the region, to the promotion of the agenda of the nonaligned movement, at the global level. But in the 1990s India has devoted greater economic and political energies to Southeast Asia, Central Asia, and the Persian Gulf, besides looking at the prospects for cooperation within the Subcontinent.

As India and the United States rethink their relations, they will have to look at their interests in the broader region comprising India's immediate neighbors, the Persian Gulf, Afghanistan, Central Asia, and Southeast Asia. The evolution of India's periphery will provide opportunities as well as difficulties in structuring a new bilateral relationship. For India, the biggest challenge is in coping with the uncertain relationship between Washington and Beijing. Given the new centrality of the Sino-US relationship in the Asian balance of power and the fact that China is its large neighbor, India needs to demonstrate extraordinary agility and wisdom in managing the consequences of the Sino-US relationship, whether it moves in the direction of a confrontation or toward a conundrum.

There is a broader agenda of cooperation awaiting India and the United States: promoting regional and subregional cooperation within the Subcontinent, beyond China and Pakistan. This should involve encouraging political pluralism in India's neighborhood, as well as combating terrorism and its connection with narcotics trafficking on India's periphery. Building a positive engagement with the Islamic world, working toward a more secure Persian Gulf, cooperating in protecting the sea lanes in the Indian Ocean, and building a cooperative energy security policy are among the areas that must then become the foci of the Indo-US strategic dialogue.

## IN SEARCH OF A STRATEGIC DIALOGUE

As the Cold War wound down at the beginning of the 1990s, there was a great expectation in India that the two sides could begin afresh at building a viable relationship. With the four-decade-old Soviet-American rivalries and their negative impact on the region behind them, it was hoped that the two democracies could move toward a new partnership. India welcomed the return of the Democrats to power in the United States after an absence of twelve years. It raised Indian expectations that the liberal internationalist vision of the American left could be finally married to the dominant Indian worldview, centered on global collective security and the primacy of normative principles in the conduct of international relations. But in the real world, the American rediscovery of Wilsonian internationalism in the first term of the Clinton administration pushed the two sides apart instead of bringing them together.

The early focus of the Clinton administration on the promotion of human rights and non-proliferation, and its emphasis on "preventive diplomacy," fused into American diplomatic activism on Kashmir. Just when the two sides needed to build trust and confidence, US diplomacy on Kashmir stirred deep anxieties in India about American intentions and motivations. What appeared to be a small US diplomatic initiative rattled Indian sensitivities on two scores: the question of territorial integrity, and the nuclear-weapon option. To India, US forays on Kashmir appeared to be both interventions on behalf of Pakistan and a signal that the US-Pakistan strategic relationship was being renewed, especially since Pakistan seemed determined to take advantage of India's troubles in the Kashmir valley during this time.

The relentless US pressures on India's nuclear and missile programs through the early 1990s and the attempt to "cap, reduce, and over a period of time, eliminate" its strategic capabilities produced a vigorous backlash in India and rejuvenated the dormant domestic debate on the nuclear weapon option. During the May 1994 summit between President Clinton and Prime Minister Rao, efforts to finesse the issue through an agreement to cooperate on the Comprehensive Test Ban Treaty (CTBT) and the Fissile Material Cut-off Treaty (FMCT) at the global level fizzled out as India began to look at the long-term security implications of the CTBT for its nuclear option. Global multilateral negotiations on the CTBT, which started out on a note of intensive cooperation between India and the United States at Geneva, ended in acrimony when India sought to block the treaty in Geneva, voted against it in New York, and set itself firmly against it in 1996.

Although the CTBT episode left a bitter aftertaste in both countries, it did provide the much-needed shock to force a rethink on the bilateral relationship in both countries. Change in key personnel in the United States at the beginning of the second term of the Clinton administration in 1997 provided an opportunity to review and recast American policy toward the Subcontinent. This allowed the introduction of a number of new elements into US policy toward the region and India.

First, President Clinton acknowledged the long neglect of the region and the need for a sustained engagement of the Subcontinent. Despite the continuing political instability in much of the Subcontinent, its potential as an important future market was seen as of some consequence in the United States.

Second, the United States assessed that India had the *potential* to emerge as a major power in the international system. To be sure, there were persistent doubts in the United States, as elsewhere in the world, about whether India was capable of realizing its inherent potential. But the prospect of India's transforming itself into one of the larger economies of the world provided some impetus for the United States to engage India in a framework that is broader than the Subcontinent and is embedded in the evolving dynamics of the Asian balance of power.

Third, there was some effort in the United States to find a way around the Pakistan factor, which had always hobbled Indo-US relations. The United States appeared to signal that it would no longer treat India and Pakistan as conjoined twins who must always be paired together in American thinking about the region. This did not mean that Pakistan had now become marginal to American political calculus in the region. As one of the world's largest Islamic countries, and strategically located on the borders of the Persian Gulf, Central Asia, and China, Pakistan is likely to remain important to the United States. What the United States appeared to offer in late 1997 was a readiness to pursue independent policies toward India and Pakistan, thus attempting to develop relations separately with the two nations on their own merits. Although there was considerable skepticism in India whether this US approach could be sustained, it was certainly seen as a welcome development.

Fourth, on Kashmir, the US emphasis appeared to shift from direct and active intervention in the dispute to promotion of an intensive dialogue between India and Pakistan. By insisting that the United States will mediate in the dispute only if both sides want it, and acknowledging that India did not seek such mediation, the Clinton administration appeared to have finally figured out how not to rub India the wrong way without totally alienating Pakistan on the issue. This new US line toward Kashmir was certainly more sophisticated than the earlier, blunt rhetoric on Kashmir, and it received a cautious welcome in India.

Finally, there were indications from the Clinton administration that although the non-proliferation issue remains at the top of the US agenda for the Subcontinent, it may not wish to see its bilateral relationship with India becoming hostage to the nuclear question. There were hints that the administration may be prepared to acknowledge the security imperatives of India's nuclear policy, will look at the issue in a broader context, and will deemphasize the rollback of Indian nuclear and missile capabilities.

For India, which saw its relationship with the United States as the most important one in the post–Cold War period, the new American approach was a welcome departure from its past policies, and raised expectations of a sustained high level of engagement between the two countries. Meanwhile the expanding commercial interaction between the two countries and the rapidly increasing levels of US direct investment in India appeared to provide for the first time a depth and stability to the relationship. The Indo-US "strategic dialogue" that began in late 1997 looked all set for steady progress, culminating in President Clinton's visit to India in late 1998, the first visit by an American president in two decades.

## NUCLEAR TESTS: CRISIS AND OPPORTUNITY

The decision by the new Indian government, led by the BJP, to go overtly nuclear by conducting five nuclear tests in May 1998 seemed to shatter the prospects for the Indo-US "strategic dialogue" and put back all efforts to revitalize the bilateral relations after the Cold War. Efforts by both sides to finesse the nuclear issue had come to naught as the United States was forced to confront the end of long-standing nuclear ambiguity in India. The administration reacted bitterly at the nuclear surprise, and the sense of betrayal at being misled by the new Indian government was strong. The United States imposed mandatory sanctions against India and led the international effort to condemn the Indian tests at meetings of the P-5 and G-8 nations and the UN Security Council.

The Indian nuclear tests, followed by those of Pakistan, seemed to challenge the entire global non-proliferation order that had been painstakingly built by the United States over many decades. It also raised sharp concerns about the stability of Indo-Pak relations and apprehensions of a nuclear holocaust in the Subcontinent. At the bilateral level, the Indian tests and the US reaction to it seemed to undermine all the progress that had been made—on both commercial and political fronts.

For all the sense of crisis that the Indian tests generated, it also presented an opportunity for India and the United States to deal with the nuclear question squarely and up front. For years both sides had tried to manage the nuclear question on the premise that India would maintain its ambiguous nuclear posture, however uncomfortably. But with India now having declared itself a nuclear-weapon power, it became possible to address more purposefully the two important issues that bothered the United States—the anomalous nature of India's relationship to the global non-proliferation regime and the importance of stabilizing the Indo-Pak nuclear dynamic. The dramatic shift in India's posture on global and regional arms control after the May tests and the American willingness to engage India opened the door for a frank and intensive dialogue between the two nations for the first time. The series of six meetings between June and September 1998 involving Jaswant Singh, the special envoy of the Indian prime minister, and Strobe Talbott, the US deputy secretary of state, provided an opportunity for India and the United States to discuss the nuclear issue head on, and perhaps put it aside and move on to build a new relationship.

The strategic objectives of India's nuclear diplomacy were radically transformed in the sweltering summer of 1998. Until May 11 the purpose was to create and sustain the option to make nuclear weapons when needed. Since mid-May the task has been to defend India's nuclear deterrent, reduce the political and economic costs of exercising India's nuclear option, eventually gain international acceptance of its new status, and learn to live in nuclear peace with Pakistan and China. The significance of this fundamental transformation in India's nuclear policy objectives has not been fully understood in the Indian domestic debate that followed the nuclear tests nor adequately appreciated at the international level.

In the past India rejected most of the global nuclear arms control arrangements, including the NPT, full-scope safeguards, regional nuclear-weapon-free zones, the bilateral denuclearization of India and Pakistan, and more recently the CTBT. India's nuclear rejectionism was built around the principles of global disarmament, equity, and nondiscrimination. But underlying these normative arguments was a powerful security consideration: that India could not allow the global arms control and non-proliferation regimes to chip away or completely rob it of the option to build nuclear weapons when it wanted.

It was inevitable that India, having finally exercised its option, would review its traditional opposition to arms control. Until now, the principal question that India had asked itself was whether an arms control treaty was global and nondiscriminatory. Since its decision to go nuclear, India has begun to look at two different issues. First, how does a treaty affect India's national security? Second, what are the political gains and losses associated with joining any particular arms control arrangement?

India is not the first country to make such a transition. China, for example, has moved from its past intense ideological opposition to all arms control, which it had branded as reflecting superpower hegemony, to pragmatic participation in global nuclear regimes. China took nearly three decades to make this transition, but India does not have that luxury. Facing a hostile international environment after its nuclear tests, India has made a rapid transition in its arms control positions in order to dent the international opposition to its nuclear weapons.

After its nuclear tests on May 11, the Indian government moved quickly to signal its readiness to find a rapprochement with the global nuclear order. It demonstrated a new flexibility on joining the CTBT, which it had rejected only two years earlier, and facilitated the resumption of negotiations on the FMCT at the Conference on Disarmament (CD) in Geneva. India reiterated its commitment to strengthen its export control policy as part of beefing up the global nuclear order. Without a radical departure in its own nuclear posture, it would not have been possible for India to become a cooperative state in relation to the global non-proliferation regime. By transforming itself into a nuclear power, India laid the basis for ending its rejection of arms control initiatives and becoming a part of the global non-proliferation consensus.

The overt nuclearization of the Subcontinent has also allowed intensive exploration of a lasting regime of arms control within the region. Until now Pakistan had emphasized regional disarmament, and India had insisted on global denuclearization. But now the two nations are beginning to talk the language of stability, arms control, and deterrence. Having come out of the nuclear closet, India and Pakistan must now figure out a new set of explicit and well-understood rules that must govern their bilateral relations and diplomacy. Such rules are essential if the two sides are to achieve their principal common security objective—the avoidance of a nuclear war in the Subcontinent.

In the wake of the South Asian nuclear tests, the great powers and their allies have made much noise about the dangers of a nuclear arms race in the region. They have delivered demarches to India and Pakistan to undertake wide-ranging military confidence-building measures (CBMs) to reduce the dangers of a war. Although the idea of an arms race finds an echo in a section of the public opinion in the Subcontinent, such an outcome is not inevitable in the Indo-Pak context. Maturity and sobriety in defining national-security strategies in the new context can and will obviate the danger of a nuclear confrontation in the Subcontinent.

Regardless of the external pressure on India and Pakistan to undertake CBMs, there is a solid case for the two nations to institutionalize a broad range of CBMs *in their own interest*—to minimize the prospects for a conventional conflict and its escalation into a nuclear one.

India and Pakistan do not necessarily need lessons or assistance from the great powers in implementing CBMs. What they do need is the political will to overcome the strong resistance from within the national-security bureaucracies to such measures. India and Pakistan did begin a process of negotiating military CBMs in 1990. A number of agreements have been reached, but there has not been enough political and institutional support in both countries to pursue them vigorously. The reason is that on both sides of the border, there is no real recognition of the importance of CBMs in managing the security dynamic between the two countries. The post-test realities have generated the possibility for a more intensive consideration of these measures.

Any suggestion that India's diplomacy must now focus on nuclear arms control and confidence building (as opposed to the traditional emphasis on total elimination of nuclear weapons) and on balance of power (in place of global multilateralism) evokes a passionate opposition from across the national spectrum. For many within the Indian political class, de-emphasizing disarmament and supporting interim arms control measures such as the CTBT is a surrender of core principles that have guided Indian foreign policy over the last five decades. They argue that it is a triumph of new opportunism over the past commitment to a principled foreign policy.

There is no need here to go into the merits of the arguments, because to some of the most articulate sections of Indian intelligentsia it is a matter of conviction. Any foreign-policy transition toward pragmatism, the critics of the new nuclear approach argue, means discarding the notion of "Indian exceptionalism" in international politics, with its emphasis on morality and on the norms of equity and fairness. By declaring itself a nuclear-weapon power and agreeing to join the CTBT, they suggest India becomes just as cynical as the other nuclear-weapon powers.

Even as the domestic debate constrains a full-blown transition from disarmament to arms control, the external reaction too has created complications. In the heat of the reaction to the Indian and Pakistani tests, the United States has once again returned to focusing on the Kashmir issue. The reaction and the statements from the United States, the P-5 group, the G-8 nations, and the UN Security Council have all renewed the emphasis on resolving the Kashmir dispute. Although all the declarations stress the resolution of the dispute through bilateral dialogue, the global attention to Kashmir has revived hopes in Pakistan for an internationalization of the dispute and reduced its stake in the success of the bilateral dialogue with India. As a consequence, the thrust of Pakistan's diplomacy is on resolving the "root cause" of tensions between the two nations, rather than on the importance of establishing a system of CBMs. It is in the interest of the United States that international energies not be dissipated again in pursuing the holy grail of a solution to the Kashmir dispute; rather, the focus should be on stabilizing nuclear deterrence between the two nations.

## COPING WITH A FAILING STATE IN PAKISTAN

The prospects for achieving a stable nuclear deterrence between India and Pakistan could be severely undermined by the deepening social, political, and economic crises in Pakistan. The decision by Pakistan to respond to India's tests with six of its own has dramatically accentuated Pakistan's troubles. Both the United States, the longtime benefactor of Pakistan, and India, its archrival in the Subcontinent, are now faced with the real danger of a failed state in Pakistan armed with nuclear weapons.

The United States has strongly encouraged India to resume the dialogue with Pakistan in the wake of the nuclear tests, and India has stepped up its own efforts to end the prolonged wrangling on the procedural aspects of the talks and begin substantive engagement with Pakistan. But the mere renewal of talks is unlikely to provide the badly needed breakthrough in bilateral relations. Far too often in the past, expectations of a major movement in Indo-Pak relations have been dashed by the many real hurdles on the ground. It is eminently sensible for India and Pakistan to go beyond discussing the shape of the table and begin talking about the issues that divide them. But the new round of Indo-Pak dialogue expected to begin in late 1998 may not go very far unless India takes into account the far-reaching changes in the context of bilateral relations.

The Pakistani economy is hurtling toward default on its international debt obligations. The fundamentals of the economy have been in bad shape since the early 1990s, and the crisis has now come to a head. The problem is not one of finding appropriate terms for an international bailout of Pakistan, led either by the United States or by the Islamic nations. Rather, it lies in the utter inability of the Pakistani political class to initiate any serious reform that could put the economy back on the rails.

Since he took charge in early 1997, Nawaz Sharif has accumulated an enormous amount of power at the expense of the Parliament, his own party, the judiciary, and the president. But he seems incapable of exercising this power to deal with the serious social and economic problems of Pakistan. For Sharif, political power appears to have become an end in itself; it is power without purpose. Unable to cope with the current crisis, he wants to further expand his own power by Islamizing the polity of Pakistan. Meanwhile the ethnic and sectarian tensions of Pakistan continue to grow. There is increasing resentment among the ethnic minorities of Pakistan that political power is now concentrated in the hands of the Punjabi elite. Sectarian tensions in Pakistan between Sunnis and Shias have grown to alarming proportions, fueled by militant organizations. Pakistani military adventurism in Kashmir and Afghanistan has put Pakistan at odds with most of its neighbors, including India, Iran, and the Central Asian states. Pakistan has become a breeding ground for international terrorism, thanks to the infrastructure of terrorist training facilities and ideological militancy established in Pakistan by its intelligence agencies. The forces of religious extremism unleashed by Pakistan are beginning to turn some of their attention to Pakistan itself and hastening the pace of the "Talibanization" of Pakistan. If the social explosion in Pakistan is likely to happen sooner rather than later, what should be India's strategy for dealing with a failed state on its borders? Five different options present themselves.

The first option for India is a policy of *status quo plus.* This would involve continuation of the present framework of engagement with Pakistan, with minor adjustments. This may be precisely the approach that was hammered out at the nonaligned summit in Durban in September 1997, where Indian and Pakistani officials apparently sorted out their differences over the modalities of resuming the talks. The details of this agreement were to be announced after the two prime ministers met in New York in September 1998. But a revival of negotiations by the two foreign secretaries under the new formula may not produce any significant results, even if it lasts beyond a couple of rounds. Since 1990 the two foreign secretaries have been engaged in on-again, off-again talks that have produced very little. These talks have largely become an exercise in scoring diplomatic points with the international community and posturing before domestic audiences. If the talks continue within the old framework and at the bureaucratic level of the foreign secretaries, they may not achieve very much.

An improvement over the policy of status quo plus would be an Indian approach that may be termed *limited engagement.* This would call for elevating the dialogue to the political level and attempting a purposeful negotiation over the entire range of issues with Pakistan. India could seek to clinch a whole range of agreements that had been finalized in earlier rounds of talks, while opening a serious dialogue on Jammu and Kashmir. But such a policy may not have too many takers in Pakistan. There is very little that India can give on Kashmir that will satisfy the right flank of Nawaz Sharif. The domestic pressure on Sharif not to agree on anything with India unless the core issue of Jammu and Kashmir is resolved to the satisfaction of the extreme opinion in Pakistan is real. Limited engagement would be helpful in convincing the world that India is serious about talking with Pakistan, but it is unlikely to change the political dynamics across the border.

A third option for India is to pursue a *benign neglect* of Pakistan. Such a policy would be based on two assumptions. It would acknowledge that Pakistan is not really interested in a serious dialogue and is seeking only to highlight the dispute over Jammu and Kashmir. It would take into account that Pakistan is absolutely unwilling to engage cooperatively with India, even when it is in Pakistan's own enlightened self-interest, for instance in areas such as trade. An Indian policy of benign neglect would limit itself to handling firmly the cross-border terrorism from

Pakistan. It would recognize the depth of the Pakistani crisis but argue that it would be presumptuous of India to believe that it can save Pakistan from itself. Such an approach would call for leaving Pakistan alone until it comes to terms with itself and the need for a cooperative relationship with India. Benign neglect may be a realistic policy proposition, but it may underestimate the fallout from a collapse of Pakistan, and it leaves the initiative on the dialogue entirely to Pakistan. There would also be some international diplomatic costs if India was seen as consciously shunning a dialogue with Pakistan.

Another option for India is to consider an *active containment* of Pakistan. It would be rooted in the assumption that the establishment in Pakistan is committed to unremitting hostilities against India, and that whatever India does to improve relations, Pakistan has little reason to reciprocate. It would argue that India must directly confront Pakistan's hostile policy through active measures on the border. It should utilize the contradictions between Pakistan and its other neighbors and step up military, political, and diplomatic pressures on Pakistan until it transforms itself into a less aggressive nation and stops being a threat to the whole region. Under a policy of active containment, India would make Pakistan engage in an arms race until Pakistan is ruined. The policy assumes that Pakistan is determined to self-destruct and all India has to do is "help" it along. The consequences of such a policy are not entirely predictable, but it is certain that tensions will mount rapidly in the region without a guarantee that India will be able to control the whole process. The danger, of course, is that as it sinks, Pakistan will take India along with it.

Of the four options discussed above, status quo plus is futile, limited engagement is unsustainable, benign neglect is too indifferent, and active containment is risky. India might consider instead a policy aimed at the integration of Pakistan into a cooperative regional order in the Subcontinent. The *regional integration* of Pakistan would call for steps, including unilateral Indian ones, that would encourage various forces in Pakistan toward cooperation with India.

Contrary to the perception that such a policy is sentimental and effete, it would involve an aggressive approach and the search for a radical outcome over the long term. It would open up the Indian market unilaterally to Pakistan, and step up the economic incentives for commercial interaction with India. Besides drawing Pakistan into the South Asian market, it would use public diplomacy to force open Pakistani society, which has been deliberately closed by the Pakistani establishment for ideological reasons. It would seek to chip away, bit by bit, at the roots of hostility against India in Pakistan. This approach would call for a boldness of vision and statesmanship. But this is a policy that it may be in the American interest to encourage. While the obstacles are huge, building a cooperative order in the Subcontinent through a joint effort of India and Pakistan is not entirely unrealistic. The recent nuclear tests in the Subcontinent have not reduced the importance of India's and the United States' pursuit of this objective.

## TOWARD A COOPERATIVE ORDER IN THE SUBCONTINENT

Expanding commercial and political understanding between India and the United States may significantly strengthen efforts within the Subcontinent to deepen cooperation. As the nations of the region unveiled policies of economic liberalization in the early 1990s, the logic of expanding trade and commercial cooperation within the Subcontinent has become apparent. This has created an unprecedented opportunity for the United States to focus on transforming the region into a large integrated market.

There is now a strong consensus within the Indian political class that pursuit of good neighborly relations is in the national interest. Inder Kumar Gujral has most vigorously articulated this policy, first as foreign minister and later as the prime minister of the United Front government (1996–98). Although the so-called Gujral doctrine has been identified with one man, there is broad agreement on its essence. P. V. Narasimha Rao paved the way for the Gujral doctrine by reducing India's tensions with its smaller neighbors. Vajpayee has largely pursued a similar policy of unilateral Indian concessions, at least on the economic front. There is a growing awareness in India that it will not be able to play a larger role on the world stage unless it brings greater harmony to its own backyard. Although relations with Pakistan remain in a category apart, it is not impossible to conceive of a scenario wherein India and the United States first encourage regional cooperation wherever possible, and slowly nudge Pakistan into that process.

In the second term of the Clinton administration there have been signs of a new approach in the United States. Pointing to the new trends in the Subcontinent, the US assistant secretary of state, Karl Inderfurth, told the US Congress on October 22, 1997:

> A sense of regional cooperation is growing, enhanced by India's new more accommodating posture towards its smaller neighbors, known as the Gujral Doctrine. The formerly moribund regional organization, the South Asian Association of Regional Cooperation is showing signs of life.... South Asia's massive energy shortages make it a major market for the US power companies. In India we are considering a special partnership to build state-of-the-art, environmentally friendly power plants. American companies are looking at Nepal's enormous hydropower resources, and possible exports of thousands of megawatts to India and other countries. Other sizable projects are being considered in Bangladesh and Pakistan.

As the United States discovers the potential for hydropower generation in Nepal and hydrocarbon resources in Bangladesh, prospects for Indo-US cooperation having wider regional impact grow significantly. The American commercial interest in Nepal and Bangladesh provides a historic opportunity for India and the United

States to work together for the first time in the Subcontinent. For far too long, India and the United States have dissipated their diplomatic energies in squabbling about the western part of the Subcontinent—their respective relations with Pakistan. The time has come for the two sides to "look east" and seize the emerging opportunity to jointly promote economic prosperity in a region that is home to the world's largest concentration of poor.

In many ways Bangladesh could become a more important economic priority than Pakistan for both India and the United States. While Pakistan refuses to grant even minimal trading privileges to India, and links trade with the "core issue" of Kashmir, Bangladesh has become one of India's most important trading partners, taking nearly a billion dollars' worth of official imports from India. Unofficial trade is estimated to be even larger. Dacca is with New Delhi and Kathmandu in seeking subregional economic cooperation both within the ambit of the South Asian Association for Regional Cooperation (SAARC) and outside it.

For the United States, too, Bangladesh has become economically attractive. Until recently the cumulative US FDI in Bangladesh stood at about $20 million. But in the first six months of 1997 this has shot up to $200 million, mostly in the natural gas sector. As American oil companies flock to Bangladesh to exploit the huge natural gas reserves, the United States is advising Bangladesh to lift its current ban on export of natural gas to India. It is being pointed out that integration with the Indian market would facilitate the quick flow of US investments into Bangladesh. For the first time in decades, American commercial interests in Bangladesh may be in tune with the political desire of the two large South Asian neighbors—India and Bangladesh—to promote regional economic integration.

India and the United States also have a common interest in ensuring that the fledgling democracy in Bangladesh—one of the world's largest Islamic nations—succeeds. A common objective for India and Bangladesh is to promote the perception that democracy and Islam are not incompatible. Rapid growth in Bangladesh is essential to prevent the flow of economic refugees from there into India—such a flow would complicate domestic politics in several Indian states. Promotion of moderate and modern Islam in Bangladesh is of considerable political value to both India and the United States. However, India and the United States could also face new complications in Bangladesh. For example, the US decision to seek a status-of-forces agreement has generated some concerns about US military intentions in the region. These apprehensions are best removed through an intensive political dialogue among all three countries involved.

India and the United States have expanding stakes in regional and subregional cooperation in South Asia. But if the United States seeks to disengage from the region—if it pursues only non-proliferation objectives and does not forcefully seek to end sanctions against India and Pakistan—the prospects for regional integration could diminish and new tensions could be generated.

## INDIA, THE UNITED STATES, AND THE ASIAN DYNAMIC

The evolution of Indo-US relations toward a greater political understanding will have considerable impact on southern Asia. At the same time, the broader political evolution of the region and the strategies pursued by the United States and India toward this part of the world will also have a bearing on Indo-US relations. The last couple of years have seen an intensive reordering of relations among the great powers in Asia. The early post–Cold War rhetoric on collective security arrangements has given way to a revival of the traditional alliance arrangements and the building of new special relationships. The Indo-US strategic dialogue must also be seen as part of this unfolding realpolitik in Asia.

The very initiation of a serious political dialogue between India and the United States has had some impact on the foreign-policy debate in Pakistan. There is apprehension about the label "strategic" being attached to the US dialogue with India. Greater political cooperation between India and the United States is likely to generate fears in Pakistan about American abandonment. Indifferent Indo-US ties over the last five decades had made it easy for Pakistan to balance India through strategic cooperation with the United States. Pakistan has been desperately hoping that the end of the Cold War would not mean an end to its special relationship with the United States. It has believed that the American interest in Central Asia, the United States' continuing tensions with Iran and Iraq, and US concerns about the Islamic world—where Pakistan sees for itself a special position—would help Pakistan retain some strategic relevance for the United States.

To cope with the uncertainties generated by an improving Indo-US relationship, Pakistan may continue to seek an alliance with the United States and keep pressing for American intervention in its disputes with India. Indian nuclear tests and the pressure on Pakistan to test have increased sympathy for Pakistan in the United States. Uneven progress in the post-test diplomacy of the Clinton administration could once again raise questions marks in India and Pakistan about the US tilt to the other side.

Pakistan's ties with China have proved to be enduring, and if Indo-US relations move forward, Pakistan and Beijing may move even closer. While Pakistan needs old and new friends, its external adventurism and its promotion of sectarian Islamic politics has complicated its relations with Iran, China, and the United States. Pakistan is likely to remain a complicating factor in Indo-US relations. But India and the United States may both have a stake in the stability of Pakistan and in encouraging Pakistan to move toward moderation in its external and internal policies and promote its integration into a regional cooperative order.

Iran has now become an interesting factor in Indo-US relations. India views Iran as an important future partner over the long term—as a critical element of its energy security policy and as the natural gateway to Central Asia. The intense American hostility toward Iran, however, has forced New Delhi to constantly look over its shoulder in considering more intensive cooperation with Teheran. But now the United States itself appears to be in the midst of a comprehensive debate over Iran, and India is keenly following it. A constructive American engagement with Iran would be strongly welcomed in India. It is in the common interest of both the United States and India to support the emerging tendencies toward liberalism in the Islamic Republic.

Central Asia and the Caucasus have emerged as new foreign-policy priorities for the United States, which is seeking to promote their political and economic independence, integrate them into the global market, build military linkages, and develop their hydrocarbon resources. India has a strong interest in the energy resources of Central Asia, too, but given the absence of a geographic border, the current turmoil in Afghanistan, and Pakistan's reluctance to build a more cooperative strategy, India is constrained in its policy toward the region. Nevertheless, India maintains an active diplomatic profile in Central Asia and cares strongly about maintaining the liberal religious orientation of the countries of the region. While there are some concerns in India about the consequences of the growing Central Asian military links with the West, it is also aware of the increasing Chinese involvement in the energy politics of the region. Enhanced Indo-US cooperation on the energy front must be accompanied by efforts to build greater political understanding between the two sides over central Asia.

In Southeast Asia, there was an enthusiastic response to India's new "look east" policy, which culminated in India's entry into the Association of South East Asian Nations (ASEAN) as a full-dialogue partner and into the ASEAN Regional Forum (ARF). Concerned about the rise of China and fearful of an uncertain US policy toward the region, the Southeast Asian nations bank upon an effective balance of power among the major powers of the region to ensure their security. They would like to see India emerge economically stronger and play a more proactive role in the regional security arrangements. A more positive framework of Indo-US policy will boost India's ties to the region and generate greater depth to American policy toward Asia. The changing political landscape in Asia has also spurred greater interest in Japan about strengthening political cooperation with India. India already has an expanding relationship with South Korea.

If there is one factor that is likely to loom large over the future of Indo-US relations, it is China. Although there is greater interaction now between China and the United States than between India and the United States, there is some concern in Beijing at the prospect of a strategic understanding between India and the United States. During his visit to the Subcontinent in late 1996, Jiang Zemin talked about the importance of Sino–South Asian cooperation in excluding "hegemonism" from the region. While China may have a clear interest in limiting the American presence in the region, the United States has been talking about mobilizing China to resolve some of the problems of the Subcontinent. India has some stake in the American policy aimed at preventing China from exporting nuclear and missile technology to Pakistan. But it has no desire to see China emerge as the "big brother" of South Asia.

Several developments have pushed Sino-Indian relations to a new low after steady improvement for a decade. These would include not just the recent nuclear tests by India, but also the remarks against China by the Indian defense minister, George Fernandes, on the eve of the tests, and India's reference to the Chinese threat in justifying its recent tests. The new Indian debate on China, in which the defense minister came in for severe criticism from the opposition, reflected India's own ambivalence about China. But it has also reflected a greater Indian assertiveness after years of passive acquiescence to China's policies in India's own neighborhood. The United States has responded to the Indian tests by mobilizing Beijing to promote its non-proliferation objectives in the Subcontinent. This has generated a severe backlash in India. The Indian strategic community is appalled that the Clinton administration is willing to bring Beijing into "managing" South Asian non-proliferation on the nuclear issue. It was, after all, the Chinese nuclear test in 1964 that triggered the Indian nuclear debate, just as it was Chinese determination to assist Pakistan in acquiring nuclear weapons since the mid-1970s that eventually forced India's nuclear hand.

India may have nothing to gain from either the US containment of China or a Sino-American conundrum in Asia. India will be the loser if it becomes a cheerleader either for an American policy to isolate China or for the Chinese rhetoric against American "hegemonism" in Asia. Instead, India must remain committed to a substantial political engagement with both the United States and China. But coping with the vicissitudes of Sino-US relations is likely to pose a major challenge to India. On one hand, India cannot afford to be part of an American containment strategy against China, which is its large neighbor. A formal alignment with the United States could complicate India's security environment in the region. On the other hand, India is concerned about US policies that work toward further boosting China's capabilities and its ambitions to emerge as the dominant power in Asia. The fundamental challenge facing India on Sino-US relations is not a question of aligning with one against the other. Rather, it is one of finding an effective balance of power in Asia. India should strive hard to insulate itself from the negative consequences of Sino-US relations—either cooperative or confrontational—while making itself an indispensable element in structuring a stable order in Asia.

# 3

# Indo-US Relations after the 1998 Tests: Sanctions versus Incentives

**Virginia I. Foran**

An interesting twist of events occurred with India's testing of five nuclear devices on May 11 and 13, 1998. For thirty years India opposed the nuclear Non-Proliferation Treaty (NPT) and more recently the Comprehensive Test Ban Treaty (CTBT) on the grounds that the treaties are discriminatory because they allow the declared nuclear weapon states to retain their nuclear arsenals and continue some level of testing (albeit computer-simulated). In the absence of "universal and non-discriminatory disarmament, we [India] cannot accept a regime that creates an arbitrary division between nuclear haves and have-nots." [1] In explaining its decision to test, the government of India (GOI) argued that it "was obliged to stand aside from the emerging regime so that its freedom of action was not constrained." [2] Much like closing the door after the horses already have left the barn, India then announced its willingness to participate in several aspects of the non-proliferation regime that it had so severely criticized.

1. India announced that it would observe a voluntary moratorium on further testing and was willing to "move towards a de-jure formalization of this declaration," indicating its willingness to join the CTBT.

2. India was also ready to participate in negotiations on the Fissile Material Cutoff Treaty (FMCT).

3. India reiterated "its readiness to discuss a 'no-first-use' agreement [with Pakistan], as also with other countries bilaterally, or in a collective forum."

4. India indicated its commitment to maintaining stringent export controls on its own nuclear know-how and technologies.

The price of India's signature of the CTBT and any further participation in the non-proliferation regime such as the FMCT or NPT itself is yet to be determined. India has indicated that the CTBT must be revised to include a time-bound framework for the nuclear disarmament of the five declared nuclear-weapon states. Other sources suggest that India wants to become a member of the nuclear export control regime—the Nuclear Suppliers Group (NSG)—and have access to high technology as the price for its signature. While this is an opportunity to gain India's participation in the non-proliferation regime, the whole world will observe the response of the regime, and of the United States in particular, to India's snubbing of widely accepted international non-proliferation norms—even if the norms are indeed discriminatory. The international response to India is no longer a simple one of imposing sanctions to punish and isolate the violator, nor is it a matter of what price the international community is willing to pay to persuade India to finally join them. Faith in the traditional non-proliferation tools of incentives and sanctions has been shaken, but there is no obvious replacement.

By reviewing the incentives offered and sanctions imposed on India in the past, this chapter evaluates the current strategy adopted by the United States and the international community toward India and assesses the likelihood of its success in discouraging further proliferation in South Asia. I conclude that the litmus test for the success of international nuclear non-proliferation is not in the willingness and ability of states to impose sanctions and punishment on transgressors of non-proliferation norms. Instead, it lies in the ability to get non-proliferation results over the longer term, even if this means that traditional non-proliferation goals appear weakened in the short term.

## HISTORY OF US SANCTIONS AND INCENTIVES TOWARD INDIA

Relations between the United States and India, as well as the history of US sanctions and incentives toward India, largely can be viewed through the twin lenses of the Cold War and nuclear non-proliferation.[3] Many of the sanctions imposed on and incentives offered to India by the United States were not designed with nuclear non-proliferation as the objective. However, they are important because they have affected the state of Indo-US relations and are likely to affect the success of targeted non-proliferation sanctions or incentives.[4] Until very recently, sanctions or the threat of sanctions, rather than incentives, dominated Indo-US relations where nuclear non-proliferation was concerned.

### Sanctions

India did not want to take sides during the Cold War, and by the mid-1950s it had developed a nonalignment policy that was designed to allow it to remain independent of both the United States and the Soviet Union. By the mid-1960s, however, nonalignment became more rhetoric than actual policy, as India began to side with the former Soviet Union diplomatically and became the beneficiary of the Soviet arms exports and technology, much of it on a barter or grant basis. There were several important consequences of India's pro-Soviet leanings. These led to the American imposition of restrictions on America's and other nations' foreign trade and economic relations with India. In particular, India's import of Western military and high technology suffered, and at times so did its ability to obtain foreign aid, especially food aid. These restrictions did little to affect India's decision to develop a nuclear-weapon option alongside its nuclear energy program, except to underscore India's perception that it could not rely on Western democracies for the kind of assistance (developmental, military, and political) it felt it needed and deserved.

The United States imposed specific non-proliferation sanctions and restrictions on India after India's first test of a nuclear device in 1974. These restrictions were designed to limit India's access to nuclear material, goods, and technology and thereby slow down or inhibit India's nuclear ambitions. However, India's response was that it would simply develop everything it needed for its nuclear program itself. For a country such as India, developing sophisticated technology, including nuclear energy and nuclear weapons, was a source of great pride. Therefore sanctions and restrictions were a headache but not an impediment. In fact, at times sanctions acted as a spur for indigenous development.

*Cold War Restrictions and Sanctions*

India was not a specific target of COCOM, an organization of democratic states that voluntarily restricted the export of military and high technology to Communist-bloc countries and countries affiliated with the Communist bloc. However, at times the United States unilaterally imposed restrictions on exports because India would not support American Cold War military objectives and politics. These restrictions also aimed to prevent reexport to the Soviet Union and Communist-bloc countries.[5]

India was not singled out, however. During the Cold War the United States had difficulty balancing its foreign-policy concerns with the liberal world economic order that it advocated as the bedrock of peace. Trade barriers were seen as a major contributor to World War II, and trade with Western Europe and Japan became "a means of helping rebuild their economies and of cementing US relations with them."[6] At the same time, the United States was preoccupied with secrecy and export controls as a way of prolonging the technological advantage it had over the Soviet Union. It therefore imposed strict constraints on technology transfer even among its own allies.[7]

During the years of COCOM, India belonged to the realm of "free world" countries. It was a category V state that was not subject to the majority of American export controls suffered by categories W (Hungary and Poland), Y (all other East European states and the former Soviet Union), and Z (North Korea, Vietnam,

Cambodia, and Cuba).[8] India did not share COCOM's objectives, however, and until the mid-1980s it was regarded by the United States as having weak controls on exports to other states.[9]

The decision to grant a license for export involves a number of US government agencies. The Arms Export Control Act gives the Department of State the authority to control the export of military equipment and technology. The regulations on these exports are compiled in the International Traffic in Arms Regulations (ITAR). The ITAR is based on the US Munitions List, which is maintained by the Department of Defense. The Export Administration Act (EAA) and its amendments provide the information to the Department of Commerce for the regulation of commercial goods and technology that are considered to be "dual-use," that is, technology that "could make a significant contribution to the military capabilities of a potential adversary." Until India's test of a nuclear explosive device in 1974, the United States had no need for country-specific export controls that would apply to India. According to Department of Commerce officials, decisions for exports were made on a case-by-case basis, more often than not ending in the approval and granting of a license. This assessment, however, does not distinguish between the different categories of exports—pure commercial, dual-use, and military equipment and technology—but lumps all requests for export licenses to India together.[10] This optimistic evaluation by American officials is contested in India, where discussions of US-India trade relations are dominated by popular perceptions of the United States as a discriminatory hegemon preoccupied with preventing the export of technology to India.[11] Recently these popular perceptions have been challenged by some Indians who found that there was little data to support the contention that US restrictions have caused extensive damage to India's development, commercial trade with the United States, or even technological progress.[12]

Perhaps this is because in India, technology has always been seen as a development tool.[13] India sought technology from outside, but would retreat to indigenous development if it deemed the conditions for acquiring the technology to be burdensome or restrictive. The Indian government refused to allow the import of technology unless the transaction was accompanied by a license to reproduce the technology domestically. These highly unusual expectations surfaced vis-à-vis several US commercial firms, for example, Coca-Cola for its patent and American defense producers for design and production information.[14] When requests for technology transfer licenses were denied, Indian firms would endeavor to develop the product from scratch.

Besides restrictions on technology, the United States varied the amount of foreign aid it provided to India and made efforts to influence India's other trade partners. These measures were seen as a way to convey disappointment in India's neutralism and its not-so-veiled support of the Soviet Union. During the 1950s and '60s, Indo-US relations focused on economic development, with the United States providing half of the total foreign assistance India received. Half of the US aid came in the form of grain and agricultural commodities, but loans were also provided for industrial expansion and infrastructure, including transport, irrigation, and energy.[15] As expectations for growth accelerated during India's third five-year plan, begun in 1961, actual economic performance stagnated due to rising prices, population growth, and budget constraints. The United States called for a redirection of India's development strategy (toward agriculture and away from heavy industry) and a general liberalization of controls on foreign investment, already weighed down by restrictions and bureaucratic regulations.[16] The US Congress was not inclined to continue the economic program during this period, but was persuaded to postpone changes to the program when India suffered the worst drought in a century, followed by a monsoon failure in 1966. President Johnson responded personally by campaigning for a massive grain assistance program (14 million tons during the period 1965–67). In exchange, President Johnson hoped to persuade India to change its economic and foreign policy to a position closer to that of US interests. During 1965–66, India's government listened and responded, amending foreign-investment regulations to permit majority control of certain industries in the agricultural sector.

From the American perspective, these objectives were deemed to be reasonable given India's perceived dependence on the United States for economic assistance. In India, however, the prime minister faced anger and criticism for agreeing to such terms. When changes in India seemed to slow down, President Johnson increased the pressure by delaying some of the grain shipments and requiring that each shipment have his personal authorization. The strategy backfired, and the Indian government began purchasing grain from other sources in order to reduce its dependence on American goodwill. Prime Minister Gandhi wrote to the president to explain how "national pride made her country reluctant to accept foreign aid." Gradually it became clear that India's policies on direct foreign investment would not change and would continue to discourage American investors.[17]

Episodes such as this one characterized Indo-US economic and trade relations in particular as well as diplomatic relations between the two countries throughout most of the Cold War. The United States was able to coerce most states (some more gently than others) into accepting the conditions for US assistance, convinced that the state preferred to depend on the United States rather than on some other less well-intentioned state. India did not like being coerced by any state, disagreed with many of the American conditions, and was suspicious of American intentions as well, because even US food aid was subject to political conditions.

The view that the United States was an unreliable partner in trade and food assistance only underscored India's experience with the United States as an unreliable supplier of military equipment and informal ally. It began with the US decision to sell arms to Pakistan in 1953, its subsequent formation of a defense alliance with Pakistan, and the inconsistent and ineffective US military support after the October 1962 invasion by China. This trend continued with an arms embargo during the Indo-Pakistan War in 1965 and the perceived "tilt" toward Pakistan during the war in East Pakistan in 1971. Prime Minister Nehru responded somberly to the US-Pakistan alliance:

> A military pact between Pakistan and the United States changes the whole bal-
> ance in this part of the world and affects India more especially. The United
> States must realize that the reaction in India will be that this arming of Pakistan
> is largely against India or might be used against India, whether the United
> States wants that or not.... They imagine that such an alliance between
> Pakistan and the United States would bring such overwhelming pressure on
> India as to compel her to change her policy of nonalignment. That is a rather
> naive view because the effect on India will be just the opposite, that is, one of
> greater resentment against the United States.[18]

India viewed President Kennedy's response to the Chinese invasion in 1962 as limited, and noted that the promises of additional military assistance from the United States and the UK were not fulfilled.[19] K. Subrahmanyam estimates that between 1962 and the 1965 war with Pakistan, the United States provided approximately $80 million worth of equipment. All major weapon systems were prohibited from export to India.[20] The American embargo on arms sales after the 1965 war enraged many Indians, given that much of the equipment Pakistan used against India was of American origin. British prime minister Harold Wilson asked that British equipment supplied to India since 1962 for defense against China be returned. From the Indian perspective, it appeared that the West was applying a double standard to India.[21]

It is against this background of trade restrictions and disappointing military and foreign policy collaboration with the West that the United States made its appeal in 1966 to India to sign the NPT. Not surprisingly, India was concerned about the treaty's consequences on its security. India argued that in exchange for the promise to be a non-nuclear-weapon state, nuclear-weapon states should either promise to defend non-nuclear-weapon states from nuclear attack or agree not to use nuclear weapons against them. How else, India queried, could a sovereign state agree to adhere to the NPT in the face of unknown, future nuclear threats?[22] India also requested specific joint "security guarantees" from the Soviet Union and the United States in order to increase its security vis-à-vis China.[23]

The only response to India's requests came in June 1968, when the United States, the United Kingdom, and the Soviet Union jointly offered UN Security Council Resolution 255. This promised that they would assist any non-nuclear-weapon state that was a party to the NPT if it was "a victim of an act or an object of a threat of aggression in which nuclear weapons are used."[24] However, Resolution 255 was not satisfactory to India or to many other non-nuclear-weapon states because there was no stipulation regarding what kind of assistance would be provided and which conditions would activate this assistance. Given India's very recent experience with the unreliability of British and American military cooperation during the 1965

Indo-Pakistan War, how could India have faith in their promises to "assist" if India was subject to a nuclear attack, when the stakes would be infinitely higher? In addition, fulfilling the resolution's obligations was subject to the Security Council veto and was tied to signing the NPT. India believed that its security should be ensured, regardless of whether it signed the NPT.[25]

### Nuclear Non-proliferation Restrictions

The United States was disappointed with India's decision not to sign the NPT, but it was India's test of a nuclear explosive device in May 1974 that triggered the passage of a number of laws. These laws restricted the sale or export of high-technology products perceived to contribute to a non-NPT-member state's nuclear-weapon capability. This further restricted American exports to India (as well as to other non-NPT-member states).

A comprehensive treatment of all non-proliferation legislation would not be appropriate here. The legislation that is most pertinent to India is complex, though much of it is well known, as the details are repeated in nearly every article concerning Indo-US relations. It includes the following:

1. the Atomic Energy Act of 1954 (AEA)

2. the Nuclear Non-Proliferation Act of 1978 (NNPA)

3. Sections 101, 102, and 73(a) of the Arms Export Control Act (AECA), which incorporated parts of the Foreign Assistance Act of 1961

4. the Export Administration Act (EAA)

5. the Nuclear Proliferation Prevention Act of 1994

6. the Export-Import Bank Act of 1945

In general, the AEA and the NNPA set out conditions for US nuclear cooperation agreements. These include the requirement that US-origin equipment or technology be used only for peaceful purposes and must be subject to full-scope International Atomic Energy Agency (IAEA) safeguards.[26] Under section 101 of the AECA, the United States cannot provide aid to any country that transfers or acquires uranium enrichment facilities that are not under IAEA safeguards.[27] A very similar Section 102 of the AECA prohibits the United States from providing most forms of economic and defense assistance to states that transfer or acquire uranium reprocessing materials or technology, or that transfer or explode a nuclear device.[28] Since India developed its enrichment and reprocessing technology indigenously, it has not been subject to this legislation. The same, however, cannot be said for Pakistan.[29]

Section 73(a) of the AECA and the parallel section 11(b) of the EAA provide that sanctions will be imposed against foreign persons, firms, and government entities that violate the Missile Technology Control Regime (MTCR) if they are involved in transferring missiles or components controlled by that regime. If the transfer involves a Category II violation of the MTCR, the sanction requires suspension of all US government contracts and export licenses relating to missile technology or equipment for two years. If the transfer involves a Category I violation, then all US government contracts and export licenses for *all* items on the US munitions list and *all* items controlled by the Department of Commerce will be suspended for two years.[30]

The Export Administration Act of 1979, section 5, authorizes the president to regulate the export of "goods or technology for sensitive nuclear uses." The Export-Import Bank Act of 1945 provides that the bank can deny credit to states when the president determines that it is in the interest of nuclear non-proliferation. The bank is prohibited from engaging in transactions that will support exports to states or parties that have violated non-proliferation agreements or norms.[31]

With a few notable exceptions, because of the indigenous nature of India's nuclear and missile programs, India was not subject to the majority of this legislation until the 1998 Pokharan tests. Nevertheless, India was affected by it even before the tests. In addition to the unilateral US prohibitions, the United States has pressured other states against assisting India in any way in the area of nuclear technology. In 1992 the NSG agreed that transfers of nuclear technology, equipment, or materials would require that the recipient state agree to full-scope safeguards.[32] Since 1993 India has been unable to receive some of materials it needs to keep its nuclear facilities operating at full capacity. Now that India has conducted tests of nuclear devices, and if there is no dramatic change in India's nuclear ambitions and negotiation with the NSG, this legislation is likely to continue to affect India, especially given India's desire to expand its nuclear program to help meet an anticipated increase in domestic energy demands.[33]

### Effectiveness of Sanctions

That the restrictions and threat of sanctions did little to change India's ambitions (despite driving up the cost) is not a surprise to most observers of Indian foreign policy. This behavior is consistent with recent evaluations of the usefulness of sanctions to achieve foreign-policy goals. These studies have concluded that sanctions are unlikely to bring about a change in the behavior of the target state (in this case the nuclear weapons program of India). However, sanctions may provide some influence over the behavior of the target without incurring the costs normally associated with more radical forms of interference such as military intervention.[34] In addition, the power of sanctions can be "broken" if the target state finds an alternative source of supply; that is, sanctions imposed unilaterally by one state usually fail because the target state finds the good(s) someplace else.[35] The effectiveness of sanctions is weakened by interesting (though unintended) responses to sanctions by both the sender state and the target state.

### IN THE TARGET STATE

- Sanctions can unify the citizens of the target country to support the precise policy or behavior that is considered undesirable by the sender state. This is the rally-around-the-flag effect.

- Sanctions tend to compel the target state to look for alternative sources of supply.

- If the alternative sources of supply are created internally, the groups who benefit (in this case, the scientists and firms involved in the nuclear program) will have a stake in ensuring that the sanctions continue.[36]

In the case of India, the first two responses have been clearly observed. The nuclear program has always enjoyed vast popular support, and the Indian government simply decided to produce all the necessary components for a nuclear weapon themselves.[37]

### IN THE SENDER STATE

- Sanctions create conflicts between the sender state government and its society when implementation of the sanctions imposes losses due to interrupted trade and financial contracts.

- Even if public opinion for the sanctions is strong at first, it dissipates over time as the costs of the sanctions accrue.[38]

Criticism of using sanctions to achieve foreign-policy objectives has not just been a subject of academic debate, but has reached policy circles as well. An investigation by Richard Haass concluded that "economic sanctions are increasingly being used to promote the full range of American foreign policy objectives. Yet all too often sanctions turn out to be little more than expressions of US preferences that hurt American economic interests without changing the target's behavior for the better." [39] Lobbyists, taking full advantage of the swing in opinion, began to advocate the use of incentives as better tools to persuade states to change their policies toward a desired direction.[40] However, incentives are not a new tool for foreign policy, nor are they new to nuclear non-proliferation efforts.

## Incentives

The amount of attention sanctions receive in the non-proliferation literature does a disservice to the role that incentives have played in persuading states to forgo nuclear weapons.[41]

### US Global Initiatives on Incentives

In the postwar period, there were two major incentive initiatives that were offered to all states by the United States. The first was the US Atoms for Peace program, launched in 1953. President Eisenhower hoped to discourage states from beginning nuclear programs unless they were subject to international regulations and inspection. In exchange, the United States offered to share nuclear equipment, materials, and technology with states that agreed to use such imports exclusively for peaceful purposes and to subject them to monitoring. The inspections would be carried out first by the United States and then later on by the IAEA. The second global initiative was offered to all states that would become party to the NPT of 1968. Similarly, in exchange for accepting IAEA inspections on all of their nuclear activities, non-nuclear-weapon members of the NPT were guaranteed broad access to peaceful nuclear technology.

In the early years of the nuclear age, until approximately the mid-1970s, access to nuclear material and technology was highly valued, and this incentive was sufficient to persuade most countries of the world that sought nuclear energy-generating capability to renounce their intention to develop or acquire nuclear weapons. As the benefits of nuclear energy became more uncertain (due to unanticipated costs and risks of nuclear energy plants), nuclear commerce declined and the incentive began to lose some of its appeal. In addition, the biggest suppliers of nuclear material began to hedge on the promises made in Article IV of the NPT to provide peaceful nuclear technology under safeguards to non-nuclear-weapon states party to the treaty. This occurred after India's test of a nuclear device in 1974 demonstrated the gaps between the looser inspection agreements negotiated under the Atoms for Peace program and the more comprehensive monitoring agreements required by the NPT. Two volunteer supplier organizations were established, the NPT Nuclear Exporters Committee and the NSG. They sought to prevent the export of a wide range of nuclear commodities to states suspected of seeking nuclear arms (even if they were members of the NPT), and restricted other commodities newly believed to be "sensitive." Practically speaking, members of the supplier organizations were unilaterally altering the incentive structure that the NPT originally provided to all members that were non-nuclear-weapon states.

At the same time, other less-than-global incentives in the form of security guarantees and alliances were being offered to certain states as the result of overarching competition and rivalry between the United States and the Soviet Union. American incentives of this variety were particularly persuasive to most members of the North Atlantic Treaty Organization (NATO), Japan, Australia, and South Korea.

Finally, the United States offered incentives, including not just security guarantees but also political and economic benefits, to a number of specific states in exchange for non-proliferation commitments. These states include Taiwan, Ukraine, North Korea, Pakistan, and most recently India. The effectiveness of the incentives offered to all these states except India have been assessed elsewhere, so we will concentrate exclusively on India here.[42]

## US Incentives to India

India benefited from the Atoms for Peace program to the extent that it may have discounted the benefits of guaranteed nuclear supply offered by the NPT, which it declined to sign. It later suffered the consequences when fuel shipments to one of its largest nuclear energy facilities (Tarapur) became subject to the new American export control law created in the wake of India's 1974 test. From then on, exports of high technology, including all military equipment, to India were watched very carefully.

In 1982 an exception to the rule was made when President Reagan and Prime Minister Indira Gandhi signed the Science and Technology Initiative, which culminated in the 1984 memorandum of understanding (MOU) on sensitive technologies, commodities, and information. These agreements provided for a transfer of American technology that, most significantly, would be used to develop India's light combat aircraft (LCAs).[43]

It was not a coincidence that these agreements occurred at this time. Both states had strategic and practical reasons for wanting to cooperate in these heretofore sensitive areas of military equipment and technology. The United States was busy trying to justify providing economic and military assistance to Pakistan, which was prohibited at the time by the Glenn and Symington Amendments to the Foreign Assistance Act. These prohibitions were triggered by the import of unsafeguarded uranium enrichment equipment by Pakistan. The waiver criteria were redrafted to allow the president to waive sanctions if he could certify that it was in the "national interest of the United States."

The high-technology initiative to India was a way to balance the assistance going to Pakistan, ostensibly because the United States believed that it would increase American influence over Indian military programs by decreasing the country's reliance on indigenously developed technology. In addition, the United States wanted to try to pressure the Soviet Union by trying to "woo the Indians away from them."[44] This latter reason is somewhat similar to the strategic rationale behind American rapprochement with China in the 1970s.[45] This US effort coincided with India's desire to move closer to the United States in order to lessen the effect of a perceived US-Pakistan-China axis during the Afghanistan war. India was also concerned about becoming too dependent on the Soviet Union for military hardware.[46] There is some evidence to suggest that in exchange the United States sought some accommodation from India on nuclear proliferation. However, this was limited to developing new procedures to ensure that the technology would not be used for building nuclear weapons or missiles in India, and that no technology would be leaked to the Soviet Union.[47]

The cooperation was neither robust nor long-lasting. There were substantial disagreements over specific types of systems and technology to be exported.[48] In general, from the American perspective, the GOI made requests for the newest technology available, for projects that did not necessarily require it. This fueled existing American suspicions about India's intentions regarding the technology. In one instance the government of India requested the Cray XMP-24 supercomputer in order to study the Indian monsoon. The XMP-24 was also capable of making computations useful in developing nuclear weapons and missiles and in deciphering cryptographic codes. The US government decided to offer to India a smaller super-computer instead, the XMP-14. It was capable of conducting the analysis of the monsoon but would not be able to be used for projects involving nuclear weapons, missiles, or cryptography. India interpreted the offer as a lack of US credibility in fulfilling the terms of the MOU and yet another instance of unreliability of American promises.

In 1985 many other exports became more difficult due to the implementation of the MTCR, as additional categories of technology suitable for missiles, but also for space launchers and satellites, were added to American export control lists. India's test of the Agni intermediate-range ballistic missile in 1989 resulted in serious concern in the United States because it was believed that American high-tech exports ostensibly for use in India's space and satellite programs were being adapted for missiles.[49] Despite the desire of executive leadership in both countries to continue the military and technological cooperation, the effort was overwhelmed by mutual suspicions regarding intentions. In addition, the end of the war in Afghanistan removed one of the rationales for cooperation. The United States decided it could no longer certify that Pakistan did not possess nuclear weapons, triggering sanctions and halting the end of US military and economic assistance to Pakistan. The United States no longer had any need to balance its assistance to the region. The sanctions also meant that India could be less concerned about a three-way axis between the United States, Pakistan, and China.

### Post–Cold War Situation

Since the end of the Cold War, there has been more of a balance between US sanctions and incentives toward India, though the relationship got off to a bumpy start in 1992 when the United State pressured Russia not to transfer cryogenic rocket engine technology to India. The United States imposed nearly meaningless sanctions on Glavkosmos, the Russian export organization for space-related goods and technology, though the sanctions on the Indian Space Research Organization (ISRO) had quite an impact.[50] Until 1995 it appeared that the relationship would return to the negative dynamic of the Cold War, but that year the secretary of defense, William Perry, met with government officials in New Delhi and began to establish military-to-military relations there. Though the Indo-US Cold War was over, Secretary Perry acknowledged the difficulty of overcoming the prism that remained in their relations. He stated, "We want to build on our shared security interests and deepen our defense cooperation, even though we disagree on the nuclear issue." [51]

The Department of Defense initiative was one of several efforts to engage India and was similar to those made toward Pakistan, though the latter remained limited by the Pressler Amendment. The US Department of Commerce officially designated India as one of the world's big emerging markets, encouraging and supporting American firms that invested in Indian commercial projects. The Department of Energy, prohibited from cooperation in the sensitive area of nuclear energy until the

United States and India had an official nuclear cooperation agreement, nonetheless investigated ways of initiating cooperation in some areas of nuclear safety the law allowed. Many of these efforts bore fruit.

On the commercial side, as part of an overall American post–Cold War policy, the administration dismantled COCOM and removed the controls from a number of items that were unilaterally prohibited from export to India (although India was not a direct target of COCOM controls). The burdensome licensing procedures that were developed during the 1980s were mostly done away with or streamlined. The most significant changes to the COCOM-era controls involved the scope of the controls and the relevant end-user list. Current controls are relevant only to countries that do not adhere to the MTCR or to countries that support international terrorism. Licenses are required only for controlled items or components that contribute up to 25 percent of the value of the system.[52] These new criteria reduce the number of overall controls that are applicable to US exports and provide increased opportunities for technology transfer.

The changes in US export controls did not come easily. The US Congress and the Clinton Administration made the changes only after conducting a number of hearings and interagency reviews evaluating the costs and benefits. The debate focused on reevaluating threats to US security in the post–Cold War environment. Many experts argued that American global economic competitiveness needed to be given a higher priority than in the Cold War era, for American security now depended more "on economic performance of US companies, especially those specializing in the development of advanced technology." Further, unilateral controls only drove the target state to purchase the technology from an American competitor, resulting in lost sales on top of undesirable technology transfer and loss of leverage. Export controls needed to be revised so that they were not a hindrance to US economic growth and technological advancement.[53]

Others argued that in the post–Cold War era, the proliferation of weapons of mass destruction was the single most important threat not only to American security, but also to the security of US friends and allies. Thus export controls were an essential component of American non-proliferation and national security strategy. Moreover, the existing export control system already had significant weaknesses, especially in preventing the export and diversion of dual-use goods that could be used to develop weapons of mass destruction. Revising the current export control system to accommodate increased international commerce would only increase this risk even more.[54]

The result was a hybrid effort: to reduce or eliminate controls that could be changed without incurring increased proliferation risk, and at the same time to streamline the existing export controls and strengthen the reporting procedures within the bureaucracy. India, however, remained a target for non-proliferation-related export control legislation. There was evidence of improvement in relations in sensitive areas such as military cooperation and nuclear energy assistance. Although the cooperation was still at low levels, there was interest in both governments to gradually broaden this cooperation.

Other signs of improvement in relations between the two states include an increase in the funding for international military exercises and training (IMET). During the Cold War, relations between the two state militaries were limited, and the budget for IMET was kept at $200 million. Since the end of the Cold War, that amount has been more than doubled, although US Defense Department officials have struggled with Indian counterparts on how to use the funding and what programs could be cooperated on.[55] During 1997 the United States sold precision guided munitions to the Indian air force and agreed to provide India with a submarine rescue facility.

In the sensitive area of nuclear energy cooperation, in September 1997 the chairman of the US Nuclear Regulatory Committee (NRC), Shirley Ann Jackson, confirmed to P. Rama Rao, chairman of the Indian Atomic Energy Regulatory Board (AERB), that three joint nuclear safety projects would be undertaken.[56] After nearly two years of discussions and delays that involved GOI efforts to make the agreement with the US Department of Energy, negotiations between the two nuclear regulatory agencies were completed. The projects had to develop within the limits set up by the fact that the two countries did not have a nuclear cooperation agreement, because it is prohibited by US law unless India accedes to the NPT. It was hoped that this small but important first step at cooperation on nuclear issues would broaden once the Indian government and its public experienced the benefits of international collaboration while still respecting the technical sovereignty of the Indian civilian nuclear program. All of these projects and collaborations came to a grinding halt on May 11, 1998.

## APPLYING INCENTIVES FOR COOPERATION: THEORY AND PRACTICE

What went wrong? Why, in the midst of an improving relationship with the United States, did the GOI decide to do precisely the thing that would most damage that relationship? Did Indian policy makers believe that the United States would not impose the sanctions required by the 1994 NNPA because of this new policy of engagement? Are the Indian (and Pakistani) tests evidence that incentives are poor foreign-policy tools?

The Clinton administration had been arguing for improvements in Indo-US relations right up to the time India conducted its tests. One month before the tests, the assistant secretary of state for South Asian affairs, Karl F. Inderfurth, noted that changes occurring in the region demanded a "greater openness" in US policy toward the region. Listing the important objectives for the region, Inderfurth included reducing the threat of conflict, strengthening democracy, furthering Indo-US commercial relations, settling the Afghan conflict, and encouraging an economic opening up of Central Asia. He noted that the nuclear weapon and ballistic missile programs were "a particularly difficult issue because [they arise] from very real national security concerns." [57] Such statements are profoundly different from US policy toward India just a few years ago, when the emphasis was still on "rolling back" both India and Pakistan's nuclear programs. Just before the May 1998 tests, the United States sought to "encourage India and Pakistan to exercise restraint and accept limits on their nuclear and missile programs." [58] It was hoped that the gradually increasing levels of cooperation offered by the United States would encourage India to look for ways that their nuclear and missile programs could be limited. In the months before the tests, there were some signs that the new American attitude and policy toward India would (eventually) be successful. There also were some warnings that American diplomats (and businessmen) should not hope for too much too soon. A brief look at what a successful incentive policy requires highlights why the conditions were much less than perfect in the case of the United States and India.

### Incentives and Bilateral Cooperation in Theory

There have been two recent efforts to understand the factors and conditions under which the engagement/incentive approach can be successful. Foran and Spector focused on incentives applied for non-proliferation purposes, while Long examined the use of economic and technological incentives for achieving more general political objectives. Both analyses are useful in assessing the case considered here, and the principal findings are summarized briefly below.

In his valuable work *Economic Incentives and Bilateral Cooperation,* William Long describes three "necessary and favoring conditions for success" of incentives.[59] First, incentives require that there be potential for a "bilateral exchange relationship" between the state providing the incentive (the sender state) and the state receiving the incentive (the recipient state). The exchange relationship emerges because the sender state has impeded trade gains of the recipient state through an embargo, tariffs, or some other nontariff barrier. Some influence accrues to the sender state if it decides to release those trade gains, and in many cases it will use the influence to seek a change in the recipient's political behavior. For the exchange to be successful, the sender state must value the political concession more highly than the recipient, and the recipient state must value the potential economic benefit more highly than the political concession.[60] Second, incentives require that there be potential for a "political market" between the sender and recipient states. Long describes this market as the existence of a minimum degree of trust between the states such that both have some confidence that each understands the quid pro quo of the incentive. If trust is lacking, then steps should be taken to build confidence before an incentive strategy is attempted. Countries may need to build confidence and cooperation in stages. Incentives are not likely to be successful in a hostile environment.[61] Third, incentives require that both the sender and the receiver state have the ability to implement them. The sender state has to have the institutional capability to coordinate the bureaucracy and see that the incentives are provided in a timely fashion, and the receiver state has to have the institutional strength to implement the political changes sought by the sender. An incentive strategy, therefore, may not be appropriate for very weak states.[62]

The results of Foran and Spector's analysis overlap with one of Long's factors almost perfectly, while other aspects are consistent with Long's findings. Foran and Spector identified three variables that appear to influence whether an incentive strategy for non-proliferation is likely to be successful or not. These can be summarized as follows:

1. the level of political and financial investment by the potential proliferating state in the development of nuclear weapons at the time an incentive is being contemplated

2. the degree of friendliness between the potential proliferating state and the state offering the incentive

3. the strength of the motive to proliferate[63]

Thus, in the model, the three variables interact with one another to increase or decrease the likelihood of success or failure. An incentive strategy is more likely to be successful when the potential proliferating state's level of investment in obtaining nuclear weapons is low, its motive to proliferate is on the low end of the continuum, and its relationship with the state providing the incentive is friendly. An incentive strategy is less likely to be successful when the level of investment in obtaining nuclear weapons is high, the state's motive to proliferate is on the high end of the continuum, and the relationship between the incentive provider and the potential proliferating state is poor and unfriendly.

Using these criteria, this author conducted an evaluation of the potential of incentives for the case of India and the United States just prior to the tests, and the results were cautiously mixed. I concluded that incentives of the type offered to Ukraine and North Korea would fail because of India's posture toward the non-proliferation regime, its high level of investment in its nuclear program, the well-entrenched bureaucracy, and the substantial public support for maintaining a nuclear option. Further, India's mostly inconsistent, and at times acrimonious, relationship with the United States was also likely to have an impact on such processes.[64] Although very difficult to implement, there were indications that indirect incentives might have some success over the long term. I note my conclusions at length here:

> Current US efforts to engage India on a number of foreign policy and trade issues, and its more flexible non-proliferation strategy, are unlikely to be sufficient to generate a dramatic transformation of Indian attitudes towards the United States, or towards India's nuclear ambitions.... US efforts may

strengthen the coalition over time, but no non-proliferation bargain should be expected in the near term, even if high technology is offered as an incentive. At best non-proliferation benefits may "trickle down" from the coalition as Washington targets its incentives to individuals and groups supportive of cooperating with the Unites States.[65]

As the quote mentions, indirect incentives in the form of high-technology products and technology transfer were thought to have particular promise because of India's interest in fueling its economic development and furthering its regional and global prestige. In addition, many Indian policy makers believe that access to high technology would contribute to India's future goals.

Specifically, the opening of India's economy had positioned India on the brink of rapid development. India could not take full advantage of this position without becoming more of a participant in the world's trade organizations and lessening the restrictions it encounters due to its positions on non-proliferation and protectionist trade policies. In addition, India had not been able to replace the technology transfer relationship it had with the former Soviet Union with a new relationship with another country or countries.[66]

Researchers evaluating the role of technology on productivity agree that technology plays a dominant role on increasing productivity. Robert Solow estimated that "more than half the historic increase in US productivity was attributable to technological change." [67] While Indian economists are not likely to admit it publicly, India's ability to continue to develop fast enough to compete with other states in the region may depend on improved access to high technology.[68] In addition, in a study evaluating incentives, technology incentives proved very effective in the past because the states valued the technology for its contribution to economic and political goals and for alleviating technology scarcity problems.[69]

The analysis suggested that if the United States were to improve cooperation in areas where technology has been denied in the past, it might have created an appropriately large enough change in the relationship. This might have altered India's assessment of the costs and benefits of its relationship with the United States, perhaps enabling it to reconsider other areas of disagreement such as its position on its nuclear program. These are two very big "ifs."

### Incentives and Bilateral Cooperation in Practice

The potential for the United States and India to make an agreement based on incentives was there, but there were several conditions needed for success that had not yet come about and were cause for concern. First, the United States government had to be willing to reduce export controls (particularly on high-technology items) beyond those that resulted from the revision of the COCOM-era controls. Second, the Indian government had to have the institutional and political strength to implement (eventually) what the United States sought in terms of cooperation on foreign policy and muting of India's nuclear ambitions.

As of April 1998, wide-ranging legal barriers to unrestricted exports to India remained. Nearly all of them were tied to India's proliferation status. Even presidential support for improving relations with India could not undo these legal barriers. If the efforts to reduce the effect of the Pressler Amendment sanctions on Pakistan indicated waning congressional support for non-proliferation sanctions, then some special, one-time exceptions to the sanctions might have been made in the near future.[70] The Clinton administration's engagement policy toward India was not based on the understanding that any incentive strategy would include a wholesale reversal of existing export control laws, because that would represent the weakening and reversal of American non-proliferation goals. Exceptions made to the export controls were meant as a show of good faith toward India and as a reward for past Indian restraint in nuclear proliferation. It was understood that such good faith would be severely tested if India took steps toward making its nuclear capability more overt, that is, testing and deployment of missiles, conducting a nuclear test, or even declaring its nuclear-weapon capability without testing.[71]

The second condition for a successful incentive strategy between India and the United States was even weaker in the months before the 1998 tests. The Clinton administration dealt with no less than three different Indian prime ministers and governments since initiating its new engagement effort in 1995. The first two governments were highly constrained by their weak political positions and were subject to demands from coalition partners regarding the future direction of Indian foreign policy. Any potential cooperation with the US government, or US firms for that matter, was viewed as suspicious, and those leaders who supported it were vulnerable to being characterized as submitting to US pressure.

It did not help that during this period, even as the United States was trying to pressure India to sign the CTBT, it chose *not* to impose sanctions on China despite Chinese violations of the Missile Technology Control Regime (MTCR). The violations included Chinese transfers of five thousand ring magnets to an unsafeguarded nuclear facility in Pakistan and of M-11 missile systems. By 1998 there were some positive aspects to Indo-US relations, but these were only recent improvements and, judging from past experiences, might not have been long-lasting. One could not characterize Indo-US relations as "friendly" during this time. At best, they were less acrimonious.

The Bharatiya Janata Party (BJP) won the right to form a government by winning the most seats in the March 1998 elections. The elections were held after the United Front (UF) government fell in November 1997 following the withdrawal of the Congress Party from the fourteen-party governing coalition. The BJP has publicly supported India's declaration of its nuclear capability for many years. In the months leading up to the elections, there were signs that the BJP would keep its promise. The BJP's National Agenda for Governance stated that it would "re-evaluate the [country's] nuclear policy and exercise the option to induct nuclear weapons." [72] Most analysts did not agree on what precisely was meant by "exercise the option to induct nuclear weapons," but none (including this author) assumed or predicted that it included conducting a series of nuclear tests less than a month after assuming power.

The BJP government was in many senses weaker than the preceding UF government, needing fifteen parties to form a government. Furthermore, it was assumed that now that the BJP had successfully formed a government after failing to do so when given the chance in 1996, it would want to concentrate on consolidating its power at home and portraying itself as stable leadership to the outside world. Finally, India's nuclear program has suffered from tremendous financial and technical difficulties over the years. This has combined with a reluctance to integrate the military into either the operation or the conceptualization of the nuclear strategy, despite the apparent popular support and advocacy for an overt nuclear capability by certain bureaucratic groups. Given these factors, what kind of nuclear weapons capability could the BJP actually produce if they did make good on their promise?[73] Testing, therefore, would not make sense.

Given the state of affairs in the months leading up to the test, continuing the US policy of engagement toward India made sense, even in light of the BJP coming to power. While a compromise in India's nuclear program did not seem likely in the near future, neither did it seem that the GOI would decide to overtly "exercise its nuclear option" immediately. Incentives in the areas of trade and technology could still contribute to strengthening of a coalition within India that would support continuing cooperation with the United States.

> This coalition may grow as the stake in Indo-US relations grows larger. The current trend of US policy towards India in emphasizing overall relations, particularly economic ones, may also help to decrease the high profile of the nuclear issue between the two states and enable a genuine internal debate by Indians on the merits of their nuclear program.[74]

Finally, the analyses indicated that because neither condition for success existed, improvements in Indo-US relations on the nuclear proliferation issue were not likely at the time and that this should not even be an expectation of the US engagement policy in the short term. Clearly, however, the analyses did not predict that Indo-US non-proliferation relations would change so radically, either.

### A Failure of Analyses?

Even though testing did not make sense for all the reasons enumerated above, the analysts failed to appreciate the accuracy of one of their own predictions. The BJP did want to consolidate its power at home. Testing and declaring India's nuclear capability not only fulfilled what BJP leaders had been promising to the people of India for years, but also ensured that their domestic critics would be silenced for some time. No political party could criticize the tests without criticizing India's right to be recognized by the world as a powerful, technologically advanced nation.

Predictably, many individuals and groups criticized the *timing* of the tests, though not the tests themselves.

A number of studies estimated that the cost of sanctions would be approximately 1 percent of India's GNP for the first few years and would decline thereafter, because it would become increasingly difficult to prevent other countries and US firms from wanting to sell to the growing Indian market. Sanctions, many Indian analysts assert, can hurt only rich nations, not poor ones. There were also a number of studies estimating the cost of an overt nuclear capability. Most reflect the conception of minimum deterrence with little or no attention paid to the need for command, control, communications, and intelligence systems ($C^3I$).[75] Financial estimates of the future costs of India's nuclear weapons capability that have been made (by Indian organizations) reflect this minimalist approach and range from Rs. 5,000 crores to Rs. 20,000 crores over the next decade. This is equivalent to a range of $119.47 million to $477.88 million.[76]

The analysts were correct about the factors the BJP government would consider, but miscalculated how these factors would be evaluated—hence their conclusion that nuclear proliferation was not imminent.

## CURRENT US RESPONSE

The world was taken by surprise on May 11, 1998, when India conducted a series of nuclear tests at its testing site in the Pokharan Desert, and even more surprised on May 13, when India conducted a few more and then announced that the testing "series" was concluded. There was no warning—usually provided by sophisticated technical intelligence agencies observing the test site—to enable the international community to dissuade the GOI from going ahead with the tests. No last-minute offer and no last-minute threat was possible, because there was a deliberate (and successful) effort to hide the test preparations from satellite view and an equally important effort to not inform or tip off any foreign government in any way.[77]

The United States had little choice in its response. The 1994 NNPA requires that strict, comprehensive sanctions be imposed automatically on any non-nuclear-weapon state that either receives or detonates a nuclear explosive device. It would take between several months and one year to ascertain which Indian firms, individuals, existing and pending contracts, loans, and sales of goods and services would be affected by the sanctions. At the same time, the Clinton administration embarked on a policy of negotiation and engagement with India (and Pakistan) in an effort to head off a nuclear arms race in the region. The strategy was simple. The United States would impose sanctions, but obtain the ability to waive them, gradually if necessary, to support either state's demonstration of nuclear restraint. The conditions for "restraint" and for the corresponding lifting of American (and other international) sanctions were laid out in the statements made by the five permanent members (P-5) of the United Nations Security Council (and declared nuclear weapon states) and eight advanced industrial nations (the G-8).[82] Many of the steps or conditions mirror the GOI's own statement of its non-proliferation intentions, noted at the beginning of this chapter, indicating that negotiation was a realistic possibility.

Under these conditions, India must:

- stop all further tests and agree to adhere to the CTBT

- refrain from manufacturing warheads or bombs, or attaching them to ballistic missiles

- refrain from testing or deploying nuclear-weapons-capable missiles

- halt production of fissile material

- confirm policies not to export equipment, material, or technology relevant to missiles or weapons of mass destruction and enter into commitments in that regard

- participate constructively in the negotiations of the FMCT

- reestablish direct communications with Pakistan and address the basic causes of tensions including the issue of Kashmir[79]

For the record, Secretary of State Madeleine Albright also announced that neither India nor Pakistan will be allowed to join the NPT as a nuclear-weapon state, because the treaty specifically defines a nuclear-weapon state as one that "has manufactured and exploded a nuclear weapon or other nuclear explosive device prior to January 1, 1967." Amendments to the NPT are unlikely, as they have to be approved by a majority of all parties to the treaty, including all nuclear-weapon states, and then ratified by individual nations.

Many disagree with the US efforts to continue to engage India and Pakistan. They believed that the United States imposed its own sanctions halfheartedly and did not work hard enough to persuade other nations to support US actions. Members of the non-proliferation community were critical of the Clinton administration and Congress for supporting waiver legislation and indicating that negotiation was possible before waiting for the sanctions to have their full effect.

On the other hand, sanctions, particularly unilaterally imposed ones such as those imposed on India and Pakistan, have been criticized as an ineffective diplomatic tool in persuading a state to change an undesired policy, and particularly ineffective in changing a state's nuclear proliferation policy. French president Jacques Chirac confirmed that he and other European leaders believe that "sanctions alone will make India and Pakistan more desperate and determined to pursue their nuclear policies." He stated:

> [W]e can see that the tests occurred, and therefore the threat of sanctions did not work. We have to talk together and then talk to India and Pakistan, in a more understanding way, even as we make clear that we disapprove of what they have done.[80]

In the United States, Richard Haass's commentary summed up what many policy makers and analysts thought about the automatic sanctions imposed on India and Pakistan. He stated, "[I]t is difficult to see how the same sanctions that fail to deter India from testing will now cause it to back away from a nuclear weapons option." [81] Haass and others recommend that only "targeted sanctions" be imposed—those sanctions that block the provision of technology that could contribute to Indian and Pakistani nuclear and missile programs. In Pakistan, broad punitive sanctions may actually weaken domestic political authority and undermine important American interests in the region, including the promotion of democracy, human rights, and expanding economic cooperation. In addition, Haass recommends that the US offer assistance to help them manage their "new nuclear challenge," including intelligence and technology, as this would contribute to nuclear stability in the region.

There is tremendous concern that such recommendations will signal to other potential proliferators that the consequences for going nuclear in the future will be mild and can provide an opportunity to extract benefits (blackmail) from states that do not want them to go nuclear. Haass's response, which was echoed by some members of Congress, is that not all proliferation is equal. Nuclear weapons in the hands of Iraq, Iran, North Korea, or Libya are far worse than nuclear weapons in India and Pakistan (or Israel). Providing incentives and engaging India and Pakistan to help minimize a nuclear arms race between them does not mean that incentives will be or should be offered to all states.[82]

### Will the Current Strategy Work?

The debate between whether sanctions, on one hand, or incentives and engagement, on the other, will work to persuade India (or Pakistan) not to move further up the proliferation ladder cannot be conducted without assessing India's ability to respond to both strategies. Would India simply find substitute external and/or domestic suppliers to replace those lost to the embargo? Will the sanctions simply cause India to promote its nuclear ambitions aggressively to demonstrate its resolve not to succumb to international pressure? Can the fragile BJP-led coalition government stop from shoring itself up in the near term and consider the long-term implications of its decision to conduct the tests and negotiate an agreement with the United States? Finally, given that the opposition would want to take advantage of the situation, will the national government in India be able to implement any agreement that places limits on India's nuclear weapons future?

As noted, many of the conditions laid out by the P-5 and G-8 are consistent with the GOI's publicly announced intentions. However, various elements of the Indian elite ranging from the scientific community to the military to the political and intellectual leaders are engaged in a debate about India's nuclear future. It remains to be seen what the outcome will actually be, though as of December 1998, some positions are becoming clear. Let's trace the impact of sanctions and evaluate India's ability and willingness to accept the conditions specified in the P-5 and G-8 statements.

## Impact of Sanctions

In May 1998 it was estimated that the cost of sanctions to India would be approximately $20 billion in loans, guarantees, and other economic aid. The estimate, however, did not include indirect costs associated with losses in consumer confidence, capital flight, or foreign investment in the Indian stock market.[83] Many Indian journalists forecasted that the impact of the sanctions would be minimal and emphasized instead the costs to American companies.[84] In the meantime, the prime minister advocated stoicism and "not buckling" under the pressure.[85] However, it was not too long before reality started to set in.

In June 1998 one report described how an Indian investment banker watched a foreign client pull $20 billion out of India's main stock market in Bombay.[86] During the summer months, seven Indian scientists working at the National Institute of Standards and Technology (NIST) in Maryland were asked to leave the United States. This was only the tip of the iceberg as the Department of Energy then identified 62 Indian institutions that could no longer work on cooperative projects with the US government.[87] The sanctions were not just limited to professionals, students studying in the United States on programs such as the Fulbright scholarships or other academic awards could also be targetted.

With the support of the US Congress, however, it was going to be largely a matter of discretion which sanctions were imposed and it depended on whether India was showing "restraint" as indicated by progress on the P-5 and G-8 conditions. Soon after initial sanctions were announced (but before they were implemented), the Congress passed the South Asia Sanctions Flexibility Act. The Act gave President Clinton the authority to waive sanctions imposed on wheat credit transactions and trade financing.[88] This was done largely to reduce the impact the sanctions would have on American farmers, but it was also consistent with the administration's policy of engagement and incentives. Further authority to waive all sanctions, up to one year, was provided to the president by the Brownback Amendment in October 1998.[89] Temporary lifting of economic sanctions in early November (until November 1999) permitted U.S. commercial banks as well as the US Import-Export Bank, the Overseas Private Investment Corporation, and the Trade Development Agency to resume lending. Senior US government officials stated that the action was taken to reward India and Pakistan for "restraint" by refraining from "weaponizing" by not installing nuclear warheads on missiles or bombers and for promising to sign the CTBT.[90] Soon after, however, the US Department of Commerce released the list of 300 Indian and Pakistan government agencies and private companies that would be prohibited from doing business with the US without a license.[91]

Indian Defense Minister George Fernandes reacted angrily to the American strategy: "The United States has an agenda for India which is not acceptable. . . . The United States should understand India's security concerns and reconcile itself to the obvious. . . . India is too big and potentially a very powerful country to be subjected to a carrot and stick treatment."[92]

Fernandes was as angry about the strategy as the fact that the United States had made some of the details of the negotiation public. Sensitive to criticism from opposition parties, the Indian government made a series of statements about production and deployment of missiles (Prithiv and Agni) and even announced willingness to sell some of its short-range missiles (Nag, Trishul, Akash) and about the imperative of "maintaining a minimum credible deterrent." [93] This response is interpreted further below.

Whatever the actual costs of the sanctions turn out to be, it is clear that the waivers the United States has made in some special areas will not reverse the majority of the costs. Indeed they will impart real hardship on several aspects of the Indian economy in the near term, at least requiring Indian policymakers to make appeals to other countries which will be under pressure not to do new business with India. US efforts to make its sanctions global do not have to be perfectly successful for the sanctions to cause economic confusion and political upheaval.

## India's Willingness and Ability to Comply

India and Pakistan continue to have great difficulty even discussing the Kashmir issue, leave alone resolving it. The first post-test bilateral discussions broke off having made little progress. Indian president Narayanan has indicated that India will continue to try to "normalize" relations with Pakistan even though differences continue to hamper the process. [94] The differences involve not only the substantive issue of the territory of Kashmir, but the process of the discussion as well. Pakistan has long wanted the United States or the United Nations to mediate the discussions, a condition that India has always refused. [95] Prime Minister Nawaz Sharif reiterated Pakistan's desire for third-party mediation in talks with President Clinton, but the latter politely declined, noting that both parties would have to agree—something that is not likely. [96]

Nevertheless, the US was inclined to cast in a positive light what small progress India and Pakistan have made toward reducing tensions. Perhaps this is because it was becoming more difficult to see India's positions on fissile material production and future nuclear weapons development as positive.

Through the summer and into the fall months, Indian defense intellectuals debated India's nuclear future and whether or not India should negotiate with the nuclear weapon states. How India participated in the global discussion was as much a part of India's internal debate as how many bombs India should build and how they should be deployed. In fact, in addition to questions of cost, the degree of weaponization was debated because of its intimate connection with India's international nuclear policy, particularly its position on CTBT and FMCT. If the consensus emerged that India should develop more bombs than it has fissile material for, then India would be unwilling to agree to a FMCT, or would not agree to a moratorium on fissile material production while the FMCT was being negotiated. If India should decide that it needed different warhead designs, then the testing might be needed and India's position on the CTBT would be affected. [97]

There are now several different estimates of what the costs of building and deploying nuclear weapons will be. Most still rely on unrealistic assessments of a nuclear-weapons arsenal devoid of a C³I system for early warning and to prevent accidental launch. One recent estimate, by C. Rammanohar Reddy, is more realistic and is based on developing a second-strike capability with China and Pakistan as targets. Like earlier estimates, it included 150 warheads and a triad of delivery systems (aircraft, land-based ballistic missiles, and submarine-launched ballistic missiles), but added provision for a modest C³I system. The total future expenditure on these items was estimated to be at least Rs. 40,000 crores to Rs. 50,000 crores (equivalent to $10 billion to $10.25 billion) over the next ten years. Reddy then tallies what the Indian government could purchase in the way of health care, housing, and, education with these funds if they were not spent on nuclear weapons. One Agni missile could finance the annual operations of thirteen thousand health centers. The annual budget for weaponization would pay for universal primary education in India for two years.[98] Put in these terms, the nuclear debate will create real fissures between those who see Indian nationalism in terms of weapons that cannot be used and thus impede welfare objectives, and those who see it in terms of gains from aggressively asserting India's technological capabilities.

Reddy is not the only Indian speaking out about the opportunity costs of India's decision to go nuclear.[99] For some, the tests violated India's high moral principles for disarmament and added insult to injury because they were conducted on Buddha's birthday *and* in the fiftieth year after Gandhi's death.[100] Several prominent members of the foreign-policy elite have indicated that the tests need not entirely reverse the more peaceful aspects of India's history. Former foreign secretary J. N. Dixit states that "becoming a nuclear weapon state does not in any way diminish our commitment to global nuclear disarmament." He advocates that "India should actively participate in multilateral discussions to bring about global nuclear disarmament in a non-discriminatory fashion." [101] Retired air commodore Jasjit Singh, now director of the Institute for Defense Studies and Analyses in New Delhi, advocates that India should propose a nondiscriminatory, verifiable global treaty to abolish nuclear weapons.[102]

Dixit warns that not moving from weaponization to deployment would make the tests a meaningless political and strategic exercise. At the same time, he advocates

> negotiating with the five nuclear weapon powers and other important countries like Japan and Germany to see how we can become part of the mainstream of non-proliferation process without compromising on our vital national security interests.[103]

Other intellectual leaders have specified possible trade-offs in such negotiations that may have implications for the outcome of India's nuclear debate. Jasjit Singh advocated that India should negotiate its accession to the CTBT if all "negative effects" (sanctions) of the test are removed and India has access to nuclear technology and materials. India should also commit to a unilateral policy of no first use and a pledge of nonuse against a non-nuclear-weapon state. In contrast to those who advocate deployment of warheads, Singh advocated maintaining a recessed deterrence capability that quickly could be made more overt in the event the security environment deteriorates. Testing and deployment of delivery systems, however, should continue.[104] P. R. Chari has described other aspects of a "grand bargain" that include Indian moratoria on testing and further weaponization in return for some agreement requiring the nuclear-weapon powers to proceed more quickly toward nuclear disarmament.

By September, there was a consensus within the GOI for negotiation with the nuclear weapon states, and with the United States in particular. Bilateral discussion began to take place regularly between Assistant Secretary of State Strobe Talbott and the prime minister's special envoy, Jaswant Sigh. For the most part, the GOI has been silent on their content. However, the official characterization of the discussion as "positive," "on the right track," and most recently, "constructive," is interpreted as indicating that India is open to signing the CTBT and, eventually, the FMCT.[105] Analysts suggest that the GOI's silence on the discussions is to minimize criticism of the negotiations. Not all criticism was avoided, as a scathing indictment appeared in July 1998.

> [T]he BJP-led Government is no longer fundamentally opposed to the Unequal Global Nuclear Bargain (UGNB), "nuclear apartheid" expressed in the NPT division of the world into a nuclear weapons club and the rest, the NPT's corollaries such as the CTBT and the FMCT to come, the obnoxious and pseudo-scientific doctrine of nuclear deterrence pioneered and practiced by the United States and the non-proliferation control regime.[106]

The criticism went to the heart of the government's electoral Achilles heel—the weak majority: "Questions could justifiably be raised about the extent to which a Government so unsure of its mandate could go in [on] negotiating changes to the country's foreign policy doctrine." The changes the article refers to are weak responses of the BJP government to US missile strikes in Afghanistan and Sudan; although, "once India would not have hesitated to denounce the US invocation of the right of retribution against any country deemed culpable for a random act of terror, the BJP-led Ministry today shows a curious reticence." The BJP response to the strikes is seen as too cautious, in order to avoid frictions with the United States.[107]

On the other hand, two events in November indicated that the more extreme nationalist positions on India's nuclear posture may not be widely supported by Indian citizens. First, an opinion poll conducted by *The Hindu* newspaper indicated that support for an ambitious nuclear weapons development and deployment program would be lukewarm. The issues of highest import to the citizens polled were "population control" and "poverty elimination," and not "national security" or "globalization." Interpreting the results, S. Swaminatham concludes, "[T]he survey has given lie to the vastly exaggerated claims about the Pokhran-II blasts raising India's image to the world outside and about people in India exulting with a new-found sense of achievement." [108] Second, the Congress (I) Party dramatically won back seats held by the BJP in state elections demonstrating the public discontent with BJP leadership. Although the strong showing did not eliminate the BJP's majority in Parliament, the losses were dramatic enough to require Prime Minister Vajpayee to announce that a new government would not be formed as a result. While many analysts interpreted the election results as a reaction to recent domestic inflation and flagging consumer confidence, it was clear that any dramatic increases in any government spending, including defense spending, would be closely scrutinized. [109] The two events may serve to quiet nationalist criticism of the governing coalition's interpretation of India's nuclear future.

Alert to maintaining balance in his domestic coalition, in mid-December 1998, Prime Minister Vajpayee announced that India would maintain some "credible minimum deterrent." There also were indications that some minimal command and control system would accompany the "minimum deterrent." [110] This need not be a repudiation of the GOI's earlier negotiation position as it was still unclear how much deployment would take place. As of December 7th, the debate was still going on in the Indian press, as evidenced by an article by K. Subrahmanyam interpreting what "minimum nuclear deterrence" meant. [111] If actual deployment of warheads to missile or bomber sites takes place, then it will be difficult for any American administration to lift the sanctions that remain.

The announcement also seemed to be in reaction to the release of the entity list naming Indian firms and government agencies that are barred from doing business with the United States, and more importantly, the revelations of the Indian negotiating position by American negotiator, Assistant Secretary of State Strobe Talbott. To justify the temporary lifting of economic sanctions, Talbott stated that India has promised to sign the CTBT by September 1999 and has refrained from weaponization. Muchkund Duby noted that Talbott's statement was "in sharp contrast to the extreme secrecy maintained by the government of India on the ongoing diplomatic parleys." [112] Dubey goes on to propose what India's position should actually be. To clarify the GOI position in the negotiations, Talbott's Indian interlocutor, Jaswant Singh, revealed the government's position. Mr. Singh stated bluntly, "[I]ndia's nuclear weapon status is a fact, and the US government cannot dis-invent it." Furthermore, he indicated India's readiness to negotiate a non-discriminatory FMCT, and strengthen export controls on sensitive technology. India's position on the CTBT would be "guided by national consensus," and did not rule out that Rajya Sabha might be able to add conditions to India's signature of the treaty. [113] Without being privy to internal deliberations in the Indian government, I can only speculate that the GOI had to cast doubt on Talbott's statements in order to ward off criticism from the more extreme nationalist members of the BJP or other members of the governing coalition.

## CONCLUSION

Whatever the outcome, however, a few things seem clear. First, the sanctions imposed by the United States do not undermine either the engagement policy or the incentives it may offer India to reduce tensions in the region and ward off a nuclear arms race in the region. In fact, the incentives themselves will appear more valuable because of the effect of the sanctions. Second, the incentives do not undermine the sanctions, for there is significant evidence that the sanctions will still cause hardship for India, its people, and its government. Finally, the Indian government is under pressure due to coalition weakness to strike a strong bargain with the nuclear powers—a bargain that will turn the decision to test into greater status for India. This means joining the international community by providing leadership on disarmament issues while keeping its nuclear capability at existential levels and receiving long-awaited access to high technology in exchange.

## NOTES

1  "Paper Laid on the Table of the House on Evolution of India's Nuclear Policy," June 1998 (www.Indiagov.org/govt/evolution.htm)

2  Ibid. The "freedom of action" includes India's right to evaluate its "supreme national interests" including its legitimate security interests. The government explained that had India's 1988 proposed action plan, which called for a "phased elimination of all nuclear weapons within a specified time frame," been received positively by the nuclear weapon states, "India need not have gone for the current tests."

3  Portions of this section of the chapter originally appeared in Virginia Foran, "The Case for Indo-US High-Technology Cooperation," *Survival,* vol. 40, no. 2 (summer 1998), pp. 71–95.

4  For further explanation, see Virginia I. Foran and Leonard S. Spector, "The Application of Incentives to Nuclear Proliferation," in David Cortright, ed., *The Price of Peace: Incentives and International Conflict Prevention* (Boulder, CO: Rowman & Littlefield, 1997): 21–53, especially pp. 30–31.

5  COCOM was made up of the members of NATO minus Iceland, plus Japan. It was dismantled in 1996 and a more inclusive organization with less restrictive controls, called the Wassenaar Arrangement, was created to replace it.

6  I. M. Destler, *Making Foreign Economic Policy* (Washington, DC: The Brookings Institution, 1980); pp. 132–37. Destler notes that from 1945 until approximately 1967, the United States allowed foreign policy concerns to dominate trade policy. Change in this dynamic came slowly due to the increase in competition from Europe and Japan and from regional economic arrangements that increasingly placed the United States at a disadvantage.

7  One source notes, "[F]rom the start . . . the items on which the United States imposed controls differed from those controlled by COCOM. In addition to those items that all COCOM members agreed to control, the United States controlled many items unilaterally." For an excellent overview explaining the rationale behind US export controls, including design and production technology transfer, see *Balancing the National Interest: US National Security Export Controls and Global Economic Competition,* Report of the Panel on the Impact of National Security Controls on International Technology

Transfer, Committee on Science, Engineering, and Public Policy, National Academy of Sciences (Washington, DC: National Academy Press, 1987); pp. 7–14. For quote mentioned here, see page 73.

8   Ibid. See pp. 84–85 for the map of country groups.

9   The National Academy of Sciences report notes "growing concern in the Intelligence Community about the extent to which the Soviet Union and other Warsaw Pact countries have been or may be able to obtain controlled technology in the Free World countries that do not cooperate in national security controls. This concern applied both to the industrialized neutral countries of Europe and to some of the more advanced newly industrializing countries (such as India, Singapore, and Brazil)." Ibid. p. 5.

   An excellent overview of the Indian export control system is by S. Chandrashekar, "Export Controls and Proliferation: An Indian Perspective," in Gary K. Bertsch, Richard T. Cupitt, and Steven Elliot-Gower, eds., *International Cooperation and Nonproliferation Export Controls* (Ann Arbor: University of Michigan Press, 1994): 261–94.

10  Telephone interviews with Department of Commerce officials, April, June, and July 1997. The US Department of Commerce regards specific information on export licenses as proprietary and does not make it available to the public. In addition, while one can request information on licensing by item, this information is not collected by state, making it very difficult to assess overall approvals and denials for individual states. The only way to obtain more than very general statistics is to make a Freedom of Information Act request to the department, which would take several years for the department to respond to, and then conduct the evaluation oneself. Information may be more forthcoming from the government of India.

11  Brahma Chellaney, *Nuclear Proliferation: The US-Indian Conflict* (New Delhi: Orient Longman, 1993), p. 191.

12  Author's discussion with Jasjit Singh, director, Institute for Defense Studies and Analyses, September 24, 1997, New Delhi, India. The lack of data does not mean that the perception does not reflect reality, but that thus far, at least, the perception is driven by rhetoric rather than by data that has been collected and evaluated.

13  Brahma Chellaney writes, "[A]fter two centuries of foreign colonial rule, the creating of a broad based science and technology infrastructure was given one of the highest priorities by the national policymakers, who believed technological backwardness made a nation politically and economically vulnerable. . . . Policymakers believed a nuclear program that was predominantly self-reliant would help spur technological development in other sectors of the Indian economy." Chellaney, *Nuclear Proliferation,* pp. 2–5. See also Rikhi Jaipal, "The Indian Nuclear Situation," *International Security,* vol. 1, no. 4 (spring 1991): 45–46. Dr. Homi Bhabha also argued in favor of indigenous efforts, explaining the "technological fallout" that would result from atomic energy and the impact it would have on economic and scientific activity in India. See *Atomic Energy and Space Research: A Profile for the Decade 1970–80* (New Delhi: Government of India, 1970); p. iii, as cited in Chellaney, *Nuclear Proliferation,* pp. 4–5.

14  The US government has been reluctant to share defense production and design information even with its allies. NATO alliance required the United States to transfer military hardware to its allies, but the United States imposed unilateral constraints on those countries, and required them "to obtain prior approval of—or to account periodically to—the US government for re-exports of US-origin products, US-origin parts and components incorporated into foreign equipment, and foreign products manufactured with US-origin technology." *Balancing the National Interest,* p. 11.

Regarding Indian demands on the Coca-Cola Corporation, see Dennis Kux, *India and the United States: Estranged Democracies, 1941–1991* (Washington, DC: National Defense University Press, 1992), p. 363.

15  P. J. Eldridge, *The Politics of Foreign Aid in India* (London: Oxford Univ. Press, 1969), p. 11, as cited in Surjit Mansingh, "India and the United States: What Price Partnership?" *Towson State Journal of International Affairs,* vol. 13, no. 2 (spring 1979): 62.

16  Mansingh, "India and the United States," p. 62, citing "Clay Committee Report on Foreign Aid to the US House of Representatives," March 25, 1963, and David Bell, "Confidential Report to the World Bank," August 1964.

17  Mansingh, "India and the United States," pp. 66–67, citing a letter from *Indira Gandhi to Lyndon B. Johnson,* May 12, 1967 (White House Confidential File, Pakistan, White House Central File, LBJ Library).

18  Jawaharlal Nehru, *Letters to Chief Ministers,* 1950–1952, vol. 3 (New Delhi: Jawaharlal Nehru Memorial Fund, 1986), p. 442, letter of 15 November 1953, as cited by Kux, *India and the United States,* pp. 108–9.

19  President Kennedy and Prime Minister MacMillan agreed during their meeting in Nassau in December 1962 to jointly provide $120 million in military assistance. In 1963 MacMillan and Kennedy agreed to a further $50 million from the United States with a lesser amount from the United Kingdom. During discussions with Secretary of Defense Robert McNamara in mid-1964, Defense Minister Y. B. Chavan discussed the possibility of buying twenty-four to thirty-six F-104s. Out of concern for its relationship with Pakistan, the United States decided against supplying combat aircraft to India, and India pursued purchasing MiG fighters from the more willing Soviet Union. See K. Subramanyam, *India's Problem of Security* (Jaipur: University of Rajasthan, Department of Political Science 1969) p. 14. See also Shivaji Ganguly, "US Military Assistance to India, 1962–63: A Study in Decision-Making," *India Quarterly,* July-September 1972, pp. 6–7, and a cable from Bowles to Dean Rusk, March 31, 1965 (Country File, India, National Security Files, Lyndon Baines Johnson Library).

20  K. Subramanyam, "Military Aid and Foreign Policy," *Foreign Affair Reports,* vol. XVII, no. 11 (Indian Council of World Affairs, November 1968): 117.

21  A. Appadorai and M. S. Rajan, *India's Foreign Policy and Relations,* (New Delhi: South Asia Publishers, 1985), pp. 242, 330; memorandum, September 6, 1965 (Country File, United Kingdom, National Security Files, LBJ Library); Surjit Mansingh, "India and the United States," p. 70.

22  *The Near Nuclear Countries and the NPT* (Stockholm: SIPRI, 1972), pp. 19–21; George H. Quester, *The Politics of Nuclear Proliferation* (Baltimore: The Johns Hopkins University Press, 1973).

23  India received no positive response to these specific requests. See A. J. Noorani, "India's Quest for Security Guarantees," Asian Survey, vol. 7, no. 7 (July 1967): 490–502.

24  *The Near Nuclear Countries,* p. 21.

25  Ibid.

26  The term "full-scope safeguards" means that all of a country's nuclear facilities and activities are inspected by the IAEA. The United States suspended its 1963 nuclear cooperation agreement with India in the early 1980s after India refused to agree to full-scope safeguards. These laws also require termination of an agreement if a non-nuclear-weapon state (any country but the United States, the Soviet Union (now Russia), France, China, and the United Kingdom) detonates a nuclear explosive device. India was in violation of both.

27  This provision can be waived by the president (subsection b(1)) if it is determined that the aid termination "would have a serious adverse affect on vital United States interests" and if "he has received reliable assurances that the country in question will not acquire or develop nuclear weapons or assist other nations to do so." Arms Control Export Act, chapter 10, section 101; 22 US Code Sec. 2799a (1994).

28  This provision has a weaker waiver condition. The president can waive the implementation of the law if it is determined that "the termination of such assistance would be seriously prejudicial to the achievement of United States non-proliferation objectives or otherwise jeopardize the common defense and security" of the country in question. Arms Control Export Act, Section 102; 22 US Code Sec. 2799 (1994).

29  See Rodney Jones and Mark McDonough, *Tracking Nuclear Proliferation 1998*, (Washington, DC: Carnegie Endowment for International Peace, 1998). See also Richard P. Cronin, *Pakistan Aid Cutoff: US Nonproliferation and Foreign Aid Considerations*, CRS Issue Brief 90149 (Washington, DC: Congressional Research Service).

30  The MTCR applies to the transfer of missiles or components capable of carrying at least a 500-kg warhead 300 km. Category I violations include violations on complete missile systems, major subsystems, rocket engines, guidance systems, and missile production facilities. Category II violations apply to smaller components, machinery, and equipment, such as electronics and other dual-use items. See Leonard Spector, Mark McDonough, and Evan Medeiros, *Tracking Nuclear Proliferation 1995* (Washington, DC: Carnegie Endowment for International Peace, 1995), p. 185.

31  This information on non-proliferation legislation has been compiled from the following sources: Foreign Affairs and National Defense Division, Environment and Natural Resources Policy Division, *India-Pakistan Nuclear and Missile Proliferation: Background, Status, and Issues for US Policy* (Washington, DC: Congressional Research Service, 1996); *Export Administration Legislation, Report for Congress*, CRS Report No. 96–492 E (Washington, DC: Congressional Research Service, 1996).

32  Members of the NSG include Argentina, Australia, Austria, Belgium, Bulgaria, Canada, the Czech Republic, Denmark, France, Finland, Germany, Greece, Hungary, Ireland, Italy, Japan, Luxembourg, Netherlands, New Zealand, Norway, Poland, Portugal, Romania, Russia, Slovakia, South Africa, Spain, Sweden, Switzerland, the United Kingdom, and the United States. Also during meetings held in 1991 and 1992, the list of items that would be controlled was expanded to include uranium conversion plants and equipment, and expanded controls on dual-use items: "The dual use Guidelines require exporting states not to ship items on the list if they are for use in non-nuclear-weapon states for unsafeguarded nuclear fuel cycle facilities or in a nuclear explosive activity." Also, the Guidelines specify that states not "transfer items on the list 'when there is an unacceptable risk of diversion to such an activity, or when the transfers are contrary to the objective of averting the proliferation of nuclear weapons.'" See Spector, McDonough, and Medeiros, *Tracking Nuclear Proliferation 1995*, pp. 181–82, and INFIRC/254/Rev.1/Part 2.

33  R. Chidambaram, Anil Kakodkar, and Placid Rodriguez, "Nuclear Technology: Power to the People," *IEEE Spectrum: Technology in India,* March 1994: 36–39.

34  See David Baldwin, *Economic Statecraft* (Princeton, NJ: Princeton University Press, 1985); M. S. Daoudi and M. S. Dajani, *Economic Sanctions: Ideals and Experience* (London: Routledge & Kegan Paul, 1983); Gary Hufbauer, Jeffrey Schott, and Kimberly Ann Elliott, *Economic Sanctions Reconsidered* (Washington, DC: Institute for International Economics, 1985); Stephanie Ann Lenway, "Economic Sanctions and Statecraft," *International Organization,* vol. 42, no. 2 (spring 1988): 397–426.

35  Lisa L. Martin, *Coercive Cooperation: Explaining Multilateral Economic Sanctions* (Princeton, NJ: Princeton University Press, 1992), p. 3, as cited in William J. Long, *Economic Incentives and Bilateral Cooperation* (Ann Arbor, MI: University of Michigan Press, 1996), p. 29.

36  Long, *Economic Incentives,* pp. 27–30.

37  Sunil Jain, "What Indians Think, Opinion Poll: Yes to the Bomb," *India Today,* December 31, 1995, pp. 48–49. Results of surveys conducted over the years by the Indian Institute for Public Opinion indicate that over 50 percent of the respondents favor continuing with a bomb option (though the support has declined since a high of 75 percent in 1974 following India's test at Pokharan). See Thomas W. Graham, *India's Nuclear Program: A Briefing,* as cited by W. P. S. Sidhu, *Enhancing Indo-US Strategic Cooperation,* Adelphi Paper no. 313 (London: Institute for International Strategic Studies, 1997), p. 28. Polls of Indian reaction to the May 1998 tests were overwhelmingly supportive.

38  Long, *Economic Incentives,* pp. 24–27. This is what has occurred with the 1990 Pressler Amendment sanctions on Pakistan. See Virginia I. Foran, "Were the Experts Wrong? US Engagement Policy Towards South Asia Before and After the Tests," unpublished manuscript, September 1998.

39  Richard N. Haass, *Economic Sanctions: Too Much of a Bad Thing,* policy brief no. 34 (Washington, DC: The Brookings Institution, June 1998), p. 1.

40  "The Foreign Policy Effects of Unilateral Sanctions," *USA Engage* (http//:www.usaengage.com).

41  Leonard Spector and I make this case in Virginia I. Foran and Leonard S. Spector, "The Application of Incentives to Nuclear Nonproliferation," in David Cortright, ed., *The Price of Peace: Incentives and International Conflict Prevention* (Boulder, CO: Rowman & Littlefield, 1997), pp. 21–53.

42  Ibid.

43  For details on the LCA project and the US role, see Satu P. Limaye, *US-Indian Relations: The Pursuit of Accomodation* (Boulder, CO: Westview Press, 1993).

44  Various accounts of these events can be found in Stephen P. Cohen, "The Reagan Administration and India," in Harold A. Gould and Sumit Ganguly, eds., *The Hope and the Reality: US-Indian Relations from Roosevelt to Reagan*; Kux, *India and the United States;* and interviews with US State Department officials, April 1997. The Indian side of the events is described in Limaye, *US-Indian Relations.*

45  See Long, *Economic Incentives.*

46  Sidhu, *Enhancing Indo-US Strategic Cooperation,* pp. 39–50.

47  Limaye, *US-Indian Relations.* For further discussion of the MOU and its implementation, see Santhanam, "Indian Defense Technology Infrastructure and Prospects of Indo-US Cooperation," paper presented at the Indo-US Defense Workshop, National Defense University, Washington, DC, September 19–21, 1989.

48  According to one Ministry of Defence official involved in negotiations for equipment and technology during this period, despite the high level of executive involvement, no requests for significant military systems by India were approved by the United States. Interview with the author, Neemrana Fort, India, September 1997.

49  In one particular case, since approximately 1985, India had made requests for an American testing system known as the US Combined Acceleration, Vibration, and Climatic Test System (CAVCTS). This system could be used to test a re-entry vehicle's ability to withstand the high temperatures and stress related to launching and re-entering the atmosphere. After many delays, the United States formally denied the sale in 1989. See Alexander A. Pikayev, Leonard S. Spector, Elina V. Kiritchenko, and Ryan

Gibson, *The Soviet-Russian Sale of Cryogenic Rocket Technology to India and Russia's Adherence to the Missile Technology Control Regime*, Adelphi Paper (London: International Institute of Strategic Studies) paper #317, 1998.

50  As Pikayev et. al. note, Glavkosmos was one of a number of organizations under the Russian Ministry of General Machine Building and only one of many partners within the Russian space industry that was involved in the sale to India. US law would have permitted extension of the sanctions to these other organizations, but it was not done. The sanctions had a political impact, but they had little effect on the manufacture or design of rocket systems in Russia. ISRO, on the other hand, was responsible for all aspects of the Indian space and missile program resulting in a defacto freeze of all US assistance in this area. France restricted its cooperation with India's space program in concert with the American action. See "Six Major Projects Likely to be Hit by US Sanctions on ISRO," *News India*, May 29, 1992, p. 14; "France Gives Conditions for Rocket Technology," *Delhi All India Radio Network*, July 17, 1992, in JPRS-TND, July 22, 1992, p. 19, cited in Pikayev et al., *The Soviet-Russian Sale of Cryogenic Rocket Technology to India.*

51  "Establishing Strong Security Ties with India and Pakistan," prepared remarks by Secretary of Defense William J. Perry to the Foreign Policy Association, New York, January 31, 1995, *Defense Issues*, vol. 10, no.10, 1995.

52  *Export Administration Legislation*, CRS Report for Congress (96–492 E), updated August 27, 1996, especially pp. 8–11; Foreign Affairs and National Defense Division and Environment and Natural Resources Division, *India-Pakistan Nuclear and Missile Proliferation: Background, Status, and Issues for US Policy*, CRS Report for Congress (97–23 F), December 16, 1996.

53  Trade Policy Coordinating Committee, *Toward a National Export Strategy: US Exports = US Jobs*, Report to Congress, September 30, 1993; J. David Richardson, *Sizing Up US Export Disincentives*, Institute for International Economics, 1993; Council on Competitiveness, *Economic Security: The Dollar$ and Sense of US Foreign Policy*, February 1994; and Glennon Harrison, *The Economics of Export Controls*, CRS Report to Congress, 95–575, May 9, 1995.

54  Office of Technology Assessment, *Export Controls and Nonproliferation Policy*, OTA-ISS-596, June 1994; *The Federal Government's Export Licensing Processes for Munitions and Dual Use Commodities*, Special Interagency Review, Final Report, Conducted by the Offices of the Inspector General at the US Departments of Commerce, Defense, Energy, and State, September 1993; *Export Licensing Procedures for Dual-Use Items Need to Be Strengthened*, General Accounting Office, GAO/NSIAD-94–119, April 1994. All cited by Dr. Zachary S. Davis, *National Security and Nonproliferation Implications of Reduced Export Controls*, Congressional Research Service, Testimony provided to Senate Armed Services Committee, May 11, 1995.

55  To a certain extent, the technical cooperation is limited by the strategic relationship. Both countries are assessing how far the cooperation can go. Progress on the Indian side is limited by the domination of the Ministry of External Affairs in all foreign-policy decisions, even ones that involve the Indian military. Interview with Department of Defense official, February 1997, and telephone conversation update, July 1997.

56  Rao replaced A. Gopalakrishnan, whose term of office was not renewed in 1996 after releasing details of safety problems at nuclear facilities to the Indian press.

57  Karl F. Inderfurth, "Article on US Relations with South Asia," Department of State, Washington, DC, April 1998.

58  *Report to Congress: Update on Progress Toward Regional Nonproliferation in South Asia*, April 1998, available at www.state.gov/www/regions/sa/non-proliferation.html

59  Long argues that an international exchange model can be used to understand how economic incentives, particularly trade and technology incentives, can alter the international payoff structure representing the strategic interaction between states and the formation of domestic preferences (i.e., domestic coalitions) within them, to produce a political concession. Long, *Economic Incentives,* pp. 19–33.

60  Ibid., p. 77.

61  Ibid., p. 78.

62  Ibid. p. 80.

63  Foran and Spector, *"Application of Incentives,* pp. 27–34.

64  I argue that there are two general types of incentive approach strategies that can be discerned, direct and indirect. Direct incentives have received the most attention and criticism. Belarus, Kazahkstan, and Ukraine negotiated a package of direct incentives that included security guarantees, money, and raw materials, in exchange for agreeing to send to Russia weapons they inherited from the former Soviet Union for dismantlement and acceding to the NPT. As the term implies, direct incentives generate explicit expectations, indeed, even contracts that stipulate changes in behavior that will be exhibited in exchange for extending the incentives. The acceptance of the incentive creates an obligation that change will take place. In the negotiation of direct incentives for nonproliferation, the obligation would be to dismantle existing nuclear weapons, or to somehow take steps back down the proliferation ladder.

    Indirect incentives are incentives that are provided with less explicit changes in behavior being a condition of the incentives. These work by slowly persuading the state (or appropriate individual, groups, or policy makers) that the behavior is no longer desired or preferred by influencing the cost/benefit function associated with the behavior. Indirect incentives are less confrontational and are designed to work within the self-interest of the states involved. This type of incentive strategy might be termed a market-based strategy because, similar to the law of supply and demand, it is designed to rely on the invisible hand of costs and benefits to facilitate the target state reaching its own decision—for example, of what non-proliferation objective it can agree to—rather than the persuader state(s) setting an objective in the negotiation. The length of negotiation also is not specified with this strategy, occurring when the participating states are jointly motivated to do so. See Foran, "The Case for Indo-US High-Technology Cooperation," pp. 78–79.

65  Ibid., p. 87.

66  Eric Arnett, "Military Technology: The Case of India," *SIPRI Yearbook 1994* (Oxford: SIPRI, 1994).

67  Robert M. Solow, "Technological Change and the Aggregate Production Function," *Review of Economics and Statistics,* vol. 39 (1957): 312–20; and "Productivity and the Economy," *Bulletin of the Bureau of Labor Statistics,* no. 1926 (Washington DC: GPO, 1977), p. 63, as cited in Long, *Economic Incentives,* pp. 21–22.

68  Energy is one sector where technology is needed the most. As one researcher concluded, "As in a number of other successful developing nations, the hope embodied in rapid economic growth is beginning to bump up against the realities of infrastructure limitations, political constraints, and a simple lack of energy. Without important progress in the energy sector, India's impressive economic boom of recent years could quite literally run out of gas." Raju G. C. Thomas, "Policy Forum: Energy Futures," *The Washington Quarterly,* vol. 19, no. 4 (autumn 1996): 99.

69  William Long, *Economic Incentives,* p. 21. Long notes ". . . strong total utility is more likely when advanced technology is part of the package as technology is integral to the state's overall productive capability."

70  In addition to the Brown Amendment, passed in 1995, in July 1997 the US Senate passed the Harkin Amendment to the Foreign Operations Authorization Act without opposition. This amendment re-establishes authorization for Pakistan to receive IMET assistance funds from the United States Government and makes Pakistan eligible again for foreign direct investment insurance provided by the Overseas Private Investment Corporation (OPIC), a US firm that has been prohibited from insuring investments in Pakistan since 1990, when the Pressler Amendment was triggered.

71  Foran, "The Case for Indo-US High-Technology Cooperation," pp. 79–80.

72  See Bharatiya Janata Party (BJP), "National Agenda for Governance," March 18, 1998, point 26, available at http//:www.bjp.org/vagenda.html

73  On the difficulty of developing a nuclear strategy and integrating the military, see Brigadier Vijai K. Nair, "Nuclear Proliferation in South Asia: The Military Implications," *Indian Defense Review*, vol. 10, no. 1 (January/March 1995): 34; Lieutenant General K. S. Sundarji, *Blind Men of Hindoostan: Indo-Pak Nuclear War* (New Delhi: UBS Publishers, 1993). On the difficulties of funding and technical problems, see Arnett, "Military Technology," p. 343; Ian Anthony, "The 'Third-Tier' Countries," in Herbert Wulf, ed., *SIPRI: Arms Industry Limited* (Oxford: Oxford University Press for SIPRI, 1993), p. 362.

74  Foran, "The Case for Indo-US High-Technology Cooperation," p. 87.

75  See Neil Joeck, "Maintaining Nuclear Stability in South Asia," *Adelphi Paper no. 312* (Oxford: IISS, 1997), p. 55.

76  C. Rammanohar Reddy, "The Wages of Armageddon, parts I, II, and III, *The Hindu*, August 31, September 1, and September 2, 1998.

77  One news account reported that India's tests were "a kick in the teeth" to the United States because not only had India ignored a very recent "series of appeals" for not testing, but top Indian cabinet aides had assured the US ambassador to the United Nations, Bill Richardson, that they wanted to improve relations with the United States. No hints were given that underground tests were being contemplated. Thomas W. Lippman, "Defiance Endangers US-India Relations: Administration Had Urged Cooperation," *Washington Post*, Tuesday, May 12, 1998, p. A15.

78  Paul Blustein, "US Policy on India Questioned: Experts Skeptical About Sanctions' Value," *The Washington Post*, May 15, 1998, p. A32.

79  Both France and Germany stated that sanctions "after the fact" are not useful. Blustein, "US Policy"; Jim Hoagland, "Incentives Considered to End Tests in S. Asia," *Washington Post*, May 30, 1998, p. A1; Stephen P. Cohen, "Nuclear Breakout: How Should Washington Respond to the South Asian Bombs?" *San Diego Union Tribune*, June 8, 1998 (made available by the Brookings Institution at http://www.brookings.edu).

80  Wheat credit transactions are not covered by the exemption for food assistance because they are conducted by private institutions, and the waiver was designed to rectify that. The waiver for trade financing was designed so that India could continue payments on trade loans owed to US banks.

81  The legislation was initiated to try to provide "flexibility" to the administration as it began its negotiations with India and Pakistan for restraint on their nuclear weapons programs. Some senators strongly objected to a general waiver bill, with Senator Glenn threatening to filibuster if additional waiver provisions were kept. See Thomas W. Lippman, "Senate Votes to Exempt Food Exports from Sanctions on India, Pakistan, " *Washington Post*, July 10, 1998, p. A5; Thomas W. Lippman, "Senators Seek to Ease Nuclear Test Sanctions," *Washington Post*, July 3, 1998, p. A32; Sridhar Krishnaswami, "Another US Bill for Sanctions Waiver," *The Hindu*, July 18, 1998, p. 1.

82  The members of the P-5 are Britain, China, France, Russia, and the United States. The G-8 countries are Britain, Canada, China, France, Italy, Japan, Russia, and the United States.

83  Paul Blustein, "US Policy on India Questioned: Experts Skeptical About Sanctions' Value," *The Washington Post,* May 15, 1998, p. A32.

84  This includes emphasizing the waivers proposed to US sanctions law that allow for continued wheat sales, narrowly interpreting the banking sanctions to only apply to loans and credits made to the Government of India, not to private banks, corporations, and individuals, the delay in implementing sanctions blocking loan applications at multilateral financial institutions, etc. See G. Balachandran, "US Sanctions Against India," *The Hindustan Times,* June 21, 1998, available at http://www.indiagov.org/govt/nuclear/ht21.htm; N.C. Menon, "Rethinking on Sanctions?" *The Hindustan Times,* June 22, 1998, available as above at indiagov.org/govt/nuclear/ht22.htm; Inder Malhotra, "Sanctions: Signs of Second Thoughts," *The Observer,* June 24, 1998, www.indiagov.org/govt/nuclear/obs24jun.htm.

85  "India Will Withstand Sanctions, Says PM," *The Hindu,* July 23, 1998, p. 1.

86  $20 billion was the original American estimate of the total impact of the sanctions before they were imposed. Molly Moore, "Bomb Tests Wound India's Economy; Sanctions Investor Anxiety Speed Decline of Sluggish Markets," *The Washington Post,* June 20, 1998, p. A1; "Nuke Rebukes Spook India," CNN, July 23, 1998; Alok Mukherjee, "Can We Take On the Sanctions?" *The Hindu,* May 17, 1998, p. 11.

87  "7 Scientists From India Told to Leave," *The Washington Post,* July 25, 1998, p. A1.

88  Wheat credit transactions are not covered by the exemption for food assistance because they are conducted by private institutions and the waiver was designed to rectify that. The waiver for trade financing was designed so that India could continue payments on trade loans owed to US banks.

89  Adam Entous, "Clinton Wins Power to Lift India-Pakistan Sanctions," Reuters, October 21, 1998.

90  "U.S., India Begin Nuclear Talks," Associated Press, November 10, 1998; Arshad Mohammed, "Clinton and Sharif Discuss Nuclear Issues, F-16s," Reuters, December 2, 1998; Thomas W. Lippman, "Clinton, Pakistani Prime Minister Meet, U.S. Outlines Conditions for Upgrading Relations," *The Washington Post,* December 3, 1998, p. A34.

91  The "entity list" specifies three categories. The first contains government nuclear and missile entities. All trade is banned with them except for spare parts needed for commercial aircraft. The second category includes government-affiliated entities and private companies. Again, all trade is prohibited, although exemptions can be made on a case-by-case basis. The third category are military entities, which have a complete ban. Alexander Ferguson, "India, Pakistani Firms Face U.S. Sanctions," Reuters, November 13, 1998.

92  "Little Progress in India/US Talks," Associated Press, November 20, 1998.

93  "India Says Prithvi Missile Inducted into Army," Reuters, December 2, 1998; "Agni in Full Production," Reuters, December 2, 1998; Y.P. Rajesh, "India Willing to Sell Short Range Range Missiles," Reuters, December 9, 1998; "India Still Committed to CTBT Deadline," Reuters, December 15, 1998.

94  Ibid.

95  Reddy, "The Wages of Armageddon."

96  Thomas W. Lippman, "Clinton, Pakistani Prime Minister Meet, U.S. Outlines Conditions for Upgrading Relations," *The Washington Post,* December 3, 1998, p. A34; Sridhar Krishnaswami, "Mediation on J & K Only if India, Pak. Desire: U.S.," *The Hindu,* December 4, 1998, p. 1.

97  Arjun Makhijani, "A Legacy Lost," *The Bulletin of Atomic Scientists* (July/August 1998): 53–56; Ashis Nandy, "Decline in Euphoria," *Hindustan Times,* July 4, 1998.

98  J. N. Dixit, "After the Bomb, What?" *Economic Times,* June 23, 1998.

99  "India should commit to a unilateral no-first use pledge," comments by Jasjit Singh, on the release of Jasjit Singh ed., *Nuclear India* (New Delhi: Knowledge World & Institute for Defence Studies & Analyses, 1998). Reported by UNI, July 28, 1998.

100  Kenneth J. Cooper, "Nuclear Dilemmas: India; New Power Raises Crucial Questions," *Washington Post,* May 25, 1998, p. A1.

101  Reddy's assessment states that India's current plutonium stocks will only be enough for fifty bombs and that 800 kg of plutonium more will be needed for the additional one hundred bombs. No existing research or power reactor in India can yield this amount of plutonium in the time needed. See Reddy, "The Wages of Armageddon," part III.

102  Dixit, "After the Bomb, What?"

103  "India should commit to a unilateral no-first use pledge" (see note 99).

104  Sridhar Krishnaswami, "Jaswant-Talbott Meet Sets Positive Tone for Talks," *The Hindu,* August 25, 1998, p. 1; K. K. Katyal, "Indo-US Talks on Right Track," *The Hindu,* July 21, 1998, p. 1; K. K. Katyal, "Optimism on Eve of Jaswant-Talbott Talks," *The Hindu,* July 20, 1998, p. 1; "Secrecy Shrouds Meeting Between Jaswant, Talbott," *The Hindu,* July 10, 1998, p. 1.

105  Sridhar Krishnaswami, "Jaswant-Talbott Meet Sets Positive Tone for Talks," *The Hindu,* August 25, 1998, p. 1; K.K. Katyal, "Indo-US Talks on 'Right Track,'" *The Hindu,* July 21, 1998, p. 1; K.K. Katyal, "Optimism on Eve of Jaswant-Talbott Talks," *The Hindu,* July 20, 1998, p. 1; "Secrecy Shrouds Meeting Between Jaswant, Talbott," *The Hindu,* July 10, 1998, p. 1; K.K. Katyal, "Jaswant, Talbott Talks 'Constructive,'" *The Hindu,* November 21, 1998, p. 1.

106  N. Ram, "What the Vajpayee Government Is Up To," *Frontline,* vol. 15, no. 15 (July 18–31, 1998).

107  "India Acting Cautiously to Avoid Frictions with US," *The Hindu,* August 24, 1998.

108  S. Swaminathan, "Pokhran II agony or ecstasy?" *The Hindu,* November 15, 1998, p. 25.

109  "Vajpayee Rules Out Change of Govt.," *The Hindu,* November 29, 1998, p. 1; "Congress (I) Wins in Delhi and Rajasthan, Ahead in M.P., Lags Behind in Mizorara," *The Hindu,* November 29, 1998, p. 1; "Cong. Gets Absolute Majority in Rajasthan," *The Hindu,* November 29, 1998, p. 7.

110  C. Raja Mohan, "PM Rejects Demands to Limit Nuclear Capabilities," *The Hindu,* December 16, 1998, p. 1; Kenneth J. Cooper, "India Rejects Some Weapons Restraints, U.S. Praises Premier's Promise to Embrace Nuclear Test Ban, Tighten Control," *The Washington Post,* December 16, 1998, p. A37.

111  K. Subrahmanyam, "Not a Numbers Game," *The Times of India,* December 7, 1998.

112  Muchkund Dubey, "Nuclear Elimination, A Disarming Argument From India," *The Times of India,* November 19, 1998; Donna Bryson, "U.S. Helps India Manage Nukes," Associated Press, December 17, 1998; "India Still Committed to CTBT Deadline," Reuters, December 15, 1998.

113  C. Raja Mohan, "PM Favours More Stable Relationship with U.S.," *The Hindu,* December 17, 1998, p. 1.

Part II

SECURITY AND
NON-PROLIFERATION ISSUES

# 4

# Up in the Air
## Prospects for Indo-US Space Cooperation

**Anupam Srivastava**

In the post–Cold War period, the United States has stepped up its efforts to stem and reverse the proliferation of weapons of mass destruction (WMD) and their means of delivery. The collapse of the Soviet Union has removed the central ideological bone of contention that undergirded the East-West rivalry. There is thus greater consensus on the need to "win" the proliferation battle. At the same time, with the restraining impact of superpower rivalry having been removed, regional as well as other contentious issues have resurfaced, prompting former US senator Sam Nunn to remark that the world has moved from an "era of high risk but high stability" to one of "low risk, but also low stability." [1]

US attempts at devising national as well as multilateral policies to tackle the aforesaid proliferation problem have been questioned on several grounds, from selectivity in the application of rules to double standards in its national versus global perspectives on the issue. In South Asia, for instance, rated as a region of prime proliferation concern to the United States, Indian policy relating to its missile program has been at variance with the US position on the matter. The area of policy divergence has been brought into sharper focus with the setting up of the Missile Technology Control Regime (MTCR) in 1987. With one of the more advanced ballistic missile programs in the world (perhaps after the United States, Russia, France, Britain, Ukraine, and China), and an equally impressive civilian space program, both of which continue to receive top policy priority by the government, India presents a major challenge to the United States in the matter.

79

## NUCLEAR TESTS AS A WATERSHED

This matter has acquired added salience in the aftermath of the nuclear tests conducted by India in May 1998. The United States, as a prime mover in the nuclear and missile non-proliferation regimes, has demanded that India clarify its defense posture following its decision to establish a "minimum nuclear deterrent," sign the Comprehensive Test Ban Treaty (CTBT) immediately and unconditionally, and agree to be party to the proposed Fissile Material Control Treaty (FMCT). Moreover, India should freeze all missile tests that would further refine and advance its missile arsenal.

The Indian response, as it has evolved after the tests, demonstrates willingness to sign the CTBT, participate in good faith negotiations leading to the speedy conclusion of the FMCT, and maintain strict national control over exports of sensitive technologies and materials relating to WMD. However, it has clearly rejected any attempt to halt all missile tests. It argues that missiles, as delivery vehicles, are essential to erecting a minimum nuclear deterrent. As such, the demand to freeze its missile programs is untenable for meeting legitimate threats to the security of the realm.

Clearly, the track record of Indo-US interaction on issues relating to international security has at best been a mixed one. The Indian position on how to tackle the proliferation challenge has differed from the US one in both conceptual and procedural domains. Further, the missile issue presents greater problems because as means of delivery, they do not invoke international moral censure in and of themselves. It is what one mounts on them—whether conventional or nonconventional warheads—that effectively determines the lethalness, and (im)morality of the missile system in question.

India's civilian space program has engaged in extensive collaboration with the United States dating back to the 1960s. It is only since the late 1980s that the missile component of the Indian space program has caused policy divergence between the two countries. As India embarks upon developing its intercontinental ballistic missile (ICBM) and cruise missile (CM) capabilities, and inducts ballistic missiles (BMs) into its force structure, the implications for regional force stability and Indo-US cooperation deserve to be examined in greater detail.

This chapter proceeds in four sections. The first section provides a brief description of the MTCR and its institutional mandate/capacity to curb global missile proliferation. The next section discusses India's burgeoning civilian space and missile capabilities. This provides the substantive context within which to examine the need for India and the United States to identify the common ground between their respective policies in the matter. The third section discusses the costs and benefits of bringing Indian space policies into line with the existing norms and guidelines of the MTCR and attendant institutional architecture. The concluding section enumerates specific recommendations on how the two countries can reconcile their policy differences in order to promote US non-proliferation goals in South Asia without undermining India's legitimate security concerns in the process.

## INSTITUTIONAL CAPACITY AND LIMITATIONS OF MTCR

Established in 1987 by the G-7 countries,[2] MTCR comprises guidelines for sensitive missile-relevant transfers that member states voluntarily undertake to follow in their national export controls, accompanied by an equipment and technology annex (ETA) specifying the technologies to which the guidelines apply.[3] Member states commit themselves to taking these guidelines into account in implementing their export controls, but the decision about whether or not to grant an export license is in each case a national prerogative. Thus the legal force behind the MTCR stems from national legislation enacted by individual states, and not an overall treaty wherein all signatories undertake certain obligations that impart it a de jure force. This is in contrast to regimes that seek to control the proliferation of nuclear, chemical, and biological weapons and related technologies.

The annex of the MTCR divides missiles, components, and related technologies into two categories. Category I comprises complete rocket systems (including ballistic missile systems, space launch vehicles, and sounding rockets)[4] and unmanned air vehicle systems (including cruise missile systems, target drones, and reconnaissance drones)[5] capable of delivering at least a 500-kg payload to a range of at least 300 km as well as the specially designed production facilities for these systems. Category I also includes complete missile subsystems. Category II covers all items not listed in Category I and includes components, designs, and related technology.

If a nonmember seeks outright purchase, or assistance in production, of a Category I item, the members are advised to proceed with "a strong presumption for denial." For Category II items, requirements are less restrictive. Nevertheless, members are advised to proceed with caution and carefully scrutinize the import request, particularly as regards its end-user verification. In each case, members should report fully and without delay their action to all other member states.

The original guidelines of the MTCR applied to a missile capable of delivering at least a 500 kg payload to a distance of at least 300 km. Since mid-1993 the technical parameters of the guidelines have been changed to include all missiles intended for delivery of WMD.[6] Further, members agreed in October 1994 to a no-undercut policy on license denials: If one member denies a missile technology to a country, other members must do the same.[7]

During the twelve years that the MTCR has been in existence, its membership has grown from seven to twenty-nine. In addition, seven other states have either applied for membership or formally declared their adherence to the norms and guidelines of the regime. These include Israel, China (PRC), Ukraine, Romania, Taiwan (ROC), South Korea, and Egypt (see Table 1 in the appendix to this chapter). To an extent, then, MTCR can be said to have exercised an inertial restraint on the global proliferation of missiles and related technology. However, it has had little impact on curbing the missile capabilities of the MTCR members themselves, or the national missile programs of India, Pakistan, North Korea, and Iran.[8]

In addition to the lack of treaty status, MTCR suffers from one crucial built-in contradiction: It is not clear whether the regime is an internal policy coordination arrangement among its members or a global missile proliferation control regime. Clearly, the regime faces trade-offs between the need to widen both its membership and the scope of its activities and the need to deepen them. Further, since the regime can be formally classified as a technology control arrangement between a group of suppliers (i.e., an oligopsony), it lacks the institutional capacity and mandate required to emerge as an effective counterpart to regimes governing state and interstate behavior in the spheres of nuclear, chemical, and biological weapons.

To this can be added the growing problem of technology becoming an increasingly fungible commodity, such that it becomes harder to control the flow of a dual-use item on security grounds. This is especially true in the case of civilian space technology, whose linkages with missile technology only keep growing. Finally, as stated earlier, whether one mounts a conventional warhead on a missile or a WMD ultimately determines the lethalness and (im)morality of missiles as means of delivery; as such, missiles are not a cause of moral repugnance in and of themselves.

## INDIAN CAPABILITIES

### The Civilian Space Component

India's space program dates back to the creation of the Indian Space Research Organization (ISRO) on August 15, 1969, under the Department of Atomic Energy.[9] It may be noted, however, that the Indian National Committee for Space Research (INCOSPAR) was set up in 1962, and work on establishing the Thumba Equatorial Rocket Launching Station (TERLS) had started the same year. Indeed, the first sounding rocket was launched from TERLS on November 21, 1963. But the commissioning of ISRO (1969) and the creation of the Space Commission (1972) and the Department of Space (1972) provided the critical organizational impulse. It was on April 1, 1975, that ISRO was upgraded from an autonomous status to a Government Organization, and soon after, the first Indian satellite, Aryabhatta, was launched (April 19, 1975).[10] From then, Indian civilian space programs have displayed a phenomenal track record of achievement and are regarded as one of the most successful manifestations of domestic priority being given to the pursuit of excellence in advanced science and technology.[11]

India's civilian space program has two important components: the Indian National Satellite system (INSAT) and the National Natural Resources Management System (NNRMS). The INSAT seeks to provide uninterrupted services for telecommunications, meteorological observation (including disaster warning) and data relay, nationwide direct satellite television broadcasting to augmented community TV receivers in rural and remote areas, and nationwide TV program distribution for rebroadcasting through terrestrial transmitters.[12] The NNRMS is aimed at optimal utilization of the country's natural resources by a systematic inventory of resource availability using remote sensing data in conjunction with conventional techniques. Thus its major elements encompass conceptualizing and implementing space segments with necessary ground-based data reception, processing, and interpretation systems, and integrating the satellite-based remotely sensed data with conventional data for resource management applications.

The INSAT program has conceptualized three successive stages of development and use of its satellite systems, the third one in advanced stages of definition of roles and requirements. Under the INSAT-1 and INSAT-2 series, India has placed into orbit nine satellites that are capable of complex, multi-role functions. Under the NNRMS program, for which the Indian Remote Sensing system (IRS) has become the mainstay, India has launched six satellites from the IRS-1 and IRS-P series that are currently in operation. There is a complex web of ground control systems—from telemetry, tracking, and command networks to spacecraft control systems, and now increasing use of the Global Positioning System (GPS) and Geographical Information System (GIS)—that support the space missions and augment ground-based applications of these services.

The Department of Space (DOS) has also pursued the ambitious program of providing an indigenous launch vehicle facility to support the tasks performed by the satellites. The result has been the successful development, testing, and launch of the Satellite Launch Vehicle (SLV), Augmented SLV, and the Polar SLV (PSLV, placing 1,000-kg payload-bearing Indian satellites into polar sun-synchronous orbit). The PSLV is a four-stage launch vehicle that uses both solid and liquid rocket fuels. Buoyed by the success of the PSLV, and using the data generated by the flight performance of the PSLV, India plans to launch the Geo-Synchronous Launch Vehicle (GSLV) in late 1999 (see Table 2 in the appendix).

The GSLV is intended for launching 2,000–2,500-kg INSAT-class satellites into geosynchronous transfer orbit. In addition to the indigenous rocket engine for the GSLV that is nearing completion (the engine, and components thereof, have been successfully tested),[13] India had contracted the Russian space agency, Glavkosmos, for supply of the engine and technology.[14] Citing export control violations, the United States had banned Glavkosmos and ISRO from receiving US technological assistance, and forced Glavkosmos to cancel the Indian deal in July 1993. After protracted negotiations, the United States agreed to a one-time waiver of the ban, to permit the sale of the engine only (not the technology), since the deal predates Russia's joining the MTCR (in 1995) and being bound by its export control regulations. Accordingly, on 23 September 1998, ISRO headquarters in Bangalore received the first of the seven cayogenic engines developed at the Krunichev space construction center near Moscow. The rest of the six engines will be supplied within the next three years.

**Growing Commercial Potential**

A brief survey of the growing success of ISRO's programs will serve to highlight its tremendous commercial potential. Thus, one instance relates to the increasingly high-tech nature of Indo-US cooperation in the area of satellite imagery.[15] Another instance, relating to the diversification of the collaborators, is the contract that enables the (Korean and German) Tuffsat satellite to "piggyback" the indigenous IRS-P4 satellite, scheduled for launch by early 1999.[16] Similarly, European interest in ISRO has grown markedly over the years. Dr. Rupert Haydn, chairman of Germany's IRS ground station, Euromap (which is an ISRO collaborator), feels that the "Indian barrier" has been broken: "We hope to get about 20 to 30 percent of the market over the next 4–5 years, as many European users who had initially refused to take the IRS data have found it useful for use in telecommunication and road navigation sectors." [17] Further, ISRO runs the largest commercial satellite-monitoring program in the world, and its black and white image-resolution capacity (of 6 m) is one of the sharpest available in the commercial market.[18]

Likewise, Spain has evinced keen interest in using IRS-1C-1D data for preparation of its annual mapping assessment. Ground stations to receive IRS data are being built in Australia and South Africa, while similar stations are expected to come up shortly in Saudi Arabia, Japan, South Korea, Ecuador, and either Brazil or Argentina.[19] Also, on March 12, 1998, the Host Country Agreement between the UN-affiliated Center for Space Science and Technology Education in Asia and the Pacific (CSSTE-AP) and the Government of India (GOI) was signed at the Space Application Center (SAC) in Ahmedabad (India). The CSSTE-AP is an educational institution that enables the member states to build indigenous capabilities in space science and technology. It offers postgraduate degrees in remote-sensing and geographical information systems (GIS), satellite meteorology, satellite communications, and space sciences to students of twelve countries in the region. The governing board of the CSSTE-AP, consisting of representatives of the twelve member countries and the United Nations, reelected K. Kasturirangan (chairman, ISRO) as the chairman of the board for the term 1998–2000.[20]

**The Missile Component**

India's missile development program dates back to the creation of the Defense Research and Development Organization (DRDO) in 1980, which enunciated the Integrated Guided-Missile Development Program (IGMDP) in 1983. Since their inception, ISRO and IGMDP have received top policy priority and relative autonomy from the elaborate maze of governmental (legislative and bureaucratic) controls. This has permitted the IGMDP to embark upon a systematic and time-bound program of research, development, field testing, (serial) production, and deployment (including induction into the force structure) of a range of BMs.[21]

Currently the IGMDP consists of five core missile systems: Agni ("fire," the intermediate-range ballistic missile, or IRBM); Prithvi ("earth," the short-range ballistic missile, or SRBM); a medium-range surface-to-air missile (SAM) named Akash (sky); a short-range SAM named Trishul (trident); and an anti-tank guided missile (ATGM) named Nag (cobra). In addition, recent reports mention ongoing projects, including extending the range of Agni to make it an intercontinental ballistic missile (ICBM), to be designated as Surya (sun); development of a submarine-launched ballistic missile (SLBM) named Sagarika (ocean's daughter); [22] and a phased array radar system (Rajendra).[23] Moreover, IGMDP has been engaged in the development/modification and production of an entire range of other missile systems: surface-to-surface missiles (SSMs), surface-to-air missiles (SAMs), air-to-surface missiles (ASMs), air-to-air missiles (AAMs), and antiship missiles and antitank missiles (see Table 3 in the appendix).

## Synergy between Space and Missile Programs

The missile program of India has over the years established synergistic linkages with the domestic civilian space program. Assessment of the extent of this linkage is not an easy task, because information on the subject is highly classified, and where such information is available, it is of a level of technical complexity that is clearly beyond the scope of this study.

It is important to stress, however, that the analytical parameters of the study are designed in a manner such that any limitation of the ability to precisely determine the extent of this linkage does not prejudicially impinge upon the robustness of the study. It is sufficient for the study to determine that the linkage with the civilian space program has so far had a beneficial spin-off effect upon the development of India's BM program.[24] In this context, it bears mention that the level of technological sophistication (and the gestation period) required to convert a space launch capability into missile capability is relatively modest.[25] The success of the PSLV launch, and the optimism surrounding an early launch of the GSLV, creates speculation that India will soon utilize the experience to produce an extended IRBM-range Agni, and follow it up with an ICBM (strategic) missile.[26]

Recent scholarship on the subject, however, argues persuasively that further advances in India's space program would be severely impeded if access to advanced technology and material becomes difficult. [27] The Prithvi (battlefield support) missile that was deployed in 1994[28] comes in three variants, depending upon the trade-off between range and payload.[29] Software permits target updating and in-flight maneuvering, and Prithvi's unitary and cluster payloads can be changed in the field. Its role can be similar to that of the US Army Tactical Missile System (ATACMS).[30] But Prithvi is somewhat less flexible, being limited in particular by the decision to use liquid fuel and the Indian army's limited battlefield surveillance capabilities at the missile's full range (350 km).[31] Further, Prithvi still relies on some foreign components and alloys.[32] Even if the simplicity of Prithvi's design makes its indigenization possible, other programs (such as an ICBM-range Agni) would not necessarily progress as smoothly if more complex technologies were involved.[33]

### Growing Commercial Potential and Intent

While the technical debate on issue linkages remains inconclusive, some recent developments signal India's desire to enhance national defense capabilities as well as harness them for commercial purposes. It is significant that this developmental trajectory brings the country into greater clash with the objectives of the MTCR. Thus in September 1995 India established a Defense Export Board, which is charged with the responsibility to pursue "an aggressive new marketing plan to offer complete missile systems to overseas customers, rather than subsystems or spare parts." [34] It is not clear, however, how India wishes to compete in a saturated global missile market, particularly when the indigenous demand has not been fulfilled. There are media reports that the DRDO intends to sell its antitank missile, Nag, to South Africa's Denel armament company for mounting on its Rooivalk antitank helicopter.[35] However, there have been no reports to suggest that the government is seeking export destinations for its longer-range missiles.

In the aftermath of the recent nuclear tests, the government has clearly enunciated its resolve to maintain its missile arsenal, as it constitutes the delivery component of the "minimum nuclear deterrence" sought to be maintained against China (and Pakistan). Accordingly, the government is reported to have authorized the completion of the developmental phase of Agni, leading to its eventual induction into the force structure.[36]

In an important gazette notification issued by the Directorate General of Foreign Trade (DGFT) in March 1995, the government has made a statutory amendment that would permit, under license, the sale of a range of missiles, subsystems, components, designs, materials, and relevant technologies.[37] This has two critical implications: the government, as per statute, can now sanction the sale of delivery systems and related "know-how" and "know-why"; and notwithstanding the overarching political considerations, license granting now resides within the authorized administrative realm of the central bureaucracy.

It scarcely bears underlining that the above legislation has far-reaching domestic and international implications. It is equally crucial that despite this amendment, India has refrained from any attempt to export any item to any country that is engaged in any suspected indigenous BM program of regional or global concern.

## COSTS AND BENEFITS OF INDIA JOINING THE MTCR

See Tables 4 and 5 in the appendix for a summary of this section.

### Costs to India of Noncompliance with MTCR

At the outset, it needs to be clarified that the Missile Non-Proliferation Regime (MNPR) is not as strong as the Nuclear Non-Proliferation Regime (NNPR). The NNPR is undergirded by a near-universal treaty (the Nuclear Non-Proliferation Treaty, or NPT), and comprises an interlocking web of regimes that make the pursuit of clandestine nuclear weapons programs increasingly untenable.[38] In contrast, the MNPR is comprised of only the MTCR. The Wassenaar Arrangement (WA), which seeks to control the transfer of dual-use goods and technologies, acts as an additional filter to impede the horizontal and vertical proliferation of BM programs worldwide.

For India, however, despite all its institutional weaknesses, the effectiveness of MTCR is not diminished. This is so because the technologies that India requires for further development and refinement of its missile program reside mainly with the United States, Russia and France. As members of the MTCR, these countries have explicitly rendered their commitment to observe the guidelines of the regime in deciding upon technology transfers that might increase the incidence of missile proliferation. As such, even without a legally binding mandate, MTCR is just as effective a technology-denial regime for India as the nuclear regimes can be or have been.

By not joining the MTCR, India will at best remain a marginalized voice of dissent outside of the regime framework; more likely, it will remain a target of the regime. It will thus lose the opportunity to constructively shape the regime's agenda and approach toward tackling the non-proliferation problem worldwide.

Technology denial has certainly impeded India's missile program. Continued technology embargoes have, on an average, delayed India's missile programs by about five to eight years. In the long run, such approaches augment the country's indigenous resolve (and capacity), while also making any rapprochement more difficult down the road—exactly opposite to the intended objectives of the embargo in the first place. In a sense, this approach is quite similar to the multilateral security regimes' experience in negotiating with India in the nuclear sphere.[39] At the same time, the longer India remains outside of the regime framework, the more difficult it becomes for it to enter into profitable collaborative arrangements with member states, particularly in the peaceful applications of space sciences. In sum, India's BM programs and ambitions have proceeded up to a certain point in the face of all technology embargoes, but any further progress is likely to be severely jeopardized.[40]

The global market in satellite imagery is fast becoming a buyers' preserve, with supply rapidly outstripping demand. This has serious implications for price setting as well as quality control. India has certain comparative advantages in this area, particularly relating to the spectral resolution of imagery. It would certainly be expensive and difficult for India to explore, secure, and maintain market niches for its products in the medium to long term if it opts for an independent path.

The experience of the aerospace industry has clearly revealed the nature of the competition and the decision of erstwhile market leaders to join hands and work together. Likewise, although it has not amounted to much, certain European industries have attempted to pool their R&D budgets (and efforts) to explore competitive niches for select products rather than attempt defense autarky within their national markets. According to one estimate, this European R&D budget is $12 billion, compared to the US Department of Defense's R&D budget of approximately $35 billion.[41]

The figures are not important, what is of significance is that market compulsions, including product differentiation, costs and research lead times, volatility of capital and investment flows, and the growing role of technology with regard to competitiveness, crucially impinge on national latitude for decision making in these strategic sectors of the economy.

India has long differed with the piecemeal approach to disarmament. It thus perceives arms control agreements as a flawed demonstration of resolve by the technological "haves" to pursue comprehensive global disarmament. Nevertheless, as these overlapping agreements make transfer of technology to outsiders progressively difficult, India's costs for noncompliance will grow over time. Specifically, with the WA tightening the definition and control of dual-use goods and technology, India will be at the receiving end of these technology-denial regimes.

### Costs to India of Joining the MTCR

India will not be able to export any of its medium- to long-range missiles (i.e., Agni, and others that it might develop over time, e.g., Surya and Sagarika). It will also not be able to sell Prithvi, since it is capable of delivering nuclear weapons.

India will have to put a verifiable cap on vertical proliferation of its ongoing BM programs. Further, it will have to dismantle all the BM programs that are mentioned above, because they cannot be retained even to meet national security threats (since India will have to join MTCR as a non-nuclear-weapon state). Of course, the shorter-range missiles, which are not capable of delivering nuclear weapons, can be retained. However, this will heighten India's strategic dilemmas given the growing BM capability of Pakistan and the demonstrated capability of China.

On April 6, 1998, Pakistan test fired a medium-range (1,500-km) missile, Ghauri.[42] There are reports that Pakistan is planning an early flight test of a longer-range missile, Ghaznavi.[43] Following its nuclear tests, Pakistan announced that it was mounting nuclear warheads atop Ghauri. Experts, however, estimate that it will take Pakistan at least two years before its nuclear-tipped missiles can achieve operational readiness.

A review of the expanding membership of MTCR (in the appendix) reveals that between 1987 and 1993 it went from a G-7 club to an Organization for Economic Cooperation and Development (OECD) club. This study submits that consolidating the security architecture of Western Europe was considered to be an important cementing influence without which differences of opinion on the economic and monetary agenda of the European integration process would have become extremely difficult to manage—divergence of opinions ranged from farm subsidy and common agricultural policy, to a common monetary system and single currency.[44] Further, the inclusion in the Maastricht Treaty of the opt-out clause relating to the "ladder" that specified the ever-narrowing bands within which individual currencies would be allowed to float is testimony to severe differences on key economic and monetary issues. The trade-offs between deepening versus widening of the European Union (EU) membership became painfully evident in the process.

Coterminously, debate on the ability and willingness of the United States to underwrite NATO's existing Cold War responsibilities were balanced against the possible increase in the roles of Organization for Security and Cooperation in Europe (OSCE) and West European Union (WEU). The accession of the non-G-7 OECD members into the MTCR fold should be understood in this context.

Of the other entrants to MTCR, the cases of Hungary, Portugal, and Turkey can be explained as guided by the desire to become part of the EU. South Africa, with the reins of power transferred to a multiracial African National Congress, can also be easily explained. Likewise, one can explain the simultaneous joining by Argentina and Brazil, and also Russia.

Thus, the test cases that India will notice with greater interest are Israel and Ukraine. Israel's Lance missiles were supplied by the United States, while its Jericho I and II missiles have been developed in collaboration with France. It will be instructive for India to examine the terms of Israeli accession to MTCR (it has already applied for membership).

The Ukrainian case presents even more insight for India. As the largest and oldest producer of ICBMs in the world (while part of the Soviet Union), Ukraine has already forsworn and dismantled its nuclear-weapons program and joined the NPT. However, it would still like to retain the right to produce and deploy ICBMs for national-security purposes. At the same time, it has expressed clear interest in building institutional bridges with the West, both as a function of its closer identification with the liberal, Western system of governance and as a bulwark against a possible downturn in its relationship with Russia. Further, as Ukraine searches for its rightful place in the post-Soviet space, it also wishes to harness its satellite launch capabilities for commercial purposes. The terms of Ukraine's possible induction into the MTCR would have important lessons for the Indian policy makers.

### Benefits to India from Noncompliance with MTCR

If India remains outside the MTCR, it can retain its BM programs, continue to refine and upgrade them, and produce and deploy them as per the dictates of its national-security imperatives. This would enable India to decisively alter the strategic force balance against Pakistan and augment its deterrent capability against China in the medium term.

Scholarship on the subject persuasively argues that the mode of deterrence in the future would increasingly be sea-based. Submarines, especially when they are at or near the ocean bed, are difficult to detect and destroy. Equally difficult is to destroy submarine-launched missiles during the underwater stage of their flight. Further, nuclear-powered submarines are capable of remaining submerged for months, enabling them to conceal their location and enhancing their ocean-prowling capacity. If equipped with nuclear-tipped SLBMs, they can serve as deadly offensive weapons, acting either singly or in tandem with the rest of the attack/counterattack formations.

It is in this context that India's efforts at developing its nuclear-capable submarine assume added significance. At the end of the Cold War, as the United States and

Russia began withdrawing from the Indian Ocean, China has been increasing its naval presence. Thus India's pursuit of a blue-water navy can be understood partly as an attempt to correct this asymmetry, and partly as a way to acquire/augment its power-projection capability in the Indian Ocean and the littoral region. There are reports of Russian assistance to India in improving the accuracy of the underwater stage of the launch of its SLBM (Sagarika).[45]

According to recent reports, IGMDP is engaged in developing a capacity to produce cruise missiles (CMs), which, as unmanned air vehicles capable of flying at extremely low altitudes and slow speeds, have certain advantages over BMs as delivery systems on specific military missions. For instance, CMs that are capable of flying at ocean-skimming (or ground-kissing) altitudes and made of radar-absorbing material, are extremely difficult to detect, making it considerably harder to initiate countermeasures.

India might sell its BMs to a range of countries, particularly those that are not unduly concerned whether Indian BMs can compete with the best in the world (e.g., larger Circular Error Probable (CEP), or restrictions relating to mobility and/or storage).[46] Such buyers might include those that cannot receive missiles from MTCR members or wish to pursue clandestine BM programs.

As stated earlier, until mid-1993 the MTCR threshold permitted sale of missiles with a range of less than 300 km and a payload of less than 500 kg. India could easily have sold missiles within that threshold to countries such as Libya or even Iraq. Where adversaries occupy contiguous territories, as is generally the case in the Middle East (or even the Korean peninsula), even a 100-km-range missile acquires a strategic dimension. Further, as a nonmember of MTCR, no restrictions applied to India against such sales, nor do they apply now.

India has a significant expatriate population residing in the Middle East. If the domestic leadership decided to use missile exports, among others, to extract leverage from the importing state(s), it could easily do so. But as a senior diplomat commented, "The Indian government has never elected to use military as a tool of political statecraft—whether in the domestic context, or abroad." [47] Thus, if a "political" decision to use arms sales as a foreign policy tool were to be taken, India could use its BM exports for dramatic leverage, in addition to generating revenue that could finance further weapons development and export programs.

Finally, India's indigenous BM program is a proud demonstration of a developing country's achievements in a high-technology sector, despite technology embargoes from advanced countries. This prestige factor also translates into greater credentials for primacy in the region, as well as leadership of the developing world.

### Benefits to India from Joining MTCR
India can receive technological and other assistance from advanced space powers for further development of its civilian space program. These include weather forecasting (e.g., disaster warning); ocean bed exploration, mapping of forests, denudation patterns, and desertification; and a host of other domestic priorities.

It can collaborate with other countries in the commercial launch of civilian satellites for other countries. Evidence of India's interest in harnessing this potential is abundant. Thus in March 1998 ISRO invited global tenders for the construction of its first geostationary launcher-class launch pad at Sriharikota. The launch pad, costing an estimated Rs. 2 billion, will include an umbilical cord, a control station, and support systems. It is expected to be ready by the end of 1999, in time for the launch of ISRO's first GSLV for placing large communications satellites into orbit. According to the defense budget for 1999–2000 announced on February 27, the government has allocated $20.16 million toward construction of a second launch pad at Sriharikota.[48] ISRO plans to optimize at six to eight launches per year, with anticipated revenue averaging $50 million per launch although this target might be too optimistic in the medium term.[49]

As noted earlier in this study, India and United States have over the years entered into several important and commercially significant collaborations. India's joining the MTCR and renouncing BM capabilities might induce greater cooperation from the United States in the civilian space sector, since it removes the threat that India would divert these resources into its offensive programs.

At different times, Russia and China have raised the demand for negotiating a global treaty on outer space that institutionalizes norms and guidelines for the responsible use of common human resources. In a sense, such a treaty would complement existing agreements on outer space, the deep sea, and Antarctica. MTCR, as a technology control regime, would then become a valuable subset of this treaty.

India has expressed an interest in this overarching treaty, particularly if it subscribes to the principle of common rules for all members for the use of common resources.[50] This includes low-cost access to outer space using vehicles capable of multiple reentry. By becoming an MTCR member, India could participate in this effort from within the regime.

Russia and China have long argued that they were never party to the deliberations that led to the formation of the MTCR, its scope, and other procedural aspects. They should not, therefore, be denied the right to voice their concerns and reshape the regime from within. By joining MTCR, India would also get the chance to play a constructive role in shaping the regime from within, because membership raises the stakes of both parties in making the arrangement work.

### Costs to MTCR and the United States of Marginalizing India

The hawkish segment of the policy spectrum in India is arguing more persuasively that the West has not adequately acknowledged Indian restraint in exporting WMD-related equipment, materials, and technology. The same case is being made about missiles as delivery vehicles for WMDs as well as high-explosive conventional warheads. In other words, the international arms control community does not distinguish between India as a *domestic* proliferator versus an *international* proliferator.[51] Lack of external acknowledgment of this distinction, and the continued voluntary restraint on the Indian side, has polarized national debate in recent years.[52]

The polemics surrounding the NPT Review and Extension Conference (May 1995), the fractious CTBT negotiations (June-September 1996), and the proposed FMCT negotiations accentuated this polarization. Following the nuclear tests, India has clearly rejected the US demand to dismantle its BM program, arguing that it constitutes a vital delivery component of the evolving nuclear doctrine, which would seek a "minimum nuclear deterrent" against China (and Pakistan). Perceived via the lens of India as an international proliferator, this would greatly undercut the cherished goal of MTCR to curb global missile proliferation.

It has been argued that Pakistan's flight testing of Ghauri (on April 6, 1998) might have triggered the Indian decision to conduct its recent round of nuclear tests (May 11–13, 1998).[53] With a range of 1,500 km, Ghauri has considerable strike potential relating to counterforce as well as countervalue targets in India. Further, given the technical parameters of Ghauri, it is widely believed that it is based on the North Korean No Dong missile design. It is also plausible that China may have assisted in the design of the (dummy) warhead that was tested, so as to generate necessary data for configuration of the warhead that will eventually be deployed.

Regardless of the impact of Ghauri on the Indian nuclear decision, it has clearly imparted an urgency to revive the Agni program, leading to its expeditious deployment. The BM race that has begun in South Asia clearly represents a setback to the MTCR, even though the two countries are not party to it.

As the web of technology controls grows, the hawkish element in the Indian security debate argues for merging the activities of ISRO and IGMDP.[54] It is a well-known fact that in the early years IGMDP drew its resources, in both human and physical terms, from ISRO.[55] Over the years, as IGMDP has gained maturity and stature, it has established its credentials as a highly successful entity distinct from ISRO.

A broader point bears mention here. Research collaboration and synergistic linkages between India's civilian and offensive space programs, whatever the extent may be, are neither country-specific nor sector-specific.[56] Indeed, in the aftermath of the nuclear tests, the domestic debate in India has questioned the wisdom of duplicating research in two independently operating institutions, given the resource constraints that a developing country faces. This segment argues that just as the roles and functions of the Atomic Energy Commission (AEC) and the DRDO are being coordinated, so also should the roles of the ISRO and IGMDP.

As mentioned earlier, India possesses one of the more advanced BM programs in the world. A failure to bring it into the MTCR would create a serious lacuna in the attempt of the regime to stem the proliferation of BMs worldwide. Further, unlike the nuclear regimes, there is no moral repugnance associated with the possession and export of BMs. This might make it easier for India to defy the missile regime.

### Costs to MTCR and the United States of Inducting India

It is difficult to speculate on the terms of India's induction into the MTCR. If India decides to dismantle its BM programs, the gains in the area of civilian space

collaboration are quite easy to enumerate and project. However, if the Indian negotiating posture is similar to the Ukrainian one, as is more likely, and it insists on
retaining specified categories and quantities of its BMs for the defense of the realm,
but agrees not to export them, speculating on the outcome of this negotiation
becomes much more difficult.

Aside from the psychological considerations, mounting a conventional warhead
atop India's IRBMs would hugely diminish their military significance. It is also not
cost-effective to use IRBMs (or ICBMs) to launch conventional weapons against an
enemy target, not to mention their relative lack of accuracy.[57] It is clear, then, that
since India has decided to induct nuclear weapons into its arsenal, the military value
of missiles as delivery vehicles will remain critical. Therefore, it is more realistic to
assume that the minimalist posture of Indian negotiation for joining the MTCR
would include its sovereign right to retain its BM capacity for national security
purposes. Clearly, the terms of India's induction into the MTCR would test the
regime—in relation to both its functional domains and its implications for other
aspirants to the regime.

Since India's views on arms control versus disarmament issues are well known, as
are those relating to the use of technology denial as a policy instrument, it is quite
likely that India will find itself closer to the position taken by Russia, China, Israel,
and Ukraine, among others, in the attempt to clarify and reexamine the scope and
mandate of MTCR. This will present further institutional challenges to the regime.

### Benefits to MTCR and the United States of Marginalizing India

Continued, and enhanced, technology denials will serve to impede India's indigenous BM program. The threat of sanctions, economic and otherwise, will deter India
from conducting further flight (and engine) tests of its BMs. These tests are crucial
to determine the reliability and accuracy of the missiles, without which even the
domestic armed forces would be reluctant to purchase and induct these systems.

The objective reality, however, is that India has traversed virtually the entire
technological spectrum as far as its civilian and offensive space programs are concerned. If it is willing to risk or defy the threat of sanctions, it might not be prevented from going it alone. If the experience of sanctions and admonitions in the
nuclear sector is any indicator, this negative approach might not yield expected positive results when dealing with India.

If the MTCR is able to significantly retard India's missile programs and attendant
aspirations (e.g., using missile exports for leverage with buyers), it might set an
example of institutional effectiveness with regard to stemming missile proliferation
worldwide. Nevertheless, as the failure in impeding the vertical proliferation of missile programs of Israel, Ukraine, and others discussed in the study shows, technology
embargo regimes are a necessary but not sufficient condition for securing non-
proliferation objectives. It is equally important to analyze the demand side of the
equation that propels countries to defy certain rules of international regimes, even if

they share the underlying norms of the regimes. In general, a finely calibrated policy of "sticks" (i.e., use or threat of sanctions) and "carrots" (promise of incentives) might be more effective in the long run, both for dealing with individual countries as well as for setting a precedent for dealing with subsequent cases.

### Benefits to MTCR and the United States of Inducting India

Influential voices within the policy/strategic community and academia have argued that incentives have a better probability of securing desired goals than sanctions. The value of incentives over sanctions as a policy tool has been analyzed and largely accepted in the economic sector. Since defense of the realm is a highly sensitive issue for any political leadership, relenting on security issues at the negotiating table becomes even harder, particularly in the age of "open summitry" and "open covenants, openly arrived at."[58]

Moreover, borrowing again from the discipline of economics, it is easy to quantify and prove that when sanctions are invoked, the inefficiencies of the industry (or market) in question, as well as the production process, are passed on to the consumer in the target country. On the other hand, the benefits of incentives are passed on to the consumer in the target country and strengthen the prospects of improving bilateral trade, which can then serve as leverage for improving relations further, including rationalizing policies in the target country. The same logic of the market extends itself to the security domain. In short, inducting India into the MTCR would raise the stakes of the country as well as the regime in managing differences rather than risking suboptimal returns on a broad range of issues of mutual concern.

If India is accorded membership into MTCR, it will enable the regime to monitor the country's activities in the missile sector, and adherence to the obligations undertaken therein.

If one examines India's adherence to the guidelines and norms of the regimes to which it has acceded without any reservations, one will find the record to be unblemished. Indeed, if one can accept India's distinction between it being a domestic and not an international proliferator, one will find its record of voluntary restraint in the nuclear, chemical, and biological spheres to be strikingly good. It would then be reasonable to extrapolate that if Indian conditions for joining the MTCR are met, its record of participation will be up to the mark.

Finally, given India's existing capabilities in the BM sphere, securing its membership would remove a major challenge to the effectiveness of the regime by co-opting a significant outlier.

## CONCLUSIONS AND POLICY RECOMMENDATIONS

Having celebrated the fiftieth anniversary of its independence, India is embarked upon integrating itself into the global economic matrix. It wishes to become a significant actor in regional as well as global affairs. On the regional front, efforts to revive and energize SAARC, striving for full membership in ASEAN and ARF, and other bilateral agreements (with Bangladesh and Nepal) signal an Indian desire for engagement. It has sought to diversify and deepen its trade and technology relations with South Africa, the Middle East, and of course the East Asian economies. After the United States, the EU has become India's second largest trading partner and lender of institutional finance, as well as an export destination for Indian products. India is also seeking a permanent seat in the UN Security Council.

The national debate as well as the negotiating posture that India has adopted relating to the NPT, CTBT, and FMCT dialogue demonstrate the country's willingness to clearly enunciate its preferences and policies. The recent decision to open up its civilian nuclear sector to external collaboration, and scrutiny, is another sign of the country's determination to produce viable results in priority sectors. Laws governing patents and so forth are being actively redressed to enhance adherence to the obligations undertaken by joining the World Trade Organization (WTO).

Within the domestic context, the leadership has legislated numerous far-reaching changes to attract advanced technology and capital, such that infrastructural bottlenecks (particularly in telecommunications, electricity, ports, and surface transport sectors) do not skew the trajectory or slow the pace of economic growth. The exponential growth in the software sector is a testimony to the earnestness of this endeavor. Likewise, details of the export-import policy and the new budget (FY 1998–99) signify that the new government is committed not only to sustaining economic reform, but also to taking bold steps to increase total exports in FY 1998–99 by about 20 percent (from $34 billion to $41 billion) in dollar terms, and to recapture a GDP growth rate of 7 percent or higher.[59] Yashwant Sinha, India's new finance minister, has reiterated his government's resolve to reduce the federal deficit from 6 percent to 5.6 percent of GDP and accelerate other institutional reforms to set the stage for the rupee to become completely convertible on the capital account.[60]

Of course, these targets have become harder to realize in the short run in light of the sanctions imposed following the nuclear tests. Further, the economic recession of the Asia-Pacific region is bound to retard the overall domestic growth trajectory. Nevertheless, the fundamentals of the Indian economy remain strong, and as such the prospects for viable long-term growth remain fairly bright.

It is noteworthy that the BJP-led coalition government has not made any significant policy departures from the trajectory of economic reforms undertaken by the earlier governments in this decade. Indeed, the only manifestation of assimilating "*swadeshi*" (or made in "Indian") into the policy framework is in the area of foreign investments. The new government has pledged to encourage foreign investment in the "priority" (infrastructure) sector and discourage investment in the consumer goods and so-called luxury sectors.

The same pragmatism increasingly animates India's defense sector.[61] The original defense outlay for FY 1998–99 presented before the nuclear tests was only 10 percent higher than the previous year, with nearly half of it going into salaries and pensions, as per the recommendations of the Fifth Pay Commission. While this left little room for financing force modernization, a priority review of the defense sector is under way.[62] The DRDO, as the chief technology generator for the defense sector, is gearing for an enhanced role in this endeavor.[63] Following the nuclear tests, the government made fresh budgetary allocations for priority sectors within the defense establishment.[64] Further, in July 1998, the three-member task force that the government had set up to conduct the country's first-ever strategic defense review submitted its report. The report recommended the formation of the National Security Council.[65] Further, following the nuclear tests, the demand has been revived for the inclusion of the military top brass in the formation and implementation of national-security policy.[66]

On the US side, the end of the Cold War and the search for a new paradigm of strategic engagement with South Asia has resulted in a perceptible shift in the negotiating posture. Although the nuclear tests have hobbled the process, the Clinton administration is still seeking to recast its relations with India and Pakistan in positive-sum rather than zero-sum terms.

Strobe Talbott, the US deputy secretary of state, is engaged in wide-ranging negotiations with Jaswant Singh, external affairs minister and the special envoy of the prime minister of India, and Shamshad Ahmed, the new foreign secretary of Pakistan. While the denouement of these deliberations is still awaited and bears more directly on the nuclear-weapons issue, it also has significant implications for the Indian missile program. During the talks, Washington has signaled its willingness to permit India to maintain a nuclear-capable missile force, although it is likely that in return India would refrain from "mating" its missiles with the warheads.

It is in this strategic context that this study has explored the common ground between India and the United States as regards the prospects for collaboration in the space sector—both civilian and offensive variants. The preceding section of the study provided detailed analysis of the various options facing the two countries. The following two subsections will recapitulate them and distill the central recommendations for the two sides.

### Recommendations for India

1. India should seriously evaluate the military value of inducting BMs into its force structure. The short-range missiles in its armory are capable of delivering advanced conventional weapons to enemy targets. Much of this arsenal is also deliverable by the advanced, fourth- and fifth-generation aircraft that it possesses, although missile delivery against targets in China might operationally be a superior option. India's security leadership will therefore have to clarify whether missiles are part of the strategy for meeting security threats or part of the country's power-projection capability. It is imperative that the leadership clearly enunciate the new security doctrine of the country, particularly following the nuclear tests.[67]

2.    Prithvi and Agni are nuclear-capable missiles. Their value, if used with conventional warheads, is somewhat limited. But in order to use them with nuclear warheads, India will have to conduct sufficient flight tests of the missiles (particularly Agni) to ascertain their flight path, maneuverability after crossing the boost phase, and ability to use decoys (e.g., chaff dispensers and electronic signal jammers) and submunitions (cluster payload) in order to determine its viability. Next, sufficient miniaturization of the nuclear warhead and mating with the head of the missile will have to be done. Only then, and after sufficient tests, will Agni (and Prithvi) realize their true military potential. Despite the recent nuclear tests (five in all—"different weapon designs tested for different yields for different delivery systems"), it is not clear whether sufficient data has been generated to pursue this option and satisfy requisite operational parameters.[68]

3.    Prior to the nuclear tests, a nonweaponized or existential deterrence had existed between India and Pakistan.[69] This implied that in the absence of reliable information about the adversary's command, control, communications, and intelligence (C$^3$I) network, as well as its nuclear deployments, neither side could incontrovertibly conclude that it could neutralize all offensive nuclear capability of the other. The residual ability of the other side to launch an attack in the second-strike mode exerted an inertial restraint on the decisional calculus of each side, creating a situation of dynamic stability.

After the tests, this deterrence is in transition. As such, both India and Pakistan need to develop an explicit nuclear doctrine and all attendant operational structures. In the meantime, each side has to be extremely careful that a precipitous adversarial exchange does not escalate to open warfare where the threat or use of nuclear weapons becomes a possibility. In this context, India should be particularly mindful of Pakistan's growing BM capacity.

4.    If India intends to use its growing missile capacity to upgrade its deterrence against China, it will require serious resource and policy commitment. Further, China is a de jure nuclear-weapons power with a significant missile (delivery) capability. In recent years the two sides have striven assiduously to improve their bilateral relations. Given that both sides are currently engaged in domestic developmental efforts and have little to gain by competing in an adversarial mode, it might not be prudent for India to engage in a missile buildup that explicitly targets China.

5.    If IGMDP is planning to produce tactical short-range missiles to reduce dependence on imports, it is a step toward augmenting self-reliance objectives, in addition to saving scarce foreign currency. But if it is planning to export them, particularly in a saturated global missile market, it will have to undertake a serious market survey to weigh its options and prospects before committing vast resources to this ambitious task. Further, although India is not currently a member of the MTCR, that

possibility cannot be foreclosed for good. As such, it should be mindful that export of most of its missile armory would constitute violation of Categories I and II of the ETA of the MTCR.

6.    As the interlocking web of arms control regimes makes the transfer of technology progressively difficult, India must seriously consider all its ramifications before electing to remain outside of any regime. It should compare the costs of staying outside of the MTCR framework against the value of trying to shape the regime from within.

7.    India should consider negotiating with the MTCR from at least its minimalist posture, that is, retaining only those categories and numbers of missiles that are vital to meet the security threats to the country. This should be balanced against the potential benefits of technology collaboration and participating in the commercial market for the launch of civilian satellites.

8.    As the United States searches for modes to revive and maintain its strategic relevance in southern Asia, India has certain advantages over Pakistan and China.[70] This consideration could be used as leverage in negotiating with the United States, particularly while making certain technological choices in the aerospace sector.

In this context, it is illustrative to note the range of technology collaborations that DRDO has recently entered into with Russia, with several more in the pipeline. It is evident that Russia would like India not only to produce major weapon systems for its own consumption but also to meet Russian export commitments elsewhere. This raises the ability for DRDO to secure better terms of trade from Russia in these advanced-technology transfers.

At the same time, as the DRDO seeks to enhance its capacity to produce weapons systems, it is also assessing the expected rate of obsolescence of these systems (and technologies). Opportunity to procure similar production technologies from the (US-led) West gives the DRDO better leverage in dealing with Russia. Perceived in another way, it affords the (US-led) West an excellent opportunity to make inroads into the Indian market.

9.    A better public dissemination of the institutional safeguards that India imposes on the import and export of sensitive equipment, materials, and technologies, will go a long way in appeasing the hawks in the US Congress (and public policy domain) as regards the dangers of engaging with India. Concerted attempt to do so would strengthen the hands of the proengagement lobby (including the eighty-five-member-strong India caucus in the Congress) to elevate India from a "sensitive country" category to an ally category.[71] This higher categorization would permit a freer flow of technology and collaboration even within the existing confines of the (US) domestic legislation.

### Recommendations for the United States

1.   The United States considers missiles (both cruise and ballistic variants) as integral to meeting its national-security objectives. Equally significant is the policy priority placed upon the defense of the continental United States (CONUS) against incoming missiles. The vaunted Strategic Defense Initiative (SDI), or "Star Wars," antimissile program initiated under the Reagan administration was scaled down during the Bush administration to Global Protection Against Limited Strikes (GPALS) and further pruned under the Clinton administration to Ballistic Missile Defense (BMD).[72] Even under its current dispensation, the BMD, employing either space-based launchers (SBL) or multisite launchers, would violate the ABM treaty and the protocol.[73] Despite grave reservations expressed by Russia, the United States has decided to activate the National Missile Defense (NMD) component of the option. Moreover, extension of the US anti-BM "shield" to its allies and troops in regional theaters, by way of the theater missile defense (TMD)—the other component of the BMD option—is threatening to raise the "defensive shield" against an existing strategic offense parity.[74]

Using this logic, one would conclude that United States should acknowledge that other countries have a similar right to possess BMs to safeguard their legitimate security interests. A refusal to do so would mean that the deadlock with India will continue. In the final analysis, institutionalized attempts to control missile proliferation face much the same contradictions that India perceives with the nuclear regimes.

2.   The lack of success of past sanctions is a good guide for the United States in dealing with India. It should thus assess the viability of using an incentives-based approach in negotiating with India.

3.   The United States has overly emphasized the synergistic, and sinister, linkages between ISRO and IGMDP. As stated earlier, this linkage is not isolated to India, and has diminished over the years. Recognition by the United States of the legitimacy and achievements of ISRO's programs would go a long way in improving bilateral trust and prospects for future cooperation. This would be particularly profitable in the wake of numerous collaborations between the two countries in commercial exploration of outer space and satellite imagery. Their relationship, which is poised to assume greater proportions, would receive a big fillip with this gesture.

On the other hand, if the United States persists with, or increases, technology embargo measures against India, it runs the risk of pushing the country to seek alternative sources of advanced technology, and/or the risk of making rapprochement more difficult down the road. Thus from the standpoint of securing national commercial objectives as well as international non-proliferation objectives, adopting a finely calibrated incentives-based approach vis-à–vis India is likely to yield better results.

4.    Finally, the United States has long perceived India first through the lens of non-proliferation, and then as a target. Recognition of Indian restraint in the export of equipment, materials, and technology would assuage Indian pride and pave the way for greater engagement. Further, as the United States searches for a bulwark against a possible downturn in its relations with China and Russia, the post–Cold War geopolitics of southern Asia indicates the great potential that India will emerge as such a player. The United States should move forward decisively to take advantage of these opportunities and engage India in a broader strategic framework.

The emerging Asian balance of power dictates that the United States recast the parameters of its strategic entente with the regional powers, China, Russia, Japan, and India. A qualitatively superior engagement with India would yield better options to the United States, on both the economic and security axes, in maintaining and enhancing its strategic relevance in the Asia-Pacific region.

## APPENDIX

### TABLE 1.

#### MTCR MEMBERSHIP

(in order of entry)

| Year | Total membership | New membership | Nations entering the regime in each year |
|------|------------------|----------------|-------------------------------------------|
| 1987 | 7 | 7 | Canada, (West) Germany, France, Italy, Japan, United Kingdom, United States |
| 1990 | 13 | 6 | Spain, Belgium, Luxembourg, The Netherlands, Denmark, Australia |
| 1991 | 18 | 5 | Norway, Sweden, Finland, Austria, New Zealand |
| 1992 | 22 | 4 | Portugal, Switzerland, Ireland, Greece |
| 1993 | 25 | 3 | Iceland, Argentina, Hungary |
| 1995 | 28 | 3 | Russia, South Africa, Brazil |
| 1997 | 29 | 1 | Turkey |

*Source:* This list is adapted from Dinshaw Mistry, "Ballistic Missile Proliferation and MCTR: A Ten-Year Review," *Contemporary Security Policy*, December 1997.

*Note:* MTCR nonmembers who have either applied for membership or formally declared adherence to the regime guidelines include Israel, China (PRC), Ukraine, Romania, South Korea, Taiwan (ROC), and Egypt.

## TABLE 2

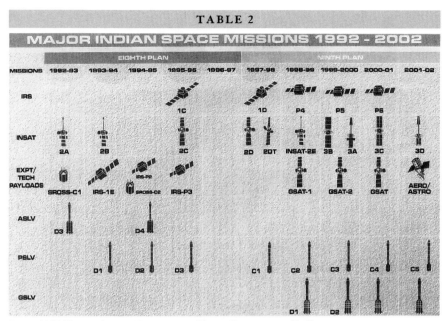

*Source:* 1997–98 annual report, Department of Space, Government of India.

## TABLE 3

### MISSILE ARMORY OF INDIA (INDIGENOUS SYSTEMS)

| Name of Missile | Missile Type | Guidance | Range (km) | Altitude (meters) | Status |
|---|---|---|---|---|---|
| Prithvi | SRBM/surface-to-surface | Inertial | 150/250/350 | | In service (with possible use of GPS) |
| Agni | IRBM/ surface-to-surface | Inertial with terminal guidance | 2,500; tested up to 1,400 | | Undergoing tests |
| Surya | ICBM/surface-to-surface | ? | ? | | Existence unconfirmed |
| Sagarika | SLBM | ? | 320 km? | | Existence unconfirmed |
| Akash (Sky) | surface-to-air | | 25 | 25,000 | User trials |
| Trishul (Trident) | surface-to-air | | 9 | 12,000 | User trials |
| Astra | air-to-air | | 100 | | Development |
| Nag | antitank | | 4 | | User trials |

*Source:* Adapted from Bharat Rakshak, http://www.bharat-rakshak.com.

## TABLE 4

### ISSUES FACING INDIA

| Issues Facing India | Compliance with MTCR | Noncompliance with MTCR |
| --- | --- | --- |
| 1. Access to advanced technology (relatively unrestricted) | Yes, some | No |
| 2. Access to advanced technology through international collaboration (relatively unrestricted) | Yes, some | No |
| 3. Retaining ballistic missiles, inducting them | Possibly not | Yes |
| 4. Upgrading existing BMs | No | Yes |
| 5. Developing new missile capability (cruise, SLBM, others) | No | Yes |
| 6. Exporting BMs | No | Yes |
| 7. Shaping the regime (MTCR) | Yes, maybe | No |
| 8. Shaping the broader regime (space treaty) | Yes, maybe | No |

## TABLE 5

### ISSUES FACING MTCR AND UNITED STATES

| *Issues Facing MTCR and United States* | *Strategy: Marginalizing India* | *Strategy: Co-opting India* |
|---|---|---|
| 1. Prospects of inhibiting India's missile programs | Very low, most likely not | Low, maybe |
| 2. Reconciling divergence of opinion with India re MTCR | No | Yes |
| 3. Positive impact on effectiveness of MTCR | Maybe, low likelihood | Yes, likely |
| 3a. Greater knowledge about IGMDP India's missile program | No | Yes |
| 3b. Prospect of merger of ISRO and IGMDP (activities) | Yes, high likelihood | No |
| 3c. Prospect of continued compliance by India to MTCR | No, progressively lower | Yes |
| 4. Prospect of renegotiating MTCR (with respect to mandate, approach, and operational domain) | No, low likelihood of other direct challengers | Yes, likely |
| 4a. Setting a (negative) precedent for others to follow (India's example) | Maybe, low likelihood | Yes, likely |
| 4b. Revisiting the issue of permitting non-MTCR and non-P-5 members to retain BMs for national defense | No, low likelihood | Yes, likely |
| 4c. Reconciling lingering, divergent opinions of dissatisfied members/ adherents/aspirants (PRC, Russia, Israel, Ukraine) | No, low likelihood | Yes, likely |
| 5. Negotiate a global space treaty (of which MTCR is a subset) or MNPR | No, low likelihood | Yes, likely |

## NOTES

1  Sam Nunn, former chairman of the Senate Armed Services Committee, speaking at the Richard B. Russell Symposium, "A New U.S. Policy Toward China," organized by the Center for International Trade and Security at the University of Georgia, November 1997.

2  Responding to growing concerns within the domestic public policy arena relating to commercial and national security interests, in October 1982 the United States revised its export control policy (NSDM-187), thereby greatly curbing its cooperation with rocket programs abroad. President Reagan's National Security Decision Directive 70 (NSDD-70) of November 1982 authorized investigation into curbing global missile proliferation. By 1985 the MTCR had been informally established (in cooperation with the G-7 states)

and was formally announced in April 1987. For details, see Jürgen Scheffran and Aaron Karp, eds., "The National Implementation of the Missile Technology Control Regime— The US and German Experience," in Hans Günter Brauch, Henry J. Van Der Graaf, John Grin, and Wim A. Smit, eds., *Controlling the Development and Spread of Military Technology: Lessons from the past and challenges for the 1990s* (Amsterdam: VU University Press, 1992), pp. 235–256.

3    *Proliferation and Export Controls: An Analysis of Sensitive Technologies and Countries of Concern* (Surrey, UK: Deltac/Safeworld), 1996, pp. 61–62.

4    A ballistic missile is defined as any unmanned, self-propelled weapon delivery vehicle that can be used in a surface-to-surface mode and which sustains a ballistic trajectory throughout most of its flight without relying on aerodynamic lift [e.g., German V-2, Iraqi Scud, British (of U.S. origin) Trident, Soviet SS-20, and US Pershing missiles, although the last named was scrapped under the Intermediate-range Nuclear Forces (INF) Treaty].

5    A cruise missile is defined as a pilotless warhead carrier, guided or unguided, that is powered like an aircraft (normally by a jet) and is supported by aerodynamic lift through at least most of its flight. That means that, unlike a rocket, it must be continuously powered as it flies through the atmosphere, and is limited to relatively low speeds [e.g., German V-1 buzz bombs and U.S. Tomahawks].

6    Jon Wolfsthal, "MTCR Members Tighten Missile Transfer Restrictions," *Arms Control Today* vol. 23, no. 8 (October 1993), p. 19.

7    Lora Lumpe, "Bans on Missile Technology," in Joseph Cirincione and Frank von Hippel, eds., *The Last 15 Minutes: Ballistic Missile Defense in Perspective* (Washington, DC: Coalition to Reduce Nuclear Dangers, 1996), p. 32.

8    Israel, having applied for MTCR membership, drops out of this group of nations. Nevertheless, it bears mention that MTCR had no effect in curbing the indigenous BM program of Israel. Indeed, the reasons for the Israeli decision to apply for MTCR membership include lack of new buyers of missile technology (as were South Africa, Taiwan, China, and Iran during the 1970s and 1980s) and growing risk of US technology embargoes to the domestic aerospace sector (triggered by US export control legislation). None of this, however, directly pertains to the qualitative upgradation of the Israeli BM program.

9    *Annual Report 1997–98,* Department of Space, Government of India

10   Ibid.

11   "Space Research," Embassy of India dispatch, Washington, DC, January 30, 1995: "In a significant step, the Department of Space, Government of India, has entered into an agreement with the Washington based International Telecommunications Satellite Organization (INTELSAT) on leasing a portion of the capacity (11 C-band transponders of 36MHz capacity) on India's satellite INSAT-2E planned for launch in the last quarter of 1997 for INTELSAT usage in providing telecom services to its customers. Under the terms of the agreement, the transponders will cost INTELSAT approximately $100 million over a period of 10 years." It must be noted that the launch date of INSAT-2E has been rescheduled to early 1999.

12   *Annual Report 1995–96,* Department of Space, Government of India.

13   The ISRO successfully tested its indigenously designed cryogenic engine for about one minute at its Mahendragiri test facility near Tirunelveli in Tamil Nadu. *The Hindu,* February 27, 1997.

14   It is important to bear in mind that the ISRO had first approached the United States for purchase of the rocket engine and technology but had been turned down.

15   Eduardo Lachica, "India Sets Ambitious Plan to sell Satellite Imagery" *Asian Wall Street Journal,* February 3–4, 1995. "A contract signed by India's Antrix Corporation and Earth

Observations Satellite Corporation (EOSAT) . . . authorizes the US firm to commercialize the output of 8 remote sensing satellites that India intends to put into orbit over the next 10 years. The agreement could be worth $1 billion for the world-wide remote sensing industry during that period."

16 "ISRO to Launch Two Foreign Satellites," *Deccan Herald,* March 18, 1998.

17 Ibid.

18 *The Military Balance 1996/97,* International Institute for Strategic Studies (London: Oxford University Press, 1997), p. 152.

19 Ibid.

20 "ISRO Signs Pact with CSSTE-AP," *Deccan Herald,* March 12, 1998.

21 For a good discussion on the deployment of Prithvi, see Greg Gerardi, "India's 333rd Missile Regiment," *Jane's Intelligence Review,* March 1994.

22 Translation from ancient Sanskrit may not be precise.

23 Vivek Raghuvanshi, "India Develops Plan to Save State-Oriented Firms" *Defense News,* Sept. 11–17, 1995, p. 6.

24 In general, technological development has reached a point where a country with an advanced industrial infrastructure can siphon off benefits from one sector to another relatively easily. In that sense, technology as an economic commodity has become increasingly fungible across sectors. For a fuller discussion, see William J. Long, "Trade and Technology Incentives and Bilateral Cooperation," *International Studies Quarterly* vol. 40, no. 1 (March, 1996), p. 77–106.

25 W. Seth Carus, *Ballistic Missiles in the Third World: Threat and Response* (New York: Praeger, 1990).

26 The Intermediate-range Nuclear Forces (INF) treaty, between the United States and the Soviet Union (adopted in 1988), calculated the shortest distance between the two countries (measured by the great circle, i.e., over the North Pole) to be 6,500 km. As such, missiles with a range of 6,500 km or more would be classified as "strategic." The ICBM version of Agni is expected to have the maximum range of 12,000 km.

27 Eric Arnett, "Military Technology: The Case of India," in *SIPRI Yearbook* (Oxford: Oxford University Press, 1994), pp. 343–65.

28 Prithvi has been deployed with the 333rd Missile Group at Sargodha in southern India.

29 The 150-km-range version has been developed for the army; a 250-km-range model is being produced for the air force; and the 350-km variant is undergoing flight testing and is targeted for the navy.

30 *Conduct of the Persian Gulf War,* (Washington, DC: US Department of Defense, 1992), Appendix T: "Performance of Selected Weapon Systems," p. T-149. Quoted in Arnett, "Military Technology."

31 W. P. S. Sidhu, "Prithvi Missile—Tactical Gap: Army Has Yet to Find a Role for the Weapon," *India Today,* September 15, 1992, pp. 84–85.

32 I. Banerjee, "Integrated Guided Missile Program," *Indian Defense Review,* July 1990, p. 101.

33 Arnett, "Military Technology."

34 Ibid.

35 *Khaleej Times,* March 16, 1997, p. 22. Note: Nag's design was fabricated by the DRDO and built by Bharat Dynamics Limited.

36 Demand for recalling Agni had grown over the recent years, with India's All-Party Standing Committee on Defense urging the government to build and deploy Agni. Finally, in August 1998, the government approved development of the second stage of Agni. See "Government Approves Second Stage of Agni Missile Program," *The Times of India,* August 12, 1998.

37   According to Public Notice 68 EXP (PN)/92–97, Ministry of Commerce, Government of India, March 31, 1995, the Directorate General of Foreign Trade (DGFT) hereby specifies "the list of Special Materials, Equipment, and Technologies, export of which shall be permitted against a license issued in this behalf." This list includes "refrigeration units and equipment capable of cooling hydrogen or helium to −250 degrees Celsius (23K) or lower." Also permitted under license are "technology, know-how and equipment for the design and manufacture of missiles and rockets and their subsystems, propulsion units and their test and evaluation." Further, permitted under license are "sub-systems and design, manufacturing equipment and know-how for subsystems, and components capable of being used in missiles and rockets such as: Re-entry systems, heat-shields; Solid or liquid propellant rocket engines; and Guidance systems and their components such as gyros and inertial reference units."

38   NNPR is the composite of an elaborate set of international institutions and guidelines aimed at controlling the development and diffusion of nuclear materials and technology. The centerpiece of such efforts is a near-universal treaty called the Treaty on the Non-Proliferation of Nuclear Weapons (NPT). Opened for signatures in July 1968, adopted in 1970, and extended for an indefinite length of time in May 1995, the NPT expressly prohibits any state outside of the current five nuclear-weapon States (United States, Russia (as the successor state to the Soviet Union), Britain, France, and China) to pursue nuclear weapons options. Its current membership is 181 states, i.e., all signatories of the UN Charter except India, Pakistan, Israel, and Brazil. Its mandate is enforced by the International Atomic Energy Agency (IAEA). The IAEA requires that a member state disclose the list of its nuclear facilities where the agency would conduct regular inspections to monitor compliance. It has the mandate, and capacity, to conduct surprise inspections, even of an intrusive nature, when it perceives that a member state is not disclosing all the information regarding its nuclear program. (A case in point is the nuclear program of Iraq.) In addition, a host of other international regimes/supplier cartels complement the effort to stem/reverse the proliferation of nuclear weapons and technologies, including: the Nuclear Suppliers Group, the NPT Exporters' (Zangger) Committee, Convention on Physical Protection of Nuclear Material, and State Systems for Physical Protection of Nuclear Material. Moreover, numerous treaties have been signed/ratified that seek to limit the testing of nuclear weapons by countries, including the Partial Test Ban Treaty (1963), the Threshold Test Ban Treaty (1974), the Tlatelolco Treaty (1967), the Intermediate-range Nuclear Forces (INF) Treaty (1988), and the Comprehensive Test Ban Treaty (CTBT).

39   For an excellent discussion on the subject, see Brahma Chellaney, "Non-Proliferation: An Indian Critique of U.S. Export Controls," *Orbis,* summer 1994, pp. 439–56.

40   Arnett, "Military Technology."

41   According to a report published in 1990 by the Frankfurt Peace Research Institute, Germany.

42   This missile is provocatively named after an infamous Muslim invader, Mohammed Ghauri, who pillaged Indian cities in the eleventh century, particularly those within the jurisdiction of the Indian king Prithvi Raj Chauhan. The Ghauri missile is intended to counter the tactical role conceived by India of its Pakistan-specific missile, Prithvi.

43   Like Ghauri, Ghaznavi is also named after a Muslim invader of medieval times.

44   For a related discussion, see Dinshaw Mistry, "Ballistic Missile Proliferation and the MTCR: A Ten-Year Review," *Contemporary Security Policy,* December 1997.

45   Igor Kudrik, "Russia Helps India Build Nuclear Submarine," *Bellona* (Norsk: Russkaya), September 17, 1998. During earlier interviews, one senior-ranking Russian foreign-

ministry official and at least one senior bureaucrat in India's Ministry of Defence tacitly admitted this. Names withheld upon request.

46  The Circular Error Probable (CEP) is defined as the radius of the circle within which at least 50 percent of the missiles will land. *Note:* The surface area of a circle is measured as $A = (\pi)r^2$, with $\pi$ being a constant. Knowing the value of the radius and calculating the area of the circle thus permits a fairly accurate assessment of the damage that a missile with a known CEP is capable of causing. The larger the CEP, the lesser the accuracy of the missile strike.

47  Interview with a senior diplomat (retired from the armed forces) serving at the Indian Embassy, Washington, DC, 1996.

48  K. S. Jayarman, "Indian Budget Increase to Benefit GSLV, Insat," *Space News*, March 15, 1999, p. 9.

49  *India News,* Indian Embassy, Washington, DC, March 16–31, 1998, p. 2.

50  For an excellent discussion on the subject, see S. Chandrashekhar, "Missile Technology Control and the Third World," *Space Policy,* November 1990, pp. 278–84.

51  This relates to the "nuisance value" that countries like North Korea (and even Iran, Iraq and Libya) have created over the years, and the consequent greater leverage that they have acquired, particularly North Korea, in negotiating with the arms control community.

52  Interview with a member of the Governing Council of the Department of Space, Government of India, December 1997. The officials stated that if the United States were to send even a dummy satellite into orbit aboard ISRO's PSLV, that would be a "clear signal" that the United States accepts the legitimacy of ISRO's programs and activities, and that it can distinguish between the civilian programs of ISRO and the military programs of IGMDP. This would clear the air and greatly improve prospects for bilateral cooperation in the civilian space sector. It might be noted that Germany and South Korea are already sending their satellites aboard the PSLV, as stated earlier in the study.

53  Seema Sirohi, *The Telegraph,* April 10, 1998.

54  "National Command Structure for Nuclear Weapons Required," *Deccan Herald,* June 22, 1998.

55  Interview with Dr. Abdul Kalam, scientific advisor to the defense minister and head of DRDO. Quoted in W. P. S. Sidhu, *Enhancing Indo-U.S. Strategic Cooperation,* Adelphi Paper 313 (London: IISS, 1997).

56  This common theme featured prominently during separate interviews with the author of senior Indian policy makers within the DRDO and various government agencies in Delhi, Bangalore, and Hyderabad, November–December 1997.

57  According to 1990 constant rupees, one Agni-I IRBM costs approximately 1 crore (10 million) rupees.

58  Distinctive theme of Woodrow Wilson during World War I days and the term of his presidency.

59  Various reports in the Indian media, especially *The Hindu* and *The Economic Times.*

60  Statements to this effect have been widely reported in the domestic and international media. He reiterated these points during his April 1998 trip to Washington to attend meetings at the IMF and the World Bank (that reviewed the aggregate level of financial and policy support to be rendered to India's economic reforms). He also had a series of meetings with private business interests.

61  For a related discussion, see Paul Dibb, "The Future Military Capabilities of Asia's Great Powers," *Jane's Intelligence Review,* vol. 7, no. 5 (1995).

62  The recently constituted Defense Minister's Committee recommended newer budgetary

allocations for force modernization, especially for the army and navy. See *The Hindu,* April 24, 1998.

63  Interview with the director, Aeronautical Development Establishment, Bangalore, December 1997.

64  The finance minister increased the budget for the Department of Atomic Energy (60 percent), the ISRO (52 percent), and the DRDO (48 percent). He also announced that further allocations will be made as and when necessary so that defense preparedness is not compromised. Reported in *The Hindu,* July 17, 1998.

65  It bears mention that as per the statute, NSC was created during the prime ministership of V. P. Singh (in 1990), and two gazette notifications to that effect still obtain with the central government. However, that NSC idea remained in a moribund state until now. The new NSC is expected to play a critical role in defense strategy formulation and implementation. The Task Force that recommended it was comprised of K. C. Pant, former defense minister (chairman), Jaswant Singh, former finance minister and current deputy chairman of the planning commission (member), and Jasjit Singh, director, Institute for Defence Studies and Analyses (convenor).

66  "Army Chief Wants to Be Part of the NSC," *The Hindu,* September 11, 1998.

67  Prior to the nuclear tests, various scholars had distilled what was called the implicit military doctrine of India. See, for instance, Raju Thomas, "India's Military Strategy and Potential," paper presented at "Beyond the Technological Frontiers of Force XXI," an Army After Next Project Conference, Atlanta, September 1996; B. K. Bishnoi, "Airpower and Changing Security Perspectives in South Asia," *Indian Defense Review,* vol. 12, no. 3 (1997) p. 50; and Anupam Srivastava, "India and the Emerging South Asian Geopolitics," *The Monitor,* vol. 2, no. 4 (fall 1996), pp. 15–17.

68  Excerpted from the official text of the statement of the prime minister following the tests.

69  Prior to the nuclear tests, analysts such as Jasjit Singh, K. Subrahmanyam, and K. Sundarji had distilled central elements of the nuclear security doctrine. The new doctrine will need to formulate a robust command, control, communications, and intelligence ($C^3I$) network both within the country as well as with the potential adversaries to avoid accidental nuclear exchange.

70  For the purposes of this paper, "southern Asia" refers to South Asia plus China (PRC), but excludes western and Central Asia. Inclusion of China is considered vital to any comprehensive appraisal of the South Asian strategic scenario.

71  According to a Department of Commerce classification relating to export controls in the mid-1990s.

72  So far, at least $99 billion has been spent on the NMD program since 1963, with considerably more earmarked until the year 2005. Figures from *The Last Fifteen Minutes: BM Defense in Perspective.* Experts have raised serious doubts about the effectiveness of the NMD (as it may operate without violating the ABM Treaty). There are equally serious doubts about its effectiveness in destroying long-range (strategic) missiles after the boost phase.

73  The 1972 ABM Treaty, and the subsequent 1974 ABM Protocol, limits the U.S. and Russia to no more than 100 interceptors at one location to defend against long-range BMs. Space-based interceptors are forbidden under the treaty. Both the NMD and the TMD, as currently envisaged, would violate the ABM Treaty, long considered the corner stone of all subsequent bilateral arms control agreements. For details, see the *1997 CDI Military Almanac* (Washington, DC: Center for Defense Information, 1997), pp. 9–10.

74  See, for example, "A New Low in US–Russian Relations," *Proliferation Brief,* vol. 2, no. 1 (February 3, 1999). This is the statement issued by Alexander Pikayev, Director, Non-Proliferation Project (Moscow Office), Carnegie Endowment for International Peace, Washington, D.C.

# 5

# *Reenergizing the Debate: Indo-US Nuclear Issues*

## Seema Gahlaut

In the 1990s a consensus appeared to be emerging in the United States that notwithstanding the near-universal acceptance of the Nuclear Non-proliferation Treaty (NPT) and the Comprehensive Test Ban Treat (CTBT), it is unrealistic to expect that India and Pakistan will give up their nuclear weapons option in the near future.[1] The nuclear tests conducted by India and Pakistan in May 1998 have had a mixed effect on this consensus. To most observers, the tests meant a worsening of the regional security situation, and a clear indication that the provisions of the CTBT are essentially unverifiable. The surprise Indian tests were seen, above all, as representing an intelligence failure. Others, however, believe that the tests only formalized the strategic reality that has prevailed in South Asia at least since the 1980s. These analysts also believe that the tests underscored yet again the inability of the international community to solve the problem of proliferation solely by focusing on the supply-side strategies of technology denial. Now that Indian (and possibly Pakistani) capacity to weaponize at will has been publicly and unambiguously demonstrated, a range of options is being explored to restore the nuclear order. The United States, as the leader of the multilateral non-proliferation efforts, is understandably heavily involved in this effort.

The United States, bound by the Nuclear Non-proliferation Act (NNPA) of 1994, imposed automatic sanctions on India and Pakistan. However, given the broad sweep of this law, the exact scope of the sanctions was determined slowly and painstakingly. It had to take into account the objections and recommendations of a range of domestic political groups, many of whom stood to lose economically or politically if the sanctions were broad-based. At the international level, too, there was a lack of consensus among the European allies of the United States regarding the utility of sanctions as an instrument of non-proliferation. Several of these states indicated that the forcible expansion of the nuclear club should be seen as an opportunity to stabilize South Asia, to engage the dominant states of the region in confidence-building measures (CBMs), and to bring Pakistan and India into the fold of the CTBT and the proposed FMCT. The resolution of the problem of sanctions in the United States and at the global level are interconnected. Neither can be seen in isolation. But for the purposes of this chapter, I will consider only the various means available to the United States and India to resume their interrupted "strategic dialogue," especially as it relates to the knottiest problem—the issue of civilian nuclear cooperation.

The post-test dialogue between India and the United States, however, is confined to the issue of Indian response to the nuclear non-proliferation regime.[2] The initiation of bilateral cooperation in nuclear energy is being considered too remote a possibility, even after a satisfactory outcome of the current dialogue. Considering the objective facts on this issue, this appears quite puzzling.

First, the tests have only confirmed overtly what the US strategic community and US national laws have always assumed: that India is a nuclear-capable state. Second, the current thinking in the United States appears to have already placed nuclear energy technology on the dust heap of history. Yet there are clear indications that India, like China and several other Asian states, will continue to be committed to nuclear energy as one of the means of alleviating its energy insecurity in the future. Third, given the size of the current and predicted energy shortfall in India, its nuclear sector can be a large market for external investors. Fourth, as late as 1997, US officials have admitted that, even assuming that India planned to build up its fissile inventory, they do not believe India needs to depend on new, externally supplied nuclear power projects for its supply of weapons-grade material. Fifth, there is no evidence to date that nuclear supplies to India have been reexported or diverted to other states, nor is there reason to believe that indigenously developed materials and technologies were exported by India in the past. Sixth, given the recent agreements with China and North Korea, it is unlikely that the issues of nuclear energy economics and nuclear safety are insurmountable problems for the United States. Finally, in a similar vein, if India can agree to facility-specific safeguards on the proposed Russian power plants, there is little reason to oppose such arrangements with other suppliers.

I submit that images and perceptions have dominated Indo-US relations in general and nuclear relations in particular. The literature and political rhetoric of proliferation from both sides has served to harden positions and reduce flexibility, and has thus impeded bilateral movement in this issue area. Given the domestic public support that each position enjoys, there appears little scope for convergence. This has limited the utility of dominant national rhetoric(s) for becoming the basis for a sustained policy dialogue aimed at problem solving. On the other hand, the situation is ripe for initiating nonrhetorical public dialogue in both countries. As changes in their respective domestic and international environment have crystallized, for both sides there are diminishing returns from the policy of nonengagement.[3]

This chapter will discuss the context of India's search for partners in nuclear energy cooperation in the 1990s, analyze the reasons why Indo-US cooperation in this area has been minimal, and examine the political feasibility and theoretical viability of Indo-US nuclear cooperation. Specifically, it will address the following questions:

1. Why has there not been as much cooperation between India and the United States as objective conditions would warrant?

2. Can and should India and the United States initiate cooperation in the nuclear energy sector?

3. What lessons, if any, can be drawn from the history of US nuclear cooperation with countries such as North Korea and China?

Accordingly, the first section provides a brief description of the nuclear capacity in India, makes forecasts about its future, and discusses the intertwined concepts of energy security and national security that have provided the foundation for the Indian nuclear program. The second section will be an examination of how Indo-US cooperation in the past has been affected by the existence of images that have magnified the role of perception and misperceptions in their relationship. The third section will examine how the United States has been able to modify its images and consequently its policy toward countries such as North Korea and China. The fourth section will explore how domestic and international changes in the 1990s are changing the images that India and the United States have of each other. Finally, the conclusion will recommend some intermediate steps to accelerate this process toward meaningful cooperation.

## THE OBJECTIVE REALITY

### Nuclear Power: Projected Growth in Asia and in India

Electricity demand has been growing much more rapidly than overall energy use, doubling in the last twenty years. World Energy Council projections suggest a doubling from 1990 to 2020, assuming much-increased energy conservation and no increase in average primary energy per capita.[4] Nuclear power is an established part of the world's electricity mix, providing 17 percent of world electricity (compared to coal at 39 percent, oil at 11 percent, natural gas at 14 percent, and hydro at 19 percent).[5] There are now 438 commercial nuclear power reactors in thirty-two countries, and their efficiency is increasing, mainly because over 8,600 reactor-years of experience has been gained with civil nuclear power. In addition, there are some 270 research reactors operating in fifty-nine countries, and more are under construction. These are used not only for research but also for production of medical and industrial isotopes, and some are used in training.[6]

However, there has been a continuing debate about the future of nuclear power. Many in the United States and Western Europe have pronounced it the "twilight technology." The basis for this is the concern regarding the operational safety of nuclear power plants and the requirement of large investments coupled with the long periods necessary to get such plants built and operating. Other concerns relate to the problem of environmentally safe disposal of nuclear waste and the proliferation of weapons capability. On the other side are those who see many of these problems as difficult but not debilitating: "The very limited level of radioactive emissions from commercial plants since the inception of nuclear power suggests that in practice the environmental risks from nuclear power can be made small. Still the risk of a catastrophic accident causes significant public concern despite the record of operation."[7] Further, "the efforts of research and development made today by the nuclear power industry, in particular in Europe, give grounds for thinking that the outlook for new equipment is positive. . . . Resumption of nuclear investments, in Europe, between now and the 10 to 15 year horizon is not therefore to be discounted, founded on newly perceived merits of nuclear power in terms of cleanliness."[8]

Nuclear power is thus one of the renewable energy sources, along with hydro, solar, tidal, wave, geothermal, and biomass. Apart from hydropower in a few places where water is very plentiful, none of these is suitable, intrinsically or economically, for large-scale base-load power generation.[9] Nuclear power, therefore, appears to be an attractive option for energy-poor economies. In the short to medium term (i.e., between now and 2010) it retains a competitive advantage in relation to fossil fuels, because nuclear plants indeed produce electricity at the lowest price per kilowatt-hour.[10] A further advantage being discussed is that on a global scale, nuclear power currently reduces carbon dioxide emissions by some 2.3 billion tons per year (relative to the main alternative of coal-fired generation, though natural gas would produce about half as much).

"Asian countries are expected to expand electricity generation by more than 5% a year during the next 20 years, as compared with 1% in most OECD countries."[11] The power capacity of Asia is bound to continue to grow substantially over the next twenty-five years because of the supply-demand deficit compared with the West and the sheer scale of population growth in the region. This conclusion has emerged from numerous sources, and it is projected that total capacity in Asia will rise by 740,000 megawatts (MW) to 2,002,000 MW by 2020. As of February 1998, most reactors on order or planned (sixty-two of the seventy-nine) are in the Asian region. According to the US Energy Information Administration (EIA), there is a genuine desire for building new plants in Asia, primarily South Korea, China, Japan, Taiwan, and India, because these countries, with the exception of China and India, are without an abundance of natural gas or coal and face the alternatives of importing fuels at relatively high cost. Over 70 percent of the world's new nuclear capacity is anticipated in these five countries.[12]

India's population will soon pass 1 billion and, according to some, could match that of China by 2025. This would mean only a marginal improvement in its supply-demand gap of 269 MW against a population of 1.5 billion. At a ratio of 1:5, this will still be below that of China. In 1995, India had an installed electrical generating capacity of 94.3 million KW, significantly less than peak demand. At the end of 1997 the total energy shortage was about 14 percent.

### TABLE 1

**INDIA: ECONOMIC AND SOCIAL INDICATORS**

| | |
|---|---|
| Population (millions) | 984 (1998) |
| GDP per capita (US$) | 449 (1997) |
| Urban population (% of total) | 26% (1997) |
| Electricity consumption per capita | 12 million Btu (1996) |
| Energy imports (% of merchandise exports) | 26% (1997) |
| Energy import dependency | 21% (1994) |

*Sources:* Country Report, US Energy Information Administration, July 1998, and Economic and Social Indicators, World Bank, 1998.

According to a Standard and Poor report, currency depreciation will have a strong impact on project profitability throughout Asia, and since both coal and oil are traded internationally in dollars, it will raise the cost of imported fuels in most countries.[13] India is the fourth largest coal producer in the world, with around 270 million tons of output in 1996. Huge coal reserves, of around 200 billion tons, give the country the potential to meet almost 72 percent of its energy requirements from domestic sources. On the other hand, oil and natural gas imports take up almost a quarter of its annual earnings from exports.[14]

Given that India ranks third in the number of operating nuclear power plants in Asia (behind Japan and South Korea) yet ranks fifth in the actual generation, it is clear that the nuclear power plants are not operating efficiently. Despite this, as the following table shows, capacity expansion in the nuclear sector has been planned for the future.

### Problems: Present and Future

Policy makers and the majority of the general public in Asia have viewed the expansion of nuclear power programs with equanimity, in contrast to the pessimism surrounding the nuclear power sector in most Western countries. In fact, the criticism faced by the nuclear bureaucracy in India has been that it has *underutilized* both the financial and the institutional resources given to it for power generation.[15]

## TABLE 2

### NUCLEAR POWER PROGRAM IN INDIA

(As of September 4, 1997)

| | | |
|---|---|---|
| In operation | 1,695 MW | 10 plants |
| Under construction | 808 MW | 4 plants |
| Planned | 5408 MW | 12 plants |
| Total | 7911 MW | 26 plants |

*Source:* "Status Summary For Power Reactors > 30 Mwe (Net)," *Uranium Information Center Ltd.*
[http://www.uic.com.au//nip07.htm]

The major problem of the nuclear power industry in India has been inefficiency: all the power stations run at low capacities, ranging from 40 to 65 percent. The plant load factor (PLF) has been on the lower side, though the last few years have seen improvements. The explanation from the Indian side is that problems are related to more conventional areas. Further, "given the need to totally indigenize nuclear power production, slow growth is the price one has to pay." [16] Another reason cited for slow growth of the power sector is the great emphasis on safety. Nuclear safety problems have been common, even though they have been identified and fixed indigenously.

However, if the contribution of nuclear energy to national electricity demand has to be increased, significant amounts of financial and technological investment will be needed. Financial investment is crucial because nuclear power projects have long gestation periods, and neither the government nor the domestic industry has the necessary resources. According to Indian sources, the country's nuclear power program has not grown due to this financial crunch.

> Unlike other infrastructure, proposals to set up nuclear plants with foreign technology and soft loans from the international financial institutions, is not available for the nuclear sector due to technology regime controls. Financial borrowing from the domestic market are for a limited period of five years only, which is too short a period considering the gestation period of power plants, even at the international level. Long term financing is therefore a necessity. [17]

Additionally, the embargoes on export of nuclear technology to India have been cited as having stretched the gestation period and are creating problems in developing technologies for in-service inspections, life-extension programs, and spare parts for imported plants. So far, the nuclear power program is owned and largely funded by the Government of India, with limited finances from the domestic market. Implementation has been the responsibility of the Nuclear Power Corporation and the DAE. To consider various other options for growth, the Indian Atomic

Industrial Forum (IAIF) was launched in 1996. It is an association whose membership ranges from the NPC and DAE to nuclear industries, R&D organizations, and consultancy and financial institutions.

The IAIF is the forum where the options of participation in the Indian nuclear power program by private parties, both Indian and foreign, are being considered. Some active options are: (a) loans from industries in the form of suppliers' credit; (b) equity participation by private parties, both Indian and foreign; (c) joint ownership, with NPC/DAE responsible only for the nuclear island of the plant, while the entire conventional and utility system rests with the other partner; and (d) expand the model of functional distribution in (c) above to entire project management. [18]

In addition, the IAIF is charged with exploring avenues for mutual coordination and technical cooperation with developed and developing countries. It has established contacts with international agencies, industrial groups, and organizations engaged in similar activities, and with countries that already have a nuclear power program or plan to have one. Among these, the Philippines, Indonesia, Vietnam, and North Korea have been identified for possible collaboration.

## LIMITED INDO-US NUCLEAR COOPERATION: ROLE OF IMAGES AND PERCEPTIONS

### Differing Worldviews

Both India and the United States are essential cases in studies that seek to understand the factors that promote international cooperation on trade, foreign policy, and security issues. These are countries that have traditionally displayed contradictory behavior: despite broad agreement on the nature of challenges to regional and global security, they have had markedly divergent perceptions regarding the means of responding to these challenges. From the US perspective, membership in the NPT/CTBT is the cornerstone of responsible behavior regarding nuclear nonproliferation. The Indian perspective has traditionally protested that both the structure and the actual operation of the NPT has emphasized differing approaches for the nuclear "haves" and "have-nots." Thus, for the "nuclear five" an arms control approach is considered feasible, while for the rest only the disarmament approach is considered valid.

India's decision to be outside the NPT framework has led the international community to categorize it as a "proliferator" and nearly a "rogue state." However, India's behavior has been irreproachable insofar as the goal of nuclear non-proliferation is concerned: it did not export nuclear materials and technology to others. In that sense, it has forced the international community to disaggregate its category of "proliferator" into "domestic proliferators," and "international proliferators," that is, those that develop this capability for their own legitimate (national-security) uses, and those that seek to diffuse it to others. Further, unlike a host of other states that had developed this capability, India's nuclear program and "option" has always had nearly unanimous public support, an amazing feat in a democracy characterized primarily by diversity.[19]

Recent proposals about "islanding" the Indian nuclear power industry are a product of both the changed international energy environment and the changing domestic political and economic situation in India. Given that the United States has a large unused capacity in nuclear power generation, such proposals represent commercial opportunities. Nuclear energy cooperation is thus an issue area where the trade, security, and non-proliferation concerns of both countries converge. Yet even before the May 1998 tests, movement on this issue, even in terms of an unofficial dialogue, was absent.[20] Most of the reasons that accounted for weak relations during the Cold War no longer exist,[21] and several reasons for greater cooperation have emerged since the beginning of the economic liberalization program in India during the 1990s.[22] The absence of movement is thus worthy of greater attention.

Several distinct features have characterized Indo-US relations. Accommodation to each other's views has occurred, but in very diffuse ways;[23] rhetoric plays an important part in setting the context of any negotiations;[24] and finally, most cooperative projects in security-related areas have been successful as "islands."[25] On the nuclear issue specifically, the problem can be summed up as follows: "All US rhetoric is policy for India, while all Indian policy is rhetoric for the US."[26]

Images and perceptions therefore appear to have played a very important role in the Indo-US interaction on nuclear issues.

**Importance of Images**

Images of self, of others, and of the situation are cognitive organizing devices that help policy makers interpret and understand the complex reality. National images influence policy preferences and thus generate a propensity toward certain policy choices.[27] Images are based upon the characteristic attributes that the policy makers presume to be important. "The attributes that combine to form political images are those that are useful to the perceiver as he/she attempts to understand and predict the actions of the other states."[28] For the images of self and the other, attributes can be arrayed along three dimensions: intentions, capabilities, and domestic structures and norms.[29]

*Intentions* refers to orientation toward structural change, that is, whether the policy makers see self or other as expansionist or revisionist or status-quoist. *Capability* refers to comparison of resources and capacity for their mobilization. The primary focus is almost always on military power, but economic power is also considered important. Domestic structures and norms are considered relevant as the bases for determination of similarity with self, either in terms of degree or in absolute terms.[30] The characterization of the situation is done along the axis of possibility for state action: thus, policy makers can see the situation as a window of opportunity or as a constraint.[31] This will affect their choice to embark on policy innovation or to maintain the status quo.

### Perceptions and Misperceptions

There is widespread agreement among scholars that durable, noncomplex, and internally consistent images have the most influence on policy choices. These characteristics are interrelated; thus images that weather a number of external challenges become increasingly robust, and this increases their influence.[32] Similarly, it is difficult to live with conflicting images for longer periods, and so actors strive for consistency.[33] This may, in turn, induce reductionism and simplistic images.

Given the tendency toward persistence of simplistic images of the other, there is a possibility that images very often act as information filters and may distort any incoming information. This means that images help filter out information that challenges existing perceptions (and the associated policies).

A related influence of images on interaction is that actions by self or by an ally are always evaluated differently from those by a hostile state. Bad behavior by self or ally is perceived to be the result of unavoidable circumstances, whereas, similar action by nonfriends is perceived as being rooted in their innate characteristics. Changes in the image of others therefore influence how their actions are perceived and how we respond to them.

### Images and Indo-US Relations

Several characteristics of image-based interactions can be easily discerned in Indo-US interaction over the years. First, accommodation is not publicly acknowledged or accepted by either side. For example, the distinction that is often ignored in India is that although Indian actions may have provided the learning experience for global US policy on non-proliferation, most US laws are not always directly aimed at India. On the other hand, it is only in the 1990s that there has been an acknowledgment in the United States, almost as an afterthought, that India is not an international proliferator or even a security threat to the United States.

Second, new information about changing external and internal dynamics is not incorporated into images of the other. Such policy stagnation can of course be explained by several interrelated factors. Thus, for the United States, South Asia's marginal importance to US strategic objectives has dampened the need for policy innovation. Further, given the dominance of national-security concerns in its own domestic discourse on nuclear weapons, it has been far easier for the United States to accept nuclear-weapon programs that are justified in terms of rational deterrence (Israel and Pakistan) than those based on identity and prestige concerns.[34]

For India, the United States has been far too important to ignore, in as much as the United States has always been seen as both a source of advanced technology and a global hegemon. Given India's regional ambitions, it has always felt the need for recognition of this role by the United States. In all bilateral negotiations, it has indicated its expectation to be treated as an equal. Yet its need for technology has always put it in the position of a supplicant vis-à—vis the United States. Worse, India's emphasis on self-reliance and an independent foreign policy have clashed with this supplicant role. Therefore, an overemphasis on form, rather than substance, has been the norm in bilateral negotiations.

Finally, there is little attempt by either side to view the other's actions as rooted in anything but innate nature. Whether it is technology transfer, monitoring, or accomodation with third parties, each has preferred to ignore the systemic and institutional realities that may be causing a particular behavior or posture.

Cooperation between India and the United States on nuclear energy issues has a long but undistinguished history. As an outgrowth of President Eisenhower's Atoms for Peace initiative, which promised US assistance to peaceful nuclear programs, the two countries concluded an agreement in 1956. Under this, United States agreed to sell heavy water to India to operate the Canadian-assisted research reactor (Cirus). Later, the 1963 commercial agreement permitted the construction and operation of India's Tarapur Atomic Power Station (TAPS). Yet US hopes of influencing the direction of India's nuclear policy were belied because, as one analyst observed, "Tarapur became not an entering wedge for the United States but an island of cooperation divorced from the mainstream of India's program and affording little leverage over India's policy." [35]

The main concern of the United States in South Asia has been the maintenance of regional stability. The area has been viewed as most volatile and dangerous because of the existence of two nuclear-armed rivals, India and Pakistan. A further concern of the United States has been that any help to India that may boost its war-making capabilities will generate insecurities in Pakistan and propel it to lower the nuclear threshold. This zero-sum view has been dominant in the United States until recently, and has hampered more meaningful cooperation with India. [36] On the other hand, India's main concerns have been national sovereignty and self-reliance. The policy of non-alignment was underscored as the means to express India's right to freely determine its foreign policy, unhindered by Cold War alliances. Acceptance of conditional assistance, whether it be food aid in the 1950s or dual-use goods in the 1980s, has generated fierce passions and been considered "unbecoming" for a self-respecting nation.

Before the tests, some proposals were discussed regarding the utility of limited nuclear cooperation with India and Pakistan. [37] These proposals emphasized that it is in the interest of the global community of nations to assist them in the areas of nuclear safety and nuclear power generation. [38] There had also been some discussion about the need for the United States to move beyond the prism of non-proliferation in dealing with proliferation problems in South Asia. One of the ideas in this regard was the creation of an intermediate category (between nuclear-weapon states and non-nuclear-weapon states) in the current international nuclear hierarchy and recognize Israel, India and Pakistan as "nuclear-capable" states.

Indeed, the longstanding US policy of asking India and Pakistan to cap, freeze, and roll back their capability was modified in 1997. It now urged them "to take steps to reduce the risk of conflict and to bring their nuclear and missile programs into conformity with international standards." [39] Some scholars had suggested that instead of a technology-denial approach toward India, an incentive-based approach would have a greater chance of success.[40] Assistance via limited cooperation in the area of civilian nuclear programs had been suggested in this regard.[41]

These ideas, however, continued to float freely and failed to find any takers in the US government. The bilateral agreement on nuclear safety, concluded a few weeks before the nuclear tests, was a first hesitant and circumspect step from the US side. The outcry against the tests was therefore even more strident because many in the US government felt betrayed at the surprising timing of these tests. The Indians, for their part, continued to justify the secrecy by quoting earlier US initiatives that had effectively pressured India to abort its plans for the tests. Each side reverted back to its earlier images of the other and found comfort in brazenly denying that the tests represented a new strategic reality that required nonemotional, nonrhetorical responses.

## US IMAGES OF INDIA

Policymakers who have dealt with Indian diplomats in bilateral and multilateral negotiations have formed distinct images of India and Indians. Among these are images of acute moralism, an aspiring hegemon, ungratefulness, stubbornness, and misplaced pride.

Moral indignation and mutual recriminations have been an intrinsic part of Indo-US relations since the 1950s. Striking accusatory postures and aiming for the moral high ground has been the option used by India many times in negotiations with the United States, including those regarding the continuing supply of nuclear fuel to Tarapur in the 1980s.

> American negotiators tend to be intensely irritated by Indian moralism, the assumption that India is somehow the repository of righteousness and objective truth in the world. Of course they are irritated; many Americans perceive that select role for themselves. . . . Paul Kriesberg, . . . comments wittily that negotiating with Indians is intensely frustrating because it is "like negotiating with yourself!" [42]

Similarly, India's aspiration to be a regional hegemon and an important player on the global scene has long been recognized. Indeed, according to some scholars, it was easier for the United States to accept the Israeli (and possibly the Pakistani) nuclear-weapons program because it was based in national insecurity. "Unlike the Chinese and the Indian cases, the Israeli case did not involve a country attempting to parlay its nuclear capability into great power status." [43] A similarly sympathetic characterization of Pakistan's helplessness dominated expert opinion in the United States after Pakistan conducted the tests.

Yet another obstacle in Indo-US relations has been the American perception that Indians have a misplaced sense of pride that urges them to take umbrage at real and imagined insults to their national dignity. Examples of this include Ambassador Allen's comment regarding the "Indian inferiority complex," and later observations by foreign service officials that Indians walk around "with a chip on their shoulder." [44] This has been especially hard for the United States to deal with, as most other states have chosen to accept the role of the supplicant in their bilateral relations with the United States. India has received US assistance in diverse forms over the years, yet "with an acute sense of national pride, India has evolved a unique strategy for saving face: it would accept needed assistance, but it would not say please or thank you." [45] The Indian position, based in neo-Marxism, was that the rich Western nations had achieved success by exploiting the riches and labor of the colonies and were thus merely repaying the old debts.

## INDIA'S IMAGES OF THE UNITED STATES

In India, like most postcolonial societies, a conflictual yet enduring nationalism has guided policy and relations with the outside world. "On the one hand . . . nationalism emerged in the periphery as an oppositional force, with a potentially counter-hegemonic historical project. On the other hand, the reigning models of the future in these colonial struggles were themselves clearly derivative of the Western experience and its three pillars of Science, Reason, and Capital." [46] This is the bedrock of India's aspirations toward the same liberal democratic ideals as the United States and its insistence on substantive and procedural equality in bilateral negotiations. Because the United States, like some other Western nations, does acknowledge a vocation to act as a moral arbiter, spreading justice and aid to the developing world, India has found ample reason to point out numerous moral shortcomings in American behavior. [47]

Other cultural norms have shaped Indian images of the Unites States as well. Among these is the Indian belief that in a complex world, disembodied generalizations cannot deal with concrete circumstances. A case in point would be the Indian insistence that both the rigid structure of the NPT and the relevant sections of the US Nuclear Non-proliferation Policy Act (NNPA) of 1978 aim to overlook distinctions among the so-called nuclear proliferators. [48] American officials, in the best Anglo-Saxon legalistic tradition, assert that they cannot make an exception for India, no matter how nonthreatening its behavior for the United States and for the nuclear regime. Indians retort that "India already exists as an exception" to all their formulaic definitions of good guys versus bad guys, and it would be logical for US policy makers to accept this. [49] Indians have cited the fact that the United States has made exceptions for strategic or commercial purposes (with regard to countries such as Israel, Pakistan, and China) as proof that the United States has a flexible sense of legality.

Similarly, the American "can-do" approach, emphasizing technological solutions to political problems, coupled with this attitudinal proclivity toward broad generalizations, is seen by Indians as patronizing and overbearing. Several Indian officials have mentioned the "catch-all" requirement in US export control laws as the example of just such an attitude. They saw this as based in the (erroneous) faith in technical solutions to what are clearly problems based in political motivations and the inevitability of technological diffusion.[50]

Another image of the United States is that of an overbearing upstart that has no sense of history and prescribes policies without any regard for the sensitivities of others. Some scholars of negotiation exemplify the American attitude that the other party needs help (to solve the problem that prevents good and beneficial relations), often against his own will and perception.[51] As P. K. Iyengar, the former chairman of the Atomic Energy Commission of India, saw it:

> Although the post–world war period did witness considerable growth of nuclear power in a number of developed countries, this promising technology was not shared with the rest of the world. The main reason . . . was the fear of the members of the oligopolistic nuclear weapons club, that the bad example *they* had set . . . might prove to be contagious." [52]

In India, as in other interdependent cultures, a negotiation is not an end in itself but simply one episode in an ongoing relationship. American efforts to extract concessions in return for aid, forced by the congressional demand for specific reciprocity, have been seen as an example of opportunism. The United States' emphasis on short-term, limited commitments also makes it an unreliable partner. Above all, there is the image of the United States as an unabashedly materialist nation, which, when it comes to other nations, considers everything, including national pride, as negotiable. This image is further strengthened by the fact that the United States has used different theories to explain the same phenomena in similar contexts: rational deterrence (and arms control) to justify why it needs to retain nuclear and advanced conventional weapons, and non-proliferation (and disarmament) to justify why the others need to give up the same.

Several scholars have noted this tendency in US officials at the highest levels.[53] Bundy, for instance, noted that "Johnson treated Third World leaders like Senators. . . . He presumed that they were all reasonable men who could be persuaded to compromise on almost any issue if the right combination of threats and incentives was employed." [54] Indeed, the utility of sanctions as a non-proliferation tool was the cornerstone of United States policy throughout the Cold War, and it is only recently, when dealing with extreme cases such as North Korea, that there has been official acceptance of the notion that sanctions limit the United States' ability to influence events.

America's ability to punish North Korea for proliferation is limited due to the strong actions taken in the past to isolate Pyongyang. The United States maintains an economic embargo on the North and does not have diplomatic relations with the DPRK. These conditions rendered the Clinton administration's proliferation-related sanctions on two North Korean organizations in June 1992 and a third in May 1996, purely symbolic. The United States does, however, have significant positive leverage, or incentives, which, which if used appropriately, could influence North Korean behavior.[55]

## CHANGES IN THE 1990S

The end of the Cold War, the rise of Islamic fundamentalism in Pakistan, the success of economic liberalization in India, and the lessons learned by the postindependence generation in India, have combined to modify the images these two countries have of each other.

### Lessons Learned by the Postindependence Generation in India

Generational change has not been emphasized as an important variable in policy research, yet it has significant impact on the ideas, interests, and identities of states. In India, such a change can be correlated with the end of state-guided socialism, which has set the context for the current domestic debate about both the ends and the means of Indian foreign policy. This has also brought to the fore open criticisms of past policies, which are seen as having been too moralistic and not pragmatic enough. Though the overall aims of foreign policy—self-reliance, regional dominance, and global activism—have not lost their relevance, the means are under severe scrutiny. Some of the criticism clearly draws upon the lessons of past interactions with the world in general and the United States in particular.

For instance, the cooling off of US relations with Pakistan after the Soviet withdrawal from Afghanistan has been noted as a vindication of India's image of the United States as an unreliable, unprincipled ally.[56] On the nuclear issue, it is increasingly accepted that India has been ignored and/or berated by the United States because it had only a nuisance value and was not a real threat. While North Korea has been rewarded for blackmailing the international community, the China-Pakistan nexus has been overlooked altogether.[57] Thus, the Indian policy of unilateral restraint (no bomb, no export, no blackmail) is seen as having produced a "sucker's payoff." The more nationalistic opinion actually saw an open declaration about nuclear-weapons capability as the only alternative that would help India build upon and use its capability for real diplomatic and strategic gains.[58]

Several important lessons have been drawn from Chinese diplomacy. China has been extremely successful in forcing the United States to deal with it on China's own terms. Human rights, dumping, nuclear and missile exports, the show of force over Taiwan—all these have all been overlooked by the United States in its pursuit of the

Chinese market. This underscores the need for India to concentrate on building its economic strength and helping the international community to have a greater stake in the Indian economy.[59]

Beyond these extreme lessons, there has also been a realization among the moderate group that no matter what the non-proliferation rhetoric and technical facts actually are, cooperation with the United States will be based on US domestic political considerations regarding Indian utility in the Asian strategic theater.[60] In other words, the changing US outlook toward South Asia in general, and India in particular, will determine the magnitude and direction of cooperation. However, this pragmatism is tinged with caution, because many, both in the government and outside it, believe that the United States aims to control capability, not proliferation.[61] The overall understanding, however, is that India must learn to engage with the global market, albeit at its own pace. Further, India has to deal with the United States as though it is like any other party in commercial transactions, and not as the instigator of a grand conspiracy against India.

### US Learning about India

Recent studies from the United States reflect changes in US perceptions of India. There is a growing demand that the United States move beyond its zero-sum approach toward India and Pakistan and aim to redress the imbalance by engaging with India.[62] Even before the nuclear tests, an important RAND Corporation study had suggested that future instability in South Asia may be caused by Pakistani insecurity from Indian economic and technological growth, and not necessarily by any overt Indian attempt to establish military hegemony over Pakistan.[63]

There is also the realization that with determined countries such as India, sanctions prove to be counterproductive. Indeed, there is open acknowledgment by many scholars on both sides that multilateral sanctions may have been instrumental in undermining larger non-proliferation concerns vis-à–vis India: first, it solidified the political will to attain self-sufficiency at all costs; second, it fostered greater domestic and international secrecy (and lack of public accountability) in the nuclear and missile programs; and finally, it ensured that a shared siege mentality and the imperative to cut R&D costs actually deepened the linkages between the civilian and defense programs in both the nuclear and missile spheres.[64] Some scholars are therefore suggesting that instead of a technology-denial approach toward India, an incentive-based approach would have a greater chance of success.[65]

On the other hand, as noted earlier, the long-standing US policy of asking India and Pakistan to cap, freeze, and roll back their capability was modified in the 1990s. It urged them "to take steps to reduce the risk of conflict and to bring their nuclear and missile programs into conformity with international standards." [66]

But some images persist. In 1997 India approved the construction of two nuclear power generating units, Kudankulam I and II, due to start operation in 2006 and 2008, respectively. In June 1998 India signed a $2.6 billion deal with Russia for the construction of the reactors (1,000 MW each) in southern India. The United States reacted against this deal. The perception and policy of US administration was explained thus:

> We have opposed it, frankly, less because we think that the transfer would contribute materially to India's nuclear weapons program than because we think that the transfer would be inconsistent with Russia's commitment as a member of the NSG. . . . The transfer itself probably does not involve substantial proliferation risks, because we doubt the Indians, who have their own access to unsafeguarded plutonium, would actually divert plutonium from the safeguarded reactors.[67]

## LESSONS FROM US INTERACTIONS WITH OTHER COUNTRIES

The previous discussion demonstrates how certain images and perceptions about the self, others, and particular situations can crystallize, and how their persistence over time often limits the scope of policy innovation. But as the following discussion will show, images can and do change, and may be a factor in policy shifts.

### US Relations with North Korea

According to a recent report, "there is little reason to expect the North Korean appetite for ballistic missiles sales to diminish. Moreover, though the LWRs promised by the United States are not capable of producing weapons-grade plutonium, American tests have demonstrated that 'non-weapons-grade' plutonium is sufficient for nuclear weapons." [68] Yet the administration has leaned in favor of providing energy security to North Korea, via oil sales and LWRs, so as to keep North Korea within the NPT. This has been done despite the questionable track record of the country in keeping its promises, and in spite of concerns, raised by the testimony of high-ranking defectors, that many underground nuclear facilities remain beyond the reach or even the knowledge of inspection teams. Clearly, there seems to be a change in the way the problem of North Korean proliferation behavior is being perceived. The solution appears to suggest that the US desire to cap proliferation has not precluded the option of considering energy needs, even if these are the needs of a "rogue" regime.

### US Relations with China

A 1998 congressional report had examined China's record of honoring nonproliferation pledges only when convenient. The report stated categorically: "China is the principal supplier of weapons of mass destruction and missile technology to the world, and US government's efforts to turn Beijing against international proliferation have met with little success." [69] Yet the China-US Nuclear Agreement of 1985 was revived in 1998. The reasons given by the officials reveal how images of China have changed over the years, such that infractions are considered minor and there is an attempt to both explain the domestic context of illegal exports and highlight the positive changes. Thus, according to Robert Einhorn, the deputy assistant secretary of state:

> China, in the past several years, has taken a number of steps to demonstrate its commitment to non-proliferation. In 1992 it became party to NPT, signed CWC in 1993 (ratified 1997), and is party to BWC. In the 1990s it has taken a variety of important steps to support non-proliferation agreements and has cooperated with the United States in supporting non-proliferation goals in various regions of the world. It worked with the United States to promote an effective solution to the North Korean problem in 1994. Dramatic changes in its behavior are apparent since the 1960s when its declared policy was to support nuclear proliferation, to "break the nuclear hegemony of the super powers." Now it sees itself more as a major power with important responsibilities. It is a member of the UNSC and P-5, it has come to realize that one of the important attributes of great power status is to abide by international non-proliferation norms. So we think that China is more and more becoming a responsible player.[70]

Further, when there were reports indicating that China had transferred five thousand ring magnets to the AQ Khan Research lab in Kahuta, Pakistan,[71] Einhorn downplayed it by saying: "But I have to say that China's evolution is not yet complete. It has made important progress, but in certain areas of proliferation it is still engaged in activities that are problematic for us. The ring magnets are relatively unsophisticated pieces of equipment. The more we looked at this, the more it became very believable that the Chinese entity involved was operating on its own without government oversight. The commercial value of the transfer was something less than $70,000. These are general purpose goods but they nevertheless contributed to Pakistan's nuclear enrichment program."[72] However, according to the congressional report cited above, the state-owned exporter, the China Nuclear Energy Industry Corporation, is a wholly owned subsidiary of the China National Nuclear Corporation, a firm under the direct control of the State Council, whose head is the Chinese premier.[73]

Mr. Einhorn's emphasis in the interview was on the positive development: that China has adopted a nuclear export control system, a nationwide comprehensive system that it never had before and which, for the first time, will give China the ability to control effectively both nuclear items and dual-use nuclear-related items that go to foreign countries.[74]

These cases provide enough support for the argument that nuclear cooperation, even with countries of concern, is possible. Compared to both North Korea and China, the United States should have fewer proliferation concerns about India either on actual export or on the institutional ability to control exports. If there is already an understanding in the United States that safeguarded Russian nuclear power plants in India will not contribute to India's existing plutonium stock or to its ability to get the technology for generating weapons-grade plutonium from power plants, then proliferation by India does not appear to be a reasonable justification for non-cooperation. In both the pre- and post-test periods, the United States was concerned that India would set a bad precedent by demonstrating to other aspirants that recalcitrance pays. Beyond this, there are the US non-proliferation hawks who favor punitive action against India, to make an example of it. This group has found support from those who consider nuclear technology too dangerous to be used even for energy purposes.

## CONCLUSION

The above discussion demonstrates the importance of perceptions and misperceptions as important variables affecting cooperation. Despite shared interests in the maintenance of democracy, regional stability, and global non-proliferation, India and the United States have been unable to agree on the means to achieve these ends. Mutually antagonistic images on each side have hindered the assimilation of new (though contradictory) information regarding the other. This was exacerbated by divergent national priorities during the Cold War: South Asia remained an area of marginal economic and strategic significance for the United States in its war against global Communism, while India restricted its interactions with the global market (and the United States), because of its belief in state-guided development. In the absence of public debate, cultural stereotypes have dominated bilateral interactions. This suggests a two-step model of interaction for enhancing future cooperation.

**FIGURE 1**

**MODES OF FUTURE COOPERATION**

*Step 1: Overcoming the problems of misperceptions*

- Disseminate detailed positive information about each other
- Generate national dialogue that reflects this information
- Commence bilateral dialogue on outstanding issues of concern

*Step 2: Changes in national legislation to allow for limited cooperation*

- Based on specific reciprocity, to engender institutional trust and foster habits of cooperation
- Use examples of incentives from bilateral cooperation between the United States and other countries, i.e., North Korea, China
- Use examples of the conditions accepted by India in its cooperation with other countries, i.e., Russia

## Why Step One?

The possible impact of a dialogue regarding nuclear cooperation would help in the identification of preferences, that is, it might help prioritize the goals of each country regarding nuclear technology and proliferation. For the United States, it will clarify the answers to the following questions:

1. Is it more interested in ensuring that no further proliferation takes place, (that is, accepting that India already has the capacity but asserting that it should not be given any more incentives to export and profit) or in continuing to accept a procedural view that equates NPT membership with non-proliferation?

2. There is growing acceptance by the international community that the safety of nuclear power plants should be a global concern and an incentive for transnational cooperation. Should the United States eschew cooperation in this area because it is more concerned with certain principles regarding unauthorized proliferation?

3. The large market represented by the nuclear power sector in Asia, and India in particular, will be a powerful magnet for commercial interests worldwide. Besides, the reasons for adopting nuclear energy as one of the means to tackle the energy deficit in Asia are real and legitimate. Does the United States really hope to overcome commercial incentives and prevail over not only its own nuclear industry but also the nuclear industry worldwide?

4. Why are the exceptions under which cooperation with North Korea and China has been possible not applicable in the Indian case?

On the other hand, similar national dialogue will clarify the following issues for India:

1. There is agreement among scholars that India cannot establish effective deterrence against the Chinese nuclear and missile capability in the near to medium term, and it already has both nuclear and conventional superiority to Pakistan. Therefore, how useful will it be for India to continue to hide behind the withering fig leaf of diffuse national-security objectives and refuse to clarify the role of nuclear capability in its national defense?

2. How can India justify the developmental focus of its nuclear energy program given the dismal performance of the nuclear power sector so far? How much of this failure can be reasonably attributed to external technology denial regimes?

3. When all is said and done about national sovereignty, what is India willing to do to allay the reservations of those who may want to help in the nuclear energy and nuclear safety spheres?

4. Given the need for power for future economic growth, the heavy expenditure on the nuclear sector is likely to generate public pressure in India for increased bureaucratic accountability on nuclear matters. Will the current nuclear institutions be prepared to face foreign competition at home? Will they be able to maintain their status as unquestioned instruments of national development?

### Why Step Two?

Laws and legislation formalize a relationship, implying national commitment. Given the preference of both India and the United States for legally binding agreements, and given the level of distrust between them, such agreements would set the boundaries of mutual expectations clearly. Further, nuclear power projects have long gestation periods, requiring long-term commitment of resources, and agreements enshrined in laws provide checks against arbitrariness and shifting political expediency.

Thus, an analysis of US regulations regarding atomic energy cooperation with foreign countries under 10 CFR 810 would help set the context of domestic political debate in the United States regarding the legal and technical limits to such cooperation. An overview of 10 CFR 810 is presented in Figure 2.

### FIGURE 2

*10 CFR 810 USG, Assistance to Foreign Atomic Energy Activities*

Generally Authorized Activities Under 810.7

In accordance with section 57b (2) of the Atomic Energy Act, the following activities are generally authorized, provided no sensitive nuclear technology is transferred:

> a) furnishing public information

> b) furnishing information or assistance to prevent or correct a current or imminent radiological emergency

> c) furnishing information or assistance to enhance the operational safety of an existing civilian nuclear power plant in a country listed in 810.8(a)

> h) otherwise engaging directly or indirectly in the production of special nuclear materials outside the US in ways that (1) do not involve any of the countries listed in 810.8(a) and (2) do not involve production reactors, enrichment, reprocessing, fabrication of nuclear fuel containing Pu, or production of heavy water.

*Source:* Code of Federal Regulations, United States Government, 1997

Under 810.10: Grant of Specific Authority, section (b), the Secretary of Energy with the concurrence of State, ACDA, NRC, DOC, and DOD can determine that the activity will not be inimical to the US national interest. The following conditions are taken into account:[75]

1. whether the United States has an agreement for nuclear cooperation with the concerned country

2. if the country has signed the NPT (or a regional equivalent like the Treaty of Tlatelolco)

3. whether the country has agreed to IAEA safeguards on *all* its peaceful nuclear activities

4. if it has agreed to accept IAEA safeguards when applicable to the proposed activity

5. other non-proliferation controls or conditions applicable to the proposed activity

6. the relative significance of the proposed activity

7. foreign availability.

Any nuclear cooperation with India must therefore pass muster under the various conditions set forth by 810.10, and these are where politico-legal interpretations will be important. It is fairly obvious that conditions 4, 6, and 7 are easily fulfilled by India, given the following: (a) the proposals about "islanding" new private investment in the nuclear sector, (b) the realization by US officials that India is not looking at such cooperation as a source for its supply of weapons-grade uranium and plutonium, and (c) that France and Russia are interested in cooperation with India.

Condition 1 would follow from agreement on the relative importance of other conditions. Further, conditions 2 and 3 would be the major hurdles. But, to put things in perspective, the United States has already accepted the Chinese position that on its supply of nuclear material to Pakistan and Iran, it is the Zangger Committee guidelines (i.e., condition 4) that apply, not the NSG guidelines (i.e., condition 3). If this distinction is not important in one context, it would be hard to justify it in another. Finally, condition 5 appears to have been put aside in dialogue with Israel and dealings with North Korea, and can be similarly reevaluated for India.

However, even though US laws allow exceptions, based mostly on determination by the executive branch, India does not favor such a relationship. The reason for this is past experience: exceptions and executive agreements represent the temporary nature of commitment from the United States, subject to the whims and vagaries of US domestic politics. On the other side, given the possibility of coalition governments in India in the next few years, and given the changing compositions of coalitions, specific national laws and bilateral agreements would ensure policy continuity. Precedence for such agreements exists in other fields of Indo-US cooperation, such as the 1984 memorandum of understanding (MOU) and the Defense Production Group (DPG) and Joint Technology Group (JTG) process in the 1990s.

The options facing India in the 1990s can be summarized as the choice between emphasizing national security or energy security as the prime (though not exclusive), concern of its nuclear capability. Similarly for the United States, the choice is between emphasizing non-proliferation as the primary goal of its policy toward India and a nuanced shift toward limited, mutually beneficial nuclear engagement. The first choice would highlight for both countries issues of sovereignty, self-reliance, and national goals and would set the boundaries of discussion. The second choice, on the other hand, would highlight issues of pragmatic cooperation, a long-term vision of economic growth, and a proactive approach to multilateral technology control regimes, and will expand the ambit of cooperation.

## NOTES

1  *A New US Policy towards India and Pakistan,* Council on Foreign Relations Task Force Report, 1997 (henceforth CFR Report 1997). See also Ashley J. Tellis, *Nuclear Stability in South Asia,* RAND Report, 1997.

2  For example, the Strobe Talbott–Jaswant Singh talks throughout the summer and fall of 1998 were aimed at negotiating some compromises on the CTBT/FMCT issues. India started contributing to the FMCT debates in the CD in August 1998, and newspaper reports indicate the growing likelihood that India will sign the CTBT in the coming months.

3  For the United States, ignoring a growing Asian economy with the largest scientific/technical manpower pool, minimal linguistic barriers, and a legal system compatible with Anglo-Saxon tradition would not make economic sense. Arguments have also been made about the possibility of using India as a counterweight to China and of not losing ground to Russia in South Asia. For India, the compelling reasons for engagement would be access to advanced technology and foreign capital, and the ability to influence technology-related regimes from within.

4  Nuclear Issues Briefing Paper 11, September 1997, Uranium Information Center (UIC) Ltd., Melbourne, Australia.

5  Ibid.

6  Nuclear Issues Briefing Paper 7, Uranium Information Center, Australia, February 1998.

7  Jean-Marie Bourdaire and John Paffenbarger, "Nuclear Power and Sustainable Development," *Uranium Institute Symposium Abstract,* 1997 (http://www.uilondon.org/uiabs97/bourd.html).

8  Chritian Waeterloos, "The Competitiveness of Nuclear Power in Relation to Natural Gas," *European Commission, Directorate-General XVII (Energy),* September 15, 1997.

9  Even in China and India, where hydropower potential is plentiful, the ecological costs of large dams have generated widespread opposition, both from the environmental lobbies and from the large populations that will be displaced.

10 However, due to the higher initial investment costs and longer gestation period of nuclear power plants, the current attractive price of natural gas indicates that within a decade, construction of new nuclear production capacity will only result from conscious choice by the investor to give priority to the long-term over immediate profit, and to insure himself against possible future disturbances on the natural gas market. Christian Waeterloos, "The Competitiveness of Nuclear Power in Relation to Natural Gas," *European Commission, Directorate General XVII (Energy),* September 15, 1997.

11 Kun Mo Chung, Korean academic, quoted in "Power in Asia," *Financial Times Energy Publishing,* February 23, 1998 (http://www.financialtimes.com).

12 *Nuclear Power Generation and Fuel Cycle Report 1997,* Energy Information

Administration, September 1997 (http://www.eia.doe.gov/cneaf/nuclear/n_pwr_fc/front-ov.html).

13   Quoted in "Power in Asia."

14   An excellent overview of how India's decisions on nuclear energy have been affected by the variable availability of petroleum and coal can be found in Raju G. C. Thomas, "India," in Raju G. C. Thomas and Bennett Ramberg, eds., *Energy and Security in the Industrializing World* (Lexington, KY: University Press of Kentucky, 1990), pp. 13–34.

15   See, for instance, *Reports of the Standing Committee on Energy (1996–97),* Eleventh Lok Sabha, New Delhi.

16   Deepa Ollapally and S. Rajagopal, eds., *Nuclear Cooperation: Challenges and Prospects* (Bangalore: National Institute of Advanced Studies, 1997), p. 111.

17   Y. S. R. Prasad, "Nuclear Power Development: The Indian Experience," in Ollapally and Rajagopal, *Nuclear Cooperation,* p. 100.

18   Atul Kohli, "Centralization and powerlessness: India's Democracy in a Comparative Perspective," in Joel S. Migdal, Atul Kohli, and Vivienne Shue, eds., *State Power and Social Forces: Domination and Transformation in the Third World* (Cambridge: Cambridge University Press, 1994).

19   For a discussion that moves the traditional preoccupation of political science with procedural aspects of democracy, see Arendt Lijphart, "The Puzzle of Indian Democracy: A Consociational Interpretation," *American Political Science Review* 90 (June 1996), pp. 258–68. See also Atul Kohli, in Joel S. Migdal and Atul Kohli, eds., *State Power and Social Forces: Domination and Transformation in the Third World* (Cambridge: Cambridge University Press, 1994).

20   Some officials have pointed out that US relations with India seemed to be worse than objective conditions would warrant. Ron Lehman's remarks, reported in Edward Fei's *India Trip Report,* US Department of Energy, March 16–22, 1998.

21   The reasons for this have been documented in numerous books and articles over the years. Most explanations focus on the rational description of US and Indian national interests: that the United States was concerned about horizontal proliferation of nuclear weapons capability; that US Cold War concerns subsumed all bilateral relationships; that South Asia as a whole had a marginal position in US global strategy; and that the United States was favorably disposed toward Pakistan, which was being used as a base for support for the *mujahideen* fighting against Soviet invasion of Afghanistan. On the Indian side, reasons included the fact that the United States was not its *only* supplier of technology; that development of nuclear capability, though aided by others, was largely indigenous; that India did not see why China's nuclear capability could be accepted by the United States in 1964 (even though its motives were clearly suspect) whereas India was given only the choice to join the NPT as a non-nuclear-weapon state; and that India always had regional hegemonic ambitions, and nuclear capability, including the weapons option, was one of the means adopted to quickly achieve this end.

22   Charles Wolf, Jr., K. C. Yeh, Anil Bamezai, Donald Henry, and Michael Kennedy, *Long-Term Economic and Military Trends, 1994–2015: The United States and Asia* (Santa Monica: RAND, MR-627-OSD, 1994).

23   See for instance, Dennis Kux, *India and the United States: Estranged Democracies, 1941–1991* (Washington, DC: National Defense University Press, 1992), and Satu P. Limaye, *US-Indian Relations: The Pursuit of Accommodation* (Boulder, CO: Westview Press, 1993).

24   Selig Harrison, "Dialogue of the Deaf: Mutual Perceptions in Indo-American Relations," in S. R. Glazer and Nathan Glazer, eds., *Conflicting Images: India and the United States* (Glendale, MD: Riverdale Co., 1990).

25  For example, the LCA, Tarapur, space, military-to-military.

26  "Summary of Roundtable on Confidence Building," in Ollapally and Rajagopal, p. 107.

27  Keith Shimko, *Images and Arms Control* (Ann Arbor: University of Michigan Press, 1991), pp. 34–36.

28  M. L. Cottam, "Recent Developments in Political Psychology," in M. L. Cottam and S. Chih-yu, eds., *Contending Dramas: A Cognitive Approach to International Organizations* (New York: Praeger, 1992), p. 6.

29  This is similar to R. Hermann and M. P. Fischerkeller, "Beyond Enemy Image and Spiral Model: Cognitive-Strategic Research After the Cold War," *International Organization* 49, no. 3 (1995).

30  See, for instance, the democratic peace literature that examines the reasons why democracies do not fight each other. See also T. Risse-Kappen, "Democratic Peace—Warlike Democracies? A Social Constructivist Interpretation of the Liberal Argument," *European Journal of International Relations* vol. 1, no. 4 (1995).

31  This is of course more relevant for the smaller/weaker states than for the great powers, though it may be applicable in situations where the smaller power may have great power aspirations. M. Handel, *Weak States in the International System* (London: Frank Cass, 1990).

32  J. W. Legro, "Which Norms Matter? Revisiting the 'Failure' of Internationalism," *International Organization,* vol. 51, no. 1 (1997).

33  R. Jervis, *Perception and Misperception in International Politics* (Princeton: Princeton University Press, 1976), p. 117.

34  An examination of the US attitude on British, French, and Chinese weapons programs in the early postwar period would support this view. On the other hand, it is interesting to note that there is an automatic acceptance of the view that the United States, as the leader of the free world, must have nuclear weapons, i.e., the correlation between a particular status and the weapons capability remains unquestioned.

35  Peter A. Clausen, quoted in Satu P. Limaye, *US-India Relations: The Pursuit of Accommodation* (Boulder, CO: Westview Press, 1993), p. 93.

36  Kanti Bajpai, Stephen P. Cohen, Devin Hagerty, eds., *Brasstacks and Beyond: Perception and Management of Crisis in South Asia* (New Delhi: Manohar, 1995).

37  "An Appropriate Role for Nuclear Energy in Asia's Power Sector," policy paper, The Atlantic Council of the United States, December 1997.

38  Deepa Ollapally and S. Rajagopal, eds., *Nuclear Cooperation: Challenges and Prospects* (Bangalore: National Institute of Advanced Studies, 1997).

39  White House, *A National Security Strategy for a New Century,* May 1997.

40  CFR Report 1997.

41  Such a proposal was forcefully put forward by Ambassador Naresh Chandra during his visit to the University of Georgia, March 1997. See also C. Raja Mohan, *The Hindu,* January 1998.

42  Raymond Cohen, *Negotiating Across Cultures* (Washington, DC: United States Institute of Peace Press, 1991), p. 73. See also, Hans Binnendjik ed. *National Negotiating Styles* (Washington, D.C.: Foreign Service Institute, 1987); Ashok Kapoor, *International Business Negotiations: A Study in India* (New York: New York University Press, 1970).

43  Avner Cohen, "Israel and the Evolution of the US Non-proliferation Policy: The Critical Decade (1958–68)," *The Non-proliferation Review,* vol. 5, no. 2 (winter 1998), p. 17.

44  Cohen, *Negotiating Across Cultures,* pp. 34–35.

45  Ibid., pp. 71–72.

46  Sankaran Krishna, "Inscribing The Nation: Nehru and the Politics of Identity in India,"

in Steve Rosow, Naeem Inayatullah, and Mark Rupert ed. *The Global Economy As Political Space* (Boulder, London: Lynne Rienner, 1994), p. 197.

47  Cohen, *Negotiating Across Cultures.*

48  The NNPA requires the US government to negotiate new agreements for nuclear partners as a condition for the granting of export licenses for nuclear materials by the US Nuclear Regulatory Commission. Under this, agreements for cooperation must grant the United States "consent rights" not only for each transfer of US-origin material, but also for enrichment or reprocessing and for the storage or alteration in form and content of HEU or plutonium derived from such materials. This consent also extends to the proposed use of non-US-origin nuclear fuel irradiated in a US-supplied reactor.

49  This argument has been used generally to explain the slow pace of Indo-US dialogue on technology transfer. One specific instance was during discussions at the workshop in Athens, GA, April 1998.

50  Interviews and informal conversations with the author, November-December 1997.

51  For instance, I. William Zartman and Maureen R. Berman, *The Practical Negotiator* (New Haven, CT: Yale University Press, 1982).

52  Saurabh Kumar and P. K. Iyengar, *Atoms for Peace: Retrieving a Lost Ideal* (New Delhi: Rajiv Gandhi Institute for Contemporary Studies, 1995).

53  Norman D. Palmer, *The United States and India: The Dimensions of Influence* (New York: Praeger, 1984). Also, R.V. R. Chandrashekhara Rao, "Searching for a Mature Relationship," *Round Table* 263 (1976), pp. 249–60; O. P. Diwedi and R. B. Jain, "Bureaucratic Morality in India," *International Political Science Review* 9 (1988).

54  McGeorge Bundy, quoted in Cohen, *Negotiating Across Cultures,* p. 34.

55  *The Proliferation Primer,* Majority Report of the Subcommittee on International Security, Proliferation and Federal Services, Committee on Governmental Affairs, United States Senate, January 1998, pp. 31–36.

56  Despite the traditional rivalry, there was considerable sympathy in India for the Pakistani position vis-à–vis the United States on the issue of F-16s.

57  This includes the issue of Chinese supply of both M-11s and ring magnets to Pakistan, which has not hindered the US nuclear deal with China.

58  See for instance, K. Sundarji, "Strategic Stability in the Early 2000s: An Indian View of the South Asian Model," in Melvin L. Best, Jr., John Hughes-Wilson, and Andrei A. Piontkowsky, eds., *Strategic Stability in the Post-Cold War World and the Future of Nuclear Disarmament* (Washington, DC: Kluwer Academy Press, 1995); K. Subrahmanyam, *Indian Security Perspectives* (New Delhi: ABC Publishers, 1982); Brahma Chellaney, "The Challenge of Nuclear Arms Control in South Asia," *Survival,* Autumn, 1993, pp. 121–36.

59  Author's interviews with a range of officials and analysts at nongovernment and government (MEA, MOD, and DRDO) establishments in New Delhi, Bangalore, Hyderabad, November–December 1997.

60  C. Raja Mohan, "US and India's Periphery," *The Hindu,* April 16, 1998; Amitabh Mattoo, "India's Nuclear Status Quo," *Survival,* Autumn 1996, pp. 41–57; and C. Raja Mohan, "Non-proliferation, Disarmament and the Security Link," in Ollapally and Rajagopal, eds., *Nuclear Cooperation.* Some of these fears appeared to have come true after the nuclear tests. See C. Raja Mohan, "Sino-US Tilt towards Pakistan," *The Hindu,* June 1, 1998.

61  Interviews by the author in New Delhi, Bangalore and Hyderabad during November–December 1997. Most interviewees pointed to the differing deals offered by the Nuclear Supplier Group (NSG), Missile Technology Control Regime (MTCR), and Wassenaar Arrangement (WA) to recent entrants, including Russia and Ukraine, the

"new friends." Besides this, the "catch-all" requirement of the US export control policy is seen by all as a means of industrial espionage, in order to anticipate needs of developing countries, and to impose controls on crucial technologies.

62   CFR Report 1997.

63   Ashley J. Tellis, *Nuclear Stability in South Asia* (Santa Monica: RAND, 1997)

64   Itty Abraham, "India's 'Strategic Enclave': Civilian Scientists and Military Technologies," *Armed Forces and Society,* vol. 18, no. 2 (winter 1992), pp. 231–52.

65   Virginia Foran, "The Case for Indo-US High-Technology Cooperation," *Survival,* vol. 40, no. 2 (summer 1998), pp. 71–95.

66   White House, *National Security Strategy.*

67   Mr. Einhorn's testimony, quoted in *Proliferation Primer,* pp. 19–20. This refers to the negotiation for the sale of two nuclear power reactors to India. The $2.6 billion deal calls for construction of two 1,000-MW LWRs at Kudankulam in Southern India. The reactors are the same type as those being supplied to Iran. Though India has not signed the NPT, the reactors will be under IAEA safeguards. The deal was originally signed in 1988 (Gorbachev–Rajiv Gandhi) period, and is now revived under a clause that allows pre-NSG deals to go through. Since 1992 (Soviet disintegration), India has been unable to finance the reactors, and according to Einhorn's estimates of June 1997, will not be able to do so, either. But the deal was finalized in December 1997 nevertheless. If they are built, India's nuclear power capacity will be doubled. India has an ambitious plan to expand its current nuclear power capacity to 5,000 MW by the year 2000. The administration has raised concerns, saying it violates the spirit of the 1992 NSG agreement.

68   *Proliferation Primer.*

69   Ibid, pp. 3–5. Although China acceded to the NPT in 1992, it has refused to join the NSG. It instead agreed in October 1997 to join the Zangger Committee and announced its implementation of an export licensing system for specialized nuclear equipment and its intent to regulate exports of dual-use goods in September 1997. Zangger is similar to NSG except that it does not require *all* nuclear-facilities of the recipient to be under IAEA safeguards, only those facilities for which the exports are destined.

70   "China and Non-proliferation: Interview with Senior US Official," (Robert Einhorn, deputy assistant secretary of state for non-proliferation), *USFP Agenda: The electronic journal of the USIA,* January 1998.

71   *Washington Times,* February 5, 1996.

72   "China and Non-proliferation."

73   *Proliferation Primer,* p. 5.

74   "China and Non-proliferation."

75   This is based on the *Code of Federal Regulations,* United States Government, 1997. There is no claim to this being a *reproduction* of the said section, as only the relevant information has been presented here in an abridged form.

# 6

# Indo-US Convergence on CWC and BTWC: Assessing the Possibilities of Cooperation

## Aabha Dixit

The most obvious benefit from the underground nuclear tests conducted by India at Pokharan on May 11 and 13, 1998, is that Indo-US relations will be underwritten by a certain sense of realism. Up until now, bilateral relations were being conducted by both countries at different levels, which made a common meeting ground between the world's largest and greatest democracies extremely difficult. Realism has been the basis of US security policy, and this has been reflected particularly in its approach toward securing international agreements on weapons of mass destruction (WMD). India, on the other hand, sought to secure its interests in the multilateral arena in negotiations on WMD by raising the debate to a moral high point. Put simply, from a national standpoint, the United States has conducted its foreign policy on WMD with a positive sense of creating agreements that would perpetuate its advantages and minimize the concessions that it was required to make. The overriding priority that underlay these efforts was to allow the United States to play its global role. In contrast, India engaged in multilateral diplomacy and negotiating tactics that seemed to prevent the legitimization of the existing realities.

Consider the Indian approach to the Nuclear Non-proliferation Treaty (NPT), or even the Comprehensive Nuclear Test Ban Treaty (CTBT). Rather than spell out why India could not subscribe to either, or ensure that the treaties take its concerns seriously in their eventual forms, India pursued a negative approach to negotiations. It created an initial reasoning that was entirely inconsistent with its security calculus. This positive-negative focus has been, in many ways, the reason why Indo-US strategic relations have failed to make any headway in the past fifty years.

The United States has consistently exhibited a sense of realism and put forward its objections to specific elements in any negotiations on WMD, even to the extent of acknowledging that the end result of such negotiations would be a discriminatory treaty. It has not shied away from acknowledging that such arrangements would be at great variance with the principles underlying the creation of the United Nations itself, because the preservation of US national-security interests has remained paramount. India, on the other hand, continuously focused on raising the moral issues concerning WMD, with little regard for its own national-security interests. A detour of the histories of the internationally negotiated treaties on WMD—NPT, BTWC, CWC, and CTBT—would show that India was able to rally enough support, particularly from the developing world, to prevent the adoption of patently discriminatory clauses. Yet in each case the end game in the negotiations saw this support base vanish, leaving India with two options: either refuse to subscribe to the treaty (as it did with the NPT and CTBT), or accept the treaty in its entirety, along with the objectionable conditions inserted by the others (as in the case of BTWC and CWC). This need not be seen as a failure of Indian diplomacy, but it does highlight the consistent flaw in the approach adopted by successive Indian governments. This approach perpetuated the impression not only that India overestimates its own global role but also that it always seeks to prevent the conclusion of such agreements. More important, it failed to amplify adequately those of its security interests that might have found resonance among the key negotiating countries.

After Pokharan II, India appears to have made a giant leap, almost reinventing itself in the process. By conducting the underground nuclear explosions and justifying its intention to be recognized as a nuclear weapon state, India has cast its lot decisively with one side. It has sent out an unambiguous message that irrespective of its acceptance as a de jure nuclear-weapon state, any attempts by other nuclear-weapon states to "engage" India will have to be cognizant of this reality.

In the interim, this decision by India might seem to be a frontal challenge to the global non-proliferation architecture, which is admittedly based on discriminatory treaties, *ad hoc* regimes, and unilateral national export legislation. From this perspective India would be seen as attempting, as always, to prevent the strengthening of an international norm. But a closer look at the diplomatic activities after Pokharan II would suggest that the tests have fundamentally altered the manner in which India is going to perceive, articulate, and pursue its foreign and security interests. It is a case of better late than never.

There is a sense of realism in the present Indian approach, and a lot of it has been forced by the need to deal effectively with the impact of sanctions. The shift in approach is popularly characterized as "coming out of the closet" and involves actively working toward accepting the multilateral export control regimes that were earlier criticized for being ad hoc, and agreeing to be co-opted by the members of such regimes, without being formally inducted. This appears to be the preferred quid pro quo for signing the CTBT, and would harmonize India's negotiating posture with its image and security interests in international forums. It would create the basis for a stronger, more vibrant, and meaningful strategic dialogue that does not fight shy of the core issues in the Indo-US bilateral relationship. In future international agreements as well, Indian negotiators can be expected to pay less attention to the moral dimension of issues, and focus instead on the trade-offs that are directly relevant to India's security interests.

The next logical question that needs to be addressed in this context is how this changed reality impinges on Indo-US strategic relations in the context of the Chemical Weapons Convention and the Biological and Toxins Weapons Convention.

## BIOLOGICAL AND TOXINS WEAPONS CONVENTION (BTWC)

The significance of the BTWC emerges from the fact that this was the first multilateral treaty designed to tackle one category of WMDs. But it was designed during the Cold War period and therefore failed to receive the recognition that it should have for incorporating elements that would eventually become fundamental to all subsequent treaties relating to WMDs. Both India and the United States are parties to the BTWC, and the commonalities of their approach toward supporting it have been highlighted as a shared concern for working toward general and complete disarmament.

However, their respective motivations for agreeing to the BTWC were entirely different. From the US point of view, the nuclear question had assumed dangerous proportions during the 1950s and 1960s, following an unbridled arms race with the USSR. Even though the strategic focus of the Cold War had a nuclear orientation, this did not prevent either side from researching and developing biological agents and toxins for possible use, if considered necessary. The motivation to engage in multilateral negotiations on a BTWC in the Committee on Disarmament (as it was called in the 1960s), however, was prompted solely by the non-proliferation element. Technology to develop biological agents and toxins had improved exponentially after the World War II and countries with a relatively modest research and production base could develop biological warfare agents and toxins.

BTWC was the first US attempt to build non-proliferation architecture through the multilateral route. It was important in that it was crafted as a declaratory text, with no verification provisions, and the overall approach to the treaty was nondiscriminatory. By banning the development and production of BW agents and toxins, the treaty contributed to the goal of disarmament. These aspects of the treaty, along with its multilateral emphasis, made it acceptable to India.[1] Significantly, neither India nor Pakistan insisted on any linkage in signing the treaty. Remarkably, the treaty has survived through the years despite the absence of a verification provision. No use of biological warfare agents and toxins in interstate conflict has been reported since the BTWC came into force. A few national incidents, however, have been reported.[2] A collective norm against these agents and toxins has deterred most countries from activating or pursuing an overt biological warfare program.

Despite its success in preventing the spread and use of biological warfare agents and toxins, the BTWC has been revisited in the post–Cold War era. Several reasons can be cited as justification for this. First, the Iraqi experience and the US insistence on applying the "trust but verify" principle has led to renewed negotiations in the Conference on Disarmament (CD) in Geneva in the past few years to develop a verification protocol to the existing treaty.[3] Second, some Western intelligence reports indicate that several other countries are in a position to mount an active biological warfare program. Finally, the developed countries, including the United States, insist that despite the success of the BTWC in containing the use of agents of biological warfare, the possibility of its continued success cannot be taken for granted. They argue, therefore, that by putting into effect a verification regime, the BTWC will emerge stronger and play a more forceful role in preventing the development, production, storage, and use of biological warfare agents and toxins.

The point of departure between India and the United States on the BTWC is how each views the reasons behind its successful operation so far. India insists that the BTWC can continue to be successful in its present form. Verification is essential and may be the shape of all future treaties; nevertheless, one needs to highlight the moral dimension of the treaty.[4] Its universal and nondiscriminatory characteristics need to be maintained because these have prevented the use of BW agents even after the outbreak of hostilities. Rather than seek mandatory verification regimes, which are even more difficult to implement than in the chemical weapons area, efforts should be aimed at enhancing confidence-building measures (CBMs) and provisions for the voluntary supply of information.

The other major element where the United States and India disagree is the preservation of ad hoc export control and technology denial regimes such as the Australia Group. The Australia Group requires members to collectively deny export of dual-use technology and equipment relating to chemical and biological weapons to any country. India is vigorously opposed to this, and submits that Article X of the BTWC explicitly permits full access to equipment, technologies, and related items by all states parties for purposes not prohibited by the convention. There has been a growing concern in India that the non-proliferation aspect, which includes the perpetuation of export control regimes, is gaining greater salience than the disarmament aspects of both the CWC and the BTWC.

This divergence is perhaps the outcome of a difference in the philosophical approach to the concept of seeking multilateral treaties banning WMDs. It is increasingly being projected by the United States that disarmament and a permanent condition of nonproduction and nonuse of biological and chemical weapons is a utopian idea. The best and most feasible choice is to limit efforts to proliferation. This promotes the belief that only through constant monitoring will it be possible to prevent a breakdown of such treaties. Therefore, while the goal would be in the direction of disarmament, operationally it must stop short at ensuring non-proliferation.

### Similarity in Indian and US Perspectives

The common points and the differences between the positions of the Indian and US delegations in developing the verification protocol at Geneva are summarized as follows.

1. Being open societies with large private-sector industries, both countries have sought more stringent measures to protect commercial proprietary information (CPI), which would also have a bearing on the legitimate national-security interests of states parties. Both countries want states parties to provide mandatory declarations, which would avoid providing information under CPI or in disclosing national-security information by any state party.

2. In a major turnaround, the United States has supported an Indian position on the manner in which a decision for investigations is taken. Earlier, the US had insisted on an easier route (red light approach), based on its experiences in the CWC. The US and India now support the position that the Executive Council of the proposed BTWO would need to give approval by simple majority before any investigation is actually launched (green light approach).

3. Significantly, the United States and India have similar positions on investigations of the nature of challenge inspections. The United States appears to have abandoned in the BTWC negotiations the "anyplace, anytime" principle that it had so passionately advocated during the CWC negotiations in Geneva. Instead, it now appears to be backing the managed-access route.[5]

### Differences in Indian and US Perspectives

In broad terms, the two countries share the same objective—of outlawing the development, production, storage and use of agents of biological warfare. However, India insists that such efforts must be part of a larger plan for achieving general and complete disarmament. This, in turn, would allow for removal of restrictions on free trade in equipment, materials, and technologies that might have dual uses. The verification protocol, therefore, must inspire sufficient confidence among all states parties for the elimination of all agents of biological warfare. It should also perpetuate a nondiscriminatory application of the treaty provisions, to make it morally unjustifiable for any state to contemplate the use of such weapons. The United States wants a dilution of commitments under Article X of the BTWC because of its non-proliferation concerns, while India wants categorical language in the verification protocol that leads to operationalization of this article. This difference of approach leads to fundamental difficulties between the United States and India in the negotiations in Geneva.

## THE CHEMICAL WEAPONS CONVENTION

Negotiations in Geneva were halted interminably during the 1970s and 1980s owing to American and Russian intransigence over destruction of all chemical weapons stockpiles. The United States, as part of its larger policy of deterrence, had insisted on retention of 2 percent of its stockpile. For countries from the developing world that participated in the CD negotiations, it was difficult to accept the creation of yet another treaty, after the NPT, that sought perpetual differentiation among members. This deadlocked progress on negotiations, until the United States and Soviet Union reached a bilateral agreement in Jackson Hole, Wyoming, in 1989, under which the demand for retaining 2 percent stockpiles was dropped.

The removal of this demand was once again perceived to be in the US national interest. With chemical weapons technology almost sixty years old by then, fears of its proliferation to over a dozen countries, and in particular to radical states, made President Bush finally agree to remove the objection.[6] In the process, the United States sought a firm date of 1992 to conclude negotiations. After two decades in limbo, CWC negotiations assumed enormous urgency between 1989 and 1992.

The convention was a first in itself for many reasons. It proposed a truly non-discriminatory treaty with universal application. It also sought to develop a verification regime that was an improvement over all the existing verification activities conducted multilaterally by the IAEA, or developed bilaterally under the INF and START treaties. The artificial deadline of 1992, however, meant that apart from resolving the superstructure of the convention, over 125 items that required technical and political attention were pushed into the Preparatory Commission (PrepCom) of the Organization for the Prohibition of Chemical Weapons (OPCW), located in The Hague.

Significantly, after the convention entered into force in April 1998, and through the four years of PrepCom (1993–97), differences between India and the United States have reemerged on issues that were mentioned in the context of the verification protocol for the BTWC. Several reservations were added into the US ratification and implementation legislation under the Iran Missile Proliferation Act. Though vetoed by the US president on June 24, 1998, these efforts once again highlight the differences in positions taken by the two countries. The Senate has added some conditions to US ratification of the CWC in April 1998. These include, among other things, a commitment from the US administration to aggressively pursue the non-proliferation aspect of the convention through strict reporting measures for noncompliance by other states parties as a condition for the United States remaining a party to the convention. The other precondition is to secure a commitment from the administration for the preservation of the Australia Group mechanism despite the entry into force of the CWC. The conditions imposed by the US Senate have a direct bearing on the Indian position.

Unlike the United States, India has ratified the convention without reservations, as mandated in the treaty. There are analysts in India who believe that the US Senate conditionalities constitute an implied reservation, given the fact that international obligations are given precedence over domestic legislation. In fact, most implementation legislation is designed to bring domestic laws in line with accepted international obligations. By preserving the Australia Group, India believes that the United States is attempting acts that are expressly prohibited under the convention. Article XI of the convention envisages free trade in technologies and equipment for purposes not prohibited under the convention. The retention of the Australia Group, outside the purview of the convention, in itself violates this principle enshrined in Article XI.

The fall out of this position has become evident in the negotiations on unresolved issues. The greatest distance between the Indian and US positions is over free access by all states parties to equipment that is to be used for inspections and training. India has been insisting that such equipment be commercially available and therefore accessible to all states parties. The United States, on the other hand, in pursuance of its non-proliferation objectives, has put forward the objective that equipment required for inspections, if accessed by all countries could in itself become an agent for proliferation. This difference continues to be unresolved and is related to basic positions adopted by both countries in their larger national strategies.

In the implementing legislation, the US Congress has attached a conditionality through Section 237 (National Security Exception) of the Iran Missile Proliferation Act that virtually precludes the conduct of a challenge inspection. The National Security Exception states that the president may deny a request to inspect any facility in the United States if such an inspection posed a threat to the national-security interests of the United States. This is in total violation of the text and the spirit of the convention, which is based on the philosophy of challenge inspections "anyplace, anytime," denies states parties the right to refusal, and makes it incumbent on them to accept such inspections without conditions. It is clear that this congressional legislation is exclusively focused on non-proliferation. Further, it introduces an element of discrimination by invoking domestic legislation to prevent the taking on of obligations that affect US national-security interests. If other countries were to follow the US example in prohibiting challenge inspections, it would completely wreck the convention, whose underlying principle has been "trust but verify."

## CONCLUSION

At a broad conceptual level, the Indian and US positions in relation to the CWC and the BTWC appear to converge. In the past few years, as efforts to initiate a strategic dialogue have gotten under way, the similarity of perceptions on the CWC and BTWC has been highlighted as part of the existing common ground upon which the edifice of a stronger security relationship can be built. This tendency has seen greater amplification in the post-Pokharan period as well, largely on account of the differences that emerged on the nuclear front. As the ground underneath the evolving relationship started breaking, the CWC and BTWC approaches have been used as short-term glues to keep the bilateral strategic dialogue going.

But prospects for cooperation between the two countries within the ambit of the CWC and the BTWC will continue to remain limited until broad agreements can be reached over the thorny issues of technology transfer and verification. In the CWC, with operationalization of the convention, the relative importance of differing goals espoused by the two countries may well become more apparent. The United States is likely to insist on going slow in fulfilling obligations and commitments provided under Article XI. On the other hand, the United States will attempt to highlight that the CWC, because it has become a model agreement, must retain its non-proliferation character, to ensure that future security-related treaties become as secure as the CWC. Such an approach, apart from stressing the verification aspects of the convention, will also strive for the retention of the Australia Group and other controls on exports of dual-use technologies, equipment, and materials.

This will contrast with the Indian stand that the CWC, given its model disarmament character, needs to be a judicious blend of non-proliferation and CBMs. This can be done by the implementation of Article XI, which would make other countries accept similar treaties to rid the world of all WMD. Such a position is presaged on the dismantling of all export-control-related restrictions external to the CWC, including the Australia Group. In the BTWC context, a similar difficulty will be encountered on the verification protocol presently under negotiation. At the very root of such differences is the contrasting world vision that both countries hold about weapons of mass destruction and the relevance they have to national security.

From the point of view of broadening the Indo-US strategic dialogue to include meaningful lessons and experiences from other treaties, it must be remembered that the BTWC and the CWC were negotiated in a phase when India remained a nuclear-weapon-capable country. With Pokharan II, the situation has altered immeasurably. The United States is likely to find it difficult to accord a de jure nuclear-weapon status to India, but in negotiations there will be greater appreciation of India's security concerns, which in part prompted the 1998 nuclear tests.

In the context of current negotiations between US and Indian officials, it would be reasonable to assume that realistic bargains are being suggested. There is talk of India signing the CTBT in its present form, and in return the US would accept, tacitly, a minimal deterrent force by India. Another complementary deal is to remove ad hoc export control restrictions on India in return for allowing civilian nuclear power plants to develop through the "islanding" concept. What shape the negotiations will eventually take is beyond the scope of this paper to predict. However, the differences in the BTWC and CWC will fall by the wayside if, in the words of Karl

Inderfurth, deputy assistant secretary of state for South Asia, "an acceptable compromise or reconciliation" can be agreed upon. Rather than the CWC and the BTWC becoming the catalysts for bringing about an understanding on the nuclear question, it would require tackling the nuclear question in an acceptable manner, one that will ensure that Indo-US strategic relations are based on a sense of realism.

## NOTES

1   India did not consider the back-room wrangling between the US and Russian delegations as a defining characteristic.
2   This includes the Sverdlosk incident in the Soviet Union.
3   In Iraq, the heavily politicized UNSCOM mission has reported that Iraq developed biological warfare agents including 50,000 liters of anthrax and botulinum at the Al-Hakam factory. It is estimated that 100 kilograms of anthrax released from the top of a tall building in a densely populated area could kill up to three million people.
4   India has been a votary of an effective multilateral verification regime since it presented its Action Plan for A Nuclear Weapon Free and Non-Violent World Order to the UN General Assembly in 1988.
5   This shift in the US position has occurred after difficulties attached to the passage of the CWC implementation bill in the US Senate. One major pre-condition attached to the bill virtually forecloses the possibility of a challenge inspection by giving the president the power to deny such inspections by citing national-security interests.
6   These were later re-defined as "rogue" states. These states insisted on developing such weapons as a poor man's response to nuclear weapons.

# 7

## The Emergence of Indo-US Defense Cooperation: From Specific to Diffuse Reciprocity

### Jyotika Saksena
### and Suzette Grillot

For more than fifty years India and the United States have been engaged in a relationship that has experienced many ups and downs. Positive Indo-US interaction began in the 1950s when the United States provided India with financial assistance, food aid, nuclear fuel for power reactors, and assistance in its space program. In the 1970s India and the United States began cooperating closely for educational purposes, for which they established a joint commission for science, technology, education, and culture. By the 1980s the United States was India's largest trading partner, with trade including such high-technology items as telecommunications, computers, and electronics.[1]

Despite such cooperative exchanges and interactions, Indo-US relations have suffered from a number of obstacles. In 1965 the United States placed an arms embargo on both India and Pakistan because of the war between the two. In 1968 India refused to sign the Nuclear Non-Proliferation Treaty (NPT), which heightened US concerns about nuclear proliferation in South Asia. During the 1971 Indo-Pakistan conflict, US support clearly tilted toward Pakistan and away from India, and continued to do so particularly after India's explosion of a "peaceful" nuclear device in 1974.[2] In the meantime, India drew closer to the United States' chief rival, the Soviet Union, and became increasingly reliant on Soviet military equipment for national defense.[3] The United States' increased pressure regarding non-proliferation issues in the 1990s further frustrated Indo-US relations and culminated in India's refusal to sign the Comprehensive Test Ban Treaty (CTBT) in 1996. Finally, India's test of five nuclear devices in May 1998 alienated the United States, which chose to impose economic sanctions in response.

Indo-US relations therefore, have not been free of difficulty. Nonetheless, cooperation has emerged even in the sensitive area of military and security relations. Strong bilateral ties and a sense of mutual trust between India and the United States have, however, remained elusive. To determine how and why India and the United States have found it possible to cooperate in some areas, yet found it difficult to solidify strong ties, this paper takes a closer look at the history of Indo-U.S. cooperation, especially in the most critical area of defense. Its central focus is on the development of cooperative Indo-US defense relations—specifically on how these relations emerged and how, based on such experience, they may develop. The paper suggests that Indo-US defense cooperation was possible on the basis of specific reciprocity, and that through such specific exchanges the pattern of cooperation may deepen and evolve, leading to stronger relations based on trust.

Indo-US relations have experienced many highs and lows—especially recent lows in light of the 1998 nuclear tests. Today's post–Cold War environment offers both the United States and India new opportunities, as well as new challenges, to expand their strategic cooperation. It is, therefore, important to look more specifically at the numerous factors that may have influenced Indo-US cooperative efforts in the past. In doing so, we may be better able to indicate how the two countries can move ahead and work together more closely on matters of security and defense. A focus on the methods used to achieve defense cooperation, therefore, may offer solutions to old and new problems as the two countries attempt to reconfigure their relations after India's nuclear tests.

The rest of this chapter is divided into four sections. The first provides a brief historical overview of Indo-US relations, focusing on the numerous challenges they have faced throughout their fifty-year experience. The second section offers a theoretical framework based on state interaction and international cooperation. Specifically, the framework focuses on reciprocity as a means for achieving cooperation among nations. From the basic theoretical tenets, research questions regarding Indo-US cooperation are offered. The third section offers a case study of Indo-US defense relations to determine how and why defense cooperation emerged. For clarity and focus, we pay special attention to the modalities of cooperation. Several cooperative defense agreements made between India and the United States are discussed in detail so that we may better understand the factors that either enhanced or inhibited them. The fourth and final section provides a discussion of the study's findings and their implications for the future of Indo-US defense cooperation.

## HISTORICAL OVERVIEW

The history of Indo-US defense relations must be examined in the broad context of India's postindependence foreign, security, and economic policy, America's Cold War compulsions, and the consequent emergence of Soviet-Indian and US-

Pakistan relations. While some of these compulsions have lessened, or no longer exist and the relationships have considerably weakened, what remains is a history of distrust that may not necessarily govern, but continues to affect Indo-US cooperation.

One of the basic differences between the two countries has been their strategic and security views.[4] In 1947 India, as a newly independent state, decided to pursue a policy of nonalignment, which meant that it would not join military alliances created by either of the two superpowers. This policy was derived from its desire to pursue an independent foreign policy free of external influence and the realization that the developmental needs of a newly independent state would not permit heavy defense expenditure. Moreover, Indian leaders, particularly Jawaharlal Nehru, the first prime minister and primary architect of India's foreign policy, hoped that India would be able to acquire an international political and moral role by abstaining from bloc politics. For the United States, on the other hand, South Asia as a region acquired importance only after the advent of Communist China and the Korean crisis. The United States, therefore, was looking for a strategic partner or an ally in the region. Before the Sino-Indian war of 1962, however, India considered China to be a friend and not an enemy.[5] Hence, rather than looking for an ally, India preferred a minimal superpower presence in the region.

The United States then turned to the only eager ally in South Asia, Pakistan. What followed was almost forty years of strategic partnership between the two countries. Pakistan provided the United States with a reliable friend in the region, and the United States in turn provided Pakistan with a security umbrella, including military and financial aid. The US-Pakistan relationship became one of the main sources of conflict between the United States and India. Pakistan became a member of US-sponsored security alliances—the Southeast Asian Treaty Organization (SEATO) and the Central Treaty Organization (CENTO)—and a recipient of US technology and arms. Indian policy makers perceived any US assistance as being tied to the objective of nudging Indian defense capabilities in the direction of particular American strategic objectives (the containment of China) while at the same time protecting Pakistani interests.[6] India also felt that the United States sided with Pakistan on the sensitive Kashmir issue.

Indo-Soviet friendship was yet another factor that considerably soured relations between India and the United States. Under Nehru's leadership, India opted to follow a socialist form of democracy, and the Congress Party under him and subsequent leaders remained partial to the Soviet Union. Further, after US reluctance to supply India with weapons and defense technology, Indo-Soviet relations grew closer, as the Soviets were willing to supply India with both weapons and technology. Although India purchased military-related items from the Soviet Union as early as the mid-1950s, and MiG-21 aircraft before the Sino-Indian War, substantive Indo-Soviet military ties developed only after the United States refused to assist

India's defense modernization effort beginning in 1964.[7] In subsequent years India received the majority of its military equipment from the Soviet Union.

Divergence in the nuclear policy of the two countries was yet another factor that inhibited Indo-US defense relations. Western countries, led by the United States, have for decades limited the spread of nuclear weapons and technology based on the 1968 Nuclear Non-Proliferation Treaty (NPT). According to the NPT, only Britain, France, China, the Soviet Union, and the United States are allowed to maintain nuclear weapons. India, however, refused to sign this treaty on the grounds that it was discriminatory and unfair, and considered 1968 an arbitrary date for eligibility to possess nuclear weapons.[8] India's "peaceful nuclear explosion" in 1974 and its refusal to be a member of any of the multilateral export control regimes made matters worse in the upcoming years.[9]

India's refusal to sign the NPT and its friendship with the Soviet Union became the main hindrance to Indo-US relations. This created a feeling of distrust between the two countries. The United States was concerned that its technology could be diverted to the Soviet Union and that India could use any possible dual-use technology for its nuclear program. India was suspicious of the United States because of its partnership with Pakistan and its attempt at preventing India from developing peaceful nuclear and space programs. Hence, transfer of technology remained minimal. India, unhappy with US nuclear policy and in need of technology, began interacting more with the Soviet Union. The connection between Indo-Soviet relations and the US Defense Department's reluctance to transfer sensitive technology was explained by a former chief of the Office of Defense Cooperation in India (ODCI): "This friendship [Indo-Soviet] is the most significant factor inhibiting better bilateral Indo-US relations and is the major factor restricting military equipment incorporating advanced technology being released to India." [10]

These were the basic factors that created feelings of distrust between the two nations and inhibited cooperation. Nevertheless, the two countries continued to make efforts to cooperate on matters of defense. India sought to cooperate with the United States because it desired Western technology and did not want to be completely dependent on the Soviet Union. The United States continued to engage India because it did not want to lose India to the USSR, considered India a potential ally against Communist China, an important market, and wanted to persuade India to sign the NPT.

The most recent setback to Indo-US relations emerged on May 11, 1998, when Indian officials announced that they had successfully conducted three underground nuclear explosions in the desert state of Rajasthan. Two days later, on May 13, Indian officials disclosed that they had tested two additional nuclear devices. The initial shock in the United States resulting from the first series of tests was compounded with disbelief after the second set of explosions. After much condemnation, the United States imposed economic sanctions against India and vowed to oppose any World Bank or IMF loan for which India was being considered. Moreover, the United States ceased all military cooperation with India. Future defense relations, therefore, remain in question.[11] Concrete ways through which India and the United States might put their relations back on track, therefore, may be exceedingly valuable as the two countries attempt to mend fences in the coming years.

## THEORETICAL FRAMEWORK

Among international-relations scholars, there is much disagreement about the nature and possibilities of cooperation among states. Some suggest that because the international system is full of self-interested, egoistic actors operating in an anarchic self-help environment, state cooperation is rare and unexpected. Moreover, when states do cooperate, such cooperative measures are unlikely to be durable or permanent.[12] However, others argue that cooperation occurs among nations regularly and commonly, and that cooperation is indeed durable and persistent.[13] For those who believe that states can and do cooperate, the concept of reciprocity as a standard of behavior is thought to be a means by which cooperation can be achieved, especially among egoistic states whose goals or motives may be, in some respect, conflictual.[14]

In an attempt to clarify the concept of reciprocity in international relations, Robert Keohane delineates two kinds: specific and diffuse. Specific reciprocity refers to "situations in which specified partners exchange items of equivalent value in a strictly delimited sequence. If any obligations exist, they are clearly specified in terms of rights and duties of particular actors." [15] Actors who engage in diffuse reciprocity, on the other hand, are less concerned with the specific and precise definition of equivalence, may view one's partners as part of a particular group rather than a single actor, and are more flexible concerning the sequencing of reciprocal actions.[16]

Based on such understandings of specific and diffuse reciprocity, two aspects of the concept are essential—contingency and equivalence. Contingency or conditionality suggests that cooperative actions depend on the rewarding *re*actions of partners. Cooperation ceases when expected reactions or reciprocation ceases.[17] Furthermore, the contingency aspect of reciprocity suggests that cooperation is met with cooperation and defection is met with defection.[18]

The second aspect important for reciprocity is equivalence. For partners to cooperate, in other words, "rough equivalence" is usually and commonly expected—especially among equals. Among those who are unequal, cooperative relationships are "characterized by exchanges of mutually valued but non-comparable goods and services." [19] Although precise measurement is rarely possible in social relations—and particularly difficult in terms of state actions—specific reciprocity requires that cooperative partners perceive there to be a degree of "bilateral balancing" in order for cooperation to continue.[20] Based on the aspects of contingency and equivalence, therefore, reciprocity—primarily specific reciprocity—may be best understood as "exchanges of roughly equivalent values in which the actions of each party are contingent on prior actions of the others in such a way that good is returned for good, and bad for bad." [21]

It is important to note three factors that may affect, either positively or negatively, whether states may actually agree to reciprocate—even when specific exchanges are mutually acceptable. First, partners may be excessively concerned with relative gains. States are more likely to reciprocate, in other words, when it is unlikely that their partner(s) will "acquire a permanent decisive advantage" over them.[22] Second, actors find it difficult to reciprocate actions that are perceived to have ulterior motives. If one state perceives that another is making concessions based on some hidden, alternative agenda, it will be less likely to acknowledge the action and reciprocate in kind.[23] Finally, if a recipient state considers its partner's actions to be costly and voluntary, the recipient will be more likely to reciprocate. Just like people, states feel less compelled to return favors that were not provided voluntarily. Moreover, states are more impressed by actions that are perceived to be costly and somewhat sacrificial. Ultimately, actions that are both intentional and valuable are indicative to the recipient that they are well intended, thereby facilitating reciprocation.[24]

Where specific reciprocity is based on the self-interest of states to achieve cooperation (i.e., one gets when one gives), diffuse reciprocity rests on the importance of norms, obligations, and trust. Keohane suggests that states engaging in diffuse reciprocity "contribute one's share, or behave well towards others, not because of ensuing rewards from specific actors, but in the interests of continuing satisfactory overall results for the group of which one is a part, as a whole." [25] Ultimately, partners engaging in diffuse reciprocity are less interested in the direct rewards they may receive from their cooperative actions and more interested in a long-term pattern of interaction that is mutually beneficial and based on a sense of trust and obligation. Interest in the future, therefore, helps promote cooperation.[26]

Interestingly, specific and diffuse reciprocity may not be mutually exclusive. In other words, one may lead to the other. Reciprocity based on self-interest, for example, may in the long run generate trust as a result of "recurrent and gradually expanding" social exchange.[27] States that engage successfully in specific reciprocity for a significant time period may set in place conditions that are suitable for diffuse reciprocity.[28] One additional factor may also affect whether cooperating states achieve a longer-term pattern of reciprocation based on trust, and that is the sequencing of exchange.

When partners engage in reciprocity, they may reciprocate any action either simultaneously (actors A and B exchange goods or services Y and Z at the same time) or sequentially (actor A exchanges good or service Y, then actor B exchanges good or service Z). For specific reciprocity to lead to diffuse reciprocity, actions must occur sequentially.[29] Because simultaneous exchange necessarily balances in a single moment, there never exists a "debt" or a "credit." Debts and credits must exist for a sense of obligation to exist—and a sense of obligation is what, over the long term, increases confidence and trust among partners as debts and credits are regularly balanced.[30] Marshall Sahlins even suggests that we should create societal mechanisms that not only encourage partners to fulfill their obligations and repay debts, but which also "induce people to remain socially indebted to each other and which inhibit their complete repayment."[31] Where simultaneous exchange signifies a breakdown in confidence and indicates distrust and hostility, sequential exchange exemplifies obligation, trust, and good faith. Specific reciprocity may lead to diffuse reciprocity, therefore, as actors repay specific debts and offer specific credits over the long run. The creation of obligation increases confidence and enables actors to view common interests in a wider context.

Based on the above theoretical discussion, the following research questions served as guides for this paper. Have the United States and India engaged in specific reciprocal actions concerning defense issues? What kinds of specific agreements were made? What were the specific conditions attached to such agreements? Were exchanges made sequentially or simultaneously? Were there any obstacles to making the agreements, such as a focus on relative gains and/or perceptions of ulterior motives? Is there evidence that the parties believed each were making costly and voluntary decisions in order to cooperate? Has specific, reciprocal, sequential action led to a greater sense of trust and obligation and the existence of diffuse reciprocity? Based on the answers to these questions, what can be said about the future of Indo-US defense cooperation?

The next section provides several empirical examples of Indo-US cooperative agreements on defense issues. The examples allow us to build a case as we seek to address the above research questions. The interpretation of our findings, analysis of their implications, and suggestions for further research appear in our concluding section.

## EVIDENCE

A partnership can be sustained without complete identity of interests provided there is mutual trust, goodwill, respectful hearing of different points of view, predictability of behavior, and avoidance of threats.[32]

### 1947–80: Building of Distrust

In 1947 South Asia as a region was only marginally important to the United States. It acquired importance only after the Korean crisis and the obvious success of (and consequent threat from) Communist China. There was, however, one basic difference in the two countries' perception of their friendship and of the role that the United States was to play in South Asia. While the United States expected any cooperation between the two countries to lead to some semblance of a larger security dialogue, India, on the other hand, wanted cooperation without any strings attached. This basic difference in perception and consequent expectations from a future friendship or cooperation affected Indo-US relations in the short as well as the long run. Evidence of the same is found if one examines the three factors (ulterior motive, relative gains, and exchange being perceived as costly or sacrificial) that affect relations positively or negatively, even when specific exchange is mutually acceptable.

In the early years Indo-US relations were characterized by Indian concerns regarding possible US ulterior motives. This tended to negatively affect the Indian desire for cooperation. One of the early documents dealing with the South Asian region that favored a strategic tie-up with India, National Security Council (NSC) document 98/1, stated that if India was lost to the Communists, "for practical purposes all of Asia would be lost." It proposed a more activist policy, which included the supply of military equipment along with closer consultations and an economic aid program. The United States' obvious lack of success in persuading India to be a part of its camp and Pakistan's status as a confirmed US ally raised two concerns about US motives: first, that India was important to the United States only as long as it faced possible threat from Communist China, and second, that it would always have to play second fiddle to Pakistan. A case in point was in May 1960, when the Indian defense minister, Krishna Menon, sought Sidewinder air-to-air missiles (AAMs), something that the United States had already promised Pakistan. For fear of upsetting Pakistan, the head of the US State Department Bureau for the Near East, G. Lewis Jones, recommended that India contact Britain for AAMs with a similar capacity.[33]

A similar case occurred in 1962, after India's defeat in the Sino-Indian war. Though the United States responded positively to its request for military equipment, Washington's assistance never went beyond light arms, ammunition, and communications systems—military equipment that was very mountain-specific (India's border with China is mountainous and that with Pakistan is not). There was concern on the Indian side that its military capabilities were being forced in a certain direction.[34] India's concerns about US motives is also highlighted by the fact that in his letter dated October 29, 1962, to John Kenneth Galbraith, then US ambassador to India, requesting military assistance, Nehru asked that the United States not insist on military alliance as a quid pro quo.[35]

India's concern for US motives also became evident in the differences between the two countries over the sale of F-104 Starfighter aircraft (already supplied to Pakistan). The planes were ultimately not sold to India, and several reasons have been cited for America's refusal. One was that the United States felt that such aircraft were of limited use against the Chinese and would take up one-third of a $500 million aid package it was providing to India. The second reason was that the United States did not want to sell India any advanced technology that might upset Pakistan.[36] An American chief of the ODCI concurred by stating that "the U.S. refused to consider the sale of any form of offensive military equipment, on the grounds that this would affect the security of Pakistan."[37] This further fueled India's suspicion that the United States would cooperate with India purely out of its desire to contain China while always ensuring that Pakistani sensitivities remained protected. An Indian commentator has stated that "a longer term military assistance package [after 1962] was effectively sabotaged by . . . a Pakistani inclined Pentagon." [38]

From the US perspective, it had genuine concerns in the South Asian region with the increasing influence of Communist China. What the United States was looking for was a strategic partner, an ally, rather than a no-strings-attached association. While India shied away from joining the US camp, Pakistan proved to be a useful ally and hence deserved stronger US support. As the head of the State Department Near East Bureau explained, "In becoming our whole-hearted ally, Pakistan has undertaken real responsibilities and risks, making its territory available to us for a series of projects highly important to our national security. . . . The hard fact remains that, if our mutual security system is to remain intact, we must show Pakistan . . . that substantial benefits flow from a military alignment with us against the Communist bloc." [39]

Matters became worse after India refused to sign the NPT and it began to develop a friendship with the Soviet Union. This forced the United States to perceive its association with India in terms of relative gains. Any kind of technological and defense cooperation with India raised US concerns about two very sensitive issues. The first was that technology sold to India could be diverted to the Soviet Union, or that a dual-use item could be diverted to building or sustaining India's nuclear program. The other US concern was that it did not want to negotiate on any defense deals that might upset its ally Pakistan. From the Indian perspective, getting clearance or coproduction rights on even the most simple items took such a long time and effort that it did not seem worthwhile. For example, the Indian attempt to purchase 200 lightweight 155-mm howitzers, 60 TOW launchers, and close to four thousand missiles in 1979, and then the .50 caliber Browning heavy machine gun (HMG) from Maremont Corporation in the early 1980s, were both abruptly called off by Mrs. Gandhi. Among other reasons cited, the lengthy process highlighted to the Indians the continuing resistance in some US circles to their arms purchase requests, and strengthened their perception of the United States as an unreliable business partner. [40] In addition, either the Soviet Union or European countries such as Britain, France, and Germany could far more easily supply most of the defense or technology items that India wanted from the United States. Therefore the deals that were successfully concluded did not appear to the Indians as being costly or sacrificial for the United States. This diminished any sense of obligation for future cooperation or a move toward diffuse reciprocity.

An important condition in order for specific reciprocity to lead to diffuse reciprocity—that is, to have sustainable cooperation—is that debts and credits must exist, creating a sense of obligation. It is the sense of obligation that in the long run increases confidence and trust among partners. However, the US policy of linking food and economic aid to the sale of defense items and sensitive issues such as Kashmir not only impeded the development of any sense of obligation on the Indian side but also created suspicion. For example, after the approval of NSC document 98/1, the United States approved the sale of two hundred Sherman tanks worth $19 million. However, the US government declined a simultaneous Indian request for two hundred fighter aircraft worth $150 million. The United States questioned the rationale for spending so much on defense when only the year before, the US Congress had approved $190 million in food aid.[41] In the early 1960s India again made a request for military assistance from the United States. In turn, "India was persuaded to hold a series of abortive talks with Pakistan on Kashmir, to lower its ceiling on rupee and foreign exchange outlays for defense expenses, to delay its decision on purchase and manufacture of fighter aircraft and to accept a large supervisory establishment of US personnel."[42] The widespread perception in India was that the United States was taking advantage of its weakened position.[43] Indo-US relations until the 1970s, therefore, were marked by suspicions, concerns for ulterior motives, and a complete lack of trust.

### The 1980s: A Positive Decade in Indo-US Relations, and an Attempt toward Specificity

After an unexpectedly cordial meeting between Indian prime minister Indira Gandhi and US president Ronald Reagan in October 1981, Indo-US relations experienced a positive change. In December of the same year, Secretary of State Alexander Haig secretly cabled the US Embassy in India that it should respond positively to any arms purchase requests that India might make. Defense cooperation did not, however, improve immediately.

The positive trend in Indo-US defense relations evolved gradually with a change in attitude and perception. On the Indian side was the desire to diversify its sources of defense hardware and reduce its dependence on the Soviet Union.[44] India's decision was also flavored by the fact that the very convenient terms of trade that Moscow had previously made available to India were no longer being offered. It was also felt that "Soviet weapons though durable and serviceable, [were] usually not as sophisticated and often not as effective as Western arms."[45] Further, it became evident that the resumption of US military aid to Pakistan after the Soviet invasion of Afghanistan brought new technologies such as the F-16 Falcon and the Harpoon missile to the Subcontinent. The counter to these at that time was found only in the West.[46] On the US side, there was a desire to increase arms sales and to counter Soviet influence in India.[47] Further, according to Robert Wirsing, "it seemed to some observers of Washington's developing arms policy in South Asia that its role was excessively and unnecessarily lopsided, and that a meaningful effort to interest New Delhi in US arms might enable Washington to capture a share of the Indian arms import trade."[48] However, one thing that both sides realized was that there was too much mutual distrust and that mere political will was not going to change Indo-US relations. What was important before any progress could be made was to specifically address the concerns and needs of both sides.[49]

To facilitate defense cooperation, therefore, the United States and India signed in 1984 a memorandum of understanding (MOU) on technology transfer. The MOU indicated U.S. willingness to support India's weapons procurement strategies, but only in return for assurances that the advanced technology transferred would be protected from leaks and used for agreed-upon purposes.

India has for some time emphasized the need for indigenous arms production, which gives it the ability to conduct an independent foreign policy. India has, therefore, always sought licenses to produce advanced weaponry domestically.[50] However, the MOU successfully reconciled India's weapons procurement policies with America's technology transfer conditions, and thereby expanded military links by providing the bureaucratic basis for implementing the agreement. It did so by setting out *specific* actions to which each partner must agree and by which they must abide for defense cooperation to occur. The MOU had three distinct parts. The main text, signed on November 29, 1984, contained general security assurances for transfers of sophisticated technology. Specifically, India agreed to the following:[51]

- To import military items into India and not to redirect them, or any of their parts, to another destination before their arrival in India

- To provide, if asked, verification that possession of items was taken

- Not to reexport items without the written approval of the import-certificate-issuing authorities in India (ICIA)

- Not to retransfer within India items specified in the MOU without the written approval of the ICIA

In addition, it was agreed that certain items India might wish to purchase would require "extra assurances," which could be negotiated as needed. The implementation procedures also required Indian importers to provide these general assurances to the US government through the US exporter on an import certificate—a document developed specifically for MOU transactions. If extra assurances were requested from the importer, the government of India (GOI) would give them directly to the US government.

After the implementation procedures were signed in May 1985, it was discovered that no provision had been made for certain high-technology items, such as computers that had possible end-use applications for nuclear projects. A separate commodity control agreement, therefore, was established for nuclear end uses. It was agreed that: (1) US technology was not to be used in unsafeguarded areas or facilities of India's nuclear program; (2) Indian nuclear facilities that were only partially safeguarded could not use American high technology; and (3) case-by-case agreements could be reached whereby dual-use technologies would be cleared for use in unsafe-guarded and partially safeguarded facilities, if the use involved office/administrative tasks and not nuclear material directly.[52] In essence, in the 1980s an attempt was made to establish as specific guidelines for reciprocal exchange as possible.

Although some forces within both India and the United States opposed the MOU, Indo-US defense cooperation underwent a quantitative and qualitative expansion in the 1980s. For example, in terms of value of export licenses issued by the US govern-ment in 1987, India ranked number seven.[53] Several cases pending before the MOU were signed and cleared, the value of transfers rose, and the bulk of requests for tech-nology transfer were no longer on a case-by-case basis. One of the greater contribu-tions of the MOU was the release of purely military technology to India.

A relevant case in point was the sale of an LM-2500 gas turbine engine used by the US navy, which India wanted to use to upgrade its naval vessels.[54] An interesting aspect of this transfer is that China received permission to buy five such engines in 1985, but only after protracted arguments against objections from the Taiwan lobby.[55] Whether Pakistan raised such objection vis-à–vis India is not known. But the fact that India eventually got the engines is of importance.

A significant and strictly military technology that was sold to India was night vision devices for tanks. The Pentagon's unwillingness to provide them in 1980 was one reason India had terminated negotiations for the purchase of howitzers and antitank missiles. By the mid-1980s, however, not only was the night-vision technol-ogy released, but permission was granted to India to coproduce the devices.[56] A polit-ical decision was made at the highest level to cooperate with India by specifying the details for an agreement covering this particular technology.[57]

There were also visible signs of Indo-US defense relations moving beyond tech-nology transfer. In a letter to Defense Minister Pant, Deputy Secretary of Defense Taft proposed the coproduction of the Northrop Corporation's TF-5 aircraft in India. The United States offered to India its government-owned portion of an F-5 tooling facility for 5 percent of original cost. The facility permitted India to produce 90 percent of the center fuselage, 80 percent of the forward fuselage, 50 percent of the wings and fuselage, and 40 percent of the test tools. Although the offer had little to do with strategic technology transfer given that it was not a sensitive item and the end product was a mere trainer aircraft, it did constitute a shift in the nature of defense relations in that it moved beyond small Indian purchases of subsystem tech-nology to an American offer of its own government surplus at very subsidized cost.[58]

One of the more successful exchanges of the 1980s, however, was the collaboration involving India's light combat aircraft (LCA). In 1981 India had sought to purchase Northrop's F-5G aircraft, but it was denied because of the Pentagon's reluctance to release classified information relating to the engine. Rajiv Gandhi, during his visit to the United States in June 1985, approached the US government with respect to the project. In September 1985, V. S. Arunachalam, the scientific advisor to the Defence Ministry, expressed his interest in procuring these engines. The following February, the deputy director of the Defense Technology Security Administration, Talbot Lindstrom, was sent to New Delhi to assess the areas of defense in which the United States could contribute. Subsequently, India was sold eleven of these engines, which were to be used on the initial prototypes of the LCA. The LCA is eventually going to be fitted with the indigenously developed Kaveri engine.

One of the reasons for the success of the LCA project was the ensuing Lindstrom Report, which became the single most important US evaluation of India's defense programs, their needs, and the role the United States could play in them. This was yet another attempt at specificity. The Lindstrom report set forth three specific fields (the LCA project, India's national missile test range, and antiarmor and main battle tank development) where defense cooperation was to be pursued.[59] Three reasons were provided to justify the specific limitation of Indo-US cooperation: (1) by identifying relatively precise projects and parameters, defense cooperation could be isolated from other aspects of bilateral relations, namely political, which might impede and complicate the effort; (2) the mission area approach was chosen because it could assure the United States that it was cooperating with India only in areas which would not cause regional problems—that is, not overly upset the Pakistanis (the LCA project involved a defensive system that would pose a minimal threat to Pakistan); and (3) the mission area approach to defense cooperation permitted the United States to engage in cooperation where Indo-Soviet links were not present. The mission area approach also helped avoid "time consuming procedures of individual export licenses for exports for mutually agreed area of cooperation." [60] This offered additional protection to US technology. This also eventually led to the creation of a blue book, in April 1987, that specified the guidelines to be used by US industries for military-related technology transfers to India.[61]

A change in political will and improved perceptions of common interests played an important role in the positive change in Indo-US defense relations. An important result of this positive trend was the signing of the MOU and the Lindstrom Report. Both of these documents concentrated on providing specific guidelines for cooperation. Such specific guidelines allowed Indo-US defense relations to move ahead even further because each country could now be more certain of the other's interests and specific concerns. Moreover, an increase in certainty ultimately helped decrease some of each country's concerns regarding the ulterior motives of the other.[62]

## The 1990s: Increasing Interaction and Emerging Trust

While the 1980s saw a positive trend in Indo-US defense relations in terms of addressing the specific defense and technological concerns of both sides, there was also the realization that there were other issues that had not been dealt with. For example, as always, there remained a difference in perception between the two countries as to the expectations from this growing relationship. For India it was a five-tier pyramid, with technology transfer at the base, followed by joint development, coproduction, purchase of weapons and at the top, military-to-military cooperation. The US perception of the pyramid is an exact inverse.[63] As a Pentagon official explained, "While India is playing Chess, the United States is playing Checkers. We are not even on the same board." [64] It therefore became important to address these differences in interests and expectations. It was also felt that if any sustainable progress was to be made in the bilateral relationship, especially in areas as sensitive as defense and technology transfer, confidence-building measures (CBMs) were needed. This was especially crucial given the history of distrust that the two nations shared. Richard Haas, special assistant to the president and senior director for Near East and South Asian affairs, National Security Council, also stressed the need to establish and regularize consultation with India on matters of regional and global security in order to better understand India's foreign and defense policies (which was important if any serious defense and technology exchange between India and the United States was to take place).[65] What was needed was an effort toward more social exchange, as Alvin Gouldner points out, "recurrent and gradually expanding" social exchange can in the long run generate trust as a result.[66] So defense and technology cooperation in the 1990s focused on building trust and goodwill by more social interaction, on one hand, and efforts to increase cooperation by working on the specifics of cooperation, on the other.

In the 1990s, therefore, efforts were made not merely toward increasing sales based on specific reciprocity but toward reciprocal exchange of information and personnel. One of the first attempts at initiating interaction and exchange was made by Lieutenant General Claude M. Kickleighter, in what later came to be known as "Kicklighter proposals." The proposals included:[67]

• Army chief of staff reciprocal visits, alternating annually between the United States and India, that would support the move of the Indian and US armies toward a new and closer partnership for the future.

• Continued US and Indian army participation in the Indo-US strategic symposium, which would provide an informal, unofficial forum for US and Indian analysts, officials, military officers, and scholars to discuss the current state and future possibilities for US-Indian security relations. The symposium has been held on an annual basis since it began in 1989.

• An Indian/US Army Executive Steering Council was set up to "review, refine, and redefine the agreed upon goals and objectives put forth in the strategic plan to ensure greater future coequal cooperation, consultation, collaboration, and interoperability between the two armies."

• Senior command and staff reciprocal visits and exchanges were established to serve as a way of exchanging views and information on military matters of common concern.

- Staff information exchanges were set up to serve as the backdrop for the reciprocal flow of information.

- Reciprocal schooling and individual training of commanders, leaders, and staff officials was established.

- Mutual attendance and participation in regional conferences in order to improve the ability to work together was emphasized.

An army Executive Steering Group (ESG) was established in January 1992, and the navy and the air force followed suit in March 1992 and August 1993, respectively. This led to the first ever military-to-military exercises on a regular scale. In February 1992, Indian and US army and air force personnel participated in a joint training exercise—named Teak Iroquois—for the first time. This exercise was followed by a second one in October 1993. The Indian and US navies also held a joint naval exercise named Malabar I in May 1992. By mid-1997 the two countries had sponsored three rounds of joint naval exercises—Malabar I, II, and III.[68]

One of the cooperative successes of the 1990s was the signing of the Agreed Minutes On Defense Relations Between the United States and India in January 1995. Such defense cooperation covered service-to-service and civilian-to-civilian cooperation, as well as cooperation in defense production and research. The civilian-to-civilian group was to provide overall guidance to the other two elements; existing bilateral steering groups within the service of both countries were to expand on their existing programs; and the defense production and research cooperation elements were to include a new joint technical group that would follow the policy guidelines established by the civilian-to-civilian group.[69] In order to promote defense cooperation activities, the two sides were also to begin early consultations with a view toward arriving at a bilateral agreement on the mutual protection of classified information.[70] While the basis of cooperation remained the same as under the MOU signed in 1985, the agreed minutes on defense cooperation further formalized and expanded the specifics of such cooperation.

Three separate groups were established to foster more interaction and facilitate discussion: the Defense Policy Group (DPG), the Joint Technical Group (JTG), and the Joint Steering Committee (JSC). In addition to issues of defense cooperation, the DPG also tackled sensitive issues like the CTBT and Kashmir. The JSC (like its predecessor under the Kickleighter proposals) continued to discuss personnel and information exchange, as well as joint exercises. The JTG, on the other hand, consisted of defense technocrats and discussed issues related to defense research. The purpose of the JTG was to provide a forum in which the US and Indian defense departments could coordinate and discuss research and development, production, procurement, and logistics. "Its goal was to establish a framework for bilateral technology cooperation, to monitor progress and to provide a forum in which the policies, plans and requirements of both sides could be aired."[71] An important component of the

Agreed Minutes was building of trust between the two countries, and one way to build trust "is by helping both sides understand each other's defense policies and strategic intentions." [72] Initially the major task was to identify the specific areas for cooperation. However, Secretary Perry also made it clear that arms transfer and joint technology development were not going to be the primary areas of cooperation.[73]

The first DPG/JTG meeting was held in September 1995, when both countries engaged in wide ranging discussions on, among other things, the transfer of technology, testing of defense equipment, simulation of war scenarios, and management of defense activities. The second meeting, in October 1996, had a more limited agenda that included issues such as defense evaluation. A third meeting held in January 1998 assessed more closely the kinds of defense items that India needed, as well as the establishment of a test-and-evaluation directorate in the DRDO.[74]

As expected, after the Agreed Minutes, Indo-US defense cooperation did indeed grow. In the first half of 1997, the United States sold precision guided munitions (PGMs) for use by Indian air force strike aircraft. In April of the same year, the Indian and US navies signed a letter of agreement regarding a submarine rescue facility. New Delhi has made an initial payment of $500,000 for this deal, which involves the United States aiding the Indian navy in submarine rescue. The Indian navy also gained US-made Chukkar pilotless target aircraft (PTA) and periscopes for the German-made HDW submarines. The two navies are currently exploring the possibilities of US vessels undergoing servicing and repairs at Indian navy dockyards.

The Indian army also received confirmed offers for the sale of Hydra-70 anti-tank and incendiary rockets. Other deals made to India include sale of the latest Janus simulation system to simulate brigade-level military exercises, a low-intensity-conflict operations (LICO) spectrum for use in simulations, equipment for war gaming, and various weapons systems ranging from tanks and artillery to light weapons such as machine guns.[75]

An important highlight of Indo-US defense relations in the 1990s is an increase in personnel exchange and interaction between the two sides. In 1995, for example, Indian and US air forces exchanged for the first time combat pilot instructors at their respective air force academies. In 1996 US army officers attended, again for the first time, a low-intensity conflict (LIC) course in India, as well as other officer training courses. The two armies also began exchanging medical officers for short capsule courses. The increase in such exchange and interaction in the realm of defense and security suggests that specific reciprocal actions on the part of India and the United States may have enabled the two countries to overcome somewhat the obstacles of distrust and negative perceptions. A foundation of successful cooperation based on specific reciprocity may have been laid, allowing the parties to move ahead gradually in search of better relations.

While several issues have been resolved or provisions have been made to put them on the table for discussion, Indo-US defense relations have not been without trouble. According to the Indian side, the main problem has been that even after the items are approved for export, each item has to go through several US departments for clearance. From the Indian perspective, if any agency holds the request, it clearly indicates an intent to deny.[76] The journey to approval or actual clearance is fraught with too many hiccups.[77] This has given the United States a reputation of being an unreliable supplier.[78] What therefore is needed is more transparency in the licensing process.

From the US perspective, one of the biggest problems is that is it very difficult to work with India on any classified information, since there is no government assurance that information will be safeguarded.[79] India is not a signatory to what the United States terms a General Security of Military Information Agreement (GOSMIA). Even though the agreement places reciprocal responsibilities in sharing information and pertains to the Agreed Minutes, India has been reluctant to sign it. For the United States, "the process and result will contribute significantly to the growth of trust and confidence that are fundamental to the relationship sought by both [our] countries." [80] The United States feels that without GOSMIA the US side cannot be assured that classified information is safeguarded. It updates its assessment every five years for each country and accordingly raises or decreases the level of classified information to be shared. Right now India has access to only declassified information.[81] Indians, however, feel that there "is no reason to sign the GOSMIA because the Defense Department already has a veto on the Commerce Department list, the dual-use technology control list, and the State Department's Office of Munitions and Control List.[82]

Differing perceptions on the interpretation of the 1984 MOU have also been a large part of the problem. India believed that the MOU addressed all US concerns and reservations regarding India's requests to purchase advanced dual-use technology. The US government, particularly the Pentagon, felt that "more detailed assurances of, and systems for, protecting US technologies were needed on a deal-to-deal basis." [83] In the JTG meeting, Americans also expressed frustration in dealing with the Indian bureaucracy.[84] According to Indian sources themselves, the third annual meeting of the bilateral Defense Policy Group (DPG) was postponed for mere reasons of "protocol." [85]

However, despite these hiccups, the two sides had made progress. Three areas of cooperation were identified: (1) aircraft technology, (2) a third-generation antitank system, and (3) testing and evaluation. Not much progress has been made on the third-generation antitank system, and the JTG has so far concentrated on testing and evaluation as a more benign area. As Martin Ischinger explained, "you must crawl before you walk and walk before you run." [86] The United States has been pushing for more R&D cooperation, and the two sides have identified five points of contact: war gaming and simulations, embedded software, aircraft engines, commercial off-the-shelf technology, and electronic radar systems. The JTG meeting held in January 1998 opened up different avenues for potential cooperation and has resulted in agreements to review several technology plans. These include an aerial target drone (India has developed one and wants US opinion), anechoic chamber (a superquiet building used for the purpose of testing), removal of mines, and nonlethal weapons technology. These are all perceived as incremental steps, where increased technological cooperation may eventually lead to a close military relationship.

These steps were indeed successful, and both sides agreed that Bill Perry's visit and the consequent meetings and negotiations had helped bring the "pyramid" relationship to a platform. However, India's nuclear detonation has brought all that to a standstill. The JTG meetings have stopped, and so has work on the LCA project. From the US side, team members have been asked to continue work on the agreed items of cooperation, though it will take some time for cooperation efforts to be resumed and for trust to be rebuilt.[87]

## CONCLUSION

Defense cooperation between two friendly and like-minded countries is itself a difficult task. To foster cooperation between two countries that are not enemies but do have a long shared history of distrust is a mammoth task. Nevertheless India and the United States have managed to move in the right direction (until the May 1998 nuclear test by India) and in the past twenty years have made progress, which was elusive in the first thirty years of India's independence. This study has attempted to demonstrate how and to what extent the two countries have been able to achieve cooperative relations in the area of defense. This concluding section provides our general findings and offers recommendations for future Indo-US interaction.

In the early years of India's independence, because of differences in security perceptions, in friends and foes, and in the expectations of each other's role in the region, Indo-US relations were fraught with feelings of distrust. United States viewed South Asia, just as it did any other region in the world, through the prism of the Cold War. Numerous attempts were made to engage each other in defense cooperation. India, however, consistently believed that the United States had ulterior motives, whether it was in pushing India's defense capabilities against Communist China, placating a sensitive Pakistan, or forcing changes in India's nuclear policy. The United States, in turn, continued to be worried about India's growing relationship with its number-one foe, the Soviet Union, and about India's nuclear policy, which was in direct opposition to America's multilateral policy on nuclear nonproliferation. Therefore, US concerns of relative gain were guided by the fact that any technology transfer or weapons purchase could potentially be redirected to either the Soviet Union or India's nuclear program. Since successful cooperation took place in defense items or technologies that could be acquired easily from other Western countries with less of a problem (no strings attached, whether in terms of food aid or nuclear or security policy), it did not allow for any sense of obligation to be built up, and the exchange was not perceived as costly or sacrificial. As suggested by the theory, these three factors—concern about ulterior motive, relative gains, and whether the recipient state considers a partner's action to be costly or voluntary—affect whether states may actually agree to reciprocate even when the exchanges are mutually acceptable. In Indo-US defense relations these three factors worked negatively and constrained any positive development.

The 1980s saw a visible change in Indo-US relations in terms of genuine desire on both sides to improve defense relations. India wanted to reduce its dependence on the Soviet Union and diversify its sources of weapons supply, and the United States saw a potential weapons market in India and welcomed any attempt to minimize Soviet influence in the region. One of the most important results was the successful attempt at specificity through the MOU and the Lindstrom Report. The MOU outlined the requirements of each party *before* cooperation could occur, and the Lindstrom Report further clarified the exact areas of cooperation. Cooperation did increase after the two countries agreed to follow the specific guidelines to cooperation.

The decade of 1990s, along with an increase in defense and technology cooperation, brought in the realization that while specificity in exchange and precise outlining of interest and areas of sustained cooperation were the keys to progress in Indo-US relations, that in itself could not be the basis of cooperation. For two countries that have a shared history of distrust, what was also important was an attempt at CBMs based on increasing interaction and social exchange. Social interaction and exchange facilitate a better understanding of each others' interests, and an appreciation of each others' political and economic constraints. Such exchange in the long run facilitates the move from specific to diffuse reciprocity and eventually results in an increase in trust, cooperation, and friendship. Hence in the 1990s India and the United States no longer focused strictly on military sales but began to engage on a wider scale. Service-to-service or military-to-military cooperation occurred for the first time between them. They established joint committees to further defense cooperation in research and development. Moreover, military sales were being made based on *initial* payments rather than one-time, up-front payments. Exchange, in other words, was moving from the simultaneous to the sequential.

Although in the 1990s irritants were not absent in the bilateral relationship (e.g., India's testing of its Trishul and Agni missiles, its refusal to sign the CTBT, and, more recently, its nuclear testing), some important changes did occur. There is no question that India and the United States have, can, and do cooperate in the area of defense. However, the methods by which they have achieved such cooperation should not be overlooked. Once India and the United States agreed to specific criteria, for example, cooperation was more acceptable. As the pattern of cooperation became more sequential than simultaneous, exchange was more forthcoming. Furthermore, as interaction began to occur more regularly, despite occasional difficulties, greater cooperation and future interaction became more desirable. In other words, a longer-term focus began to create a foundation of trust upon which future cooperation and exchange could be built.

Based on this study's findings, we suggest that India and the United States continue to cooperate in the defense realm in a specific, reciprocal fashion. As the roots of such cooperation take hold, it may prosper. As another analyst argues, visible success in Indo-US cooperation will likely have important effects on the entire spectrum of Indo-US interactions.[88] Specific, reciprocal exchange has provided some success in Indo-US defense relations. As stated earlier, specific reciprocity based on self-interest may in the long run generate trust as a result of recurrent and gradually expanding social exchange. On that basis, we may be optimistic about the future of Indo-US defense cooperation.

## FINDINGS AND RECOMMENDATIONS

• The United States and India have shared a history of distrust, augmented by the recent nuclear tests. This makes cooperation a difficult task to achieve.

• Since the differences between India and the United States are major and difficult to resolve, but are not acute, a step-by-step approach dealing with specific concerns may help the two countries move in the right direction.

• Past experiences suggest that cooperation can take place if it is based on specific reciprocity, where exchange between partners is strictly delimited and any obligations are clearly specified in terms of rights and duties.

• Cooperation on short-term interests between the two sides may be the first step in this direction. It may be beneficial to examine those areas of cooperation that are noncontroversial and within the range of existing policies and in the interest of both the countries.

• The MOU in this regard has worked as a successful document in that it clearly specified the obligations and rights of both the sides, while at the same time reducing uncertainty by addressing existing concerns. A similar updated document that deals with each side's concerns and clearly identifies areas where cooperation is feasible should be drawn up. *Clearly specified directives help create certainty, maintain restraint, and help create conditions where cooperation is feasible.*

• For India, one of the most important aspects of its relations with the United States in recent years has been the issue of technology transfer. India should evaluate the merits of signing the GOSMIA. It would contribute significantly to the growth of trust and confidence between the two countries and would be a step forward in initially restoring and then upgrading the level of bilateral technology transfers.

• Problems relating to bureaucratic hurdles and protocol-related delays need to be addressed.

• While specific reciprocity makes exchange or cooperation more feasible and in the long run helps move toward building trust, it is not sufficient in itself. For cooperation to move from specific to diffuse, there needs to be more interaction and exchange.

•    Success in the 1990s in Indo-US cooperation has been possible after Bill Perry's visit, the Agreed Minutes on Indo-US cooperation, and the Kickleighter proposals. They allowed for mutual exchange of ideas and more interaction, and this has helped in a better understanding of problems and concerns and brought the pyramid to a platform.

•    Develop a consultative process among senior officials for better bilateral relationship.

•    Identify and build on existing positive developments. Survey areas of disagreement, assess which are most serious, and find common ground.

## NOTES

1    For a good overview of US-Indian relations, see Satu P. Limaye, *US-Indian Relations: The Pursuit of Accommodation* (Boulder, CO: Westview Press, 1993).

2    Ibid. Also see W. P. S. Sidhu, "Enhancing Indo-US Strategic Cooperation," *Adelphi Paper 313* (New York: Oxford University Press, 1997).

3    Regarding Indo-Soviet relations, see Santosh Mehrota, *India and the Soviet Union: Trade and Technology Transfer* (Cambridge: Cambridge University Press, 1990).

4    For details on the early differences in the two countries' security and strategic outlooks, see Norman D. Palmer, *The United States and India: Dimensions of Influence* (New York: Praeger Publishers, 1984), pp. 173–83. Also see Raju G. C. Thomas, "Security Relations in Southern Asia: Differences in the Indian and American Perspectives," *Asian Survey* 21 (July 1981), p. 692.

5    See Surjit Mansingh, *India's Search for Power: Indira Gandhi's Foreign Policy, 1966–1982* (New Delhi: Sage Publications, 1984), p. 75.

6    See Limaye, *US-Indian Relations,* p. 182.

7    See Mark Tully and Zareer Mansini, *From Raj to Rajiv: Forty Years of Indian Independence* (London: BBC Books, 1988), p. 42.

8    For a background on India's nuclear policy, see Shyam Bhatia, *India's Nuclear Bomb* (Sahibabad: Vikas Publishing House, 1979).

9    For details, see Brahma Chellaney, *Nuclear Nonproliferation: The US-Indian Conflict* (Delhi: Sangam Books, 1993).

10   As cited in Limaye, *US-Indian Relations,* p. 189.

11   See "India Sets 3 Nuclear Blasts, Defying a Worldwide Ban; Tests Bring a Sharp Outcry," *New York Times,* May 12, 1998, pp. A1, A10; "Indians Conduct 2 More Atom Tests Despite Sanctions," *New York Times,* May 14, 1998, pp. A1, A8.

12   See Joseph Grieco, *Cooperation Among Nations: Europe, America, and Non-Tariff Barriers to Trade* (Ithaca: Cornell University, 1990); and Kenneth Waltz, *Theory of International Politics* (Reading, MA: Addison-Wesley, 1979).

13   See Robert Keohane, *After Hegemony: Cooperation and Discord in the World Political Economy* (Princeton: Princeton University Press, 1984); and Oran Young, *International Cooperation: Building Regimes for Natural Resources and the Environment* (Ithaca: Cornell

University Press, 1989).

14  Robert Axelrod, *The Evolution of Cooperation* (New York: Basic Books, 1984); and Robert Keohane, "Reciprocity in International Relations," *International Organization* 40 (Winter 1986), pp. 1–27. Also see Lawrence S. Wrightsman Jr., John O'Connor, and Norma J. Baker, *Cooperation and Competition: Readings on Mixed-Motive Games* (Belmont, CA: Brooks/Cole Publishing Co., 1972).

15  Keohane, "Reciprocity in International Relations," p. 4.

16  Ibid.

17  See Peter Blau, *Exchange and Power in Social Life* (New York: John Wiley and Sons, Inc., 1964), p. 6.

18  As Axelrod demonstrates, specific reciprocity, or tit-for-tat action and reaction, can have adverse effects in that "once a feud gets started, it can continue indefinitely." See Axelrod, *The Evolution of Cooperation,* p. 138.

19  Keohane, "Reciprocity in International Relations," p. 6.

20  Ibid., p. 7.

21  Ibid., p. 8.

22  Deborah Welch Larson, "The Psychology of Reciprocity in International Relations," *Negotiation Journal* 4 (July 1988), p. 291. Joseph Grieco elaborates on the relative gains problem in international relations. He suggests that states are extremely sensitive to relative gains because the result may be that "these increasingly powerful partners in the present could use their additional power to pressure them or, at the extreme, to become all the more formidable foes at some point in the future." See *Cooperation Among Nations: Europe, America, and Non-Tariff Barriers to Trade* (Ithaca, NY: Cornell University Press, 1990), pp. 28–29.

23  Larson, "The Psychology of Reciprocity in International Relations," p. 287.

24  Ibid., pp. 292–94.

25  Keohane, "Reciprocity in International Relations," p. 20.

26  Robert Axelrod and Robert Keohane refer to this as "the shadow of the future." Because of a state's interest in future relations, there is less incentive to defect during present relations. See "Achieving Cooperation Under Anarchy: Strategies and Institutions," in Kenneth A. Oye, *Cooperation Under Anarchy* (Princeton: Princeton University Press, 1986), p. 232.

27  Alvin W. Gouldner, "The Norm of Reciprocity: A Preliminary Statement," *American Sociological Review* 25 (April 1960), p. 175.

28  Keohane, "Reciprocity in International Relations," p. 21.

29  Ibid. Also see Edward L. Schieffelin, "Reciprocity and the Construction of Reality," *Man* 15 (September 1980), pp. 502–17.

30  Keohane, "Reciprocity in International Relations," p. 22. Also see Blau, *Exchange and Power in Social Life.*

31  Marshall Sahlins, *Stone Age Economics* (Chicago: Aldine-Atherton, 1972), p. 201.

32  Surjit Mansingh, *India's Search for Power: Indira Gandhi's Foreign Policy: 1966–82* (New Delhi: Sage Publications, 1984), p. 68.

33  Kumar, "Defense in Indo-US Relations," *Occasional Paper,* Institute for Defense Studies and Analysis (New Delhi: Shirl Avtar Printing, 1997), p. 17.

34  Dinesh Kumar, Defense, p. 18.

35  Dinesh Kumar, Defense, p. 17.

36  Other possible reasons cited for cancellation of deals were US insistence on dollar payment for the aircraft and its reluctance to provide an Indian company with a license for co-production. For details see P. R. Chari, "Indo-Soviet Military Cooperation: A

Review," *Asian Survey,* vol. 19, no. 3 (March 1979), p. 234. Also see Surjit Mansingh, p. 73–85.

37  As cited in Limaye, *US-Indian Relations,* p. 183.

38  S. Nihal Singh, "Why India Goes to Moscow for Arms," *Asian Survey,* vol. 24, no. 7 (July 1984), p. 711.

39  As cited in Dinesh Kumar, Defense, p. 17.

40  Some of the other reasons cited for canceling the howitzers and missile deal were American unwillingness to let India make the items under license or produce the ammunition locally with their technical collaboration and the US right to unilaterally cancel the deal without refund for initial payment as part of the standard contractual agreement. For details see Satu Limaye, p. 186–90, and for details on the .50 caliber Browning gun see pp.193–94.

41  Dinesh Kumar, Defense, p. 9.

42  Surjit Mansingh, *India's Search for Power,* p. 77.

43  The Soviets, on the other hand, were more successful with India because they kept aid and sale issues separate and did not set conditions.

44  R. J. Augustus, *In Defense of My Country: Indo-US Defense Technology Cooperation* (Universal Publishers, 1998), p. 43.

45  Richard P. Cronin, "Policy Alert: The Rajiv Gandhi Visit: Issues in US-India Relations," Congressional Research Service, no. 85-838f, June 7, 1985, CRS-6.

46  Shekhar Gupta, "India's New Defense Policy," *Wall Street Journal* (Asian edition), October 6, 1986.

47  The then US Undersecretary of State, Fred Charles Ikle, argued that India's pro-Soviet posture was predicated upon its dependence on military supplies form the USSR. If Western resources replaced the Soviet supplies and if India's high-technology and military needs were met, it would take a more "balanced" view as far as the United States and the USSR were concerned. As cited in Bharat Karnad, "Strategic Ties with US," *Hindustan Times,* December 17, 1997.

48  Robert Wirsing, "Arms Race in South Asia: Implications for the United States" *Asian Survey,* vol. 25, no. 3 (March 1995), p. 279.

49  Wirsing summed up the lack of trust in the bilateral relationship. Referring to the .50 caliber Browning machine gun deal, he argues: "After enormous labors by both American and Indian officials to accomplish the sale, neither side was willing to yield on principle in spite of the fact that both recognized its importance as a step towards a more substantial arms relationship. In the end, US insistence on maintaining 'strings' on its weapons met with equally strong feeling of distrust for the implications of American conditions. . . . New Delhi's conviction that Washington's administrative requirements were, in fact an artful disguise to influence Indian policy towards its primary benefactor, the USSR, and its major rival, Pakistan, was apparently too much to overcome." Ibid., p. 283.

50  See Raju G.C. Thomas, *Indian Security Policy* (Princeton: Princeton University Press, 1986), pp. 246–74. Also see Raju G. C. Thomas, "Prospects for Indo-U.S. Security Ties," *Orbis* (summer 1983), p. 386.

51  Limaye, *US-Indian Relations,* p. 203.

52  Ibid., p. 205.

53  K. Santhanam, "Indian Defense Technology Infrastructure and Prospects of Indo-US Cooperation," paper presented at the Indo-US Defense Workshop, National Defense University, Washington, D.C., September 19–21, 1989, p. 13.

54  David Buchan, "GE Licenses Output of Turbines for Indian Navy," *Financial Times,* January 21, 1987.

55  See Dilip Mukerjee, "U.S. Weapons for India," *Asian Survey,* vol. 32, no. 6 (June 1987), p. 602.

56  See Inderjit Badhwar, "Indo-US Relations: A Fresh Look," *India Today,* July 15, 1985, p. 53. Also see "India Agrees to Buy U.S. Computers," *Washington Post,* February 7, 1986, p. A21.

57  Mukerjee, "U.S. Weapons for India," p. 607.

58  Limaye, *US-Indian Relations,* p. 217.

59  See Nayan Chanda, "Cap Comes Calling," *Far Eastern Economic Review* (October 16, 1986), p. 44.

60  Santhanam, p. 15.

61  Limaye, *US-Indian Relations,* p. 214.

62  Santhanam points out that despite the signing of the MOU there remained a big desire for more information in export license processing and a dilution of specifications. See Santhanam, p. 15.

63  Sidhu, p. 50.

64  At a discussion during a workshop, *"Expanding the Ambit of Strategic Cooperation: India-US Interests and Initiatives,"* April 29–30, 1998, organized by the Center for International Trade and Security, University of Georgia, Athens.

65  Richard Haas, "United States Policy Towards South Asia," Address to the Asia Society, Washington, D.C., January 11, 1990, p. 16.

66  Alvin Gouldner, "The Norm of Reciprocity," p. 175.

67  USAPC Plan for Cooperation, Kickleighter Proposals, Office of Commanding General, Department of the Army.

68  Sidhu, "Enhancing Indo-US Strategic Relations," p. 57. Also see Kumar, "Defense in Indo-US Relations," pp. 44–45.

69  "Agreed Minutes on Defense Relations Between the United States and India," United States Information Service, official text, January 12, 1995, p. 1.

70  "Agreed Minutes," p. 2.

71  Sidhu, "Enhancing Indo-US Strategic Relations," p. 58.

72  Remarks prepared for delivery by Secretary Perry, United Services Institute, New Delhi, January 12, 1995, p. 2.

73  Remarks prepared for delivery by Secretary Perry, USI, New Delhi, 1995, p. 3.

74  For details also see Dinesh Kumar, pp. 56–59.

75  Ibid.

76  Discussion with R. J. Augustus, advisor (defense technology), June 12, 1998.

77  In an interview on June 12, 1998, Martin Ischinger, trying to clarify the US position, said that what usually happens is that commercial vendors provide assurance. However, if it is an item involving sensitive technology, the government is more inclined to say no. According to him, within the Department of Defense there are some that are against any cooperation with India on defense or technology collaboration, as they do not want to have a competitor in the Indian Ocean.

78  Discussion with Santhanam, chief technology advisor, Ministry of Defence, January 9, 1998.

79  According to Martin Ischinger, deputy director, Pacific Armaments Cooperation Directorate (acquisition and technology, international program), " Indians don't tell us what these procedures are and that they are in place. Only political teams are allowed to go around and check." June 12, 1998.

80  Letter by Linton Wells II, deputy for policy support, DOD, to K. A. Nambiar, Indian defense secretary, dated September 14, 1995.

81  This was ascertained in a meeting with Martin Ischinger, June 12, 1998. However,

Ischinger also admitted that signing of the GOSMIA will not necessarily change much even though it is an impediment, because of nuclear and missile issues.

82 Indian official cited in Limaye, *US-Indian Relations*, p. 208.

83 Bharat Karnad, "Strategic Ties with US," *Hindustan Times,* December 17, 1997. The difference in perception of the importance and relevance of the MOU was also evident in the fact that, in talking to most Pentagon officials, it became clear that either they were not even aware of the document or they did not consider it relevant enough to remember, while on the Indian side the MOU was constantly being referred to as the most significant document till now.

84 As Martin Ischinger explained, "For the first few years we did not even know who was in charge, K. G. Naranyanan or Santhanam," and "the frustrating thing about working with Indians is that they cannot decide on anything." According to him, it was decided to have the meeting in May 1997, then at the last minute it was shifted to June by the Indian side, then July, then September, then canceled. Finally the meeting took place in January 1998. So no meeting took place in 1997. Ischinger, in his last meeting with the other US participants of the JTG, had to admit that he "was concerned that I can't get them to the table."

85 The Indian defense secretary, it seems, canceled his trip to the United States because he wanted Walter Slocombe, the US undersecretary of defense, to co-chair the DPG session with him, and not the junior-ranked assistant secretary Frank Kramer. According to Karnad, "In the larger context this concern with the nuances of procedural correctness has, time and again, erected virtually impenetrable barriers to a genuine breakthrough in bilateral relations." See Bharat Karnad, "Strategic Dialogue or Hurdling Trifles," unpublished paper.

86 Martin Ischinger, interview, June 12, 1998.

87 Martin Ischinger indicated this during an interview a month after the nuclear tests.

88 Santhanam, "Indian Defense Technology Infrastructure," p. 16.

# 8

# Non-proliferation Export Controls: US and Indian Perspectives

**Richard T. Cupitt
and Seema Gahlaut**

India can only blame itself for coming under growing pressure on the technology front. For three decades since starting to produce plutonium, it has not been able to make up its mind on the nuclear issue. While nuclear profligate China is courted by all cartels, nuclear abstinent India is targeted by them.[1]

We would like to re-affirm categorically that we will continue to exercise the most stringent control on the export of sensitive technologies, equipment and commodities—especially those relating to weapons of mass destruction. Our track record has been impeccable in this regard. Therefore we expect recognition of our responsible policy by the international community.[2]

W hen India tested its nuclear weapons devices in May 1998, it highlighted the long-standing antipathy that characterizes Indo-US relations regarding non-proliferation and export control policies. But as the quotes above show, the tests also brought public re-affirmation of India's unilateral commitment to export controls. Although this is significant, it brings into sharper relief the puzzling fact that India and the United States have been unable to view export controls in the same light, even though each considers it an important symbol of international responsibility.

For nearly three decades the Indian nuclear program and more recently its missile program set India and the United States at odds. The United States, for example, had four Indian organizations on its published list of entities of proliferation concern for dual-use items, before the nuclear tests.[3] At the time, no other country had more. In the aftermath of the nuclear tests, controls on the transfer of US dual-use technologies to India have become even stricter. On June 18, 1998, the Department of Commerce announced it would deny all licenses for exports or re-export of any item controlled for nuclear or missile proliferation reasons under the Export Administration Regulations (EAR).[4] Commerce also revoked a license exception that permitted the export or re-export of computers with a composite theoretical performance in excess of 2,000 million theoretical operations per second (MTOPs). License applications for such computers to any Indian government entity associated with nuclear, missile, or military programs, or any Indian non-government entity affiliated with the nuclear or missile programs, faced a presumption of denial.

The United States government has imposed sanctions on India in the past. In May 1992 the United States restricted technology trade with the Indian Space Research Organization (ISRO), related to ISRO efforts to procure cryogenic rocket engines from the Russian Federation. Unlike cases involving China and Russia, the two governments could not reach an agreement that would have allowed the United States to suspend or waive the two-year sanction before it expired.

The Indian government, in turn, remains a vocal opponent to the four major US-led supplier arrangements, the Australia Group, the Nuclear Suppliers Group (NSG), the Missile Technology Control Regime (MTCR), and the Wassenaar Arrangement (WA), as well as the Nuclear Non-proliferation Treaty (NPT) and the Comprehensive Test Ban Treaty (CTBT).[5]

The persistence of the lack of cooperation between India and the United States on these issues has puzzling aspects at several levels. With the exception of India (and Israel), every long-established democratic country that can serve as either a source of supply or a point of transit for sensitive dual-use items has signed the NPT and participates in one or more of the four supplier arrangements. Each of the arrangements now includes one or more former leaders of the non-aligned movement or less-developed countries, including Argentina, Brazil, South Korea, and South Africa. The United States also seems able to cooperate on some non-proliferation issues with North Korea, a target of all four supplier-groups, and non-proliferation and export controls with China, an emerging non-democratic rival power in Asia. India, for its part, has signed most of the other key non-proliferation treaties and conventions (see Table 1). Its recent ratification of the Chemical Weapons Convention (CWC) and its somewhat surprising declaration regarding a chemical weapons program demonstrates a willingness to cooperate on overall non-proliferation issues in certain circumstances.

The discussion in this chapter is organized as follows: After briefly exploring levels of cooperation on export controls between the two states, the authors assess the breadth of the gap between US-championed multilateral export control standards and the Indian export control system. They then review the Indian perspective on the four supplier arrangements and other non-proliferation instruments as they bear on these differences (and similarities). This includes a discussion on why India chooses to cooperate in some areas and not in others. We conclude by considering what India and the United States might do together to improve cooperation, even as the exact impact of the Indian nuclear tests on this bilateral relationship remains unclear.

## INDO-US COOPERATION ON NON-PROLIFERATION EXPORT CONTROLS: A US PERSPECTIVE

Although programs in several countries rekindled US interest in non-proliferation in the 1970s, the Indian nuclear and missile programs made particularly profound impressions on US export control policy. The Indian detonation of a peaceful nuclear device in 1974 led directly to US-initiated consultations among the NPT depository states and to the formation of the NSG, as well as to the Symington Amendment in 1976 and to the Nuclear Non-Proliferation Act (NNPA) of 1978. Similarly, the launch of the Indian SLV-3 in July 1980 prompted the Reagan administration to adopt National Security Directive 70 (NSD-70) in November 1982. NSD-70 overhauled US policy regarding the transfer of missile technology and spawned the creation of the MTCR.

In addition, the Reagan administration became increasingly concerned that the Soviet Union might gain access to sensitive items by diverting US exports intended for neutral or non-aligned countries outside the multilateral structure for Western export controls. In 1984 President Reagan authorized officials at the US Defense Department to review licenses for eight categories of sensitive items to fifteen "free-world" countries of concern, including India. When the Under-Secretary of Defense for Policy, Fred C. Ikle, visited India in April 1985, he signaled a new US interest in making its military and dual-use technology available to India. In particular, Ikle reportedly agreed to release several licenses blocked by the Office of Defense Technology Security.[6]

The United States had already begun negotiations on the means of conducting trade in military and dual-use items that culminated in a May 1985 memorandum of understanding (MOU) between Washington and New Delhi, the month before the visit by Prime Minister Rajiv Gandhi to the United States. Under the MOU implementation procedures, the Indian government would issue an import license (IL) for US high-technology exports that included assurances against diversion and retransfer. In special cases, the Indian government would also supply extra assurances to the US government. India published its regulations, and the regime came into being in May 1986.[7] The MOU appeared to have a positive impact on US exports to India, mainly in terms of advanced electronics, as the value of approved export licenses rose from $522 million in 1984 to $1.3 billion in 1985, mainly because the MOU resolved several pending cases.

Unfortunately, this system proved inadequate from the US perspective. While the mandate given to Prime Minister Rajiv Gandhi probably did allow swift progress in the bilateral negotiations, the new government also wanted to ease the red tape and other bureaucratic barriers facing importers. Consequently, the Indian government exempted large numbers of importers and state-owned enterprises from the procedure, which undermined the premise of the system of assurances. The original MOU, moreover, failed to control computers and other items that had nuclear end-use applications inside India. The two governments negotiated an annex so that these items should not go to fully or partially unsafeguarded Indian nuclear operations, except if the item went for basic administrative tasks. The agreed procedure for post-shipment verification of the location and end use complicated this process even more. India agreed to conduct the checks unilaterally or jointly, but did not agree to allow US officials to conduct verification investigations on their own. In response, the US Defense Technology Security Administration (DTSA) began blocking more and more license applications, especially for computers using 32-bit microprocessors. In addition, DTSA interpreted the MOU as narrowly applying to dual-use items, not to items on the US Munitions List, although the Indian government and the rest of the US government believed the MOU did cover munitions items, which further dampened the prospects for cooperation.

India and the United States attempted to resolve these concerns by negotiating a new COCOM-like Import Certificate/Delivery Verification (IC/DV) procedure. Indian officials apparently hoped this would lead to an end to some US restrictions, such as the Department of Defense review of license applications.[8] Although the US Department of Commerce developed new regulations based on the IC/DV system in June 1988, the United States did little to ease restrictions. Starting in 1989, dramatic changes in the international environment prompted the United States to tighten its non-proliferation export controls. The first flight test of the Agni in that same year only increased US concerns regarding Indian nuclear and missile programs. Though important, the promise of improved military cooperation raised by the visit to India by Defense Secretary Caspar Weinberger proved far less interesting to either the Indian or US military establishment. Defense continued to block, for example, the pending sale of a $12 million dollar Cray supercomputer until December 1990.[9]

Despite this opposition, transfers of defense technology did take place as a result of the MOU. India, for example, obtained the LM-2500 gas turbine engine for its navy, tank night-vision devices, gyroscopic technology, and the promise of collaboration on the Indian light combat aircraft (LCA) project. While cooperation improved in the 1990s, the level of US foreign military sales contracts and the export of dual-use items remained low when compared with US bilateral relationships with other big emerging markets.

How the United States treats export licenses to India provides one indication of US concern. Under an effort to streamline and clarify the US Export Administration Regulations, for example, Supplement 1 to Part 738 matches countries with seven reasons for control (with fifteen subcategories). The supplement shows that to export to India, US firms needed to apply for a license for items controlled for chemical-biological, nuclear, or missile technology; national security; regional stability; and for two of three crime control reasons. Even before the nuclear tests, therefore, the controls that India faced were among the most restrictive for any country not under US or UN embargo.

Similarly, the approval rate for license applications for US exports to India hovered around 50 to 60 percent, far below average for all US licensed exports, before the nuclear tests (see Table 2). Processing times also exceeded the average by 30 percent (see Table 2). Most of the sixty-seven denials made for reasons of nuclear proliferation in 1997 concern the Bhabha Atomic Research Center. However, even eliminating those licenses would not solve the problem. Thirty-five of the remaining denials, for example, related to missile proliferation. With increasing concern about the ballistic missile threat facing the United States in the next century, missile proliferation issues may fracture Indian-US relations in the next decade as badly as nuclear proliferation has in recent years.

Even with this restrictive approach to licensing, however, the value of all US export licenses to India in 1996 equates to only 1.6 percent of total US exports to India that year. By itself, this hardly constitutes a "denial" regime. The impact of US export controls, moreover, has broader practical and symbolic effects. For instance, despite explicitly identifying India as a target market for US exports in its big-emerging-market strategy, the rate of US export growth to India trails that of the rest of the world by a considerable amount: between 28 percent and 46 percent over the last five years. While US export control policy toward India alone can not explain this gap, it certainly contributes to it.

Perhaps the most telling example of this perspective came in the private-sector response to the nuclear tests. Although few governments imposed sanctions, US officials claimed that many firms shied away from investing in or exporting to India.[10] Rather than risk a license denial, US exporters may look for other consumers. Although India seems involved in relatively few cases of violations of US export regulations, US exporters ignore the regulations at their peril. The Commerce Department, for example, recently imposed a fine of $450,000 on IGG, a very small Pennsylvania firm, for continuing to export electrical products to the Indian Space Research Organization (ISRO) after the US government imposed a two-year prohibition in May 1992.[11] On the other hand, recent charges in the US media that several American companies have been violating US laws by supplying technology to the Indian nuclear and missile programs have been promptly and publicly rebutted by the concerned companies.[12] Such instances would go a long way toward correcting the common perception in the United States that any technology exports to India are bound to be misused and thus violate US laws.

At the same time, Indian entities may look for other sources of supply or be even more determined to develop the technologies indigenously. The latter require no

Indian obligation as to their use or even transparency. Denying licenses for the Cray XMP-14, for example, certainly increased the incentive for India to develop its own supercomputer, the Param, as has been the case with India's nuclear fuel reprocessing capabilities. Further, according to media reports, a number of European companies had become active in seeking deals in India immediately after the imposition of unilateral US sanctions in June 1998.

Export controls have other less obvious impacts than strict denial of trade. Although the openness of Indian society makes screening by US companies and the US government for potential end-users easier, it can also make screening more complex. The initial generic listing of Bharat enterprises on the Department of Commerce Entities List, for example, generated a needlessly high number of licenses returned without action (470). Although modifications in the list more clearly targeted the process, this hindered the development of legitimate commercial activity.

Several factors besides the nuclear tests have reduced the incentives for the US government to ameliorate this source of friction in its relationship with India. The overall liberalization of US export controls during the Clinton administration reduced private-sector demands for addressing the export control issues separating the United States and India.[13] Concomitantly, the pace of economic liberalization in India continues to make it a less attractive market to US exporters and investors than several of its Asian neighbors, though the financial crises in Southeast Asia and Russia in late 1998 may change some of that. Moreover, despite palpable concerns, neither the Department of Defense, the Central Intelligence Agency, nor Congress openly asserts that India has transferred items of proliferation concern outside the region, unlike North Korea, China, and Russia.[14] This makes their concerns appear to Indian officials as even more contrived. Finally, US relations with China, the newly independent states of the former Soviet Union, and North Korea have captured the time and resources of the export control bureaucracy in most departments and agencies. The same situation prevails in the focus of the highest echelons of policy making in the United States, leaving Indian and South Asian issues at the periphery of US foreign policy. Consequently, how India and the United States might expand cooperation on export controls remains terra incognita to a significant extent. To explore this more fully and offer suggestions requires a better understanding of the Indian perspective on non-proliferation export controls, as well as a comparison of its current system with US-led multilateral standards.

## INDIAN NONPROLIFERATION EXPORT CONTROL SYSTEM

India has been exercising a degree of control over the export of materials, equipment and technology of direct and indirect application to weapons of mass destruction (WMDs) and the means of their delivery.[15] In fact, the first control over exports of such material was effected in 1947, the year of India's independence. The legal bases for such controls lie in the following laws: the Atomic Energy Act, 1962 (which replaced the 1948 act); the Customs Act, 1962; the Explosive Substances Act, 1908; the Narcotic Drugs and Psychotropic Substances Act, 1985; the Environment Protection Act, 1986; and the Foreign Trade (Development and Regulation) Act, 1992.[16]

Detailed explication of the policy and procedures governing controls on imports and exports is given in the following four documents: Export and Import Policy, 1 April 1997–31 March 2002; the Handbook of Procedures, volume I; the Handbook of Procedures, volume II, and the ITC (HS) Classification of Export and Import Items.[17] The controls on exports and imports are regulated via three "negative lists" of items: prohibited (those that may not be exported or imported at all), restricted (that require compulsory licenses), and canalized (that cannot be imported or exported by anyone except the designated public-sector enterprise).

The Directorate General of Foreign Trade (DGFT), under the Ministry of Commerce, is the sole agency responsible for granting of licenses for exports and imports. But this is done only after the application is referred to the inter-ministerial committee that meets periodically.[18] The committee sends the application to the designated reviewing authorities (relating to their specific areas of concern), for a no-objection clearance.[19] In cases that relate to atomic materials, a no-objections clearance from the DAE is required.[20]

Implementation and enforcement are the responsibility of the Department of Customs and Excise and the Directorate General of Commercial Intelligence and Statistics. The former is mainly responsible for interceptions. In addition, some designated officials of the DGFT have the authority to enter, search, inspect, and seize materials proscribed by the Foreign Trade (Regulation) Rules, 1993. In cases where the materials are nuclear-related, final investigation and decision about their sensitivity is made by DAE, but the arresting agency is responsible for bringing the charges before the courts.[21]

Customs officials are thoroughly grounded in knowledge about chemicals and narcotics, via several rigorous intra-departmental examinations, spread over a period of up to three years. No special training for customs officials regarding non-proliferation export controls regarding nuclear materials had been considered until the 1990s, precisely because the government exclusively controlled trade.[22] However, DAE is currently undertaking steps to sensitize the industry as well as customs officials about the possibility of illicit nuclear trade. DAE has begun to offer training courses for inspectors at most of the twenty-two ports of the country, though the program is in its initial stages.

End-user certification is required for both imports and exports. This is the responsibility of the importer or exporter, and inconsistencies in this statement render the person liable for punishment. The DAE is in the process of developing a database to keep track of activities of exporters and importers of nuclear materials.[23] There are a number of agencies that are authorized for pre-shipment inspection and certification of exports (in India) and imports (in Germany, United Kingdom, Italy, Netherlands, Kuwait, Switzerland and Japan), though post-shipment verification is rare, and therefore a problem in bilateral relations with the United States.[24]

The penalties for violation of laws through misleading information and/or an attempt to import or export proscribed goods range from confiscation of goods and monetary fines to imprisonment.[25] If charged under the Atomic Energy Act of 1962, espionage and treason charges might be brought against a person charged with selling/exporting information and materials on the restricted or canalized lists without proper certification and authorization. But not much publicity is given to such violations. There is more information available about import violations than about export violations.

Information does not appear to be shared on a regular basis either with external actors or with the domestic public, beyond the government publications that enunciate the policy and specific procedures.[30] In fact, the briefing notes issued in January 1998 are the first attempt to compile and make explicit the relevant laws to "assist the representatives in India of foreign governments to familiarize themselves with India's system of legal and administrative measures that enable the regulation of exports from India of such Special Materials, Equipment, and Technologies as have application or relevance to the development, production or use of WMDs." [31]

By now, most of the relevant documents, including the Handbooks of Procedure and the EXIM Policy, have been placed on the Internet. This is part of the Electronic Data Interchange (EDI) initiative, which would include not only computerization but also the inter-linking of major offices of the DGFT with Customs, so that electronic data interchange could take place. Henceforth all public notices issued by the DGFT would be on the Internet, and in order to "bring about transparency in decisions taken by various committees for issuance of licenses will be simultaneously displayed electronically." [26] Information regarding end-users and procedures for checking that imports are not diverted is shared with suppliers of foreign technology, for instance the United States, as part of the latter's end-user verification requirements.[27]

## ASSESSMENT METHODOLOGY

In this section we briefly assess the United States, Japanese and Indian export control systems utilizing a methodology developed by a group at the University of Georgia[28]. This methodology allows researchers to evaluate the development of non-proliferation export controls in individual countries. It comprises seventy-two questions involving ten elements that fit with emerging multilateral standards. Each element is broken down into three sub-parts reflecting the existence of export control: (1) policy and/or legal basis, (2) institutions and procedures, and (3) behavior (implementation).[29] In order to reflect the differing importance of the ten elements, the Georgia group got the officials and policy experts from four countries to rank the elements, permitting weights to be assigned to each (see Table 3).

Within each element, the questions address issues of policy, process and implementation. The author assigned a score of 0 for each no answer to a question and a score of 1 for each yes answer. A qualified "yes, but" answer was assigned a score of 0.5 for that question. The raw scores were added for each element. To weigh the scores, the authors divided the raw score for each element by the number of questions in that element, then multiplied by the assigned weight for that element.

The scores arrived at by this methodology, however, are *not* a measure of the effectiveness of national export control systems. These scores show the status of elements often associated with an effective export control system. In other words, *higher scores do not necessarily equal effectiveness, while lower scores do not necessarily reveal an ineffective control system.* The scores thus provide a means of comparison across national systems and can indicate areas of convergence and divergence. This can help identify areas where conflicts will be most likely and thus focus international efforts at cooperation and coordination.

## EMERGING MULTILATERAL STANDARDS: NOT JUST US EXPORT CONTROLS

The multilateral standards used in the CITS/UGA assessment methodology certainly reflect a strong US influence, but this does not mean that highly compatible export control systems in other countries are identical to that of the United States. In contrast to the United States, for example, the Japanese have separate regulatory regimes for goods and technologies, while munitions and dual-use items fall under the same legal framework. Japan limits its version of catchall controls to those items in the general categories already controlled under the NSG and other supplier regimes, whereas US controls apply to a much broader spectrum of items.

The Japanese also base their control system on their international obligations, grant licensing authority to a single agency, do not differentiate between Hong Kong and the People's Republic of China in licensing, rely heavily on quasi-governmental bodies in exchanging information on export controls, and confine their sanctions to Japanese entities. All of this differs significantly from the US approach to export controls. Systems of governments with even smaller production bases, such as Australia or Norway, or those of key transit authorities, such as Hong Kong, differ even more, as befits their particular economic (and political) structures.

Nor does the United States system always meet the emerging multilateral standards. The United States, for example, encourages countries to adopt a clear and strong law on export controls. For many years, however, the United States has proven unable to craft a new Export Administration Act (EAA). Even though it retains a strong legal framework for its export control system without the EAA, this does indicate something about the difficulties the United States has had in building a consensus on the future of its export control system. The United States also advocates a strong end-use verification regime that uses frequent post-shipment checks, but the US post-shipment verification system has come under criticism for conducting too few checks and often relying on foreign nationals to do the checks. This has produced new provisions in the National Defense Authorization Act that in essence requires post-shipment checks for exports of all high-performance computers to certain destinations, which may triple or quadruple the current program for post-shipment verification.

## COMPARING INDIAN AND MULTILATERAL EXPORT CONTROLS

The discussion regarding the Indian non-proliferation export control system given in the earlier section has been used to assess the compatibility of the Indian system with that of the multilateral regimes (see Table 3). It highlights the following aspects:

- India has an extensive system of laws and regulations regarding control over exports of dangerous materials.

- There are negative lists of exports, and there is a detailed system that identifies the extent of licensing required for exports of different categories of items.

- These are implemented as a matter of routine, and from all available information, have successfully controlled the items of concern.

- However, none of the laws are actually concerned with non-proliferation.

Even the Atomic Energy Act of 1962 authorizes the government to "develop, control and use atomic energy for the welfare of the people of India and for other peaceful purposes and for matters connected therewith." This gives a lot of latitude to the government in broadly interpreting the mandate. Yet even though proliferation concerns may have guided the policy of restraint, there is no declaration to this effect, or even a declaration regarding why some items are under greater controls than the others. The only exceptions to this are items controlled as part of the CWC agreement and those under the Montreal Protocol.

There is an established bureaucratic process to review and grant licenses for export, and for implementation and enforcement. Yet there seems to be little information regarding the actual composition and workings of the inter-ministerial committee. Thus the rationale for denial of licenses and information regarding violators, violations, and penalties are not routinely made public. Similarly, officials confirmed that training of customs officials and border guards in the specifics of non-proliferation related control has begun recently, but no information about the nature of this training can be made public.

The preceding discussion shows that India's strict controls on the transfer of sensitive materials and technology are more a reflection of the internal policy consensus than a condition of compliance with any international regimes.[32] It thus presents opportunities to engage India in multilateral negotiations such that the country seeks to constructively shape the regimes from within rather than remain a marginalized voice of dissent from the outside. Training of customs officials, development of the database, and sensitizing the private sector are areas where more information will help external actors in devising ways of encouraging India's cooperation and engagement in the multilateral efforts in non-proliferation export controls. But none of this may be possible unless the external actors also have some understanding of the perspectives that undergird Indian attitude toward multilateral technology control regimes.

## INDIAN PERSPECTIVE ON TECHNOLOGY CONTROL REGIMES

An examination of the popular and official perspective toward the nature and purposes of technology control regimes can explain some of the differences between Indian and multilateral export controls. Almost all of the current regimes (except the CTBT) originated with the explicit efforts of the United States, and all have been supplemented by separate technology control agreements among the major supplier states. From the United States' perspective, the denial of technology for unauthorized (by the regimes) purposes is a legitimate means to alter the payoff structure of the real and potential proliferators. This is based on an understanding that formal adherence to the regimes is the crucial indicator of intentions; therefore membership is the criterion for differential treatment. Membership makes a country eligible for access to advanced technology in the concerned sphere, subject to authorized and verifiable end uses.

The US argument is that *non-proliferation* has now become an international norm, whereas India argues that it is the *elimination of all WMDs,* rather than their selective control, that should be the norm underlying such initiatives. From the Indian perspective, these goals and means are being followed in the BTWC and the CWC, albeit in a limited way, but not in the nuclear and missile non-proliferation regimes.[33] The latter are inherently flawed in that they aim to disarm all but the chosen few, thus making *some* proliferators safer and therefore more legitimate than others. The technology control agreements (Zangger, NSG, MTCR, WA) are referred to by most Indian authors as "embargo regimes" [34] and are seen as a product of the Cold War, based on political and ideological division, security perceptions and latent economic interests of the advanced industrial countries.[35] As one scholar put it, the WA, MTCR, NSG, and the Australia Group have a few things in common: they were born in secrecy, continue to lack transparency, and lack international validating agreements or the sanction of the United Nations.[36] From this perspective, naming the Australia Group in CWC and NSG in NPT review and extension conferences represents back-door efforts to lend international credibility to these cartels.[37] Thus the dominant perception is that these regimes seek to justify their aims as *globally* legitimate, even though there is no global consensus on the criteria and mechanisms by which they determine to assist or deny technology to countries.

The NSG is seen as the culmination of the cartelization of the nuclear industry, which was begun by the Zangger Committee. When the NSG met in 1991, after a gap of thirteen years, and decided on a larger list of controlled dual-use items, the perception in India was that it used the two isolated cases of North Korea and Iraq to brand every other country a proliferator. "Recipient states had no say. Supplier states ensured that they provided whatever materials, equipment and technology on their own terms. Moreover, unlike the principles of conventional justice, here one is judged guilty unless proven innocent. . . . The entire trade regime has thus become discriminatory, being dictated according to the commercial interests and geopolitical strategies of the supplier states." [38] A prominent Indian analyst characterizes the WA as follows:

> The implications of WA for India are evident in its "no undercut" rule and from Russia's inclusion into it. India will therefore have to proceed prudently before signaling interest in importing a controlled item or technology. It also exposes the vulnerability to external pressures of India's conventional defense posture, heavily dependent on arms imports. . . . The biggest lesson the new regime can teach India is that it cannot secure its future with solely a conventional force posture. [39]

The end-user information required under the catch-all clause is considered by most knowledgeable Indians to be far more extensive and therefore more intrusive than that needed for non-proliferation reasons. The 93+2 program of the IAEA is seen as yet another step in the same direction: "It is clear that confidentiality of all research and development activity being carried out in a country is likely to be revealed through such intrusive measures." Similarly, "measures under the CTBT, regarding environmental monitoring and inspections are likely to have serious impact through inhibiting technology development in the NNWS." [40] The real aim of such a requirement, according to several Indian officials and analysts, is economic and technological espionage that can help predict the trajectory of economic and technological development in the recipient country. This would enable the suppliers to anticipate future demands and impose pre-emptive controls on the relevant technology. The aim of the regimes therefore is not the curtailment of WMD proliferation but that of curtailing commercial capability of the potential competitors from the developing world, at least from an Indian perspective.

Most knowledgeable Indians also see the actual operation of the cartels as being fraught with contradictions. The rights and obligations assigned to new adherents vary, based on their economic and strategic importance to the core groups (viz, the deals offered to Russia, Ukraine, Poland, Brazil, and China by the MTCR). "It is designed to allow the winners and the losers of the cold war to jointly tackle potential strategic threats from elsewhere in the world, although the western allies will continue to hold closely among themselves their most sensitive technology." [41] From this perspective, if the current members of these regimes are truly aiming for non-proliferation, then once states ratify global treaties such as CWC and FMCT there should be no prospective proliferation concerns. This would imply that the export control agreements outside of the treaties become redundant and should be dissolved. Current discussion on these agreements, however, does not even hint at such a possibility.

## IMPROVING INDO-US COOPERATION ON NONPROLIFERATION EXPORT CONTROLS

In order to improve cooperation between the two countries, one can consider strategies at several different levels. One of these would be to examine cases where a country with differing perspectives has been able to cooperate with the United States, such that even some violations on its part are acceptable to the latter. China fits the case and thus merits discussion in this context. Another approach would be to consider the success stories in Indo-US bilateral relations, and then generalize. We consider both these approaches in the following discussion.

In the past several years, China has taken a number of steps that have satisfied the United States regarding its commitment to non-proliferation. It has signed or ratified some of the major treaties, such as the NPT (1992), CWC (ratified 1997), and BTWC. It has cooperated with the United States in supporting non-proliferation goals in various regions of the world, including behind-the-scenes support to the solution of the North Korean problem in 1994. It has agreed to ban the export of any long-range surface-to-surface missiles, committed not to provide any assistance to unsafeguarded nuclear facilities in Pakistan (May 1996), and assured the United States that it was not going to engage in any new nuclear cooperation with Iran (October 1997). In addition, the PRC adopted new export control systems on chemical and nuclear items that appear more compatible with emerging multilateral standards.[42] China also became a member of the NPT Exporters (Zangger) Committee in October 1997.

These initiatives have convinced many in the US government that China now sees itself more as a major power with important responsibilities. "It is a member of the UNSC and P-5, and it has come to realize that one of the important attributes of great power status is to abide by international non-proliferation norms. So we think that China is more and more becoming a responsible player." [43] This also allows the US government to look at problematic Chinese exports in a more forgiving light as the PRC export control system moves toward completion. Thus, even though there is evidence that some Chinese entities exported missiles to Pakistan and components to Iran and Pakistan, the Clinton administration could claim that "China has not exported *complete ground-to-ground missiles* since making that agreement. We are concerned, however, that China continues to provide components and technology to both Pakistan and Iran." [44] By not acknowledging the transfer of complete missile systems, the administration could avoid determining the transfer as a violation of MTCR Category I guidelines, which would have triggered much harsher US trade sanctions. Further, the Clinton administration could discount the export of ring magnets to Pakistan as "relatively unsophisticated pieces of equipment. . . . The commercial value of the transfer was something less than $70,000 . . . and it became very believable that the Chinese entity involved was operating on its own without government oversight." [45]

A large deficit in bilateral trade, in China's favor, may be the primary explanation of such a lenient view of violations of the spirit of the agreements. However, one cannot deny that the steps China has taken to align its declared policy and procedures regarding non-proliferation have also blunted the criticism from the United States.

## RECOMMENDATIONS: SMALL STEPS TOWARD GRAND STRATEGIES

All the political fallout from the Indian nuclear tests is not yet apparent. The United States Congress, for example, quickly diluted the economic sanctions on India under pressure from farmers and other interest groups. As of September 1998 India has imposed unilateral moratorium on further testing and, according to media reports, its position on both the CTBT and the FMCT appears to be moving toward an eventual compromise. However, beyond the acrimony raised by the nuclear tests, even the significant divergence between the Indian and US-led multilateral export control systems reveals important possibilities for cooperation. Further, the success of the Indo-US defense cooperation agreement in the 1980s, for example, suggests that mission-oriented, clearly defined and delimited agreements might have a chance of making the policies of the two countries more compatible and complimentary.

## LESSONS FOR AN INDIAN GRAND STRATEGY

1. India needs to make its policy regarding opposition to WMD explicit and separate from its traditional support for disarmament. Unilateral declarations may not be impossible given that India already has an impeccable record of not supporting proliferation through exports.

2. The recent initiative of the Goverment of India (GOI) in compiling and circulating the laws governing dual-use exports is a welcome first step, as are its efforts under the EDI initiative. [46] This will indeed make its export control policy more transparent to those from whom it plans to import technology, and also help to bridge the perception gap vis-à–vis the international epistemic community.

3. Indian officials have been reluctant to engage with the United States, even at a semi-unofficial level such as visits to the Cooperative Monitoring Center (CMC) at Sandia National Laboratory. In contrast, the Chinese have avidly have reached out to the United States and significantly enhanced their institutional capabilities regarding arms controls in the Foreign Ministry and elsewhere.[47] Chinese self-confidence may have facilitated its openness to United States institutions. India may find this more difficult, given its relatively late and cautious entry into global markets.[48] Nonetheless, emulating the Chinese approach may have merit for India.

4. Over and above these specific issues, the most obvious lesson is that India needs to continue the economic reforms and make itself more attractive for foreign investment. This would help in the creation of transnational networks, both economic and political, that would be willing to devote time and energy to making the case for greater appreciation for Indian export restraints and potential Indian utility to the United States and to its European allies.

## LESSONS FOR THE UNITED STATES FROM THE CHINESE CASE

1. Prospects for cooperation improved as Chinese domestic commercial interests increased their demands for US technology, especially in the nuclear arena.

2. Prospects for cooperation improved as Chinese officials sought to enhance their international image in light of several embarrassing incidents, such as the ring magnet exports to Pakistan and chemical exports to Iran. Deregulation and privatization meant that China could not rely on its old system of export controls to avoid such incidents.

## SMALL STEPS FOR THE UNITED STATES

1. The United States could encourage commercial interests in India to demonstrate to the Indian government the benefits that could emerge from greater and more reliable access to US technology. The United States can help bring more players, especially from industry, into the process.

2. Deregulation and privatization in India may undoubtedly lead to the export from India of items of proliferation concern. The US government can prepare a joint action plan and devote some effort to forge a pre-emptive strategy to stop such potential exports. The crisis-oriented attention from the United States thus far has contributed to Indian distrust, so the United States should consider an alternative approach.

3. Sanctions have slowed Indian WMD programs, but they have increased Indian defiance and secrecy. Not only has the United States proven willing to try more cooperative strategies with North Korea and China, its own retreat on sanctions undermines US credibility on the use or threat of sanctions. Trying to marginalize India, or treat the issue as closed with the imposition of sanctions, undermines the potential for Indian cooperation on a host of non-proliferation concerns in addition to export controls, such as the CTBT and the FMCT

4. The United States may be able to increase the security and economic incentives for Indian cooperation on non-proliferation export controls by offering access to technology directly or through international collaborative projects. While the nuclear tests reinforce the need to approach this cooperation on an incremental basis with explicit and measured *quid pro quos*, they do not preclude their potential value. Investment in the Indian nuclear power sector, for example, might create long-term incentives that bind India more closely to the non-proliferation regimes.

5. Clearly, the nuclear tests have delayed opportunities for a high-level summit that could showcase such agreements. No US leader can appear to reward India for its decision to conduct its nuclear tests. Nonetheless, both India and the United States need to seek a means to demonstrate their *mutual* commitment to solve a wider range of non-proliferation issues beyond the topic of nuclear testing.

## SMALL STEPS FOR INDIA

1. The Indian government should consider making a more open explication of the actual processes, such as criteria for approval of licenses, mechanisms for pre- and post-shipment checks, and information about actual violations, violators, and penalties. This would help generate confidence that India has an effective export control system, not just a compilation of laws and regulations.

2. Even with its openness, the conglomerate character of the Indian industrial infrastructure constrains post-shipment verification procedures. These work against the interests of both exporters and importers through delays in the US export control process. Even before the tests, this problem attracted the interest of Congress. Improved cooperation, on the basis of mutual respect of sovereign rights, could forestall a dramatic increase in US restrictive trade practices directed against India. Although the Indian concept of "dual sovereignty" permits close enforcement cooperation in cases where potential violations of both Indian and foreign law occur, this narrows the scope for cooperation considerably as long as significant incompatibility exists between Indian rules and US regulations.

4. India could declare its intent to abide by some of the technology control regimes, such as the Australia Group and the Zangger Committee. India already controls

exports of most of these items of concern, which should minimize the domestic political and legal ramifications. Continued refusal to publicly acknowledge such compatibility of laws demonstrates to the international community at large that Indian ideology and pride continue to outweigh policy pragmatism and Indian interest in non-proliferation.

5. The Indian government might consider increasing the overlap between the Australia Group list of biological items and the Indian schedules of animal and human pathogens and plant pests. Although India controls the export of a large number of bacterial, parasitic, fungal, viral, and other agents, its schedules do not always match those of the Australia Group. India actually controls a vastly larger number of biological agents than are on the Australia Group lists, so it seems unclear as to why its schedule does not include all such items.[49]

6. The Indian government might also improve the correspondence between the list of forty "special materials, equipment and technologies," in Public Notice No. 68 (PN-68)/92-97 of March 31, 1995 and the control lists associated with the NSG, the MTCR, and the WA.[50] At the very least, discussion of the rationale for the structure and detail of the lists should create opportunities for cooperation and improved conditions for trade regarding some items. Initiation of dialogue aimed at explaining the basis of, if not harmonizing, the differences in these areas would go a long way in strengthening the case of those who argue for greater cooperation between India and the United States.

The recent nuclear tests inhibited the opportunities for improving Indo-US cooperation on a wide range of proliferation issues in the short-term. The long-term impact of the tests, however, may bear a more propitious theme if non-proliferation advocates in both countries use them wisely. In the case of the United States, the tests may help the growing India lobby in the Congress (buttressed by a greater involvement of Americans of Indian origin) direct more US government attention toward India. The earlier policy of neglect had played into the hands of the nuclear hawks in India, to the detriment of broader non-proliferation concerns.

At the same time, Indian advocates of non-proliferation might use the tests to engender a sustained public debate on proliferation, nuclear or otherwise, and Indian national security and welfare. Major political changes inside India, along with other factors, pushed India to declare itself a nuclear weapon state. A focused public debate on the costs and benefits of modifying the Indian posture toward export control regimes is urgently required. This might prevent India's growing marginalization from multilateral efforts that are likely to shape the rules governing technology transfers in the next century, especially as they appear to be moving steadily toward nearly global endorsement.

## TABLE 1

### INDIAN AND US STATUS REGARDING KEY
### NON-PROLIFERATION TREATIES, 1996

| Treaty or Convention | India | US |
|---|---|---|
| Geneva Protocol of 1925 | Acceded (1930) | Ratified (1975) |
| Antarctic Treaty | Acceded (1983) | Ratified (1960) |
| Limited Test Ban Treaty | Ratified (1963) | Ratified (1963) |
| Outer Space Treaty | Ratified (1982) | Ratified (1967) |
| Non-proliferation Treaty | Non-signatory | Ratified (1970) |
| Seabed Arms Control Treaty | Acceded (1973) | Ratified (1972) |
| Biological Weapons Convention | Ratified (1974) | Ratified (1975) |
| Comprehensive Test Ban Treaty | Non-signatory | Signed (1997), not ratified |
| Nuclear Material Convention | Non-signatory | Ratified (1982) |
| Chemical Weapons Convention | Ratified (1996) | Ratified (1997) |

Source: US Arms Control and Disarmament Agency, *Arms Control and Disarmament Agreements: Texts and Histories of the Negotiations* (Washington, DC: USGPO, 1997).

## TABLE 2

### US DUAL-USE EXPORT LICENSING TO INDIA AND
### THE WORLD, FY 1996–97

| Destination | Year | Licenses Processed | Approved | Denied | Returned without Action | Average Processing Time | Value (Millions of US$) |
|---|---|---|---|---|---|---|---|
| World | 1998* | 4,904 | 4,020 | 130 | 745 | 35 | NA |
| | 1997 | 10,557 | 8,717 | 318 | 1,522 | 32 (34) | NA |
| | 1996 | 8,695 | 7,102 | 256 | 1,337 | 33 (47)[51] | NA |
| India | 1998* | 394 | 219 | 83 | 92 | 46 | NA |
| | 1997 | 1,748 | 1,047 | 103 | 598 | 44 | NA |
| | 1996 | 375 | 188 | 76 | 111 | NA | 52.3 |

* Data covers only January through June 1998.

Source: Data provided by the US Department of Commerce; also see US Department of Commerce, Bureau of Export Administration, *Export Administration Annual Report 1996 and 1997 Report on Foreign Policy Export Controls* (Washington, DC: USGPO, 1997), pp. 4–5; and US Department of Commerce, Bureau of Export Administration, *Export Administration Annual Report 1997 and 1998 Report on Foreign Policy Export Controls* (posted March 4, 1998 on the BXA web page), pp. II-13-4. www.bxa.doc.gov/press/98/contents.htm

## TABLE 3

### ASSESSING THE COMPATIBILITY OF THE NONPROLIFERATION EXPORT CONTROL SYSTEMS OF INDIA, JAPAN AND THE US, 1998 (RAW/WEIGHTED SCORE)

| Element | India | Japan | US |
|---|---|---|---|
| Licensing and Legal Framework (6/7.47) | 5 / 6.20 | 6 / 7.47 | 5 / 6.22 |
| Control Lists (3/6.34) | 2.5 / 5.26 | 3 / 6.34 | 3 / 6.34 |
| Regime Adherence (12/3.2) | 0 / 0 | 12 / 3.2 | 12 / 3.2 |
| Catch-all Controls (3/1.2) | 0 / 0 | 3 / 1.2 | 3 / 1.2 |
| Training (9/3.87) | 6.0 / 2.59 | 8.5 / 3.87 | 9 / 3.87 |
| Bureaucratic Process (6/3.47) | 6.0 / 3.47 | 5.5 / 3.18 | 6 / 3.47 |
| Customs Authority (6/6.6) | 5 / 5.48 | 6 / 6.6 | 6 / 6.6 |
| Verification (9/3.67) | 6 / 2.46 | 8.5 / 3.46 | 8.5 / 3.46 |
| Penalties (6/1.8) | 4.5 / 1.35 | 6 / 1.8 | 6 / 1.8 |
| Information Sharing (12/4.2) | 8.5 / 2.99 | 12 / 4.2 | 12 / 4.2 |
| *Totals (72/41.82)* | 43.5 / 29.80 | 70.5 / 41.11 | 70.5 / 40.36 |
| *Percent of Total Score (100/100)* | 60 / 71 | 98 / 98 | 98 / 96 |

## NOTES

1   Brahma Chellaney, "The Implications of the Wassenaar Group," in Deepa Ollapally and S. Rajagopal, eds., *Nuclear Cooperation: Challenges and Prospects* (Bangalore: National Institute of Advanced Studies, 1997).

2   Government of India press release, May 11, 1998.

3   The Bhabha Atomic Research Center (BARC), Trombay; the Bharat Electronics Limited (BEL) in Bangalore and Hyderabad, with a general warning for any BEL affiliate in India; the Indian Rare Earths, Limited; and the Indira Gandhi Center for Atomic Research, Kalpakkam.

4   United States Department of Commerce, Bureau of Export Administration, "US Sanctions on the Export of Dual-Use Goods to India and Pakistan," June 22, 1998, http://www.bxa.doc.gov/ind-pak.htm. The Bureau of Export Administration (BXA), moreover, promised to produce a new list of Indian entities of proliferation concern. Under the Enhanced Proliferation Control Initiative (EPCI), Commerce would deny any license application of any EAR item to these entities. BXA also intended to prepare a list of Indian government entities involved in military activities for which any application to export or re-export an item controlled under the EAR (except the general-purpose items under EAR 99) that the BXA would review with a presumption of denial. The list appeared in November 1998.

5   See, for example, Brahma Chellaney, "An Indian Critique of US Export Controls," *Orbis*, summer 1994, pp. 439–56.

6    Dov S. Zakheim, "Developing a US-India Security Relationship," in Bharat Karnad, ed., *Future Imperiled: India's Security in the 1990s and Beyond*. (Delhi: Viking Press, 1994), p. 216.

7    "Country Focus: India," *Export Control News*, vol. 1, no. 5 (September 28, 1987), pp. 14–15.

8    "Country Focus: India, India Adopts Import Certificate Procedure," *Export Control News*, vol. 2, no. 6 (July 11, 1988).

9    Zakheim, "Developing a US-India Security Relationship," p. 217.

10   Interviews, Arms Control and Disarmament Agency and Department of State, June 1998.

11   "$450,000 EPCI Violation," *The Export Practitioner*, vol. 11, no. 8 (August 1997).

12   See for instance, the response of the CEO of IBM to Gary Milhollin's provocative article in the *Washington Post*, June 1998.

13   The recent National Defense Authorization Acts reversed this trend for some high-performance computers by bringing Congress directly into the licensing process for "tier three" countries, including India. This also gave the Indian government less incentive to cooperate, as it already gained access to new technologies while it continued to reap the security benefits of the non-proliferation arrangements that imposes limits on Pakistan, China, and other potential adversaries.

15   See the Office of the Secretary of Defense, *Proliferation: Threat and Response* (Washington, DC: USGPO, November 1997), p. 15; Director of Central Intelligence, *The Acquisition of Technology Relating to Weapons of Mass Destruction and Advanced Conventional Munitions*, June 1997; and US Senate, Committee on Governmental Affairs, Subcommittee on International Security, Proliferation, and Federal Services, *The Proliferation Primer*, Majority Report, January 1998.

15   This section is based on Seema Gahlaut, "India's Export Control Policy: A Brief Introduction," occasional paper, Center for International Trade and Security, University of Georgia, March 1998.

16   The last-named act is commonly referred to as the FTDR Act, and covers things not regulated by any other Act. *Briefing Notes on the System of Control over Exports from India*, Government of India, January 1998. [Henceforth Briefing Notes, 1998].

17   All four are publications of the Ministry of Commerce, Government of India.

18   The government agencies that routinely participate in this committee include the following: the Department of Atomic Energy (DAE), Ministry of External Affairs (MEA), Ministry of Commerce (MOC) and its subsidiary, the Directorate General of Foreign Trade (DGFT), Ministry of Defense (MOD) and its subsidiary, the Defense Research and Development Organization (DRDO), and the Ministry of Finance (MF). Other agencies such as the Department of Electronics, the Prime Minister's Office (PMO), Department of Space, Department of Science and Technology, and the Department of Industrial Policy and Promotion (Technical) are also consulted from time to time.

19   For instance, applications regarding atomic materials are sent to the DAE, those regarding materials under Public Notice 68 to the DRDO, and those involving trade with "countries of concern" may be sent to the MEA and the PMO.

20   This is based on DAE review of the end-user information supplied by the exporting agency/company and on their track-record.

21   Reports of such interdictions are routinely filed with the IAEA.

22   Telephone interview, October 1997.

23   Telephone interview, October 1997.

24   Appendix XI A, *Handbook of Procedures 1992*.

25   Both the Code of Criminal Procedure (Cr.P.C.), 1973, and civil laws (Indian Penal Code,

or I.P.C.) may apply, as also the Conservation of Foreign Exchange and Prevention of Smuggling Activities (COFEPOSA) Act, 1974.

26  Highlights of the EXIM Policy, 1997–2002, from www.nic.in/eximpol/HIGHLT.HTM.

27  According to some officials at the DGFT and the DAE, there are regular seminars and training sessions for representatives of the private industry that collaborate on DAE projects. These are designed to teach them about export controls on nuclear and nuclear-related dual-use goods. But no official documentation about the nature and scope of this training is available so far.

28  See Cassady Craft and Suzette Grillot with Liam Anderson, Michael Beck, Chris Behan, Scott Jones, and Keith Wolfe, "Tools and Methods for Measuring and Comparing Nonproliferation Export Controls," occasional paper, Center for International Trade and Security, University of Georgia, October 1996.

29  Ibid., p. 9.

30  Some senior officials of the DRDO, for instance, mentioned that they themselves would like to know exactly how one can export weapons and technology from India. This lack of knowledge of the specifics of national *export* control laws appeared to be a common factor among most interviewees until late 1997. This may have changed following dissemination via the Internet.

31  Preface to the Briefing Notes 1998.

32  This is in fact reflected in the score on the element entitled "Regime Adherence" (Table 3).

33  See the chapter by Aabha Dixit in this volume.

34  R. Chidambaram & V. Ashok, "Embargo Regimes and Impact," in Deepa Ollapally and S. Rajagopal, eds., *Nuclear Cooperation: Challenges & Prospects* (Bangalore: National Institute of Advanced Studies, 1997); S. Balachandran, "Sovereignty at Bay: The Political and Military Utility of Nuclear Weapons in the Post-Cold War Eera," in Francine R. Frankel, ed., *Bridging the Nonproliferation Divide: The United States and India* (New York: University Park of America, 1995); and Brahma Chellaney, "An Indian Critique of U.S. Export Controls," *Orbis,* summer 1994.

35  K Kasturirangan, "Globalization and Technology Sharing," in Ollapally and Rajagopal.

36  Chellaney, "The Implications of the Wassenaar Group."

38  Ibid.

39  Chidambaram and Ashok, "Embargo Regions and Impact" op cit.

39  Chellaney, 'The Implications of the Wassenaar Group."

40  Ibid.

41  Ibid.

42  Richard T. Cupitt and Yuzo Murayama, "Nonproliferation Export Controls and the People's Republic of China—1998," CITS/UGA occasional paper (forthcoming).

43  Robert Einhorn, deputy assistant secretary of state for nonproliferation, in "China and Nonproliferation: Interview with Senior US Official," *Disarmament Diplomacy,* Issue No. 22, January 1998.

44  Ibid., emphasis added.

45  Ibid.

46  *Briefing Paper*, January 1998.

47  Discussed in Ed Fei's India Trip Report, US Department of Energy, March 16–22, 1998.

48  It may be further complicated by the fact that despite its immense manpower, natural resources, and an established legal and contractual system, India's share in the global economy still remains insignificant.

49  A preliminary review of the list of plant pathogens for the export controls core list of the

Australia Group with the plant pests of the "Rules for the Manufacture, Use, Import, Export and Storage of Hazardous Micro Organisms Genetically Engineered Organisms or Cells" by India's Ministry of Environment and Forests, includes versions of *Xanthomonas* bacteria, Dothidiaceae, Pucciniaceae and Monillaceae fungi, but not *Xylella fastidiosa* (bacteria), *Pyricularia grisea/oryzae* (fungi), *Colletotrichum kahawae* (fungi), or *Cochliobolus miyabeanus* (fungi).

50   Item 30 in the public notice, for example, indicates that exporters need a license from the director general of foreign trade for "Encrypted telemetry systems, equipment and software therefor." In contrast, Category 5, Part 2, "Information Security," of the Wassenaar Dual-Use List requires three pages to denote its various controls on encryption and encryption-related items.

51   Average processing time for licenses that required referral to other agencies was forty-seven days, but this dropped to thirty days after the implementation of Executive Order 12981. Among other changes, the order imposed new time limits on license processing.

Part III

THE REGIONAL CONTEXT

# 9

# India-US Foreign Policy Concerns: Cooperation and Conflict

## Kanti Bajpai

India-US relations are entering a Copernican phase. During the Cold War, the conflict of two alliance systems was at the center of world politics. This made for a relatively simple and in some ways orderly strategic universe. After the Cold War, the United States and India are discovering that their dealings with each other are more complex than they had been in the previous fifty years. The certainties of the Cold War are gone, and neither side quite knows how to approach the other. There is a supposition that the two countries should be friendlier and should cooperate, but why and how?

This chapter attempts to chart the factors that impeded cooperation in the past, those that are encouraging the United States and India to come closer together in the present, and key hurdles to cooperation in the near- and longer-term future. In the wake of the Indian nuclear tests of May 1998, revisiting India-US relations acquires even greater significance. The key question is: What is the future of the relationship after the tests, with India insisting that it will build a full-fledged nuclear arsenal and with the United States determined to limit further proliferation in South Asia? My answer, on balance, is an optimistic one. India and the United States can surmount the political storm raised by the Indian and Pakistani tests. This is evidenced by the high-level, fast-paced talks between Jaswant Singh, the special envoy of the prime minister of India, and Strobe Talbott, the US deputy secretary of state.

My overview of India-US relations is organized in three sections. The first section deals briefly with why India-US relations were marked by discord rather than collaboration during the Cold War and why the divide between the two countries narrowed after the late 1980s. The second section then goes on to suggest that convergence on a series of geopolitical, economic, and social and political concerns are laying the basis for various programs of long-term cooperation. The third section lists six hurdles to cooperation and particularly the difficulties raised by the nuclear tests of May 1998. One key conclusion here is that the divide on non-proliferation may not be insuperable, although surmounting it will not be easy given the key role of domestic politics in both countries.

On balance, the essay concludes, common geo-political, economic, and social and political interests are advancing a cooperative agenda, which the differences over nuclear proliferation may not be able to halt. Indeed, both sides appear to have concluded that the conflict over proliferation cannot be left to a standoff or to standoffishness. Non-proliferation is a common interest. Historically, the two countries have supported different approaches to that common goal. Today, they have an interest in narrowing their differences as far and as quickly as possible.

## COLD WAR DISCORD

As the world's largest democracies, as pluralist societies, as market economies, and—dare one say it—as anti-Communist countries, the interests and approaches of India and the United States should have converged for most of the Cold War. Yet contention usually bested convergence. Why?

Three types of explanations are usually offered. The first type stresses a structural conflict at the strategic level.[1] In this view, India and the United States were ineluctably pitted against each other because of their post-1945 strategic concerns and approaches. The United States was primarily concerned about Communism as a threat, and containment of the Soviet Union and the worldwide search for allies was its response. This produced a Manichean world with little place for the strategic concerns of others or for alternative responses to the threat of Communism. India, on the other hand, while not unmindful of the dangers represented by Communism, was primarily worried about regional stability and preventing the intrusion of outside powers into local matters. Washington, in search of friends, forged an alliance with Pakistan; India, in search of balance, turned to the Soviet Union. While these alignments ebbed and flowed somewhat, over the years a basic pattern was maintained, the major exception being a convergence against China during India's border war in 1962, which momentarily presaged a strategic entente.

The second type of explanation stresses deep-seated, if not always conscious and open, antipathy, at the level of economic and cultural values, that hindered communication and set limits to the amount of mutual sympathy and accommodation.[2] Economically, the United States, as a capitalist country, insisted on economic liberalism as the proper path to economic development. India, by contrast, relied on market forces modified by planning and protectionism for its advance. The United States tended to see India's economy as backward and impenetrable, and India viewed the United States as economically predatory and inflexible. Culturally, the distance between the two, leavened by ignorance, was probably more serious. Americans found India's high culture confounding—full of abstruse "spiritual" formulations —and were bemused by or uninterested in its popular culture. Indians presumed that the United States had no high culture and were both fascinated and repelled by its popular culture. At the level of everyday engagement, Americans found Indians languid and verbose. Indians, for their part, perceived Americans as monomaniacal and shallow. Each saw the other as preachy and hypocritical.

The third type of explanation is a more political one. In this view, India-US conflict arose from the effect of internal, institutional, and personal factors in the decision-making processes of both countries. Thus, various analyses of US decision making argue that a combination of factors produced policies inimical to India: the US Congress remained unsympathetic to India; elements of the State Department and more generally the Pentagon were suspicious of India's relations with the Soviets; (or China); and various presidents and secretaries of state (Truman, Johnson, Nixon; Acheson, Rusk, Dulles, Kissinger) were indifferent, ambivalent, or hostile to India or Indian leaders (Nehru, Indira Gandhi, Krishna Menon).[3] In addition, US public opinion showed no great interest in or knowledge of India when it did not actually follow its leaders and officials in actively disliking India.[4]

On the Indian side, similar factors were operative.[5] Most Indian parliamentarians vied with each other in displaying their disdain for the United States. Suspicion of the United States was particularly deep-rooted in the Congress Party as well as the Socialist and Communist Parties. The Indian bureaucracy, with the exception of those in Economic Affairs or Commerce, was reflexively suspicious of US intentions. Indian leaders, particularly Jawaharlal Nehru and Indira Gandhi, and their close advisors seldom hid their impatience with American ways. Public opinion in India was often hostile to the United States, but in any case it generally evinced a distinct preference for the Soviet Union.

With the end of the Cold War, things have changed. The old strategic divide between the two countries is over. For the United States, the tilt to Pakistan is no longer required. Indeed, a tilt toward India is now possible, perhaps even necessary. India is the bigger country and also a possible long-term ally or balance against Muslim fundamentalism, China, and perhaps even a re-militarized Japan in the long run. On the Indian side, there is a recognition that the United States is the sole superpower for the foreseeable future and that an American presence in Asia could be a stabilizing factor.

Economically, India's reforms promise to converge with US preferences (even though Americans see the pace of change as too slow and not unambiguously market-oriented), and the country promises to be a huge market for US exports and investments. Culturally, Indian immigrants are helping bring Indian culture, high and popular, to US cities and towns. At the same time, visiting NRIs, tourists, and satellite television broadcasts are transmitting and naturalizing American culture in India, particularly among the new middle class, which, unlike its older counterpart, is not as uneasy with or apologetic about its interest in Western goods and popular culture.

At the political level, too, there have been changes. India is better received in the US Congress (though the reception could be yet better), and reflexive anti-Americanism in the Indian Parliament is probably at its lowest. In part as a result of the end of the Cold War, Indian and US officials have softened their views about each other's external policies. Furthermore, no one seriously contends that leaders and officials in India and the United States are antagonistic to each other at a personal level.[6]

The Cold War hurdles have therefore been substantially overcome. However, it is one thing to overcome hurdles and another to run a smooth race together. Why should the United States and India positively cooperate in the new world? Is there a mix of interests, concerns, motives, and forces and that can be expected to push the two powers to collaborate in substantial ways? Do these outweigh the effects of India's nuclear tests of May 1998 and the resultant US sanctions against India?

## THE PUSH TO COOPERATE: CONVERGENT INTERESTS

With the impediments of the Cold War removed or attenuated, there are a number of geo-strategic, economic, and social and political factors that are pushing India and the United States in the direction of a cooperative engagement. While cooperation is by no means inevitable, the push factors are likely to grow in importance in the years to come. By cooperation I do not mean harmony and partnership, but a systematic, sustained, and cordial attempt on the part of the two governments to communicate, persuade, and coordinate in a variety of issue areas.

### Geo-strategic Interests

Geo-strategically, the first and foremost common concern is the stability of Asia, which is beset by a continent-wide security dilemma. Asia is the largest continent on earth and has the largest population. It is inhabited by some of the most dynamic economies and the greatest military powers on earth. At the heart of Asia is China. The Middle Kingdom abuts virtually every region of Asia. It has twenty-one neighbors, more than any other country in the world. These neighbors include Burma, India, Indonesia, Japan, Pakistan, Russia, South Korea (which, when it is united with North Korea, will be an even greater power), Taiwan, and Vietnam. These are powers of some rank, in economic, military and demographic terms. China's size and economic dynamism over the past fifteen years cast a shadow over the continent. To all its neighbors, China appears like a behemoth. At the same time, surrounded by twenty-one neighbors, large and small, China perceives itself in a complex and potentially dangerous strategic environment. In addition, China has quarrels over territory and resources with many of its neighbors. Some of these have been more or less satisfactorily disposed of, while others remain contentious. Complicating

China's relationship with its neighbors are its internal vulnerabilities, particularly its regional and ethnic discontent: Beijing fears that its neighbors may well attempt to take advantage of internal weakness and divisions. In short, with China at the center, Asia confronts a gigantic security dilemma. As China builds up its defensive capabilities, it alarms the rest of Asia. As the rest of the continent arms itself, China's fear of its neighbors grows. This is a potentially explosive geo-strategic environment. If it were to explode into war in any of its theaters (East Asia, Southeast Asia, South Asia, central Asia), the violence could spread to other parts of the continent. In any case, the disruption of an economic, trading, and financial zone of this size would have consequences far beyond the immediate zone or even Asia as a whole. India and the United States have a vital interest, therefore, in the stability of Asia at a time of considerable change.

India and the United States have a second geo-strategic concern in common. Both countries would like to ensure the security of commercial and naval traffic in the Indian Ocean. A derivative concern is that the Indian Ocean region should have a naval balance of power, which prevents anyone from dominating its waters. The Indian Ocean connects Southeast and East Asia as well as Australia, New Zealand, and the South Pacific with Africa and, more important, with the Gulf and Middle East. India, with its sensitivity to sea-borne threats to its national security (the European colonial powers came from the sea), its growing stakes in international trade, and its dependence on Gulf oil, sees the security of the Indian Ocean as vital. The United States, with its naval facilities in Diego Garcia, its economic stakes throughout the littoral and Southeast and East Asia, and its interest in Gulf oil, has long held the Indian Ocean to be a key maritime theater.

This brings us to another geo-strategic interest India and the United States have in common, whether or not they will acknowledge it, namely, the unhindered supply of oil from the Gulf. India depends heavily on Gulf oil: up to one-third of its oil needs comes from the region. This dependence may well grow as the Indian economy takes off. The United States is not nearly so dependent on Gulf oil, but it has two concerns. First, key allies such as Japan and some Western European countries are heavily dependent on Gulf oil. Their economic well-being and stability are part of an extended security envelope that the United States feels responsible for. Second, the United States has an interest in maintaining a global oil regime that is regulated by market forces. Both countries want to prevent a situation where local conflict—domestic or regional—leads to an interruption of oil supplies or an "artificial" hike in oil prices.

Last but not least, India and the United States have a common geo-strategic concern in the stability of South Asia. For India, the need for regional stability is at one level obvious enough. Stability close to home is the basis for economic development, internal social and political order, and peace. It is also important for India for reasons of strategic denial. A stable South Asia will keep meddlesome external powers out of regional affairs. Beyond this, stability in South Asia frees India to pursue goals in other regions. In particular, India has diplomatic, economic, and security interests in the Gulf, Central Asia, and Pacific Asia. The importance of the Gujral Doctrine is not just the promise of development, order, and peace in South Asia, but also strategic "release" from the region. An India that is seen as generous to its smaller neighbors and can act accommodatingly is an attractive partner for those outside South Asia who might want to bring India into their locales; on the other hand, an India that is tied down by regional preoccupations and appears as a bully is a liability, if not a threat.

The United States also has an interest in promoting stability in South Asia, although one that is not altogether obvious. Some would argue that the region has been and will continue to be of minor strategic importance to Washington and that South Asia's stability or instability is of little or no moment. The one obvious, perhaps paramount, interest in South Asia is non-proliferation. Stability between India and Pakistan clearly will affect their nuclear choices. Before the tests of May 1998, the United States had hoped that greater stability in the region would reduce the incentive to go overtly nuclear and to use nuclear weapons in a military conflict. After the tests, Washington still has an interest in promoting stability in order to slow down and eventually cap India's and Pakistan's nuclear breakout and to prevent the use of nuclear weapons in South Asia. Beyond this, it could be argued, Washington has few stakes in the region. However, US interest in South Asian stability goes further. War, inter-state tensions, and internal political disarray could lead to regional collapse. A "failed" South Asia, with its more than one billion people, would be a humanitarian catastrophe. No major power could stand aloof from such a disaster, if only because the ripple effects would be felt in neighboring countries and nearby regions—Afghanistan, Burma, China, the Gulf, and Southeast Asia—in which they have vital stakes.

## ECONOMIC INTERESTS

India and the United States are being pushed to cooperate as a function of economic concerns. India needs trade, investment, and technology, and the United States is a major source of all three. The United States is India's largest trading partner, its biggest investor, and its biggest provider of advanced technology. For the United States, India is a big emerging market—with the accent on emerging. That is, India is a huge potential market for US business, although as things stand, trade with India is minuscule as a proportion of total US trade. The amount of US foreign direct investment in India is also small relative to overall US FDI. Technology transfers to India, too, are limited. However, all three transactions are expected to increase as India's economy opens up and a sustained growth rate is achieved. US interest in India economically, therefore, is for the long term. In a world that will be increasingly competitive, the United States is looking to establish a presence in markets such as India in the expectation of future returns. Given that India's population is likely to reach 1.5 billion sometime in the next century, future returns from areas such as power and infrastructure alone would be enormous.

India and the United States also share a concern over the sustainability of economic growth and development. A number of global ecological problems confront them, but perhaps the most serious is the prospect of global warming. The buildup of chlorofluorocarbons (CFCs) has been identified as one of the factors contributing to a warming of the atmosphere. This could lead to the rise of ocean levels, the submergence of vast areas of coastal land, and the massive displacement of populations as a result. The economic losses incurred plus the social tensions engendered by population movements will occur on a global scale. India and the United States will be affected directly and indirectly.

Global warming is by no means the only ecological problem both countries must take account of. There are other forms of air pollution, chemical and oil spills in international waterways and coastlines, the attendant damage to sea life, the destruction of tropical rain forests, and, as we have seen most recently in Indonesia, the spread of hazardous smoke from forest fires. All these are problems that no country, however powerful or isolationist, can control without the cooperation of other major actors. India and the United States, as large consuming economies, will contribute a high proportion of pollutants. They will be directly and indirectly affected by the actions and choices of others in controlling ecological threats, and they will have to bear much of the responsibility—along with the other major economies—of managing the ecological future of the planet. Some of these problems already demand collaboration, while others are for the long term, but the two countries must evolve structures for cooperation, bilaterally and multilaterally, which will undergird future co-action.

### Social and Political Interests

Geo-strategic and economic interests are the primary factors for India-US cooperation. In addition, there is a social and political basis for cooperation. Socially, both countries face a number of common challenges. These include drug trafficking, disease and epidemic control, and terrorism. Politically, the rising power and influence of the non-resident Indian community will encourage a more cooperative mind-set between the two governments.

The narcotics trade is a transaction in which India and the United States play different roles.[7] India serves as a production base and also a transit point in a regional and global network of drug flows. The United States, on the other hand, is the primary destination for drugs. Control of drug trafficking entails restricting supply as well as reducing demand. Since demand calls forth supply and supply creates demand, as it were, the two countries can only tackle the drug menace by acting in concert.

The spread of infectious diseases is another key area of common social concern. Given the increasing rapidity and volume of modern transportation and travel, disease and epidemic vectors will potentially connect India and the United States.

AIDS, tuberculosis, plagues, dengue fever, strains of typhoid and cholera, and various drug-resistant bacteria all could be exchanged between India and the United
States. Tracking disease and epidemic vectors, intervening to control outbreaks, and
developing treatment systems for diseases and epidemics will require conjoint
actions on the part of the governments and medical establishments of both countries.
While there are multilateral institutions such as the World Health Organization
(WHO) that deal with these problems on a more or less continuous basis, the challenges ahead may well exceed the capacity of the WHO. Bilateral coordination will
therefore also be required.

. Combating terrorism is another challenge for both India and the United States.[8]
As large, socially plural countries, both are prone to ethnic, religious, and ideological
discontent. Despite the protections of democracy, and paradoxically because of the
space afforded by democracy, some disaffected groups might use violence to express
their grievances. Both countries will also be targeted by foreign terrorists who dis-
like and fear their external policies. Given the transnationalization of terrorist
groups in terms of their political support, funding, armaments, and strategies and
tactics, counter-terrorism must be an international venture.

Islamic groups may target India and the United States. The Mumbai blasts in the
wake of the Babri Masjid demolition and, most recently, the bomb explosions in
Coimbatore during the 1998 general elections suggest that some disaffected Muslim
groups in India may take to terrorist acts. These groups may already have developed
links to transnational Islamic groups who are committed to the use of violence for
political ends. US authorities fear attacks on their diplomatic missions and on targets
within the continental United States. The World Trade Center explosion in New
York was the most dramatic instance of the latter. While the threat of Muslim terrorist violence has been vastly exaggerated, there is evidence of Islamic countries and
groups combining to perpetrate violence. India and the United States have a common interest, therefore, in tracking the activities of various countries and groups, in
exchanging intelligence information, and in mounting a diplomatic campaign
against those who aid and abet terrorist organizations.

Throughout the 1980s and 1990s, India has dealt with violence supported not just
by foreign governments but also by people of Indian/South Asian origin who have
migrated to, or found asylum in, primarily Western countries, including the United
States. Thus, Sikhs in Canada, the United Kingdom, and the United States funded
and sometimes were directly involved in the militancy in the Punjab. Tamils abroad
have remitted funds to the Liberation Tigers of Tamil Eelam (LTTE). Kashmiris in
the United States and elsewhere have supported the cause of the militancy in the
Kashmir Valley. In the case of Kashmir, non-Indian Muslims too have supported
various insurgent groups fighting the Indian government.

In the end, the activities of these expatriate groups in the United States and other
countries may affect the security of the hosts as well. For instance, there is evidence
that Tamil militants extorted money from expatriates of their own community in

Europe. These expatriates are citizens or legal residents, and host governments are bound to protect them. Militants operating in the West may well take to organized criminal activities to support their cause—narcotics, prostitution, gambling, protection rackets—and the whole gamut of "normal" criminal activity may pay better than extortion in small expatriate communities. The host countries' security may be affected in other ways. Terrorist and militant groups often develop tactical links among themselves. Thus, strategies, tactics, materials, and safe havens may come to be shared. While the survivalist, white supremacist, and right-wing anti-government groups in the United States are xenophobic for the most part, they could set racial and cultural prejudice aside temporarily to ally themselves with foreigners against the US government.

India and the United States are also being edged toward cooperation as a function of the political role of the non-resident Indian (NRI) community in the United States. The NRI community in the United States is well over a million strong. On a per capita basis, it is estimated to be perhaps the richest ethnic or immigrant community. It is a community with a high proportion of professionals and of educated, urban, and middle- and upper-middle-class migrants who maintain links with elite Indians. The profile of the average Indian immigrant to the United States is therefore rather different from that of those living in Australia, Britain, and Canada. One effect of this is the growing involvement of the Indian community in US politics. The formation of an India caucus in the US Congress reflects this change.

The NRI community also exerts political influence in India. Given its socio-economic profile, it is perhaps not surprising that a significant or at least vocal section supports the Bharatiya Janata Party (BJP). The BJP has reputedly received hefty donations from this community, as have other elements of the Hindutva coalition—the RSS and the VHP in particular. The influence of the NRIs in India is a function not only of their actual and potential economic clout; it also rests on a network of intimate family links with the Indian elite. There must be few Indian politicians and officials who do not have close relatives studying and working in the United States. Thus, the political class in India is linked to the NRI community in the United States as perhaps to no other NRI community.

The economic, social, and political influence of the NRI community having expanded in both countries, there is a new and perhaps more enduring basis for India-US cooperation. It is in the interest of this community that the two countries maintain amicable relations, and it is likely that NRIs will exert themselves to support cooperation in a number of areas. This factor should not be exaggerated, but it should also not be ignored in any audit of cooperative possibilities.

## THE EFFECT OF CONFLICT: SIX DIVERGENCES

As a function of geo-strategic, economic, and social and political factors, India and the United States are being pushed in the direction of sustained engagement and cooperation. There is nothing inevitable about this. At least six difficulties in the near and longer term may pull them apart once again.

## Proliferation

The first and greatest hurdle to greater India-US cooperation is nuclear and missile proliferation. In both countries, the proliferation issue is perhaps the most charged. Whatever else the successes of India-US relations, at critical moments the interactions between the two societies are judged by this one difference. Now that the Indian government has moved, as the Vajpayee government in its election manifesto promised, toward "inducting" nuclear weapons, such a moment has seemingly arrived. There is a distinct danger that India-US relations will rise or fall by how the issue of proliferation is handled by the two sides.

Immediately after the nuclear tests, India-US relations mostly fell. Washington condemned the tests and moved quickly to impose bilateral and multilateral sanctions. New Delhi insisted that it was a nuclear power and that there was no turning back, but it held out the possibility of signing the Comprehensive Test Ban Treaty (CTBT), observing Article I of the Nuclear Non-proliferation Treaty (NPT), and pushing for a Fissile Materials Cutoff Treaty (FMCT). In response to US sanctions, it threatened to retaliate by targeting US businesses operating in India, a threat that it apparently retracted soon afterward. After this initial phase, a more reflective process began. India sent out its envoys, Brajesh Mishra and Jaswant Singh, to explain its reasons for testing and weaponizing and to limit further damage to the relationship. The United States in turn sent Senators Sam Brownback and Charles Robb to New Delhi to find out how serious India was about further testing and weaponization and to gauge future intentions.

This was followed by a third phase in which the two sides began high-level discussions on nuclear proliferation and regional security. Four issues dominated the talks: weaponization, signing the CTBT, negotiations on the FMCT, and India-Pakistan relations. On weaponization, India repeated that its decision to deploy nuclear weapons is non-negotiable. The US position continued to be that India as well as Pakistan must stop short of deployment. Second, India proposed that it would join a test ban in some form or other in return for the lifting or easing of sanctions and, more important, the relaxation of controls on dual-use technologies, including those on civilian nuclear reactors. On the other hand, Washington insisted that India and Pakistan sign the Comprehensive Test Ban Treaty unconditionally. Third, New Delhi promised to support a faster-track negotiation on the Fissile Materials Cutoff Treaty, which Washington welcomed. Fourth, India affirmed that it would engage Pakistan in bilateral talks over a wide range of issues, including Kashmir. This addressed a vital US concern, namely, that a process of regional confidence building and communication should resume.

Clearly, the most serious disagreements between the two sides are on the first two items: weaponization and the CTBT. Even here, convergence is not impossible.

Indian commentators, in discussing the future of command and control, have already suggested that nuclear warheads should be kept separate from delivery vehicles. The United States did this in the early 1950s, with the nuclear "pits" under the control of civilian scientists and authorities.[9] Pakistan may well adopt a similar posture. It is possible that Washington could accept the "de-mating" of nuclear weapons as a posture that does not amount to deployment. After all, it is likely that before May 11, both India and Pakistan had precisely such a system in place. The difference now would be that both countries would be far more explicit about their postures in terms of numbers of weapons, procedures, and lines of civilian and nuclear authority. It may therefore be possible to reconcile the Indian and US positions on deployment.

On the CTBT, also, there is the possibility of an agreement. New Delhi has indicated that its opposition to the CTBT stands more or less nullified by the tests of May 11 and 13. That is, in principle, it is no longer against the treaty. At the third round of the Jaswant Singh–Strobe Talbott talks, the Indian position was clear enough: if the price is right, it would be prepared to sign the treaty. While the United States has publicly rejected the idea of a deal, the fact that it agreed to the high-level talks with India suggests that in reality it was reconciled to some sort of bargain before it embarked on the talks. The high level of the talks and the speed at which the first four meetings were held indicate that Washington understood quite clearly that something beyond the normal course of diplomacy was required. What is at issue, then, is not so much whether India will sign the CTBT or whether there will be a deal, but rather whether the two sides can agree on a mutually acceptable price.

Four important developments occurred in and around the Singh–Talbott talks that helped the negotiations along. First, the Indian foreign secretary, K. Raghunath, stated publicly that New Delhi understood the difficulties the United States and the other P-5 countries faced in recognizing India as a nuclear weapon state. The foreign secretary thus signaled a retreat from India's original position, namely, that it should be formally accorded the status of a nuclear weapon power. The second signal that New Delhi sent out was that it could live with US sanctions. It no longer expected the Clinton administration to altogether withdraw the sanctions, given the stringency of US laws and the pressures in Congress. This helped open up a space for dialogue, but it also did another thing. By saying that it was prepared to live with the sanctions, New Delhi suggested that US withdrawal of sanctions was not enough for India to sign the CTBT.

For its part, the United States also made two gestures. The first gesture was to move through Congress an amendment that would allow the president to waive sanctions, if the national interest demanded this, for up to a year. The second gesture came just before the third round of the Singh–Talbott talks, when Washington suggested that whereas it opposed deployment of the Agni missile, it understood the need for further testing of the delivery vehicle, which is vital to India's deterrent against China.

The analysis presented here is relatively optimistic on the possibility of an Indo-US nuclear agreement. However, nothing is certain. A number of factors, domestic and international, will play a role in the final outcome. Indeed, virtually any of these factors could derail the process.

First of all, in India there are two key domestic political factors that could unsettle the Indo-US talks and any resulting agreement. The most important factor is whether the anti-CTBT sentiment, built up so assiduously by those who opposed India's signing of the treaty in 1996, will permit any Indian government to reverse its stand. The left and left-of-center parties in India still see New Delhi's rejection of the treaty as part of an antihegemonistic, anti-imperialist fight against US power and preferences in the new world order. These parties have publicly accused the BJP-led government of "selling out" to the United States. The Congress Party has been far more cautious on the talks with the United States, but it is by no means certain that the party would support a change of policies on the test ban. To get a deal with the United States through, the BJP will likely need the support of the Congress Party. However, the Congress Party is in a dilemma. If it supports a deal with the United States, it can be accused of a sellout by the very parties—the left and left-of-center parties—whose backing it needs to return to power. Worse, if the BJP government succeeds in getting a deal, India's newfound nuclear status will be credited to its policies and political courage and not to the Congress Party. If, on the other hand, the Congress Party does not support the deal, the BJP will be able to accuse it of having sabotaged relations with India's most important interlocutor and of losing the country a profitable deal. The way out for the Congress and the BJP is to persuade the left and left-of-center parties to come around on the CTBT—but this will be no mean feat given the depth of feeling on the CTBT and the animosity of those parties for the BJP.

A second and related domestic political factor, which is vital to an agreement with the US, is the longevity of the BJP-led coalition. There is still a good deal of turbulence in the coalition. Jayalalitha, Mamata Bannerjee, Chandrababu Naidu, George Fernandes, and the Akalis—any of these could pull the plug on the government. It is worth remembering that no government, except the Narasimha Rao government, has lasted its five-year term since 1989. Should the BJP government fall, there could be a change of tack. At the very least, domestic uncertainties would cast a shadow over the talks with the United States. Washington would have to be sure that it was dealing with a government that could see the process of negotiation through, one that was also capable of implementing an agreement in the months if not years to come. In politics, timing matters. Negotiations are path-dependent. If the BJP government fell and if the Clinton administration went slow on the talks as a consequence, a decisive moment might just slip away for a long time to come.

On the US side also, domestic politics must be watched. Here the key hurdle to a nuclear agreement could be the US Congress. There are forces which, for quite different reasons, could oppose a deal.[10] These include those who are hostile to India and feel a sense of loyalty to Pakistan given the partnership of the Cold War years. Then there are the traditional antiproliferationists, who believe that the goal of non-proliferation requires everyone to sign up to the NPT and CTBT, and that deal-making amounts to rewarding those who have challenged the regulatory regime. In addition, there are those in the US government, especially the State Department, who had worked hard to support the opening to India over the past two years and feel a sense of betrayal over the tests.

Finally, one can include in the list of oppositionists inveterate critics of the Clinton administration and its liberal, internationalist diplomacy. A key figure here is Jesse Helms. More sympathetic to India will be the India caucus in Congress, those in Congress who are suspicious of China (strategically, or of the Chinese role in proliferation), and US businesses with interests in India. But it is far from clear whether these groups and the White House would prevail in a showdown.

Domestic politics in India and the United States are the most important factors in determining the future of nuclear diplomacy. However, there are at least two international factors that will also have an effect. The first of these is Pakistan. Islamabad will be watching US moves toward India very closely. Any "concessions" to India will surely elicit strong protests from Pakistan, a longtime ally of the United States, and a country that many Americans still regard as being vital for US security interests in the Gulf, Central Asia, and South Asia. There will therefore be a certain moral pressure on the United States to heed Pakistani fears. Pakistani rulers will insist on being treated equitably. Islamabad is very sensitive about its status and will press for a deal of its own along the lines of any bargain with India. The likelihood that Pakistan will protest and that it will want to cut its own rather substantial deal may strain the US ability to make concessions in the first place.

In addition, a deal with India may deepen the siege mentality of Pakistan. Pakistan holds fewer cards than India in its relationship with the United States. It therefore has an incentive to play the game with the United States somewhat differently. Whereas India has emphasized its "responsible" nuclear and diplomatic role, Pakistan has periodically signaled the opposite, namely, that it is a country under great pressure, one that may be forced into extreme measures. The Brasstacks crisis of 1987 and the Kashmir crisis of 1990 are suggestive in this respect. Two more recent incidents are also rather revealing. The first was Islamabad's accusation that India was about to attack preemptively in May 1998 and that Pakistan was forced to test as a warning to India. The second was the curious episode of the defecting Pakistani scientists. The scientists have revealed that Pakistan was ready to carry out a preemptive strike in April 1998 because it feared that the BJP-led government in India was planning to do the same thing. What the various episodes and incidents reveal about Pakistani behavior is not reassuring. Deliberately or otherwise, Islamabad is creating the impression that the India-Pakistan relationship is heading toward instability, with both sides prone to act dangerously. The United States must take account of this pattern of diplomatic and strategic signaling because it reveals something unsettling about the Pakistani state of mind, namely, a desire to play up the instabilities in South Asia in order to get international attention. In sum, that

Pakistan may become aggrieved over a deal with New Delhi and that it may become something of a "loose cannon" will cause the United States to be cautious in its approach to India.[11]

The other international factor that will have an impact on India-US nuclear diplomacy is US-China relations. If New Delhi feels that the United States is seriously trying to involve China in South Asian affairs, an Indo-US agreement would be in jeopardy. No redder strategic flag can be imagined for any Indian government than the promise of a US-China partnership in managing the region's problems. Clearly, everyone is playing a tricky game, including the United States. Washington is no doubt using the China card to warn India that the United States could turn nasty. At the same time, playing the China card too often or too crudely would only confirm India's sense of isolation and threat and push it further down the road of nuclearization.

China, for its part, may use its relationship with the United States to try to limit a deal with India. Beijing, clearly, has an interest in limiting Indian nuclear and conventional military capabilities. Any deal that lifts controls on dual-use items and, say, resumes exports of civilian nuclear technologies could cut into China's lead in conventional and nuclear arms technologies. In the wake of the May tests, it has repeatedly indicated that it does not want the Indian and Pakistani nuclear programs legitimized. Beijing could therefore put pressure on the United States.

It should be remembered that the US-China relationship is of much greater moment to Washington than the US-India relationship. First, the United States has had closer cultural and social links with the Chinese as a people. Given the long historical nature of this factor, we should not expect rapid change here. Second, the United States' stake in China's economic well-being is far greater than for India's. This too will take time to change. China has been on the path of economic reform since the late 1970s. India only began its reform process in 1991 and has been more timid in its restructuring. The United States looks at China as an economic partner in other ways, too. Thus, Beijing joined in bailing out the sinking economies of East and Southeast Asia during the crisis of 1998. Third, and perhaps most important in this context, China, however mixed its record in actual fact, has become a partner of the United States in global non-proliferation. Since the end of the Cold War, Beijing has joined the NPT as a nuclear weapon state. In 1996 it signed the CTBT. It has also promised to abide by many of the obligations of the MTCR. Most recently, in bilateral talks with Washington, it has undertaken not to export nuclear and missile technology to Iran and Pakistan. Crucially on the non-proliferation front, China has been a key player in the four-power nuclear deal involving North Korea. In addition, if and when North Korea collapses, Washington will count on China to play a steadying role. India, by contrast, is not part of the non-proliferation regime; rather, it is its object. Nor is it relevant to the situation in the Korean peninsula.

In sum, the great nuclear game in the Subcontinent is delicately poised. It is tilting to one side; India and the United States seem to be headed toward a mutually advantageous resolution of their differences. There are, however, real pitfalls along the way, and the balance could tilt back the other way. How it ends will depend on the ingenuity of leaders in both countries and their ability to deal with domestic constituencies and third countries.

### Kashmir and Human Rights

The second hurdle to sustained India-US cooperation is Kashmir and human rights. The Indian counterinsurgency effort has curtailed the militancy, and this has laid the basis for the renewal of the normal political process—minimally, elections and representative government. Human rights abuses have eased. The improvement in law and order and the normalization of politics has eased US concerns about instability in Kashmir leading to a confrontation with Pakistan and about the extent of human rights violations.

However, the Kashmir problem is not over. Ironically, the nuclear blasts of India and Pakistan may well contribute to an intensification of violence in the state. The militancy, which has been in remission, may well be emboldened by the growing international attention to South Asia and Kashmir in the wake of the tests. Militant leaders might also expect Pakistan to increase its support to the Kashmiri cause now that Islamabad has unequivocally revealed its nuclear capability. With both countries in possession of the bomb, it is no longer possible for India to escalate its counterinsurgency effort to the level of conventional war. Thus, a dissuasive, punitive attack by India on Pakistan, as in 1965, is ruled out because nuclear weapons could come into play. Under a nuclear umbrella, the Pakistani government could well step up its support to Kashmiri militants in the months and years to come. Four additional factors could lead to a renewal of militant violence: the growing numbers of foreign militants in the Valley, the possibility of new and more deadly arms being introduced into the Valley (e.g., improvised explosive devices), the rising frustration with the Farooq Abdullah government, and the continuing feeling of alienation from India.

If Kashmir explodes again, the Indian counterinsurgency effort will go back into high gear, and US concerns about Kashmir will increase. The May nuclear tests have already revived Washington's interest in Kashmir; an outburst of terrorist and counterterrorist violence would garner international attention as never before.[12] Even if the US administration adopted a moderate policy, the US strategic community, the US Congress, and US human rights organizations could well become active. Pressure on the administration to stabilize South Asia lest nuclear war break out and to restrain India's paramilitary and military forces would grow and could become hard to deflect. US activism over Kashmir, even if it came from nongovernmental organizations and the US Congress, would in turn lead to serious tensions with New Delhi. India is extremely sensitive to criticism of its handling of the militancy and of disaffection in the Valley, and finger pointing from any US source, regardless of its provenance, will make the headlines and provoke a national outcry.

In these circumstances, the prospects of the two governments working coolly and steadily together on a larger agenda would be small indeed.

### Economic Differences

Indo-US cooperation faces a number of potential economic hurdles that could set back the pace not only of economic collaboration but also of the broader agenda. How the two sides deal with certain key economic differences may become a test of their willingness and ability to carry forward the broader agenda.

There are a number of economic differences that could derail the cooperative mood between the two countries. From the US perspective, there are a number of things India should do as part of an economic reform program. These include easing quantitative restrictions (QRs); rewriting patent laws; opening up the services, power, and infrastructure sectors to foreign participation; and carrying out financial sector reforms.

From the Indian perspective, the United States is a protectionist country that uses various nontariff barriers, such as the invocation of national safety standards and—more disturbing from New Delhi's point of view—the tabling of social-cause legislation, to insulate its own producers. Thus, numerical restrictions on textile imports, safety standards on clothing, and child labor and other labor standards, as well as ecological certification on goods produced in India, are all seen as covers for protectionism.

In short, there are a number of economic disputes that could flare up if they are not settled in the next few years, and these could in turn interrupt the cooperative process. The situation is complicated by the fact that from time to time there will be bolts from the blue, such as the Enron fiasco in India, or a US company attempting to patent turmeric or neem or, as in the latest case, basmati rice. The nuclear tests of May 1998 were another kind of bolt from the blue. US sanctions on India have damaged the economic relationship between the two countries. If India and the United States do not come to a nuclear deal and the sanctions are not lifted, the costs to the Indian economy will increase. As they do, India will attempt to retaliate. Already protests against US business interests have occurred. This has included attacks on US companies. Most prominently, Coca-Cola and Pepsi trucks have been targeted. There have been calls to stop consumer items made by US companies from being sold at government-run facilities. These are relatively isolated protests, but in the longer term, retaliation may involve denying trade and investment opportunities to US businesses and favoring non-US businesses.

### Common Concerns, Divergent Approaches

A fourth difficulty in India-US relations is a basic though sometimes overlooked one, namely, that while the two countries share a number of geostrategic, economic, and social and political concerns, this does not necessarily translate into common approaches. States may share common goals and objectives but may be divided, even violently divided, over how to achieve those goals and objectives. India and the United States have often affirmed common ends but differed radically over the means to realize those ends. Nuclear non-proliferation is a very good example. Both countries have an interest in stopping further proliferation. But their approaches to the problem could not diverge more. India-US relations have been hobbled by the expectation that since the two countries are not fundamentally in conflict over goals and objectives, cooperation should be an almost natural process. When cooperation has not resulted or has been derailed, both sides have been disappointed, even exasperated. The expectation that cooperation between the world's two largest democracies should be unproblematic remains and could lead once again to impatience and frustration.

### Asymmetries

The fifth and in some ways structural—and therefore longer-term—difficulty arises from two asymmetries between India and the United States: anti-Americanism on the Indian side, and paucity of interest in the relationship on the US side.

On the Indian side, a certain degree of anti-Americanism persists, sometimes latent, sometimes more apparent, but in any case available for mobilization against any government that may want to do business with Washington. Thus, while the fear and disdain of the United States has been reduced and will continue to decline, there is little doubt that there are important residues of hostility among Indian politicians, officials, and the general public. Even relatively "normal" differences and difficulties between the two countries can therefore be blown up into major conflicts of interest. India-US relations is a handy issue in the cut and thrust of domestic politics, and cooperative agreements with the United States can be portrayed as "sellouts" on the part of any government in power. The fear of such accusations will limit the maneuverability of Indian governments, especially weak, unstable coalition governments.

The problem on the US side is not anti-Indianism—though there is a certain residue of hostility toward India in various quarters—but rather the lack of interest in India. During the Cold War, US interest in India went through seasons—at times quite high, at other times negligible. In general, the amount of attention paid to India and South Asia more generally was low. After the Cold War, things have changed, and there is a reassessment in the works. However, India and South Asia remain strategic and economic backwaters. It remains to be seen whether the events of May 1998 will cause an upgrading of the region. Ironically, if the United States reaches a deal quickly with both India and Pakistan, South Asia will likely revert to backwater status. The difficulty on the US side, therefore, is in cultivating and sustaining interest in a wide-ranging partnership with India over and above relatively momentary issues such as nuclear testing. US decision makers and analysts still view India in terms of a very narrow concern, namely, proliferation. The challenge ahead, therefore, will be to put together a coalition that is willing to put and keep India on the foreign-policy agenda long enough for long-term cooperative structures and understandings to be built.

### Policy Incoherence

Finally, Indo-US cooperation must deal with policy incoherence in both countries. In the near future, this is probably a bigger problem on the Indian side. India has had five governments and six prime ministers since 1989. All of these have been coalition or minority governments, and only one completed its five-year term. The BJP-led government of 1998 is also a coalition and is already being rocked by one of its partners, the AIDMK of Tamil Nadu. There are other sources of instability: both the Telegu Desam Party of Andhra Pradesh and the Trinamul Congress of West Bengal could also pull the plug on the Vajpayee government. The Vajpayee government must weather a fair degree of instability at the state level as well. Calls for the dismissal of state governments, the replacement of governors, and shaky ruling parties and governments in Bihar and Uttar Pradesh, all could lead to political agitation and changes in various large states around the country. In such a situation, the capacity of any central government to pay concerted attention to foreign policy, to take hard decisions on controversial issues, and to think problems through systematically and for the longer term is likely to be limited—and yet Indo-US relations, particularly after the nuclear tests, demand nothing less.

Policy incoherence is not a political affliction limited to India. US policy incoherence has rather different sources, but this also could encumber progress in India-US relations. One source of incoherence has already been mentioned, namely, the apathy surrounding the relationship. The pluralism and divisions in the US decision-making system are another source: differences between the administration and Congress and between various departments (State, Defense, Energy, and Commerce) could complicate assessments of and policies toward India. President Bill Clinton's personal political difficulties could hobble his second term to the general detriment of domestic and foreign policy.

Finally, incoherence may well stem from the inability of any agency or sector in the United States to define precisely and convincingly why and how Washington should deal with a country such as India, which is neither friend nor foe. In the evolving post–Cold War era, where the lines of cooperation and conflict among nations are far more blurred and where there is no overarching and well-accepted formulation of the nature of the international system, where the gray areas between alliance partners and enemy coalitions are ill-defined, US decision makers will find it problematic to locate India strategically and promote India-US ties.

## CONCLUSION

Indian and US interests are convergent in a number of areas, and a variety of factors are encouraging them to come together in the long term. However, a number of difficulties lie ahead—proliferation politics, Kashmir and human rights, economic differences, divergent approaches to common concerns, Indian anti-Americanism coupled with US apathy over the relationship, and policy incoherence in both countries. The nuclear tests of May 1998 and US sanctions have clouded the prospects of cooperation between the two countries. The talks between Jaswant Singh and Strobe Talbott suggest that New Delhi and Washington recognize the imperatives of cooperation. The key difficulties ahead in cutting a nuclear deal are domestic politics and the relationship to third parties. Failure in the talks could spill back onto the larger program of cooperation, but there are signs that the two leaderships want to avoid any further deterioration. There is a substantial basis for cooperation. To translate that potential into real strategic collaboration will require political craft and will.

## NOTES

1  A number of works in recent years stress some or all of these factors, more or less consciously. See, among others, Selig Harrison and Geoffrey Kemp, *India and America After the Cold War* (Washington, DC: Carnegie Endowment for International Peace, 1993); Dennis Kux, *Estranged Democracies: India and the United States, 1941–1991* (New Delhi: Sage Publications, 1993); and A. P. Rana, ed., *Four Decades of Indo-US Relations: A Commemorative Retrospective* (New Delhi: Har-Anand and the US Educational Foundation in India, 1994).

2  Harold Isaacs, *Scratches on Our Minds: American Images of China and India* (New York: John Day, 1958) plumbs the cultural issue in his illuminating study of how Americans viewed India and China. Isaacs's study showed that Americans typically prefer China and Chinese to India and Indians. Interestingly, Isaacs's findings were based on scores of interviews conducted during the height of the Cold War and after the Korean War in which the United States and China fought each other bitterly for four years.

3  That personalities count is suggested by a very interesting set of American essays on Indo-US relations that are organized by presidential terms. See Harold Gould and Sumit Ganguly, eds., *The Hope and the Reality: US-Indian Relations from Roosevelt to Reagan* (New Delhi: Oxford and IBH Publishing, 1993).

4  This generalization about US public opinion is borne out by Elizabeth Crump Hanson, "Public Opinion and Policy Choices in US Relations with India," in Harold Gould and Sumit Ganguly, eds., *The Hope and the Reality: US-Indian Relations from Roosevelt to Reagan* (New Delhi: Oxford and IBH Publishing, 1993), pp. 179–98.

5  On this, see William L. Richter, "Long-term Trends and Patterns in Indian Public Opinion Towards the United States," in Harold Gould and Sumit Ganguly, eds., *The Hope and the Reality: US-Indian Relations from Roosevelt to Reagan* (New Delhi: Oxford and IBH Publishing, 1993), pp. 199–217.

6  The one exception here perhaps was Robin Raphael, undersecretary of state for South

Asia, in the first Clinton administration. Raphael was widely perceived in India as being pro-Pakistani and anti-Indian in a personal sense.

7   One of the few American academic pieces on the problem of narcotics and security in South Asia and the interest and role of the United States is Angela Burger, "Narcotic Drugs: Security Threat or Interest to South Asian States?" in Marvin E. Weinbaum and Chetan Kumar, eds., *South Asia Approaches the Millennium: Reexamining National Security* (Boulder: Westview, 1995), pp. 167–82.

8   A number of Indian analysts have dealt with the problem and connection to terrorism, insurgency, and corruption. See, among others, K. Subrahmanyam, "Covert Operations Pose New Challenges for Indian Security," *World Affairs* (New Delhi), vol. 1, no. 4 (October-December 1997), pp. 38–49, and N. N. Vohra, "Growing Concerns About India's Internal Security," *World Affairs* (New Delhi), vol. 1, no. 3 (July-September 1997), pp. 64–77.

9   Sunil Narula, "Going Beyond the Bomb," *Outlook* (New Delhi), July 13, 1998, pp. 36–37 for the debate in India on command and control.

10  For a different breakdown of US views of India's tests, see Deepa Ollapally, "India's Nuclear Tests and US Responses: The Perception Gap and its Impact," NIAS Lecture L3-98, National Institute for Advanced Studies, Bangalore, 1998. Ollapally distinguishes between neoliberal fence-sitters, absolutist neoliberals, enlightened liberal international-ists, liberal free traders, regional neorealists, universal neorealists, Euro-neorealists, and conservative ideologues.

11  The point is not that Pakistanis are "irresponsible" and "untrustworthy" with respect to nuclear weapons in comparison with Indians and others who possess the bomb. Everyone who has had the bomb has at various times and in different ways "used" the bomb in complex bargaining processes. In some cases, they have knowingly resorted to what Thomas Schelling called the "rationality of irrationality," namely, the suggestion of lack of control and coherence in one's actions so as to induce caution in the opponent, who cannot thereby count on rational, predictable responses. See Thomas Schelling, *The Strategy of Conflict* (Cambridge: Harvard University Press, 1980), pp. 187–203, and also his *Arms and Influence* (New Haven: Yale University Press, 1966), pp. 36–43.

12  There is already evidence that the militants have shifted their focus from the Valley to Jammu and that they are targeting Hindus as never before. The most recent massacre involving primarily Hindus was in Channa and Sarwan in the Doda district of Jammu on July 28, 1998. See "17 Gunned Down by Militants in J&K," *The Hindu* (New Delhi), July 29, 1998.

# 10

## Shadow of the Dragon:
## Indo-US Relations and China

### Amitabh Mattoo

During his visit to China, President Bill Clinton and his counterpart, President Jiang Zemin, issued a joint statement on South Asia on June 27, 1998. The speech emphasized Washington's perception that Beijing should play a larger role in tackling the South Asian situation:

Recent nuclear tests by India and Pakistan, and the resulting increase in tension between them, are a source of deep and lasting concern to both of us. Our shared interests in a peaceful and stable South Asia and in a strong global non-proliferation regime have been put at risk by these tests, which we have joined in condemning.[1]

The statement went on to explicitly outline a joint US-China strategy for South Asia:

We have agreed to continue to work closely together, within the P-5, the Security Council and with others, to prevent an accelerating nuclear and missile arms race in South Asia, strengthen international non-proliferation efforts, and promote reconciliation and the peaceful resolution of differences between India and Pakistan. We call on India and Pakistan to stop all further nuclear tests and adhere immediately and unconditionally to the Comprehensive Nuclear Test Ban Treaty (CTBT). The United States and China remain firmly committed to strong and effective international co-operation on nuclear non-proliferation, with the Treaty on the Non-Proliferation of Nuclear Weapons (NPT) as its cornerstone. We will continue to bolster global nuclear-non-proliferation efforts,

and reiterate that our goal is adherence of all countries, including India and
Pakistan, to the NPT as it stands, without any modification. Notwithstanding
their recent nuclear tests, India and Pakistan do not have the status of nuclear-
weapon states in accordance with the NPT. We reaffirm that our respective policies are to prevent the export of equipment, materials or technology that could in
any way assist programs in India or Pakistan for nuclear weapons or for ballistic
missiles capable of delivering such weapons, and to this end, we will strengthen
our national export systems. Close co-ordination between the United States and
China is essential to building strong international support behind the goals to
which we are committed in response to nuclear testing by India and Pakistan.[2]

If this joint statement is good evidence of US and Chinese policies toward South
Asia, then at least three conclusions can be drawn. First, the United States now
views China as an important partner in its non-proliferation strategy vis-à–vis South
Asia, and China has accepted this role. Second, China has accepted the parameters of
the international order as defined by the United States, including the tenets of the
non-proliferation regime, and is reconciled to being a status-quoist power. Third,
India and Pakistan are viewed as problem states that need to be "managed" through
a joint US-China partnership.

This paper challenges these conclusions. It argues that China is likely to pose a
long-term strategic challenge to both India and the United States. To view China as
a benign partner that is unable or unwilling to challenge the status quo is not just
naive and shortsighted, but also dangerous for stability and order in Asia in the new
millennium. This paper, therefore, concludes that it is in the interests of the United
States to acquire the strategic space and flexibility that may be needed to deal with a
hegemonic China. New Delhi can play an important role as part of a trilateral US-
Japan-India partnership.

This paper is divided into three sections. The first section draws attention to a
recently declassified memo of 1961 and the lessons that the memo holds for contemporary relations between the United States and India in an "uncertain" Asia. The
second section critically examines the future role of China in the context of its relations with India and the United States. Finally, the third section puts forward an
Indo-US strategy for action.

## THE MEMO OF 1961

In September 1961, during the heyday of the Kennedy administration, a top-
secret memo was circulated in the US State Department.[3] The memo, from the assistant secretary of state for policy planning, George C. McGhee, to the secretary of
state, Dean Rusk, related to "Anticipatory Action Pending Chinese Communist
Demonstration of a Nuclear Capability." The memo sought "[t]o consider early
action [the United States] might take to minimize the impact on US and free world
security interests of a first Chinese Communist explosion of a nuclear device." The

initial assumptions were in line with dominant US strategic thinking of that time. "If Communist China could detonate a nuclear device as early as 1962, as has been estimated, we should consider now what actions should be taken in anticipation of the event, instead of later in reaction to it." The memo concluded that the initial impact wiould be primarily psychological, with secondary political and military effects deriving from it. This establishes the psychological field as deserving of immediate attention.[4]

The memo went on to suggest that China was likely to secure two types of "psychological dividends from its explosion":

1. Many Asians are likely to raise their estimate of Communist China's present and future total military power relative to that of their own countries, and the capabilities in the area of the United States; and

2. they are likely to see the accomplishment as vindicating claims that the Communist method of organizing a backward state's resources is demonstrably superior. Both reactions are likely to contribute to feelings that communism is the wave of the future and that Communist China is, or soon will become, too powerful to resist.[5]

But the implicit recommendations of the memo were startling, even by Cold War standards. It suggested, among other things, that it would not be possible to prevent the accrual to Communist China of such dividends, but by advance action it might be possible to reduce them. All things are comparative, and in the memo Communist China was compared first of all with the other countries of Asia. If another, non-Communist Asian state detonated a nuclear device first, the memo concluded, a subsequent and consequently somewhat anticlimactic Chinese Communist explosion would not have carried a comparable implication of Communist superiority or made quite as much impact on those who feared China's growing power.

The memo went on to state that "according to one estimate, India's atomic program is sufficiently advanced so that it could, not many months hence, have accumulated enough fissionable material to produce a nuclear explosion. While we would like to limit the number of nuclear powers, so long as we lack the capability to do so, *we ought to prefer that the first one be India and not China* (emphasis added)." The memo suggested that Nehru, given his principled opposition to nuclear tests, would be the main hurdle, but even he could probably be persuaded.

Nehru was quoted as saying, upon his arrival in Belgrade on August 31, and in the context of the Soviet decision to resume weapon tests, "I am against nuclear tests at any time in any place." The same day, however, an official spokesman in Delhi was quoted as making a somewhat less categorical statement: "We are against all tests and explosions of nuclear material except for peaceful purposes under controlled conditions." Given the context, and taken together, these statements suggest that it would have been difficult to get Nehru to agree to any proposal for an Indian nuclear test in the near future, and the chances of its acceptance would have depended upon the extent to which it met rather narrow criteria.

Nevertheless, Nehru might have been brought to see the proposal as being in India's interests. If accepted and implemented the memo hypothesized, such a proposal might help forestall Communist China's use of nuclear blackmail against India, and reduce its ability to frighten neighbors of India whose security is important to that country. Further, it might minimize the usefulness to the Communist Party of India of a demonstrated Chinese nuclear capability that otherwise could be cited as evidence that Communism, as practiced in China, was superior to India's mixed economy.

> Preliminary exploration within the [State] Department (with officers in FE, S/AE, NEA, ENA and INR), has elicited concurrence with the idea, *per se,* that it would be desirable if a friendly Asian power beat Communist China to the punch, *and it has turned up no likelier candidate than India* (emphasis added).[6]

The memo's ideas did not translate into action, perhaps because John Galbraith, then ambassador to India, was convinced that the chances were "roughly one out of fifty that Nehru's reaction would not be the negative one." But it is clear that in 1961 the Kennedy administration was seriously considering helping democratic India to test a nuclear device to offset the impact of a nuclear test by Communist China. The administration was sensitive to India's security concerns, particularly the possibility of blackmail by nuclear China, and seemed to be acutely conscious of the manner in which the rise of China could impact on international relations in Asia. This sensitivity is in marked contrast to the Clinton administration's policies, and it is the spirit of 1961, as evidenced in the memo, that this paper believes needs to be urgently revived.

## THE FUTURE ROLE OF CHINA

There are two assumptions that guide the arguments presented here. First, it is assumed that China, despite some economic problems and provincial tensions, will emerge as a great power, second only to the United States, by the first decades of the new millennium. In 1994 Richard Hornik argued that China's economic boom is more a mirage than a miracle, and the "success of China's neighbors has provided the rationale behind grandiose projections about the Chinese economy becoming the world's largest in the year 2000, 2010, 2020—take your pick." [7] However, by 1998 most of China's East Asian neighbors, including Japan, were in deep economic trouble, yet China's bubble had not burst. It is clear that China's economic success has firm foundations, and an economic collapse of the country cannot be visualized in the foreseeable future.

Similarly, Gerald Segal has argued that since the mid-1990s Beijing has been losing control over its provinces, and a possible outcome could be the breakup of China.

The fault lines of the Chinese Empire are myriad, and history is replete with Chinas of different configurations. Today one can distinguish between China's inner and outer empires. The outer empire includes Tibet, Xinjiang, Mongolia and other fringe territories, most of which have strong cases for ethnically based independence, but have reaped relatively little benefit from economic decentralization. Dialect and important cultural fault lines divide even the inner empire, which consists of areas such as Southern China, Shanghai and its hinterland, and Shandong.[8]

It is true that southern China, currently in the midst of a sustained economic boom, has one of the strongest cases for greater independence based on cultural distinctiveness. And yet, even by late 1998, there is no evidence to suggest that Beijing is losing control, or that movements for greater autonomy in Tibet or Xinjiang are threatening the political stability of China. On the contrary, despite economic decentralization, there are no obvious or strong separatist tendencies.

The second assumption is that China will remain an authoritarian state firmly under the control of the Chinese Communist Party (CCP) and that the People's Liberation Army (PLA) will remain dedicated to the regime in power. There is little evidence that China is reforming itself politically or that democracy is in sight. There is no historical example, either. As Richard Bernstein and Ross H. Munro pointed out so accurately:

> In its entire 3,000-year history, China has developed no concept of limited government, no protections of individual rights, no independence for the judiciary and the media. The country has never operated on any notion of consent of the governed or the will of the majority. Whether under the emperors or the party general secretaries, China has always been ruled by a self-selected and self-perpetuating clique that operates in secret, and treats opposition as treason.[9]

The Chinese army has emerged as the single most important institution in the country. As two distinguished analysts have suggested, in the future "the most likely form for China to assume is a kind of corporatist, militarized, nationalized state, one with similarity to the states of Mussolini or Francisco Franco." [10] In other words, the assumption that China will emerge as a military and economic power firmly under the control of an authoritarian leadership is not an unrealistic one.

But how will China as an economic superpower, firmly under the control of the CCP, behave with the outside world? Sinologists the world over are divided in their views about China's future role in the international system and vis-à–vis its neighbors. The liberal institutionalist view is that China's future role in Asia would be stabilizing and largely defensive, rather than subversive and offensive.[11]

This viewpoint identifies three different trends that seem to justify such a conclusion. First, China's foreign policy has become increasingly deradicalized. Ideology, it is suggested, no longer plays a decisive role in China's policy toward the outside world (if it ever did). China is no longer seeking to export a revolution, nor are its relations with other countries determined by the nature of their political systems. In this view, China has accepted the basic parameters of the international system as it operates today.

Second, this view holds, China has gradually become a shareholder in the world economic system. It has a stake in global economic stability, and the prudent manner in which Beijing responded to the economic crisis in East Asia is just one example of China's maturity. Proponents of this perspective pointed out that in 1980 China's exports as a percentage of GDP amounted to 8.15 percent. By 1995, this figure had gone up to 21.33 percent. The trade/GDP ratio had gone up from 18.8 percent in 1980 to 42.2 percent in 1995. China is one of the largest oil importers in the world and one of the largest investors in oil exploration in Kazakhstan. In short, China is well integrated into the international economic system.

Third, it is argued, there are increasing external constraints on China's behavior. Beijing has willingly accepted constraints by signing up for the Chemical Weapons Convention (CWC), the Nuclear Nonproliferation Treaty (NPT), and the Comprehensive Test Ban Treaty (CTBT). It might formally join the Missile Technology Control Regime (MTCR), and it is increasingly associating with regional institutions, including the ASEAN.[12]

Ideationally, the liberal institutionalist view sees Chinese strategic culture as the product of a Confucian-Mencian paradigm. In this paradigm, accommodationist grand strategies are preferred over violent defensive or offensive ones. And it is suggested that the Chinese view military force as "inauspicious," to be used only under "unavoidable circumstances," and prefer the submission of the enemy without resort to force.[13]

This liberal institutionalist view is in contrast to the more persuasive recent rereading of Chinese strategic culture that seems to reinforce a more realist view of China. The best-known and perhaps most masterly account is the one provided by Alastair Ian Johnston.[14] Based on his close reading of Chinese history and the Seven Military Classics, Johnston argues that that China has historically exhibited a relatively consistent hard realpolitik or parabellum paradigm that has persisted across different structural contexts into the Maoist period and beyond. The Confucian paradigm, according to Johnston, existed only as an idealized strategic discourse and had rarely been practiced.

On the contrary, because Chinese decision makers have internalized the parabellum strategic culture, national strategic behavior exhibits a preference for offensive uses of force, mediated by a keen sensitivity to relative capabilities. This paradigm views the external environment "as dangerous, adversaries as dispositionally threatening, and conflict as zero-sum, in which the application of violence is ultimately required to deal with threats." Most important, this paradigm explicitly embodies a key decision axiom, the notion of *quan bian,* which stresses absolute flexibility and awareness of changes in relative capabilities. The more this balance is favorable to China, the more advantageous it is to adopt offensive coercive strategies; the less favorable, the more advantageous it is to adopt defensive or accommodationist strategies to buy time until the balance shifts again.

If one accepts this view—and the empirical evidence that Johnston garners is very impressive—then China's present posture cannot be viewed in benign terms. If China is being accommodationist, it is only because the balance does not seem to be in its favor, and it will turn aggressive once that balance is altered. Indeed, as Johnston points out, "in comparison with other major powers, China was far more likely to use violence in a dispute over military-security questions such as territory." [15] China used violence as a key conflict-management technique in 80 percent of the crises in which the primary issue was territory or related to territorial security. For the United States the figure was 0 percent; for the Soviet Union, 20 percent; for Britain, 8.3 percent; for France, 27.3 percent; and for India, 33.3 percent.

## SINO-INDIAN RELATIONS

India suffered a humiliating and traumatic defeat in the war against China in 1962. The defeat deeply embedded itself in the psyche of the nation, and especially among India's armed forces. The defeat was the biggest blow to Prime Minister Jawaharlal Nehru's worldview and to India's cognitive conception about its foreign policy. It changed the way India perceived the world and formed the basis of its nuclear-weapons program.

To many Indians, the confidence-building measures (CBMs) that have been introduced since 1976 seem to have been built on a history of unilateral Indian concessions. This was quite obvious in the 1970s. In 1976 Indira Gandhi proposed upgrading diplomatic relations to the ambassadorial level, and appointed an ambassador to Beijing. China took six months to make a reciprocal gesture. In 1979 Foreign Minister Atal Behari Vajpayee attempted to normalize relations with China and paid a visit to Beijing. China rebuffed him by opening a military campaign against Vietnam, a close Indian ally, during his visit.

In 1986 and 1987 India and China nearly went to war after Indian army units established a presence in the Sumdurong Chu valley. According to one top Indian source, the Chinese even threatened to use tactical nuclear weapons during that encounter. Undoubtedly, relations in the 1990s were smoother, and the two countries had started collaborating on a number of fronts. However, there were at least a few warning signs already. By far the most serious concern was the help provided by Beijing to Pakistan's nuclear program.

The true extent of Beijing-Islamabad nuclear collusion may never be revealed, but it is clear that Pakistan's nuclear weapons program has relied enormously on China's help, and Chinese nuclear engineers might have designed Islamabad's nuclear weapons. Nuclear cooperation of this kind is unprecedented in the history of international relations since 1945. Indeed, not even the United States and Britain shared such a relationship.

Why would China want to help Pakistan become a nuclear-weapon state? According to James Woolsey, director of the US Central Intelligence Agency, "Beijing has consistently regarded a nuclear armed Pakistan as a crucial regional ally and as a vital counterweight to India's growing military capabilities." [16] No less serious is the Chinese unwillingness to settle any of the bilateral irritants to which India attaches importance.

Despite repeated promises, Beijing has still not recognized Arunachal Pradesh or Sikkim as part of India, and in 1997 and 1998 it violated the letter and spirit of the bilateral CBMs on more than a dozen occasions. Chinese inroads into Myanmar, including the reported construction of a Chinese naval facility on the Coco Islands, should be of deep strategic concern to India. Additionally, the presence in India of thousands of Tibetan refugees is an irritant that is likely to worsen as the scale of Chinese atrocities in the region deepens.

Much less is written about the direct threat from Chinese nuclear weapons. China has deployed nuclear missiles in Tibet that clearly have one target: India. Admittedly, Chinese intercontinental ballistic missiles elsewhere could also target India. But the potential political and psychological impact during a future conflict of these missiles, literally a few miles from India's border, cannot be underestimated. [17]

## EARLY WARNINGS FOR THE UNITED STATES

There are three clear warning signs for the United States. The first relates to the extent of Chinese military modernization. It is clear that China's official defense budget (only about $8.7 billion) is merely a facade. It does not include nuclear weapons development, soldiers' pensions, or the People's Armed Police. Not surprisingly, "when the Chinese purchased 72 SU-27 fighter jets from Russia in 1995 for about $2.8 billion, the entire amount was covered by the State Council and not deemed as defense expenditure." [18]

One realistic estimate suggests that China's actual expenditure is about $87 billion a year (on purchasing power parity terms). This is about one-third of the defense budget for the United States and nearly twice that of Japan's.[19] Both at the conventional and the nuclear levels, China has been modernizing its arsenal to the extent that within a few years it will be in a position to challenge American power in Asia.

The two other indications of Chinese assertiveness relate to the Taiwan issue, as reflected during the crisis in the Straits during 1996 and its intransigence over disputes in the South China Sea involving the Spratleys, Senkaku, and Paracel Islands. Together, these three signs suggest that Chinese dominance over Asia will become a reality, and the only force that can stop China's translation of dominance into hegemony is the United States.

## STRATEGY FOR COMMON INDO-US ACTION

To conclude, the possibility of a sustained long-term strategic partnership between India and China, or India and the United States, seems very unlikely. However, it is in the interests of both India and the United States to ensure that China continues to acquire and sustain a stake in the stability of the international system, including the Asia-Pacific and the southern Asian regions. Of course, the congruence in their strategic outlooks and priorities will hinge on the following factors:

- The precise nature and seriousness of the challenge that China will pose in the future

- Washington's recognition of New Delhi as one, but not the only, counterweight to Beijing

- The progress made by New Delhi and Washington in their bilateral strategic dialogue—which, one hopes, has been suspended only temporarily

In sum, China, which is making its reappearance on the world stage after what it sees as a century of Western humiliation and fifty years of postwar trial-and-error attempts to reestablish a national identity, will become increasingly assertive in regional and global affairs. India and the United States must ensure that Chinese assertiveness does not threaten the common values and interests of two of the world's largest democracies. As a first step, a substantive strategic dialogue between India and the United States that includes a comprehensive review of the Asian strategic landscape must be started. This dialogue must eschew any conscious anti-China focus and instead concentrate on the options available to promote and sustain Asian stability and prosperity in the twenty-first century.

## NOTES

1   Statement issued by President Bill Clinton and President Jiang Zemin, Beijing, June 27, 1998.
2   Ibid.
3   Top-secret memo from George C. McGhee to the secretary of state, September 13, 1961.
4   Ibid., p. 1.
5   Ibid., p. 2.
6   Ibid., p. 3.
7   Richard Hornik, "Bursting China's Bubble," *Foreign Affairs,* vol. 73, no. 3 (May/June 1994), pp. 28–42.
8   Gerald Segal, "The Middle Kingdom? China's Changing Shape," *Foreign Affairs,* vol. 73, no. 3 (May/June 1994), p. 56.
9   Richard Bernstein and Ross H. Munro, "China: The Coming Conflict with America," *Foreign Affairs,* vol. 76, no. 2 (March/April 1997), p. 27.

10   Ibid., p. 29.

11   The author is grateful to the presentation made by Dr Wei-Wei Zhang, research fellow at the Modern Asia Research Center, Geneva, at the 19th Seminar on International Security, Politics and Economics, April 14–18, 1998, Geneva. The benign view of China has relied considerably on that presentation.

12   See Jonathan D. Pollack, "Chinese Views of the Evolving Strategic System: Implications for South Asia," South Asia Futures Conference, March 20–21, 1998, New Delhi, for arguments in favor of China as a status quoist power.

13   See Alastair Ian Johnston, *Cultural Realism: Strategic Culture and Grand Strategy in Chinese History* (Princeton: Princeton University Press, 1995).

14   Ibid.

15   Ibid., p. 256.

16   Woolsey, in testimony to the U.S. Senate Governmental Affairs Committee, February 1993. China is believed to have earlier supplied Pakistan with around five thousand magnet rings, which can be used to enrich uranium in gas centrifuges. There is also evidence that China was helping Pakistan set up a plutonium reprocessing plant at Chashma. China's sale of missiles to Pakistan seems to have been proven beyond reasonable doubt.

17   For a list of Sino-Indian irritants, see Amitabh Mattoo, "India's Nuclear Status Quo," *Survival,* autumn 1996, pp. 41–57.

18   Bernstein and Munro, "China: The Coming Conflict," p. 24. Also see June Teufel Dreyer, "Chinese Strategy in Asia and the World," paper prepared for the first Annual Strategy Forum Conference on China, US Naval Academy, Annapolis, Maryland, April 27–28, 1996.

19   Bernstein Munro, "China: The Coming Conflict," p. 25.

# 11

## Coping with Insecurity:
## The Pakistani Variable in Indo-US Relations

### Milind Thakar

The nuclear tests in South Asia in May 1998 highlighted the nature of the Indo-Pak relationship. Specifically, they illustrated the insecurity within Pakistan vis-à-vis India, with Pakistan's foreign policy essentially responsive to an Indian action. Even though India's official explanations for testing cited China as the reason, Pakistan perceived the second round of nuclear testing by India in twenty-five years as endangering its security. This was not entirely surprising or unexpected, as Pakistan and India have been locked in a state of mutual distrust over the last fifty years. The existence of each has contradicted the basis of creation of the other.[1] There are differing views on the roots of the conflict, but the partition of British India itself is a significant factor. Pakistan regarded partition as *"necessary and inevitable . . . but incomplete* (without the incorporation of Kashmir), *while India regarded partition as unnecessary and tragic, but fundamentally complete* (implying that the accession of Kashmir to the Indian union was the completion)."[2] Dimensions of conflict between the two states involve territorial disputes, ideological differences, and differing perceptions of regional dynamics.

Concerns that Indian supremacy in South Asia is detrimental to Pakistan's security have shaped Pakistani foreign policy from its inception. Conversely, India has viewed its preeminence in South Asia as a natural outcome of its relative size and superior resources.[3] Therefore, while Pakistan has attempted to balance Indian superiority by seeking external ties, India has perceived this as a way of upsetting the natural balance of power in South Asia. Since 1947 this state of mutual distrust has led to three wars, numerous smaller conflicts, arms races, and crises that have brought both states close to war. For these reasons, Pakistan remains a part of any dialogue on regional stability in South Asia. At the very least, the Pakistani response to developments in the region, bilateral or otherwise, is a factor that needs to be closely examined, largely due to the "ugly stability" that characterizes South Asia.[4]

This paper will attempt to examine Pakistani choices and reactions to a widening strategic dialogue between India and the United States. The introduction of a change in the existing relationships between states may trigger instability with grave consequences for peace in the region. While the South Asian nuclear tests have cast a shadow over any kind of defense cooperation between the United States and India or Pakistan, there is evidence that the harshly critical tone characterizing US policy may be softened to deal with what appears to be a new reality. At the time of writing it is too early to predict how the United States will change its policy toward the two South Asian neighbors. Already there are signs that the initial Indian response, full of bravado and defiance, is being toned down to deal with a slowdown in growth that may worsen further if and when the proposed international sanctions come into effect. Pakistan, with a weakened economy that is highly dependent on external aid and investment, is on the verge of defaulting on loan payments.

At the same time, there appears to be a change in US policy from the harsh and moral tones that characterized American rhetoric in the immediate aftermath of the tests. The fact that the US president's South Asia visit has still not been canceled points to a desire on the part of US policy makers not to further aggravate an already somber scenario. Despite a slowdown in its growth rate, India has been less affected than other Asian countries by the economic malaise that has spread over the continent since fall 1997. A big emerging market, attractive to investors, India remains significant to the United States, perhaps simply because the lack of interest in most developed countries in pursuing the path of sanctions may lead to the United States being the loner that misses out on economic opportunity.

However, Pakistan's nuclear tests do cast a cloud over the stability of the region, in as much as they have the potential to lead to a war between states with a history of animosity. This paper aims at reviewing Pakistan's historical record of conflict with India, its cooperation with the United States, and its increasing drift towards China.

Based on the historical record, the paper will highlight the principal Pakistani options in the face of any improvement in Indo-US ties. These are:

- Following a strategy of domestic military expansion;

- Encouraging insurgency in India and building its nuclear deterrent;

- Strengthening ties with China while attempting to restore its relationship with the United States to where it was in the 1980s; and

- Attempting to recover Kashmir through a quick, decisive engagement before India maximizes its power base.

Pakistan's nuclear tests, its leaders' aggressive rhetoric, and its tests of Chinese missiles indicate that at least two of the above policy options are already being implemented.

Any attempt to increase Indo-US strategic cooperation therefore faces the primary bugbear of opposition from an insecure Pakistan. This is especially significant given the close US-Pakistani relationship over the last forty years and the differences between India and the United States.

This study suggests that accommodating Pakistani intransigence in the context of any sort of Indo-US dialogue in the future would require the following:

1. Initiating a larger dialogue that would include Pakistan and satisfy Pakistani security needs;

2. Exploring the possibility of declaring South Asia a nuclear-weapon-free zone, which will require, at the very least, that India sign the CTBT; and

3. Exploring options that enhance South Asian confidence building measures regionally, rather than bilaterally between India and Pakistan, which may have the effect of increasing chances of their successful implementation.

Accordingly, the paper is divided into four sections. The first section will deal with the motivations and roots of Pakistan's security policy. The second section will describe the Indo-Pakistani discord in historical terms. The third section will outline the importance of the United States in Indo-Pakistani relations and what the Pakistani response has been to any signs of Indo-US cooperation in the past. Based on this, the final section will seek to analyze Pakistan's choices and responses to the emergence of strategic cooperation between India and the United States. In a sense, this paper attempts to identify the costs of cooperation and its implications for regional stability.

## PAKISTAN'S SECURITY POLICY: ROOTS AND MOTIVATIONS

Pakistan's security policy aims at maintaining the territorial integrity of the Pakistani state. Cobbled together from a number of Muslim-majority states in British India, Pakistan was at its inception a truncated state, with its eastern and western wings separated by over a thousand miles of Indian territory. Born out of communal disagreement between Muslims and Hindus, the fledgling state was apprehensive that India would try to reabsorb Pakistan at some later date.[5] This threat to the Pakistani state was augmented by the cultural affinity shared by Pakistanis with people on both borders, whether Indian, Afghan, or Iranian. Cultural affinity has had a negative impact on the principle of Muslim unity, which was instrumental in the formation of the Pakistani state, and a clear example of the inherent problems is the creation of Bangladesh on the basis of a Bengali rather than a Muslim identity. The large number of Muslims in India (estimated to be equal to that in Pakistan) and ethnic strains within Pakistan itself remain constant threats in terms of diluting Pakistan's national identity.[6]

Perhaps the strongest expression of Pakistan's identity has been the negation of being Indian. As the state was born out of a divided India and its rationale was that India was not a safe haven for Muslims, this not-Indian identity is the strongest perception by Pakistanis themselves of the nature of their nation. While there is no formal enunciation of Pakistan's identity being only anti-Indian in nature, Pakistan appears to be divided along ethnic and sectarian divisions, with no concept of a Pakistani identity.[7] This does make India a formidable threat to Pakistan's identity, whether real or imagined.[8] The other major threat to Pakistan originates in the West. Part of the legacy of the British empire has been Pakistan's assuming the role of checking the Russian drive for a warm-water port in the Arabian Sea through expansion into the region. The latest such attempt was the Soviet invasion of Afghanistan in 1979.

The strategic equation against Pakistan's primary threat, India, is loaded in the latter's favor. India's natural advantages in size, population, industrial development, economic reliance, and defense forces inhibit Pakistan's capacity to deter any aggression purely on its own strength.[9] To offset this advantage has therefore been the prime goal of Pakistan's security and foreign policy. As early as 1948, the state's founder, Mohammed Ali Jinnah, had dispatched an emissary to the United States asking for a $2 billion grant spread over five years, of which $500 million would be utilized for defense.[10] While this was rejected, later attempts to balance Indian superiority through external assistance proved more successful when Pakistan sought and received admission into the American-led alliance system designed to contain the Soviet Union in the 1950s. While arms supplies were forthcoming, these arrangements did not prove very useful in terms of securing a decisive advantage against India. Defense assistance from the United States was conditional, with the understanding that the equipment and weaponry supplied would be used only against Communist aggression and not against India. In fact, during Pakistan's 1965 and 1971 wars against India, the United States declared a moratorium on arms shipments to both combatants, a step that had stronger consequences for Pakistan, as it was more dependent on US aid.[11]

The prevailing understanding of Indian foreign policy among Pakistan's scholars has been that it is based on hegemonic design within the region. Born of Pandit Nehru's worldview, Indian foreign policy was based on nonalignment, an eschewal of bloc politics during the Cold War. Pakistani scholars viewed this as being an attempt to keep the superpowers out of the region. While they were correct in this, the motives Pakistan attributed to India differed from India's self-perceptions. Pakistan saw Indian attempts to keep out external powers as a way to maintain Indian regional dominance.[12] However, the Indian position was that this would result in a loss of sovereignty for states allied with either bloc; consequently, any external power should be kept out of the region. Moreover, the Indian perspective on regional stability was at odds with Pakistan's perception. India's foreign-policy makers characterized the defense of South Asia as primarily an Indian responsibility. Therefore, the neighboring states of South Asia would have nothing to fear from India, since India would safeguard them from external threat. In return, though, they would be expected to accommodate Indian interests prior to any foreign policy action outside the Subcontinent.[13] As it happened, South Asia remained peripheral to superpower interests, barring the Afghan war, so Pakistan was not a frontline state in the war against Communism in the same way as South Korea. This meant that there was a low external presence in South Asia despite Pakistan's membership in alliances such as SEATO and CENTO.

In efforts to minimize the Indian threat, Pakistani policy makers tried the following methods:

- Balancing Indian power through alliance with the United States;

- Purchasing military equipment from the United States, France and China;

- Diversifying the base of arms suppliers when confronted by a neutral US policy with respect to both India and Pakistan;

- Attempting to neutralize India through cultivating China; and

- Fomenting insurgency in sensitive Indian provinces to prevent India from gaining a secure position.

In addition, the issue of Kashmir was kept alive by raising it in international forums, from the Organization of the Islamic Conference to the United Nations. In order to establish its Islamic credentials, Pakistan developed a strong relationship with the Islamic states of West Asia and North Africa, even sending Pakistani army troops to serve as mercenaries in some of their armies.[14]

Essentially, Pakistani insecurity is driven by the fear that secular, democratic India (a reverse image in these respects of Pakistan for most of the past fifty years) would succeed in breaking the glue that holds a fragile national identity together. The historical record vindicates such fears. In 1971 India aided Bengali militants (training their fledgling force, the Mukti Bahini) in breaking free of Pakistan and forming Bangladesh. Even though there was no attempt by India to incorporate Bangladesh, there was a feeling within Pakistan that similar attempts would be made on Pakistan's unity in the future. As a case in point, in the 1980s Pakistan claimed that India was clandestinely supporting a separatist movement in Sind.[15]

However, the linchpin of Pakistan's strategy has been to obtain Kashmir. It is considered a vital component of Pakistan (by virtue of being the only Muslim-majority state in Indian possession, it defies Pakistan's raison d'être and reinforces Indian secularism), and no Pakistani government has as yet moderated the demand on Kashmir, making its resolution a precondition for better ties with India.

The final concern of Pakistan's security policy is India's nuclear program. The explosion of a nuclear device by India in 1974 led to protests by Pakistan that this had escalated the threat potential in the region.[16] This had added impetus to

Pakistan's own nuclear-weapons program, which it was hoped would bring in a truly stable deterrence against any Indian conventional superiority. India's tests of May 1998 were answered by Pakistan's own tests with a view toward establishing parity, if only for perceptual purposes. Pakistan's quest for a nuclear device assumed seriousness after the defeat in the 1971 war (which established an irreversible Indian conventional superiority once and for all), the 1974 nuclear explosion (which left Pakistan little choice but to follow suit), and finally the Indian tests of 1998.

## INDO-PAKISTAN RELATIONS: A HISTORICAL OVERVIEW

Numerous reasons are cited for the antagonism between India and Pakistan. Apart from the disagreement over the extent of partition, there are differences in ideology, perspectives on regional security, and perceptions of each other. As discussed earlier, Pakistan has viewed India as a state aspiring for hegemony and believes that this may take place at its expense.[17] As evidence, it cites India's avowed policy of allocating to itself primacy in South Asian affairs by virtue of its preponderance in resources. This imbalance, as discussed, has played a major role in the foreign-policy calculations of Pakistani strategists, who have sought to correct it by allying with external powers.

It may be worth exploring why Pakistan feels threatened by India, given India's numerous assurances that it has no intention of reabsorbing Pakistan.[18] From a Pakistani point of view the security of Pakistan has been compromised in every conflict with India. In the aftermath of the partition, Pakistan viewed India as an aggressive neighbor that was trying to acquire Kashmir by force, a Muslim-majority state that should by the stated rules of partition have gone to Pakistan. As India holds the crucial Valley of Kashmir, where the bulk of the population of the state resides, Pakistan considers an integral part of its territory to have been in Indian possession since 1948. In the 1965 war, while both sides claimed victory, with Pakistan claiming a larger wartime seizure of territory than India, the postwar negotiations at Tashkent under Soviet auspices restored the situation under pressure from the Soviet Union and the United States.[19]

Pakistan perceived the 1971 war as being an Indian machination. To bolster its claim, Pakistan cited Indian support to Bengali militants and blamed India for dismembering Pakistan. Pakistan regards the human rights abuses in East Pakistan—now Bangladesh—as unfortunate, but not sufficient to warrant external interference and subsequent vivisection. This war was responsible for a reappraisal of Pakistan's strategy. While it reaffirmed the view that Pakistan required external support more than ever, there was a drift toward China as being a more reliable ally than the United States. Moreover, the Pakistan government under Zulfikar Ali Bhutto decided that nuclear weapons were the only viable defense against India.

In the 1980s India and Pakistan clashed over possession of the Siachen Glacier, a bleak outpost of land at the point where India, Pakistan, and China meet. This conflict, ongoing since 1986, has resulted in small-scale hostilities and high military expenditures on both sides. Later Pakistan claimed that India was assisting insurgents in the province of Sind. In turn, Pakistan supported and fomented insurgency in Punjab (India) during the 1980s and from 1989 in Kashmir, in what has been the strongest insurgency in that state to date.[20] India thus remains the principal threat to Pakistan, in the latter's view. Any changes that take place in India's strategic relationship vis-à–vis other powers alter the regional equations and are seen in Pakistan as conducive to instability. In that sense, the prospect of the United States engaging India in a strategic dialogue has profound implications for Pakistan.

While this will be discussed in greater detail in the following section, suffice it to say here that augmented ties between India, the single greatest threat to Pakistan's national security, and the United States, the largest supplier of Pakistan's defense forces, would weaken Pakistan's belief in US neutrality vis-à–vis both states. In fact, Pakistan has historically perceived the United States as favoring India at the expense of Pakistan.

The start of India's liberalization in the economic sector has had significant implications for Pakistan. First, if socialist means are discarded by India, it would lead to increased cooperation with the West, and that could happen only at Pakistan's expense. Second, the high growth rate that India had achieved in the early to mid-1990s put pressure on the Pakistani economy in terms of matching India's growing defense capability. Third, the end of the Cold War has meant that Pakistan's privileged position with the United States is now history and that it would be the existence of economic opportunities rather than ideological concerns that would govern cooperation. In this aspect, India's undisputed position as one of the big emerging markets gives it a clear advantage over Pakistan.

The point is that Pakistan's insecurity stems from perceived Indian designs on the unity of the Pakistani state, and this perception forms the basis of Pakistan's strategic calculus. Thus any change in India's capabilities, whether real or imagined, is seen to add to the imbalance in India's favor, and therefore necessitates that Pakistan try to counter it. This is why the role of the United States assumes importance in Indo-Pakistan relations.

## THE UNITED STATES IN INDO-PAK RELATIONS

In trying to address the question of Pakistan's inferiority vis-à–vis India, Pakistan had turned to the West rather than to the Soviet bloc. There are several reasons for this. The nature of the Pakistani state dictated an anti-Communist stance due to the powerful feudal forces that have played and continue to play a significant role in Pakistan. The most important organs of the state, namely, the bureaucracy, military and the political elite, are all recruited from the feudal class.[21] The ideological incongruence between this class's point of view (at least in the early days of the state) and Communism meant that cooperation with the Soviet Union was neither feasible nor desired. Therefore, the Pakistani government made it clear that they would prefer to seek help from the United States and its Western allies. Further, over time, the United States assumed the British role of being the guarantor of regional peace. Britain's retreat to east of the Suez following the 1956 debacle hastened this process.

In return for support against India (through financial and military assistance), Pakistan was ready to assume defense of the region (and American interests there) against Soviet expansion. Mention has already been made of Jinnah's attempt to secure American assistance in 1948. While this was not successful, largely due to the peripheral nature of South Asia in American policy in the 1940s and the preoccupation with Europe, a change took place with the Eisenhower administration. Secretary of State Dulles's emphasis on pacts as a means of containing Soviet power drew Pakistan's attention, and in 1953 Pakistan and the United States signed the Mutual Defense Assistance Agreement, by which the latter undertook to give training and military equipment to the Pakistani armed forces.[22] Later in 1954, Pakistan accepted an invitation to join the South East Asian Treaty Organization (SEATO). However, the treaty made it clear that SEATO would counter only Communist aggression, not all aggression, as Pakistan had hoped. A similar situation prevailed when Pakistan joined the Baghdad Pact (later CENTO).

Any flexibility in choosing between superpowers was lost after the tilt of the Soviet Union toward India.[23] Given this situation, there was little that Pakistan could do except hope for strengthened ties with the United States. Patterns of relationship between the United States and Pakistan oscillated between strong alliance and American disapproval of Pakistan, sometimes resulting in the severance of arms supplies, as in the case during wars with India. As the United States has never directly clashed with India, there was little support in the United States for augmenting Pakistan's strength purely against India. From 1957 until 1964 there was an improvement in India's relations with the United States, resulting in increased aid being provided to India. At times this surpassed the amount given to Pakistan, notwithstanding the latter's closer ties. It should be noted that US aid to India was economic and had little or no military components, except during the Sino-Indian war of 1962. In dollar figures the US aid to India was $364 million in 1957, $305 million in 1958, and $758 million in 1960, compared to $170 million, $163 million, and $301 million given to Pakistan over the same period.[24]

The American decision to boost aid to India was prompted by the belief that if India lost out to China in economic competition, it could mean millions of people lost to Communism.[25] The result of this growth in aid to India was Pakistan's growing disillusionment about an alliance with the United States. Part of this stemmed from the fact that India received US aid even though it was a nonaligned state critical of American policy, while Pakistan was treated no differently than India. Pakistan's expectation was that Pakistan would receive more favorable treatment due to its status as a US ally. Moreover, Pakistanis viewed Indian acquisition of US weaponry as being directed against them. General Ayub Khan, the Pakistani president, tried to revitalize the alliance but met with little success. This state of affairs came to a head in 1962, when India was attacked by China and became the recipient of massive amounts of military aid.[26] At this point Pakistan was in the unenviable position of being totally dependent on American aid and therefore could not voice its grievance strongly.

The 1965 war provoked a reappraisal of Pakistan's relations with the United States. The even-handed approach of the Johnson administration (he canceled both Ayub Khan's and Indian premier Shastri's visits in April 1965), infuriated Pakistan, which viewed this as an attempt by the United States to avoid its commitment to Pakistan. The Birch-Grove statement of June 30, 1963, had confirmed that the United States and Britain would continue long-term military aid to India. In 1963 the Ayub government had reached a border accord with China settling existing differences.[27] Later in 1963 the two states reached an agreement allowing Pakistani and Chinese airlines to operate in each other's territory. A trade agreement followed, drawing the two nations closer.

At the same time, there was a brief rapprochement between the Soviet Union and Pakistan. This was facilitated by the Soviet fears that India could be drawn into the Western orbit through the aid it was getting from the United States, its fear that Pakistan might become a client state of China, and its worry that India was not strong enough to withstand China on its own.[28] This did not, however, detract from the primacy of India in Soviet calculations in South Asia. India continued to receive aid from the Soviet Union and by 1963 had been granted a license to produce MiG 21 aircraft. The US response to Pakistan's move toward the Communist camp was to criticize it and later to suspend a loan to build the Dacca airport.[29]

During the period between 1965 and 1971, Pakistan continued to maintain cordial though distant ties with the United States and improve its relationship with China. The 1971 war proved to be a shock to Pakistan. Apart from demonstrating that Indian superiority was an established fact, it also drove home the message that US help would not be forthcoming even when Pakistan was in danger of being dismembered. US support was viewed as too little too late. The Nixon administration, while supportive of the beleaguered Pakistani government (Pakistan's human rights record in Bangladesh had managed to isolate it internationally), did not intervene directly, but suspended arms to both combatants.[30] The years following the war saw a weakening of the US-Pakistan relationship to its lowest level ever. There were several reasons for this dealignment. First, the assistance of Pakistan in facilitating talks for the normalization of US relations with China was a thing of the past. Second, the imperatives of the Cold War had declined with the onset of detente. Third, the new Bhutto government's leftist plank served to alienate American support. Fourth, the attempt of the Pakistani leadership to build a nuclear-weapons program met with strong opposition from the Carter administration.[31] Finally, the resumption of military dictatorship in Pakistan following the coup by General Zia ul Haq and the subsequent execution of Bhutto led to the nadir of US-Pakistani relations, when a mob of students burned down the American embassy in Islamabad.[32]

Pakistan's relations with the United States improved with the Soviet invasion of Afghanistan. Assistance flowed immediately, and during the Reagan era Pakistan developed a cordial relationship with the United States that it had never managed in the past. The reason was obvious: Pakistan had become a frontline state in the war against Communism for the duration of the Afghan War. This support continued after Zia's assassination in 1988. However, with the end of the Afghan war, the Bush administration found itself unable to certify to the US Congress that Pakistan had no nuclear-weapons program and consequently found it difficult to provide military aid. Pakistan's increased interaction with China and its purchase of sensitive (dual-use) technology from that quarter has not met with US approval. Moreover, the strengthened US presence in the Gulf in the 1990s has reduced the importance of Pakistan as a link to the Gulf states. Also, the end of the Cold War reduced Pakistan's strategic importance to the United States, and attention was increasingly focused on Pakistan's nuclear capability and its potential to destabilize South Asia.

This discussion highlights the following features of Pakistan's relationship with the United States. The relationship has oscillated back and forth between affinity and discord. From 1948 to 1953 Pakistan was not part of the US alliance system. Between 1953 to 1957 it joined the alliance system and received military aid from the United States; the relationship seemed to be mutually satisfactory. However, from 1957 onward, the gradual US tilt toward India undermined US-Pakistan relationship, leading to a move toward accommodation with China and culminating in the border and air agreements of 1963. From 1963 to 1970 Pakistan's disillusionment with the United States was reflected in its attempts to diversify arms supply by courting the Soviet Union and building ties with China. The latter was done with an obvious aim of balancing Indian superiority. There was a brief honeymoon period when Pakistan was considered essential to US dealings with China, but evidently it was not considered sufficiently important for the United States to actively intervene in the 1971 war. The weakened US-Pakistan relationship between 1971 and 1979 was sought to be compensated for by Pakistan on two fronts; the objective of acquiring a nuclear capability, and the increased cooperation with China. This situation was repeated after the termination of the Afghan war, and today Pakistan's weapons program is dependent on help from China, as is evident from the testing of the Ghauri missile in April 1998.[33]

## SUMMARIZING THE TRENDS

So far this paper has sought to establish that Pakistan is an essential part of any initiatives in South Asia and that it is crucial to regional stability. Second, it is also clear that Pakistan's perception of its primary threat is that of a strengthened India. Third, Pakistan's response to prior instances of Indo-US cooperation have been increasingly to seek help from elsewhere. This has damaging consequences for peace and stability in South Asia. It is clear that there are changes under way in South Asia. The system of bloc politics is over. The Soviet threat has receded, and with it the importance of Pakistan in US strategy. India's special relationship with the former Soviet Union is also in the doldrums, largely due to the economic downturn in Russia. To many observers, India seems to be making a serious effort to achieve great-power capabilities. These would presumably imply, at the very least, a high rate of economic growth, an enhanced military capability, and possession of sophisticated technologies. Some of these steps are already being taken in India.[34] In the early 1990s there was a major change in economic policy when the Rao government decided to initiate a program to economic liberalization, turning its back on the Nehruvian socialist model that had dominated the Indian mentality for decades. Acquiring new technology has become a national goal and is reflected in the increased dialogue being pursued by successive governments with the United States, though at the time of writing this may appear to have suffered a setback due to India's nuclear tests, which also reflect the Indian desire to achieve status. There also appears to be an objective of improving relations with key powers such as China (this process may have started almost a decade ago under the Rajiv Gandhi government), the United States, Russia, and the other countries of the West.[35]

A RAND Corporation study estimates that if India's growth continues at a rate of 5.5 percent per annum, it would find an "increase . . . [in] India's political options vis-a-vis Pakistan and other great powers." [36] Put simply, India's increased economic strength would translate into higher military expenditures and allow it to retain a more than comfortable advantage over Pakistan. The current ratio of Indian to Pakistani military power is roughly 1.5 to 1 (for all forces, but concentrating on the army and air force, as these are the crucial factors in any Indo-Pak conflict), which makes war between the two a stalemate, at least in the short term (neither side having the capability for a war longer than two or three weeks). However, a dramatic increase in Indian military expenditures would allow India's forces to dwarf the size of Pakistan's military, leading to an effective power transition in South Asia.

## FOUR FUTURE SCENARIOS FOR PAKISTAN

With the radical changes in the strategic equation that Indo-US cooperation would imply for South Asia, Pakistan would be faced with the following options:

1. Accept Indian dominance and try to develop better relations. Adopt a conciliatory attitude, as Ayub Khan did in 1960, and aim for accommodation with India.

2. Follow the current strategy of domestic military expansion, encouraging insurgency in India to keep it occupied within and acquiring missiles and nuclear weapons to provide a deterrent.

3. Follow an external policy of pressuring India through China while attempting to retain ties with the United States.

4. Attempt to recover Kashmir through a short, quick war before India maximizes its power.

In 1960, during the first period of close Indo-American ties, Pakistan found itself in a weak position. It was dependent on the United States; it had no other significant allies. Rather than weaken ties with the United States by protesting too much, Ayub Khan, the Pakistani president, decided on a strategy of accommodation with India. He accepted mediation to bring about the Indus Water Treaty (perhaps the only really successful accord between India and Pakistan), and even broached his offer to India about a common defense against Communism, on the understanding that the Kashmir issue could be resolved peacefully. Such a situation does not exist now. After two wars (1965 and 1971), there is not much hope for a spirit of accommodation. Moreover, Pakistan's ties with China go some way toward removing the insecurity that was inherent at that juncture. A third factor has been that with the increasing Islamization of the Pakistani state under Zia ul Haq, there has been a rise in the presence and activity of fundamentalist Islamic political parties in Pakistan. While these do not have a strong political base, they have introduced a religious dimension that was muted in 1960, since the governing elite of Pakistan at that time was more secular. Reaching an accommodation with India would imply putting Kashmir on the back burner, a strategy that no current Pakistan government can afford.

The current strategy of enhancing military power through high defense expenditures while encouraging insurgency within India seems the most plausible and feasible option open to Pakistan. However, this has the following problems. One, given the Pakistan economy's lackluster performance in the 1990s, sustaining such levels of expenditure would be difficult for the economy (this is especially true at the time of writing, when the Pakistan government was facing the possibility of defaulting on its loans). Secondly, pursuing the nuclear option (or missile technology, for that matter) has had the result of inviting a negative reaction from the United States and, by association, its Western allies (currently, there are rumors, not officially substantiated, that Pakistan may sign the CTBT to remove the pressure of sanctions). Finally, the insurgency within India seems to have lost momentum. The two provinces that had the maximum potential for such action—Punjab, with its disaffected Sikh majority, and Kashmir, with a Muslim majority—have both settled down after a lengthy battle of attrition with the Indian state apparatus. However, Pakistan is attempting to revive the Kashmir question in international forums. There may be few takers for Pakistani-supported insurgencies at present, especially with the nuclearization of the subcontinent and the statement by Indian home minister Advani that Indian forces would carry out "hot pursuit of militants over the Line of Actual Control."

Pakistan's alliance with China seems to be its strongest card at the moment. This relationship has withstood the test of time (and the nuclear tests), and at present both states actively trade and consult on defense matters. A large part of the Pakistani air force consists of Chinese-built MiGs, while their missile cooperation has been well documented. Also, while Pakistan's relations with the United States are no longer as cordial as they were in the 1980s, ties with India have not meant a break with Pakistan. In fact, the US line has been all along that American interests within South

Asia are not a zero-sum game between India and Pakistan. The problem with this strategy is that it does not do much to change the balance of power within South Asia, and certainly does nothing to alleviate Pakistan's central concern, which is Kashmir.

In 1965, concerned with the fact that Indian strength would outstrip Pakistan's in a few years, the Pakistani leadership, under Ayub Khan, had launched an attack on Kashmir with a view toward seizing it by force.[37] India's expansion of the war over the international boundary (rather than confining it to disputed Kashmir) resulted in the stalemate that led to Tashkent. Pakistan may attempt a similar move in the near future in view of other visible signs of Indian military growth after decades of stagnation. The advantage of such a move is that in a short war Pakistan's military inferiority would not be a serious hindrance, as geographically the compact nature of the country allows for quicker redeployment of forces than is the case with India. Indian forces are scattered over two fronts (along the Pakistani and Chinese borders); reserves are deployed in central areas of India, and would take a long time to be redeployed along the border with Pakistan.[38] However, the disadvantage of such an approach is that there is no precedent for Pakistan gaining through initiating a war. Moreover, US support would not be forthcoming; in fact, there would likely be a curtailment of US arms, as in previous conflicts. The possession of nuclear weapons by both India and Pakistan might also escalate the conflict to a level unacceptable to Pakistan. These considerations do not rule out the prospect of a war, as the scare following the Pakistani nuclear tests illustrated: a state of martial law was declared, followed by insecurity on the Pakistani side. Unconfirmed reports from Pakistan claimed the Indian side was gearing to attack Pakistani nuclear sites before the tests; a possible escalation could have started there.

The essential problem confronting any engagement of India by the United States is that Pakistan would not remain a silent spectator in the face of the obvious gains this would imply for India's military and economic potential. How, then, can Pakistan be accommodated in a way that does not compromise regional stability? The following are possible options.

One way would be for the United States to initiate similar cooperation with Pakistan, leading to a growth of defensive technologies that satisfy Pakistan's security needs without detracting from Indian needs. This may involve a larger US role in facilitating a dialogue between Pakistan and India. Another possible way would be for South Asia to be declared a nuclear-free zone, something that Pakistan has been insisting for quite some time. At the very least, this may be accomplished without compromising India's present nuclear policy. It may be possible to explore a path wherein India still remains a nonsignatory to non-proliferation regimes such as the NPT but agrees not to initiate a nuclear showdown with Pakistan. On the Pakistani side, this would require a condition that the Kashmir conflict be settled without the use of force.

It may also be worth exploring the possibility of expanding US cooperation in India into a regional plan whereby all South Asian states are able to benefit, thus replacing the specter of Indian hegemony with the prospect of regional cooperation. The implication for US policy here may be to step forward and offer some kind of a regional peace guarantee, which would perhaps go a long way in assuring South Asian states that their security would not be compromised by Indo-US cooperation.

Ultimately what matters is how any Indo-US dialogue is perceived by states hostile to India, such as Pakistan. Under the current circumstances with a nationalist party such as the BJP holding the reins of power in India, any move toward augmenting Indian power by an external tie would only seek to increase Pakistan's insecurity. Therefore, to make such a dialogue successful, both India and the United States would have to work toward reassuring Pakistan that this would not come at the expense of Pakistan. In conclusion, it may be a fair observation to make that of all the states affected by Indo-US cooperation, the strongest reaction is bound to come from Pakistan, and this is something that would have to be incorporated as a cost prior to initiating any kind of engagement.

## NOTES

1   India's claim to be a secular state where all religious minorities can coexist without governmental interference contradicts Pakistan's claim to be a homeland for the Subcontinent's Muslims. In turn, the existence of Pakistan contradicts the Indian vision of a secular state, due to the obvious reluctance of a large number of Muslims to live within India's borders.

2   Ashley Tellis, *Stability in South Asia,* study DB-185-A (Santa Monica: RAND, 1997), p. 8.

3   Hasan-Askari Rizvi, *Pakistan and the Geostrategic Environment* (New York: St. Martin's, 1993), pp. 20–21.

4   Tellis, *Stability,* p. viii. Tellis regards "ugly stability" as being one where intermittent small-scale conflicts coexist with a general stability, i.e., there are no open hostilities, but both states support and foment insurgency across the border.

5   Rizvi, *Pakistan,* p. 21.

6   It is a well-documented fact that the Indian Muslim population is as large if not larger than that of Pakistan. Taken from the CIA World Factbook, 1997

7   Interviews with numerous Pakistani officials, academics, and researchers confirm a consensus that Pakistan remained fragmented between the Punjabi, Pathan, Sindhi, Mohajir, and Baluch constituencies, the only commonality being a rejection of "Hindu India." Second, Pakistan's foreign policy is essentially a reaction to Indian actions (as a number of Pakistani officials verified in television interviews after the nuclear tests). While this may be the obvious course of action for a small state beleaguered by a larger, hegemonic state, the same is not true of any of India's other neighbors.

8   Rizvi, *Pakistan,* pp. 20–22. Pakistan's claim to be a separate nation for Muslims is threatened by India's large Muslim population, implying that if they could be accommodated within Indian borders, then perhaps the creation of Pakistan itself is an anomaly rather than a historic inevitability.

9   See Robert Wirsing, *Pakistan's Security Under Zia* (New York: St. Martin's, 1991), pp. 4, 90.

10   Ibid., p. 5.

11   Comprehensively described in Mohammad Akhund, *Memoirs of a Bystander* (Karachi: Oxford University Press, 1997). See chapters 6 and 10.

12   Rizvi, *Pakistan,* p. 20.

13   Ibid., p. 21.

14   See S. M. Burke, *Pakistan's Foreign Policy: A Historical Analysis* (London: Oxford University Press, 1973), pp.353–55.

15   Wirsing, *Pakistani Security*, p. 13.

16   Pakistan actually called off talks dealing with the repatriation of nationals after the 1971 war, in order to protest the test. See Rizvi, *Pakistan,* p.36.

17   The statements of right-wing Hindu fundamentalists that India's natural boundaries extend from the Hindu Kush to the Burma border especially worry Pakistan. While this has never been an official statement, the political vehicle of such elements, the Bharatiya Janata Party, is at the time of writing leading a coalition government in New Delhi.

18   See Morrice James, *Pakistan Chronicle* (London: St. Martin's, 1993), p. 25.

19   See Akhund, *Memoirs*. See Chapter 7 for a detailed description of the negotiations. Pakistan understood the negotiations to involve a meaningful dialogue with India on Kashmir, which did not materialize due to Indian intransigence. Thus there was a sense of loss after perceiving a military victory (which is debatable), and this was to result in the subsequent ouster of Ayub Khan as president of Pakistan.

20   James, *Pakistan Chronicale,* p. 226.

21   While there are a large number of sources for reference, a comprehensive discussion is available in Emma Duncan, *Breaking the Curfew: A Political Journey Through Pakistan* (New York: St. Martin's, 1990), chapter 1.

22   Burke, *Pakistan's Foreign Policy*, p. 164.

23   Discarding the Stalinist policy of regarding all Third World states not governed by socialist/Communist parties as "bourgeois democracies," Khrushchev's policy from 1955 onward was to cultivate all such states and maintain cordial ties where possible. This was especially successful with India, which was a founder of the nonaligned movement. Unlike Dulles's intransigence, the Soviets were more willing to support such states, in the view that keeping them out of American alliances was a goal in itself.

24   Burke, *Pakistan's Foreign Policy*, p. 255.

25   This view of any kind of economic competition was not shared by Indians and was probably an American reaction intended to prevent another "China" from taking place. However, the weakness of Indian Communist parties and the strength of the centrist Congress Party attest to this view as being a mistaken reading of the situation.

26   See Norman D. Palmer, *The United States and India: Dimensions of Influence* (New York: Praeger, 1984), pp. 26–28.

27   Burke, *Pakistan's Foreign Policy*, p. 291.

28   Ibid., p. 299.

29   Ibid., p. 312.

30   Akhund, *Memoirs*, pp. 190–93.

31   In June 1977 the Carter administration turned down Pakistan's request for A-7 aircraft, in September it suspended aid in retaliation for the planned purchase by Pakistan of a French nuclear reprocessing plant, and in April 1979 all aid save humanitarian was suspended under the provisions of the Symington Amendment. See Wirsing, p.9.

32   Rizvi, *Pakistan*, p. 94.

33   "The Ghauri," *The Hindu,* April 10, 1998.

34   Tellis, *Stability*, p. 35.

35   Satu Limaye has documented the change in Indian attitudes toward the US government as early as the early 1980s: *US-Indian Relations* (Boulder, CO: Westview, 1993), pp. 79–83.

36   Tellis, *Stability*, p. 37, quoting another RAND study by Charles Wolf Jr. et al., *Long term Economic and Military Trends, 1994–2015* (Santa Monica: RAND, 1995).

37   At that time Pakistan believed that they were at near parity, at least in military terms.

38   Tellis, *Stability*, pp. 20–22.

# 12

# Contending with the "Bear-ish" Arms Market: US-Indian Strategic Cooperation and Russia

## Igor Khripunov and Anupam Srivastava

The lattice structure of the current Indo-Russian relationship both bears striking similarities to and also constitutes a notable departure from the previous patterns of Soviet-Indian relations. The similarities stem from an impressive record of bilateral relations throughout the twentieth century. Since its inception in 1917, the Soviet Union supported the anticolonialist aspirations of the Indian people as part of its strategy to fight imperialism and promote Communist values. Both political cultures had much in common, and subsequent Soviet support for India as an independent state (since 1947) laid the groundwork for the fostering of a relationship of trust and mutual respect.

After the disintegration of the Soviet Union, both Russia and India were driven by a common vision of the new post–Cold War quality of their relations, resulting from an increased convergence that is largely nonideological, motivated by self-interest, and based on their shared concept of the world as multipolar.

## INDIA AS A VALUABLE PLAYER IN THE SOVIET FOREIGN-POLICY STRATEGY

During the Cold War years, India proved to be a valuable asset to the Soviet Union as regards two of its major strategic concerns, China and the United States. In the first case, equipped mostly with Soviet-manufactured conventional weapons but lacking any other credible deterrent, India played a pivotal countervailing role for the USSR on China's southern flank. Bolstering India militarily and otherwise was of paramount importance to the Soviet Union, which had to deploy up to one-third of its armed forces close to its border with China.

In the second case, as the leader of the nonaligned movement (NAM), India acted as a vital informal ally in the global standoff between the Soviet Union and the United States. India's foreign policy objectives (and actions) fitted perfectly into the Cold War zero-sum game, wherein what was bad or unacceptable to the United States was good and acceptable to the Soviet Union. The track record shows that on some issues discussed at the United Nations, India's position was even more antagonistic to the West than that of the Soviet Union. India was viewed as an important, though not always ideologically reliable, springboard for ideological and political expansion into the Asia-Pacific region which, being tightly controlled by the West, was basically off limits to the Soviet Union.

The moderating role that India played during the war in Afghanistan (1979–88) was deeply appreciated by the Soviet leadership, whose policies were overwhelmingly condemned by most other countries. The scale of cooperation between the USSR and India could only be compared to that with Egypt—another major Soviet ally at that time. Then Egypt finally changed sides and embraced the United States, making India an indispensable player for the Soviet Union and its leading partner in the Third World.[1]

It is hard to quantify the tangible and direct benefits accruing to the Soviet Union from transferring critical weapons systems to India. Throughout the Cold War, only one-third of the total weapons transferred outside the Soviet Union were actually sold for cash, while the rest were provided free of charge or on credit. While the pecuniary benefits from these arms transfers could have been significant, the leverage that free transfers offered the Soviet leadership in subsequent bilateral negotiations was considered to be more important. Thus, ideological and foreign-policy considerations often prevailed over economic benefits, and Russian dealings with India were no exception to this.

India was the largest recipient of Soviet weaponry and military assistance. The Soviet Union helped to build production facilities for MiG-21 and MiG-23/27 fighter aircraft, and a tank factory (in Avadi, Tamil Nadu) designed to repair T-72 tanks. All payments were made in Indian rupees, which went into the account of the USSR State Bank and were used to purchase Indian goods. Soviet weapons manufacturers were not directly involved at that time in the arms trade; revenues from abroad were channeled into the state budget, and payment for military articles always came from the state budget and was paid in rubles. The trade mechanism was highly centralized and controlled.

In addition, the Soviet Union was heavily involved in a wide range of industrial projects in India. Aside from the tangible material benefits that accrued to the Soviet Union, the political symbolism of such projects continued to dominate. On the other hand, the Indian leadership had little problem in accepting these projects, which were of relatively low technological sophistication, since much of the Indian economic sector was state-run, and they were unable to absorb more advanced technologies.

As of 1993, when a Russian-Indian intergovernmental agreement on repayment (and rescheduling) of debt was reached, Indian owed Russia between $9.3 billion and $11.6 billion, which included interest payments.[2] Not all of this debt was incurred through arms purchases. The Soviet Union supplied India with large quantities of energy, heavy industrial goods, and both new and semiprocessed material.[3]

## RUSSIA AS A SOVIET SUCCESSOR STATE AND ITS AGENDA FOR BILATERAL RELATIONS

The early 1990s dramatically transformed the bilateral relationship with India. In the first place, the relative positions of Russia and India have changed. It is estimated that in terms of GNP, Russia (which no longer ranks among the fifteen leading economies in the world) trails India. The economic and financial crises that engulfed Russia in August 1998 have further dampened prospects for robust economic growth in the near term.[4] Russia's defense budget, currently under $5 billion, lags behind India's.[5] Thus, given the state of the Russian economy, the Indian economy was not only catching up but also enjoying some important advantages.

Although microeconomic or even intersectoral comparisons between the two countries are not within the scope of this paper, a few broad points nevertheless deserve mention. Since its independence, India has systematically employed five-year plans as the basis for the allocation of governmental and private resources and for the establishment of priorities to meet developmental objectives. The inspiration for five-year plans is attributed to the visit of Jawaharlal Nehru to the Soviet Union in the 1930s, where he was exposed to the Soviet *pyatiletki* (five-year plans).[6] A review of successive five-year plans and the pattern of resource outlays reveals governmental attention to the development of the industrial and agricultural infrastructure, which would become the basis for rapid expansion in the future.[7]

Barring episodic disruptions owing to political and extraeconomic considerations, the trajectory of India's five-year plans has been to strengthen the infrastructure and, with governmental supervision, to incrementally increase the role of the private sector. As a consequence, the fundamentals of the Indian economy are fairly strong and have significant long-term growth potential. Following the economic restructuring (Indian-style *perestroika*) and liberalization since July 1991, India has taken dramatic strides toward closer integration into the global economic matrix. At its current rate of growth, according to one estimate, India would become the fourth largest economy in the world by 2020 (after the United States, China, and Japan).[8]

India possesses one of the largest pools of technical manpower in the world. The widespread use of the English language, the existence of rule of law, the longevity of financial institutions, lower wages for skilled personnel, and democracy are all factors that give it a long-term advantage over other South Asian and Southeast Asian economies. This applies to the potential for technological collaboration with, as well as investment destination for, the advanced industrial economies of the world.

It is within the above context that laudatory prognostications for the Indian economy should be situated. In comparison, as a successor state, Russia has inherited many of the advantages as well as ills of the ailing Soviet economy. It is a well-known fact that the Cold War rivalry forced the Soviet Union to engage in a disproportionate allocation of resources and priorities to the defense sector. As a consequence, the civilian sector languished. Given the current lack of domestic consensus on directions of economic growth and restructuring, Russia's ability to identify and capture global market niches is severely limited. The rate of inflation-adjusted economic growth continues to be negative, and foreign (or domestic) investments in infrastructure remain highly unsatisfactory. Both the conversion of the defense infrastructure and the definition of a minimum industrial base remain inconclusive. Add to this the August 1998 crisis, the continuous revamping of the government and the uncertain health (and leadership) of President Yeltsin, and the prospects for rapid recovery of the Russian economy appear even more illusory.

The groundwork for Russian-Indian relations was laid with the signing of a friendship and cooperation treaty during President Yeltsin's visit to India in January 1993. This was a declaratory document reminiscent of similar treaties of the Soviet period. Among other important bilateral agreements concluded during this summit meeting was an agreement on defense cooperation. Another basic document signed a year later, during the visit of Prime Minister Narasimha Rao to Moscow in June and July 1994, was the Declaration on the Protection of the Interests of Pluralistic States. This declaration enumerated the new challenges to the viability of large, multiethnic, multilingual, multicultural, and multireligious states by the forces of aggressive nationalism, religious and political extremism, terrorism and separatism, and it laid out the need to combat these challenges through democracy, secularism, tolerance, and the rule of law.

Its significance for bilateral relations was Russia's recognition of its vulnerabilities and the similarities with the problems faced by India. In other words, a new twist in the two countries' relationship was that they found themselves in the same category. This has had important implications for the manner in which the two countries have started to talk a common language and identify similar pitfalls in their future.

However, during the period 1992–94 there was a dangerous gap between the well-intentioned bilateral declarations and the realities. One reason was that the disintegration of the Soviet Union disrupted numerous cooperative arrangements throughout its territory, including defense production, which brought about a dramatic drop in Russia's exports to India. In 1993 and 1994, Indian imports from Russia were three times smaller than its exports to Russia. Irregular deliveries of spare parts and other products from Russian defense manufacturers forced the Indian government to start looking for compatible alternative resources and substitutes in other newly independent states and Central European countries. Another difficulty during this period was that an influential segment of the Russian foreign-policy elite had illusions about Russia belonging exclusively to Western civilization. Shortly, however, its honeymoon with the West ended in a bitter disappointment, propelling Moscow to wholeheartedly embrace its Euro-Asian destiny.

A report prepared by the Moscow-based Gorbachev Foundation stated that during the first several years of Russia's existence as an independent state, "Russian-Indian relations were marginalized in terms of official policy and public interest." However, the report stressed that there is a growing consensus that India is Russia's strategic partner, and close cooperation with it should become "a permanent feature" of Russia's foreign policy, regardless of its relationship with other countries and their attitudes. [9]

The steady improvement in Russian-Indian relations climaxed in 1997 with a number of important breakthroughs in areas that previously had been outside the framework of bilateral cooperation. In October, Anatoli Kulikov, the minister for internal affairs, successfully negotiated a protocol enabling the two countries to dramatically expand cooperation between their national law enforcement agencies. In November 1997, Russia's Health Minister visited New Delhi and provided a fresh impetus to the development of joint projects (Russia is becoming one of the largest consumers of India's health care products). Gennady Seleznev, chairman of the Duma (the lower houses of Russia's legislature), also came to India in November on a highly successful official visit.

Among the bilateral documents developed and/or approved in 1997 is the extension of the defense cooperation agreement, an MOU on export control, a set of documents concerning the construction of two nuclear power plants in Tamil Nadu, and so on. Thus the year of 1997 was a watershed in what can be viewed as dramatic upgrading of bilateral relations.

## VISION OF A MULTIPOLAR POST–COLD WAR WORLD

During the first half of the 1990s, Russia publicly launched its new strategy in which it envisioned a multipolar world explicitly directed against the unipolar structure dominated by the United States as the sole surviving superpower. India willingly subscribed to this theory as consistent with its own national interests. Russia's foreign minister, Evgeni Primakov, was the main architect and proponent of the multipolar concept. The thrust of his argument, as reflected in numerous official policy papers and statements, is that multipolarity would enable Russia to diversify its international relations without unduly gravitating toward any particular pole. According to Primakov, since Russia was destined in the future to become one of the poles itself, it would be unacceptable for it to operate in a global framework of leaders and followers.[10] His becoming the prime minister in September 1998 has undoubtedly strengthened the multipolarity approach as the basis of Russia's foreign policy orientation.

Though elevated to the status of a foreign policy concept, Primakov's interpretation of multipolarity was not unanimously shared by Russia's foreign-policy elite. For instance, a report submitted in early 1998 by Russia's Foreign and Defense Policy Council was based on the premise that the world is moving from bipolarity to a fluid international system, rather than a multipolar one. Participating in the discussion, Primakov responded that there was no contradiction between a fluid system and a multipolar system; the important thing is to avoid a unipolar system.[11]

Other Russian experts coined the term "functional partnership," which is particularly relevant to India. It means that Russia's foreign policy objective should be to create an environment in which countries such as India could be motivated to turn to Russia if they felt threatened or perceived a growing commonality of interests. Such functional partnership may evolve either into an independent power center or an alternative to any international coalition intended to pressure any particular state on a specific issue. However, if this convergence of interests is particularly strong, this partnership with Russia could be upgraded to the level of an alliance-type relationship. Under this option, Russia is supposed to perform a balancing act on the global stage in order to avoid a conflict with the powerful countries.[12]

In this new multipolar vision of the world, Russia formally designated India as its "strategic partner" and moved it to the top of the list of the most important countries with which it would maintain special relations.[13] Prime Minister H. D. Deve Gowda's visit to Moscow in March 1997 marked a breakthrough. Though Russia kept referring to India as its "strategic partner," New Delhi preferred at the time to use a different phrase, "strategic dimension of bilateral cooperation," lest there be a misleading impression of a security tie-up that India would like to avoid.[14] Subsequently, however, in a congratulatory message to Russia's prime minister, Sergei Kiriyenko,[15] the Indian premier, Atal Behari Vajpayee, emphasized the readiness of his cabinet to closely cooperate with the new government in Russia with the goals of elevating bilateral relations to the level of strategic partnership and maintaining stability in the world.[16]

## THE CHINA FACTOR

As regards countervailing China, India's role has evidently become much less important with the dramatic improvement in Russian-Chinese relations. Two recent confidence-building and border agreements with China—one involving Russia and the contiguous NIS states, and the other delimiting the Russian-Chinese border—introduced more stability and predictability in the region. Both countries now characterize their relationship as a strategic partnership directed toward the twenty-first century. China has become the second largest buyer of Russian manufactured weapons, including SU-27 fighter-bombers, advanced submarines, S-300 air defense systems, and so on.

Attempting to explain what might seem to be an embarrassing position of supplying modern weapons to two regional adversaries (India and China), Russian officials claim that such arms deliveries do not break the balance of force in the Asia-Pacific region but rather help restore it.[17] If one is to assume that the pursuit of Russia's security policy is effectively coordinated, then arming the two regional powers by mutually countervailing each other would make sense. However, in the wake of the nuclear tests conducted by India and Pakistan, the Russian dilemma is how to maintain China and India as Russia's major weapons export destinations if tensions on the Indo-Pakistani front should escalate. Losing one or the other (together, they account for over two-thirds of Russia's weapons exports) would deal a crippling blow to Russia's defense industry, for which export revenue comprises about 62 percent of its total budget.

At the same time, in recognition of the real and immediate threat to India from Pakistan, Russia has so far consistently declined selling weapons to Pakistan. Showing loyalty to India as a past, current, and prospective customer, the Russian government decided against providing vital parts and components for Ukrainian-manufactured (T-80) tanks under order from Pakistan.[18] In reality, it would be virtually impossible to draw a distinct line between non-Russian NIS weapons exports and Russia itself. Though the Russian military-industrial complex formally disintegrated with the collapse of the Soviet Union, contractual relations with the NIS defense enterprises are being successfully restored. For example, Russia's 100 aerospace plants regularly get over 130 high-tech components from Ukraine, almost 80 percent of which are exclusively manufactured for Russia. Efforts are on to set up an international consortium, International Aircraft Engines, which would integrate nearly a thousand production facilities in Russia and Ukraine.[19]

In the case of Ukraine's contract to deliver tanks to Pakistan, there are reports that the first shipment was equipped with Russian-manufactured components, and Russian experts shared blueprints and technologies with their Ukrainian colleagues at the Malyshev tank-building factory in Kharkiv.

Experts are ambivalent regarding Russian policy of supplying conventional weapon systems (and technologies) to both India and China. Writing in *Defense News,* Swaran Singh of the Institute for Defense Studies and Analyses in New Delhi sounds an alarm at the scale and pace of Russian-Chinese military cooperation. In addition to well-publicized deals, he claims that the least known, and even more threatening, has been Russia's contribution to China's revision of its military doctrine, which lately has shifted from active defense to fighting high-technology, limited wars which could soon influence regional and global issues.[20] The opposite view has been consistently voiced by SIPRI researcher Eric Arnett, who says that the idea of India facing a threat from China flies in the face of ten years of Chinese military reforms, the improvement in Sino-Indian relations, and the reality that—apart from rhetoric—India does not behave as if China is a nuclear threat. His conclusion is that "China does not figure in India's military planning or arms control policy."[21]

Repeated statements in the spring of 1998 by some members of India's new cabinet about China as the major threat to its national security could be conceivably construed as a well-orchestrated public relations campaign in anticipation of May's nuclear tests. On the other hand, the Chinese factor is likely to have a powerful impact on the evolution of Russian-Indian relations. Given the widening gap between the current performance and long-term growth projections of their economic sectors, political accommodation with Beijing is not a luxury but a compelling necessity for Moscow. Indeed, should there be a need, Russia would be compelled to choose China over India, however difficult the choice may be.

India's nuclear tests dampened the hopes of Russia's foreign-policy elite that the differences between New Delhi and Beijing can be reconciled and that Russia would be able to fashion an Asian triangle, consisting of China, India, and itself, that could act as a counterweight to the West, as well as a security tool for Asia. However, Prime Minister Primakov's improvised reference to this triangle during his December 1998 visit to India indicated that this idea is alive and well. In the geopolitical environment of the twenty-first century, Russia cannot afford to treat its Far Eastern borders as just one among many. Among its perceived threats and concerns from China are its growing dependence on the latter's markets; a quiet economic, if not political, takeover of Russia's Far East and parts of Siberia; rapid growth in the numerical and political clout of the Chinese minority in the Russian mainland; and interference into the affairs of the former Soviet republics in Central Asia. It seems tempting to Russia to use India for attenuating its security concerns arising from Chinese policy activism in the region.

## INDIA'S STABILIZING IMPACT ON CENTRAL ASIA

Under the broad rubric of multipolarity, Russia would like to encourage India to play a stabilizing role vis-à-vis those Central Asian republics that were earlier part of the Soviet Union. An indication of the growing alarm is an agreement reached in May 1998 between Russia and Uzbekistan to team up with the former Soviet republic of Tajikistan to keep the region free from the threat of Islamic fundamentalism.

Similarly, though Turkey is a major trade partner, Russia has concerns about its attempts to use its historic and ethnic heritage to expand its influence in the region. Further, Russia expresses concern at the virtual stampede of Western countries jockeying for maximal access to the energy resources of Azerbaijan, Kazakhstan, and Turkmenistan. A high-profile moderating role for India, either singly or in conjunction with Russia, would be a welcome move. At a recent meeting of the Indo-Russian bilateral working group on energy, Russia suggested several areas of cooperation, including supply of natural gas to India by extending a pipeline from Siberia, possibly in combination with Central Asia–based projects.[22]

India, however, has so far demonstrated a marked reluctance to assume this stabilizing role in Central Asia. Consequently, a Moscow-based think tank recommended in its report of 1997 that given the nuclear stand-off between India and Pakistan, Russia might eventually wish to reconsider its existing policy of keeping Pakistan at an arm's length.[23] At the same time, there was a renewed round of discussion among Russian nongovernmental experts about the wisdom of selling weapons to Pakistan. In addition to the fact that Indian weapons purchases from Russia would easily dwarf the import request from Pakistan, the time-tested partnership with India was also an inhibiting factor in the decision to move closer to Pakistan. Russia's leading weapons manufacturer, Rosvooruzhenie, conducted a study recently that concluded Pakistan's anticipated weapons request would comprise only about 15 percent of that from India.[24] The 1998 nuclear tests in South Asia, however, could lead to a serious reevaluation of the Russian arms transfer policy in the future.

## BILATERAL MILITARY-TECHNICAL COOPERATION

If Russia's areas of interest in India are lined up in terms of current priorities, weapons exports top the agenda, making India the largest recipient of Russian-manufactured weapons. This represents a dramatic shift in Russia's foreign-policy agenda, where erstwhile ideological considerations increasingly cede primacy to short-term economic gains. According to Sergei Prikhodko, presidential foreign-policy advisor, Russia's foreign policy is no longer geared to "slogans or abstract ideas" but rather serving the interests of industrialists, exporters, and taxpayers.[25] In this context, it is significant that Russia's leading interest groups and lobbyists, including those who represent the defense industry, wield more influence over government decisions than their counterparts in the West. [26]

A testimony to the durability of Soviet-Indian defense cooperation is that more than 60 percent of the Indian army's military hardware is Russian-made, while 70 percent of naval hardware and 80 percent of the air force hardware is of Russian origin.[27] It is estimated that Indian defense contracts and requirements kept about eight hundred Russian defense production facilities in operation.[28] Thus, any major disruption in this relationship would have dire consequences not only for Russia's defense industry, but also for the long-term modernization of its domestic armed forces. In some experts' view, the share of the domestic Defense Ministry acquisitions ranges from 10 to 20 percent of the entire defense production, while India and China regularly import up to 80 percent of the total production.[29] And within that, since India imports the larger share, there are grounds to submit that its purchases are critical to the survival of Russia's defense industry.

Both sides agreed in 1997, long before the official expiration date of 2000, that the 1994 bilateral agreement on defense cooperation should be extended through 2010. This extension was formalized in December 1998. The idea behind this initiative was to provide as much latitude for future arms deals as possible. Russian experts observe, with some satisfaction, that India has lagged in fulfilling its original target of reaching self-sufficiency in arms manufacturing. As such, its dependency on Russian supply sources will continue, and at least for the next ten years, India will remain the top customer for Russia's defense industry.[30]

As of now, the total value of the contracts concluded between Russia and India exceed $9 billion. India is purchasing forty SU-30 MK aircraft fighters at a total cost of $1.8 billion, while negotiations are on for the construction of an SU-30 production facility in India. According to the terms of this deal, Russia will supply the SU-30s in batches of eight, in component form (the first batch has already reached India), to be assembled at HAL laboratories in Bangalore, India. Indian scientists are to work on the later batches with their counterparts in Russia. The last batch, to be dubbed SU-30 MKI, will meet the specifications given by India. The earlier batches will then be retrofitted to bring them up to the current specifications, to be followed by joint manufacturing of the aircraft in India. This aircraft production is the first instance of a major collaborative research endeavor in strategic aeronautics between these two sides.

It must also be stressed that the purchase of SU-30 MKs was a well-considered decision, made after weighing other options. Writing in the *Indian Defense Review,* B. K. Bishnoi, a retired air marshall, indicated that the choice was made on the merits of the case rather than considerations of cost, traditions, and political convenience. According to Bishnoi, with the induction of SU-30 MKs, and later SU-30 MKIs, the impact of India's air power will not be only on Pakistan. Indeed, the sea lanes of the Indian Ocean, the Arabian Sea, and the Bay of Bengal could also be brought under effective surveillance through maritime operations.

Russia is playing a major role in transferring an air refueling capability (IL-76s) to India that would expand the range of SU-30s up to 5,200 km with a single midair refueling. With the acquisition and induction of aerial refueling capability, it could assume intercontinental dimensions— a major projection of India's airpower.[31]

Another large project is retrofitting and upgrading about 125 MiG-21s by integrating state-of-the-art onboard radar. Modernized MiG-21 is claimed to be comparable to the much more expensive Mirage-2000-5 and only slightly inferior to the F-16. Two more diesel-powered submarines of the 636 project are on order. Russia will embark on modernizing about fifteen previously exported submarines if the ongoing modernization of a Varshavyanka-class submarine at Severodvinsk is found to be to the satisfaction of the Indian Navy.

As of mid-1998 talks were entering the final stages for India to purchase the aircraft carrier, *Admiral Gorshkov.* Built in 1984 and decommissioned in 1995, the carrier can be equipped with a ramp to allow fixed-wing aircraft to be carried aboard, rather than only the vertical take-off planes that it had been originally designed for (namely, 24 Yak-38 short-range fighters). It was reported that a modification of the MiG-29 fighter, the MiG-29 SMT, which is yet to be inducted into Russia's armed forces, was tested for the overhauled Gorshkov. The planned sale of the carrier and the MiG-29 SMTs could carry a price tag of over $1 billion. According to the same sources, India was also buying Krivak III frigates, to be delivered by 2004.[32] India is also considering purchasing Russia's newest T-90C tanks and Msta self-propelled gun,[33] S-300 air defense systems,[34] and many other items.

A new development in bilateral military-technical cooperation (MTC) is Indian overtures to buy Russian surplus weapons. According to a report quoting Nikolai Mikhailov, first deputy defense minister, Russia was considering several Indian proposals to buy air defense systems that have been field operated in the past but are currently in storage. Such systems would be used for training purposes in India. Certainly, the systems would have to be reconditioned and sold at prices "substantially lower than those of the newer ones."[35] Such proposals were particularly appealing to Russia's Ministry of Defense because under the existing laws, such revenue would be channeled to the ministry to augment social benefits to the military, as also finance the restructuring of the armed forces.

The scope of Russian-Indian MTC goes well beyond mere transfers of weapons and military hardware, and servicing. India is entering into a phase where, whether it wants or not, its MTC with Russia acquires a semblance of closely coordinated efforts in the defense area short of a formal alliance. This evolving cooperation fits into the widest possible definition currently discussed by Russian military, which would eventually include codesigning and coproduction, joint exercises, use of each other's facilities, and so on.[36] India's advantage as an MTC partner is that, unlike China, it is perceived as the most benign recipient of weapons, posing no threat whatsoever to Russia's own security interests.[37]

## ECONOMIC AND TRADE RELATIONS

The track record of bilateral cooperation in nondefense sectors is not so commendable, however. From being a priority area during the Soviet era, this has slumped to abysmal levels and now threatens to undercut the successes of bilateral interaction in the geopolitical realm. Thus, bilateral trade had shrunk from $5.5 billion in 1990 to less than $1.3 billion in 1998, although the trade imbalance has been reversed, with Indian exports to Russia standing at $575 million and imports at $712.5 million in 1997–98.[38] Currently, India accounts for as little as 1.5 percent of Russia's foreign trade. Russia's principal exports to India are news print, ferrous, and nonferrous metals, and fertilizers. In turn, India sells pharmaceutical items, tea, coffee, nuts, rice, and other agricultural products—which account for over half of its exports to Russia. Since most of these deliveries are paid for from the aggregated debt in rupees, India has little incentive to diversify its trade with Russia by adding other items that can be easily sold in hard-currency markets.

Under the 1992 bilateral agreement, India was required to repay about $10 billion over 12 years, $1 billion of which would be used each year to buy Indian goods. But the arrangement has not worked as planned with Russia failing to buy $1 billion worth of goods from India in any year.[39] Reviewing the unimpressive status of bilateral trade relations, the Russian media sarcastically puts into question the appropriateness of calling the Russian-Indian relationship "strategic." [40]

A good case in point is Russia's lost opportunities in the Indian power sector. Originally the Soviet Union built thirteen hydroelectric power plants with a total rated capacity of 5,000 MW. However, Russia has lost a number of new contracts to its competitors from the West, some involving modernization of facilities built by the Soviet Union. Accordingly, in December 1997 the agenda of the bilateral energy group included in its discussion the possible role for Russia in modernizing the Bhakhra-Nangal hydel plant, and supplying spare parts for two thermal power plants.[41]

Russia has ceded its hitherto strong position in the Indian energy market to other suppliers because until the early 1990s the oil and oil products it sold to India originated mostly in Iraq, which is still under UN sanctions. India would like to purchase up to 2 million tons of coal from Russia, but the cost of transporting it from Kuzbass to the Far East and then shipping it to India, makes the overall selling price prohibitively high. In order to improve the situation, the bilateral group on oil and natural gas examined the prospects of channeling Indian investments into Russia's energy-related projects, and joint projects in third countries. Talks are under way to enhance Russia's involvement in joint oil and natural gas prospecting on the Indian territory.

This new trend of turning bilateral cooperation into a mutually rewarding two-way street is particularly visible in the transportation sector. Since the Russian port of Novorossiisk now plays a leading role in bilateral freight traffic, the Indian side is planning to fund the construction of some new port facilities by using its debt payments. Russia and India are also discussing a project involving the development of a mixed-mode transit route between the two countries via Iran and the Caspian Sea.

Economic cooperation between Russia and India has been hampered by the lack of trust and misperception between financial institutions. Russia has been designated as a high-risk investment destination. Its private banks, companies, and other institutions are treated with considered skepticism. However, there are some encouraging signs that Russia can resume its role in implementing long-term, large-scale projects. In December 1997 most remaining obstacles to Russia's construction of a nuclear-power station in Kudankulam, Tamil Nadu (India) were removed. This project was agreed upon and signed about ten years ago, but until very recently both sides had failed to finalize the financial arrangements. Under a compromise formula, Russia will provide a credit of over $2.5 billion, which would cover about 85 percent of the project cost. A quarter of the credit can be paid for by Indian goods, while the remainder shall be payable in US dollars. Following his June 1998 visit to India, when the arrangement to construct the Kudankulam project was formalized, Russia's minister for atomic energy, Evgenii Adamov, said that profit was not even the main motive for his industry, which is the lead agency for the project. According to him, the primary objective was to secure resources to pay the salaries of MINATOM employees, maintain work at the nuclear design bureaus and production facilities, and provide fresh momentum to the development of the domestic nuclear industry in general.[42] This amply demonstrates the significance of the Kudankulam project for the Russian side.

Cooperation in space technologies is a much less publicized area, but given India's proclaimed aspirations to become a full-fledged space power, Russia's collaboration is crucial. A good case in point is India's cryogenic engine program, developed in cooperation with the Soviet Union. The Indian Space Research Organization (ISRO) is understood to have been engaged in indigenous and Indo-Russian research on cryogenic rocket engine technology since the early 1990s.

For about three years, both Glavkosmos (a Russian space agency) and ISRO were threatened with sanctions from the United States. This stemmed from the Russian intent to transfer the cryogenic technology to India, which the US viewed as a violation of the Missile Technology Control Regime (MTCR). Finally, under a compromise formula, Glavkosmos has been permitted a one-time waiver to supply only the engines but not the technology to ISRO, since their contract predates Russia's membership joining the MTCR, and the obligations assumed thereunder relating to the transfer of technology and related equipment. Under this arrangement, Russia has begun the supply of the cryogenic engines (seven in all) to ISRO.[43] At the same time, India's indigenous R&D efforts have yielded good results, and reports of testing of the engine, or components thereof, have been available. For instance, it was reported that ISRO successfully tested its own engine for about one minute at its Mahendragiri test facility near Tamil Nadu. Nevertheless, the flight data (and other details) that will become available from the Russian engines will considerably reduce the research lead time for the indigenous version.

There is a great potential for further expansion of bilateral missile and space cooperation, particularly following India's growing budget allocation in this area. The 1998–99 budget, released in June 1998, increased the funding for ISRO by 52 percent—the largest hike in ISRO's history. The new budget for the year 1999–2000 released on February 27, 1999, continues this trend with an increase of 16 percent in the budget of the Department of Space.[44] The focus of this program is to develop a Geostationary launch vehicle (GSLV) that will use the Russian-made cryogenic upper-stage rocket. The new budget provides money for construction of a launch pad at Sriharikota, on the eastern coast of India, from where the GSLV-MK1 is expected to begin its maiden flight in early 1999. The indigenous cryogenic upper stage (MK2) is unlikely to fly before the year 2000.[45]

In September 1998 the governments of Russia and India decided to unveil their collaborative endeavor to build sea-based platforms for the Indian nuclear arsenal. A report from the Russian Defense Ministry confirms that Moscow will help New Delhi complete a submarine hull and install a nuclear reactor by the end of 1998. With this assistance, the Indian navy is expected to commission its first nuclear-powered submarine, Sagarika, by the year 2004.[46] It should be noted that the timely launch of Sagarika has been hampered on several counts. The first problem related to miniaturizing the size of the nuclear reactor, and then mating it with the design of the hull of the submarine. The second problem lay in improving the accuracy of the underwater stage of the SLBM, also designated Sagarika, that would be launched from the submarine.[47]

There are indications that, for the first time in the history of bilateral cooperation, high-technology interaction between the two countries is also becoming a two-way street. This might suggest that cash-starved Russia is developing a taste for India's innovative technologies which would have been available from Western sources at a much higher cost, and with many strings attached. A good example of this trend is Russia's interest in India's computer research and manufacturing. In recent years, Russia has imported several Indian designed Param-8600 units. The Russian media proudly hailed the recent introduction of Param-10000, making India the third most advanced computer manufacturing country in the world after the United States and Japan.[48]

Bilateral high-technology collaboration is becoming particularly visible in the area of MTC. During the visit to Russia of former Defense Minister Mulayam Singh Yadav in October 1997, both countries decided to set up a joint working group to further military-technical cooperation through joint R&D. An editorial in *The Hindu* stressed that the two countries have gone a step further to deal with the joint modernization and development of new land-based weapon systems such as artillery and rocket guns and tanks. It urged the Indian government to seize this opportunity, since "the proposal made by the Russians reflect the value they attach to the contribution India could make in a high-technology area." [49]

The fourth meeting of the Indo-Russian working group on MTC held in New Delhi in December 1997 put special emphasis on bilateral high-technology collaboration. Among other things, the group discussed the establishment of direct contacts between Russian and Indian manufacturers of weapons, including joint experiments and design projects to develop new defense technologies and weapon systems. Russian and Indian officials agreed to accelerate the modernization of the MiG-21 BIS fighter and to begin work on developing new onboard equipment for the MiG-27 fighter-bombers, which are built in India. They also reviewed the progress on the joint development of a navigational computer and other electronic components for the multipurpose SU-30 MKI, to be produced in India after 2000. [50]

## IMPLICATIONS OF INDIA'S NUCLEAR TESTING

On the day after India's nuclear-weapons test, President Yeltsin delivered a major foreign-policy address at the Ministry of Foreign Affairs in Moscow. Departing from the prepared text, he remarked briefly that India had let Russia down. Most probably the comment betrayed his personal frustration, because the tests came just as he was set to leave for the G-8 summit in Birmingham, where the advanced industrial nations were to discuss the imposition of sanctions against India.

Yeltsin anticipated being isolated because of Russian-Indian relations and hard pressed to defend them.

To Yeltsin's relief, though the G-8 leaders condemned the tests, they refrained from initiating specific measures against India. Some countries, such as Canada, Japan, and the United States, imposed unilateral sanctions, but either those have been short-lived or their impact has been limited.[51] It was reported that prior to finalizing its position against a sanctions-based approach, the Kremlin launched an urgent interagency study whose basic aim was to assess the possible negative impact of such sanctions on Russia's prospects of receiving credits and loans from international financial institutions. The conclusions of the study emboldened Russia and allowed it to decide not to join the call for sanctions.

A few months after the tests, the United States, as the spearhead of multilateral non-proliferation efforts, is engaged in an intensive dialogue with India. Following the eighth round of talks in January 1999, the two sides claimed to have covered substantial ground, and are currently engaged in "harmonizing their perspectives"[52] relating to what have been described as the five "benchmarks" in this process. These Include:

1. immediate and unconditioned signature in the CTBT;

2. participate in good faith negotiations in the proposed FMCT, and a fiss-ban in the interim;

3. halt all nuclear tests, and deployment of nuclear-capable aircraft and missiles;

4. strengthen national controls on WMD-related exports; and

5. continue dialogue with Pakistan to reduce tension through enhanced CBMs.

Russian response to the nuclear tests has operated at two levels—one for external consumption, and another for the domestic audience. Addressing the former, the Foreign Ministry dubbed the tests as unacceptable, adding that India's action had caused Russia "exceptional anxiety and concern." [53] It endorsed the approved documents issued by the G-8 and joined in strongly worded condemnations emanating from the UN Security Council and NATO.

At the domestic level, on the other hand, Russian reaction was far more muted—almost serene in contrast to the sharp criticisms issued elsewhere in the world. There was, of course, a sense of déjà vu in this reaction: In 1996, when India refused to sign the Comprehensive Test Ban Treaty (CTBT), Russian officials expressed disappointment but immediately clarified that India's refusal would not jeopardize bilateral cooperation. A high-ranking MINATOM official stressed that despite the Indian decision, the two countries would continue negotiations for construction of the nuclear power plant and several smaller projects.

Following the nuclear tests, the minister of atomic energy, Evgenii Adamov, visited India in June 1998. In a gesture of considerable symbolic significance, Prime

Minister Vajpayee received Adamov as the first member of the Russian govenment
to pay an official visit since the tests, and his visit led to the signing of an agreement
on the Kudankulam project, with facilities-specific safeguards by the International
Atomic Energy Agency (IAEA).

This business-as-usual attitude also manifested itself in the realm of MTC. In
mid-June 1998 Ajit Kumar, minister of state for defense, came to Moscow for a
series of meetings with his Russian counterpart. In addition to discussing future contracts, he also reviewed the status of existing ones, and visited a number of production facilities involved in joint weapons design and manufacturing.

It appears certain that Russian involvement in the Indian defense sector will intensify if the US does not revoke the sanctions that have frozen its defense cooperation
with India. A notable example relates to the Indian light combat aircraft (LCA) program.[54] Although the DRDO has built Kaveri engines for the LCA, it has so far used
the F-404 engines supplied by the US company General Electric on four of its prototypes. Further, under the auspices of the Joint Technology Group (a collaborative
undertaking between the United States and India), the onboard mission computers
and other components have been integrated into (and flown aboard) the F-16 to evaluate their flight performance and ascertain other technical parameters.[55] Similarly, the
Lockheed Martin Corporation has been contracted to assist in flight control and developing the fly-by-wire systems, as well as the aircraft's training programs. The current
sanctions have frozen all US cooperation with India on defense-related matters and
could seriously impair the potential for future collaboration. Indeed, given the priority
of the program, the DRDO is reported to have approached Russia's MiG-MAPO to
assist in, among other things, the avionics component of the LCA program.[56]

India's cooperative relationship with Israel also seems to have been seriously
jeopardized following allegations of the latter's clandestine involvement in the
Indian nuclear weapons program. As a result, several projects under their bilateral
MTC have been frozen, including the setting up of the Israeli-Indian Forum for
Strategic Consultations, which the two sides had agreed would serve as the basis for
coordinating future joint projects.[57] It seems probable, therefore, that an unintended consequence of the sanctions against India might be to push it into a closer
embrace with Russia.

Although Russian reaction to Indian nuclear tests has been muted, it would be
false to surmise that Russian interest in preventing nuclear proliferation is only marginal. Particularly after the Pakistani tests, the Russian security elite has been seized
with the need to reassess its regional threat scenario. Russia's southern flank, comprising the former Soviet republics of Central Asia, is particularly vulnerable. The
newly appointed chairman of the Duma Defense Committee, Roman Popkovich,
identified his top priority as assessing the imminence of Indian and Pakistani
deployment of missile-deliverable nuclear weapons. The key concern for Russia,
according to Popkovich, is to ensure Russia's security in its south and southeast.[58]
Another major worry is whether the South Asian tests might precipitate a "domino

effect" on the Korean peninsula or—although this is very unlikely—provoke Japan to reconsider its nuclear-weapons option.

An important lesson for Russia is that as its economic position worsens (most estimates place Russian GNP at the bottom of the world's twenty largest economies), its foreign-policy ambitions have to be pruned proportionately. This translates into a lack of Russian activism in the non-proliferation arena as well.

## RUSSIA AS A FACTOR IN INDO-US STRATEGIC INTERACTION

Notwithstanding its considerable interests in India, Russia occupies important common ground with the United States on the issues of nuclear non-proliferation. Thus, Foreign Minister Primakov's appeal to India following its nuclear tests included a suggestion that the countries explore steps to toward encouraging India to sign the NPT and the CTBT, and toward resolving the outstanding dispute relating to Kashmir. Coordination of US and Russian policy would be an important step in the matter. For instance, greater commitment and movement along the disarmament axis by both Russia and the United States would meet an important Indian demand before it accedes to the NPT.

Given the commonality of Russian-American interests, and the powerful leverage that Russia has in New Delhi, the United States may be better off enlisting limited Russian involvement in this endeavor. Moreover, any arms control arrangements to be introduced would require full cooperation by Russia, in its capacity as both a major weapons supplier and also as a trusted verification actor. With the United States and Russia enjoying some political trust from Pakistan and India, respectively, it might make sense to collaborate in devising future verification arrangements.

Further, Russia's strategic partnership with China gives it certain leverage in persuading the latter to get involved in the search for a lasting solution to the South Asian crisis. Beijing's special relationship with Islamabad, and Moscow's with New Delhi, provide them some maneuvering space to seek a diplomatic resolution to the crisis, with Washington playing the role of an overall coordinator in the matter.

This line of reasoning, however, will have to contend with two important factors. One is that New Delhi has consistently opposed any third-party mediation in resolving Indo-Pak disputes which it insists should be resolved bilaterally according to the terms of the 1972 Shimla Accord. Second, before embarking on his June 1998 trip to China, President Clinton made a public exhortation for China to enhance its role in solving the South Asian crisis, an appeal that he reiterated in a joint statement with President Jiang Zemin in Beijing.[59]

It is evident, however, that the US policy toward China does not enjoy bipartisan support at home. The conservatives within the US Congress are taking the administration to task on its "misconceived" policy relating to the sale of missile technology to China, safety at Chinese space launch facilities (from where some US satellites are being put into orbit), and the China's clandestine support to the missile and nuclear weapons programs of Pakistan and Iran, among other issues. For India, China has always been the link between vertical and horizontal proliferation of nuclear weapons and missiles, and components and technologies thereof. Thus, it views China as part of the problem and not as part of the solution.

Given the above, there are distinct limits to the troubleshooting role Beijing can play in the South Asian crisis. However, any meaningful and enduring solution of the South Asian security dilemma *must* bind Chinese behavior to it. In a larger sense, then, Moscow and Washington can provide their good offices in pursuing an institutional and diplomatic framework within which an integrated solution to the enduring problems in South Asia can be found.

As things stand now, there are also limits on the extent to which Russia will cooperate with the United States in pursuing non-proliferation objectives in southern Asia (a region that is defined as including China). It may be recalled that when India refused to sign the CTBT, the US brought considerable diplomatic pressure to bear upon it. Even at that time, Russia insisted on maintaining close cooperation with the Indian nuclear sector. This cooperation recently took a big step forward with the formal agreement that provides for Russia to construct the two nuclear power plants at Kudankulam. The US State Department characterizes the deal as "inconsistent" with Russia's commitments as a party to the Nuclear Suppliers Group, and that the deal "undercuts the good work" stemming from the resolutions of the UN Security Council and the G-8.[60]

In addition, Russian reaction to possible US overtures and specific actions concerning its India-related policies would be determined not only by national security considerations—provided they are adequately defined and enunciated—but by at least two additional factors. One relates to the inordinate dependence of Russian defense production facilities on exports to India. Currently, India accounts for between 30 and 40 percent of Russia's arms exports. Sustaining, and even increasing, the Indian share is currently the only viable way to prevent the national defense production base from collapsing. In that respect, Russia now suffers from what may be characterized as a supplier's dependency syndrome.

It is not clear whether Indian security planners are aware of their unique *monopsony* position and the leverage that they can exercise because of it.[61] It is nevertheless expected that the larger congruence in bilateral geopolitical and strategic outlooks will constrain any Indian proclivity to use this leverage to disproportionately benefit itself. For the time being, India's advantage manifests itself in Russia's making available to it almost an entire range of advanced weapon systems. This was underscored by the statement of Indian defense minister Mulayam Singh Yadav in October 1997: "It is up to us to decide and take from Russia whatever we want. Russia has agreed to provide new, modern and advanced, technology to India in all areas of the defense field." [62]

Another important point in gauging Russia's potential response is that its domestic decision-making process is heavily influenced by major interest groups. It is the relative weight of an influential (and interested) group, rather than an ideal case of interinstitutional information sharing, that will determine the response. According to former prime minister Yegor Gaidar, the government is organized as a representative office of interest groups: the military-industrial complex, the fuel and energy complex, the agroindustrial complex, and other lobbies. Arranged thus, "the government would not do anything that could drastically go against the interests of these lobbies." [63] As a result, one may easily predict Russia's official reaction if the arms export lobby and the nuclear industry lobby combine their efforts in the face of potential threats to their interests in India.

Given the lengthy record of cooperation between India and the Soviet Union/Russia in the defense sphere, a drastic reorientation of India's armed forces toward US and Western suppliers seems highly improbable. Even with the increased budgetary allocations for the year 1998–99 and beyond, India would require far more resources to procure expensive armory from the West. Of course, following the imposition of sanctions, many of these possibilities might not even exist for a long time. In the meantime, it might be instructive to recall the decisions of the Czech Republic, Hungary, and Poland—the three prospective NATO members—to turn westward in search of massive weapons modernization. Their experience provides a good indication of how expensive and painful such rapid reorientation efforts can be.

Prior to the sanctions, the United States had acquired some niches in India's weapons market and could have expanded them, particularly in the areas of simulation and training, where Russian technologies are woefully lagging. However, overarching geopolitical considerations would continue to constrain the United States from enhancing its defense cooperation with India. Thus the quantity and caliber of US weapons and technologies to be transferred to India will be constrained by the strategic imperative to preserve the delicate balance with Pakistan and China.

For its part, India can be expected to take steps to diversify its supplier base by deepening and widening its relationship with the United States. But it will be loath to do so at the expense of antagonizing Russia. After all, Russia's assistance to India is primarily focused on the supply of sophisticated weapons, support for its space programs, and the development of its national nuclear industry—generally recognized as the three indispensable trappings of a great power. The United States is not expected to displace Russia from this pivotal role. A new US policy toward India, if it was to materialize, would have better prospects for success if it is pursued at least partially in conjunction with Russia, and certainly not with the manifest intent to undercut Russia in the process.

## APPENDIX

| Role of India | Soviet Era (1947–91) | Russia (1991–present) |
|---|---|---|
| Counteracting China | High | Diminished; more discreet (owing to thaw in Sino-Russian relations) |
| Foreign-policy tool in the global standoff with the United States | High (in maintaining bipolar balance of power: India's leadership of NAM created synergies in outlooks and strategies) | Changed; aid in creating multipolar international system, thereby also challenging US-centered unipolar international system |
| Stabilizing role vis-à-vis Afghanistan (1979–89) | High | Neutralized or minimized |
| Crucial destination for weapons exports | High | Increased; emerging as partner in weapons pro duction and exports |
| Trade and economic cooperation | High | Diminished greatly (Russian economic ills; high outstanding Indian debt, little incentive to diversify exports) |
| Stabilizing factor in Central Asia | Nonexistent to low | High |
| Source of advanced technology | Nonexistent to low | High, and growing |

## NOTES

1   This refers to the policy switch of Anwar Sadat, president of Egypt (1969–80). His court-ing of the United States led to a rapid and marked deterioration in Egypt's bilateral rela-tions with the Soviet Union. Earlier, during the long stay at the helm by Gamal Abdel Nasser (1954–69), Egypt had cultivated a strong diplomatic and military relationship with the Soviet Union that had stood the test of time (e.g., following Egypt's nationaliza-tion of the Aswan High Dam, resulting in the Suez Crisis, and the full-blown conven-tional conflicts with Israel in 1956 and 1973).

2   Ian Anthony, ed., *Russia and the Arms Trade* (Oxford: Oxford University Press/SIPRI, 1998), pp. 82–83.

3   Ibid.

4   The dollar–ruble exchange rate has dropped from 1:6 in early August 1998 to over 1:20 by early 1999.

5   For FY 1998, India's total defense outlay was approximately $10 billion; the budget for the period 1997–2002 is estimated at approximately 2 trillion rupees ($51 billion). For details, see Vivek Raghuvanshi, *Defense News,* February 23–March 1, 1998, p. 20. Following the nuclear tests of May 1998, India's finance minister announced higher bud-getary allocations for the Department of Atomic Energy (60 percent), the Indian Space Research Organization (52 percent), and the Department of Defense Research and Development (48 percent). This trend has continued with the new defense budget announced on February 27, which increases overall defense outlay by about 11 percent. "About 11p.c. Hike in Defense Budget," *Hindustan Times,* February 27, 1999.

6  For details, see Nehru, *Discovery of India* (New York: John Day Company, 1946), and his other writings.

7  *Five-Year Plans*, Ministry of Finance, Government of India (various editions).

8  *World Penn Tables*, 1996. Quoted in Ashley J. Tellis, *Stability in South Asia* (Santa Monica, CA: RAND, 1997), p. 37–38. For details on this topic, including World Bank and IMF estimates, see Charles Wolf Jr., Long-Term Economic and Military Trends, 1994–2015 (Santa Monica, CA: RAND, 1995).

9  "National Interests and Security Problems," report by the Center for Global Problems of the Gorbachev Foundation, Moscow, 1997, p. 93.

10  Interview with Evgeni Primakov, "Our Foreign Policy Cannot Be the One of a Secondary State," *Rossiiskaya Gazeta,* December 17, 1996.

11  Dmitri Gornostayev, "Russian Foreign Minister Formulates Russia's New Strategic Objectives in the International Arena," *Nezavisimaya Gazeta,* March 17, 1998.

12  Aleksei Pushkov, "For Russia It Would Be Best to Maintain Balance Between Major Countries of Power," *Mezhdunarodnaya Zhizn,* no.3 (1998).

13  The National Security Council of the Russian Federation rates India's importance to Russia on par with that of the United States and China. Presidential Decree 1300 (dated December 17, 1997), reported in *Rossiiskeije Vesti,* December 25, 1997.

14  K. K. Katyal, "India, Russia to Enter Strategic Partnership," *The Hindu,* March 25, 1997.

15  Sergei Kiriyenko was appointed prime minister in April 1998 but was replaced in September 1998 by Evgeni Primakov.

16  ITAR-TASS, April 28, 1998.

17  Russian defense minister Igor Sergeev made a statement to this effect following a meeting with his Indian counterpart, Mulayam Singh Yadav, in Moscow in October 1997. ITAR-TASS, October 6, 1997.

18  It is interesting to note that in response to the shipment of Ukrainian tanks to Pakistan the Indian government became interested in acquiring a new generation of Russian-manufactured tanks and other military hardware to counter the new threat.

19  Vyacheslav Vashanov and Gennady Mikhalev, "National Resources Still Serve as a Basis for Integration," *Finansovyie Izvestiya,* January 29, 1998.

20  Swaran Singh, "China, Russia Join Hands," *Defense News,* March 10–16, 1997, p. 40.

21  Eric Arnett, "What Threat?" *The Bulletin of the Atomic Scientists,* March/April 1997, p. 53.

22  *RIA-Novosty Hot Line,* October 24, 1997.

23  "Evolution of the Military Security Structure: Russia's Role and Place," report of the Institute of National Security and Strategic Studies, Moscow, 1997.

24  Konstantin Makienko, "Prospects for Russia's Presence in South Asia's Markets for Weapons and Military Hardware," *Yaderny Kontrol,* March-April 1998, p. 67.

25  Interview with Sergei Prikhodko, "We Are Changing Slogans for Rubles," *Moscovskie Novosti,* February 8–15, 1998, p. 11.

26  Christian Caryl, "Who Makes Russia's Foreign Policy Anyway?" *US News and World Report,* February 16, 1998.

27  Interfax, May 31, 1996.

28  Vladimir Sergeev, "Asian Armies Provide Jobs to Russia's Military and Industrial Complex," *Segodnya,* October 26, 1995.

29  Interview with Evgeni Fedosov, director of the Research Institute of Aviation Systems, "Self-Imposed Isolation of Russian Scientists is More Dangerous than a Leakage of Secret Technologies," *Nedelya,* February 16–22, 1998, p. 7.

30  Sergei Putilov, "Choice of Favor for Russia," *Nezavisimoye Voennoye Obozrenie,* January 23–29, 1998, p. 3.

31   B. K. Bishnoi, "Airpower and Changing Security Perspectives in South Asia," *Indian Defense Review,* July-September 1997, p. 53.

32   Simon Saradzhyan, "Indian Negotiation for Russian Carrier Nears Completion," *Defense News,* June 8–15, 1998, p. 50.

33   Negotiations are in the final stages before actual signing on the deal. See, for instance, "India Plans to Acquire Russian S-300 System; Pair Renew Trade Pact," *Defense News,* June 29–July 5, 1998, p. 30.

34   "India Signs Missile Deal With Russia," *Indian Express,* June 20, 1998.

35   Interfax report, reproduced by *Segodnya* on June 24, 1998.

36   This wide interpretation of Russia's vision of military-technical cooperation is outlined in Anatoly Andreyev, "Military Aspects of Military-Technical Cooperation," *The Military Parade,* September-October 1997.

37   According to a public opinion poll, India elicited the least negative responses as an external threat by the Russian respondents (4.8 percent), followed by Japan (9.2 percent), China (21.1 percent), Israel (20.4 percent) and Iraq (34.7 percent). Source: "Mass Consciousness of Russians During Their Social Transformation," report by the Russian Independent Institute of Social and National Problems, Moscow, January 1996.

38   T. S. Vishwanath, "Double Devaluation Not To Affect Indo-Russian Trade," *The Economic Times,* August 19, 1998.

39   Reuters, December 18, 1997.

40   Andrei Tamilin, "Russia Loses Billions in India," *Nezavisimaya Gazeta,* February 19, 1998.

41   Igor Alexandrov, "Russia and India Steer Toward Long-Term Trade and Economic Cooperation," *Delovoi Mir,* December 17, 1997.

42   Press briefing by the minister of atomic energy, Evgeni Adamov (Ministry of Atomic Energy, June 24, 1998), Federal News Service transcript, June 25, 1998.

43   On September 23, 1998, the first of the seven cryogenic engines was delivered to ISRO. See "India Seeks Changes in SU-30" (PTI report) *Indian Express,* September 24, 1998. The cryo engines are to be used aboard the Indian GSLV. See, for instance, "GSLV's First Developmental Flight Likely by Year-end," *Deccan Chronicle,* April 1, 1998.

44   K. S. Jayaraman, "Indian Budget Increase to Benefit GSLV, Insat," *Space News,* March 15, 1999, p. 9.

45   K. S. Jayaraman, "India Increases Space Funding by 52 Percent," *Space News,* June 8–14, 1998.

46   "Russia Helps India Build Nuclear Submarine," as reported by *Krasnaya Zvezda,* Russia's Defense Ministry daily. Until very recently, this part of the Indo-Russian collaboration was a tightly guarded secret. Roughly translated from Sanskrit, Sagarika means "ocean's daughter."

47   The cooperation relating to the launch of the SLBM has been reported variously; for instance, *New York Times,* April 26, 1998. This was "partially confirmed" during interviews with one top-ranking Russia diplomat and one senior Indian scientist (names withheld upon request).

48   Aleksei Tamilin, "India's Computer Leap," *Nezavismaya Gazeta,* April 29, 1998.

49   *The Hindu,* October 13, 1997.

50   ITAR-TASS, December 23, 1997.

51   Barely two months after their introduction, President Clinton backed legislation ending restrictions on most agricultural products and fertilizers. The World Bank resumed aid to India with US support, and so did the Asian Development Bank. Japan did not even suspend its loans earmarked for India's infrastructure projects.

52   This was confirmed by Strobe Talbott, US Deputy Secretary of State, in a speech at the

Brookings Institute, February 1999. This was echoed by Jaswat Singh, the foreign minister of India and official spokesperson for the prime minister. See"Let's Not Take a Worms Eye View," interview with Raj Chengappa, *India Today*, February 1999, p. 11.

53   ITAR-TASS, May 12 and 13, 1998.

54   The LCA program was undertaken by the DRDO in 1984. This ambitious multirole aircraft, with fly-by-wire controls, is envisaged to perform a role similar to the F-16 aircraft. It has encountered several cost and time overruns, and is now anticipated to undergo full flight testing not earlier than in the year 2000.

55   Interview of Anupam Srivastava with the director, Aeronautical Development Establishment (wing of DRDO), and other scientists working on the program, Bangalore, December 1997.

56   Vivek Raghuvanshi, "US Sanctions to Hinder Indian Light Combat Fighter," *Defense News,* June 1–7, 1998, p. 64.

57   Aleksandr Shumilin, "Israel Did Not Develop an Atomic Bomb for India," *Kommersant Daily,* June 9, 1998.

58   Vladimir Mikheev, "Islamabad Did Not Listen to Arguments," *Izvestia,* May 30, 1998.

59   Anupam Srivastava, "Do India and China Need A 'Bear' Hug?" *The Hindu,* July 11, 1998.

60   According to Reuters, June 23, 1998.

61   Drawn from the lecture "India and the Contemporary South Asian Geopolitics," by Professor P. R. Chari (former additional secretary, Ministry of Defense, Government of India, and current codirector, Institute of Peace and Conflict Studies, New Delhi), at the University of Georgia, September 1997.

63   AFP, October 13, 1997.

63   Interview with Yegor Gaidar on the current economic situation in Russia, *Argumenty I Facty,* no. 15 (1997), p. 3.

# 13

## Conclusion: Summarizing the Next Steps

### Gary Bertsch, Seema Gahlaut, and Anupam Srivastava

The twentieth century bears the indelible imprints of two bloody world wars, a ruinous global depression, and a long Cold War. The world witnessed a technological revolution, but sadly it gave humans the capacity to annihilate this planet several times over with the use of weapons of mass destruction (WMD). Now, with the Cold War over but the architecture of the "brave new world" still at an inchoate stage, it is natural to look to the future with a sense of both trepidation and wonderment.

The experience of stemming and reversing the proliferation of WMD and their means of delivery has underlined the importance of international cooperation. On an issue so vexed as this, it is well nigh impossible for any one country to coerce others into making this a success. It is equally impractical to expect voluntary compliance on this salient matter without taking note of some of the elements that determine national behavior and responses.

One of the biggest impediments toward total elimination of WMD is their perceived operational-military value, as well as the selectivity in the application of rules enshrined within international non-proliferation regimes. It bears to recall the old truism that "what is sauce for the goose is sauce for the gander." It implies that so long as one set of countries perceive WMD as central to their defense, it is naive to believe that other countries might not perceive similar value to these weapons. The issue gets more complicated because of the element of pride that gets associated with the pursuit and acquisition of such a lethal arsenal. Since development of these weapons involves theoretical and practical knowledge of advanced mathematics, particle physics, and spatial stereo isochemistry, among other things, their possession signals a country's technological prowess.

Nuclear scientists submit that technology has grown to a point where WMD technologies are no longer regarded as among the most advanced in the world. Nevertheless, given their enormous value as instruments of deterrence, aspiring countries are loath to sidestep this path. A related problem that arises is more technologically deterministic in nature. A large and growing corpus of technology that is applied in weapons research and development also has peaceful applications. These dual-use technologies are much harder to control because attempts to do so often encounter the familiar argument that technology controls are applied by select countries to impede legitimate technological and industrial advancement of the rest of the world. Further, any technology embargoes and controls that can be applied run up against a newer challenge: the growing fungibility of technology. As technology develops, it becomes fungible across sectors, making it increasingly difficult to impose controls over its actual use or users.

Innovative advancements in information technology have dramatically altered the conduct of international trade and commerce. State sovereignty over national physical and human resources has diminished dramatically in the process, making the world more interdependent than ever before. In such a situation, the need for consensus, cooperation, and collective action becomes paramount.

It is in this analytical context that this book has examined the evolving parameters of Indo-US strategic interaction. We believe that in the coming decades, as India plays an increasingly important role in regional and global affairs, it is vital for the United States to elevate the position of India on its strategic radar and accord it higher policy priority. While their areas of mutual convergence are many, cooperation thus far has been suboptimal. And unless corrective action is taken duly and promptly, the missed opportunities might not only adversely affect their bilateral relationship but also have far wider consequences.

As such, the contemporary security dialogue between India and the United States should approach their bilateral problems in a larger perspective. It is said that enduring problems cannot be solved within existing boundaries. One should either enlarge the ambit of analysis or disaggregate the problem into its constituent units. In the case of Indo-US dialogue, there is a pressing need to explore the wider framework of their respective strategic outlooks and priorities. Having identified the areas of convergence and conflict, the countries should then set out to devise practical modalities to build upon the areas of convergence as well as to narrow the difference of opinion on the conflictual issues. In the subsequent sections we provide a summary of the central arguments presented in the book.

## PRAGMATISM ON WMD ISSUES

The issue of nuclear non-proliferation remains one of the more divisive issues between the world's largest democracies. Matters came to a head in May 1998 when India conducted five subterranean nuclear explosions, ending a self-imposed moratorium on further testing following its lone "peaceful nuclear explosion" of May 1974. Washington was quick to denounce the tests and imposed a range of sanctions. Soon after, a more deliberative stage of bilateral diplomacy was adopted to reflect upon the future course of action. Policy makers and analysts are optimistic about the outcome of these negotiations, particularly in the long run.

A distinctive element of these recent negotiations is that they are not only removed from the glare of international media—this has often hardened national negotiating postures in the past—but also imbued with a very pragmatic, problem-solving, forward-looking approach. Much of this devolves from a recent Indian foreign-policy shift that emphasizes explicit enunciation of its threat assessments and resultant national proclivities and priorities. This pragmatism in Indian foreign and defense policies is a natural outgrowth of the recent approach to integrate the domestic economy into the global economic matrix. The result has been that practical issues are vying with larger issues of morality for autonomous space on the national agenda.

This is a natural progression for an ancient civilization that barely fifty years ago emerged from centuries of colonization, and is now seeking to find its rightful place in the community of nations. The new generation of Indians is more concerned about completing the second stage of nation building, what Samir Amin referred to as the process of "national consolidation." This stage requires allocation of national resources and values toward an optimal utilization of national capabilities and potential. While moral considerations would continue to undergird the conduct of its nuclear policy, practical considerations are also not to be lost sight of. Thus, after the recent round of nuclear tests, the domestic leadership is engaged in generating a national consensus on signing the CTBT and participating in good-faith negotiations for the expeditious conclusion of the FMCT. The defining element in the domestic dialogue appears to be that India can play a much more constructive role in shaping international non-proliferation regimes by joining them rather than by remaining an increasingly marginalized voice of dissent. And if participation in regimes can facilitate access to much-needed technology to meet developmental imperatives, such as in the civilian nuclear energy sector, then an overly moralistic and exclusivist approach should be tempered with a more pragmatic outlook.

This new sense of pragmatism has informed the Indian approach toward elimination of chemical and biological weapons. While India has long abjured the use of biological weapons, it voluntarily signed and ratified the recent treaty relating to elimination of chemical weapons. At the OPCW, it disclosed its CW stockpile and is now engaged in the time-bound elimination of its existing stockpile. Since this treaty is non-discriminatory, and all signatories undertake uniform obligations relating to disclosure, elimination, and verification, analysts point out that Indian compliance with international non-proliferation regimes would be greatly facilitated if similarly uniform obligations would bind members' conduct in the nuclear weapons sphere as well.

## PRAGMATISM ON DELIVERY SYSTEMS AND
## CONVENTIONAL WEAPONS

On the issue of means of delivery of WMD, the Indian position is becoming clearer. If certain countries perceive WMD and their means of delivery as vital to meet threats to their national security, then similar options should be available to other states. To be sure, there is a great degree of synergy between civilian and offensive application of space technology. India, which has received civilian space collaboration from advanced countries of the world, has also to an indeterminate extent adapted this knowledge to further its offensive capabilities. But the crucial point is that such a synergy is not India-specific, nor is it feasible to control effectively this diffusion given the increasingly ubiquitous nature of dual-use technology. Effective control over offensive use of such capability can result only from a consensual approach that abjures its indiscriminate usage or threat thereof.

Moving beyond the WMD domain, the issue of advanced conventional weapons (ACWs) also represents an area of growing convergence between India and the United States. The lethality and the "immorality" associated with WMD render their operational usage in a situation of war fraught with numerous dangers. Although tactical WMDs of low yields have been devised, no tactical nuclear weapons have actually been used after the two atomic bombs that were dropped on the Japanese cities of Hiroshima and Nagasaki. The resultant carnage and revulsion still dog international security debates.

As such, from a purely operational-military standpoint, ACWs acquire particular potency. With the technological advances of the recent decades ushering in a revolution in military affairs (RMA), these weapons can be used to devastating effect, inflicting severe material as well as psychological damage to the enemy. This was amply demonstrated via Operation Desert Storm during the Persian Gulf crisis. Using navigational aid from satellites and high-altitude reconnaissance aircraft, the US-led multilateral offensive was able to pinpoint enemy counterforce and countervalue targets. "Smart bombs" and "surgical strikes" were then employed to overwhelm and subdue without causing unintended damage to the enemy or substantial collateral damage in the process.

By all available estimates, the role of ACWs and "psych ops" (psychological operations) are likely to grow as currencies of modern warfare. Such arsenal provides a deterrence value as well, in addition to calibrating the level of conflict and resultant damage. The Indian security leadership has taken due note of these modern trends, and domestic defense planning reflects this thinking. The Indian defense establishment has been engaged in a perspective planning process to take stock of the regional force balance and implications of the RMA for the regional theater of war. As its indigenous defense industry strives to build modern capacity to deal with the evolving challenges, cooperation with the United States becomes extremely valuable.

Indo-US cooperation in ACWs had been initiated in the 1980s and had become more institutionalized in the 1990s. The nuclear tests have suspended that process for now, but an amicable settlement of the WMD debate is likely to pave the way for resumption of that cooperation. As mentioned earlier, ACWs can bolster offensive as well as defensive capabilities of a country. Given the volatility of South Asia and its strategic periphery (Central/western Asia, Caucasus, Southeast Asia, and the Asia-Pacific region), greater Indo-US cooperation and coordination can serve to bolster the fragile balance in the region.

## PROACTIVE CONCEPTION OF THE FUTURE OF ASIA

Indo-US strategic dialogue should include sensitivity to changes in the Asian balance of power. The evolving contours of Chinese foreign policy indicate its unwavering commitment to enhance its presence in regional and global affairs. As China's economic stake in the region grows, it will augment its capacity to safeguard those interests by all means possible. The international security community remains divided on how to interpret current Chinese behavior. A benign projection of Chinese foreign policy is certainly in evidence. At the same time, elements within the Chinese strategic culture suggest that assertiveness could return once China finds the international balance of power to have shifted in its favor. As such, US (and international) efforts should be geared toward increasingly making China a stakeholder in the stability of the international system. Coterminously, however, such a strategy should involve building counterweights to insure against a possible downturn in its relations with China.

India's relations with China have improved significantly since the border conflict of 1962. However, as both the Asian powers expand their foreign and economic policy agenda, their interests can coincide as well as conflict. While both are currently engaged in the process of domestic consolidation, it is quite likely that they will seek to upgrade their deterrent relationship in the medium term. It would be of considerable strategic interest to the United States to deepen and widen its relationship with both these countries, and not necessarily in a mutually exclusive manner. Indeed, a qualitatively superior US engagement with both China and India could substantially bolster the regional security environment.

During the current decade, Russia's relations with India have gone from being a mere replacement of the old Soviet-type engagement to being a strategic entente in its own rights. This new relationship consolidates many aspects of the Soviet-era defense cooperation but has developed into a larger recognition of common strategic interests and priorities. However, in light of the diminished and still-declining Russian economic capabilities, and its altered politico-strategic presence in the post-Soviet space, Russia has considerably expanded its bilateral relationship with China.

For Russia to pursue its larger strategic objectives within the emerging Asian balance of power, improving relations with China has become an ineluctable priority. As such, the Russian elite prefers that cooperation with India and cooperation with

China do not become mutually exclusive options. Indeed, improved relations with both could possibly generate an Asian strategic alignment that could act to neutralize a disproportionate US influence in the region. As such, it would be wary of any significant tilt of either of these countries toward the United States, to the exclusion of Russia. This crucial reality needs to be incorporated in devising any long-term prospects for Indo-US cooperation.

Russia's preference for consolidating a regional entente where its interests intersect with those of China and India received a jolt with the Indian nuclear tests of May 1998. That Pakistan elected to follow suit with tests of its own further complicated matters. Russia and India recognize China's interest in propping Pakistan as a counterweight to India in South Asia. This would keep India "pinned down " south of the Himalayas and prevent it from enhancing its profile in the larger Asian affairs.

In this context, Moscow and New Delhi hope that Beijing would be persuaded to eschew this option in favor of larger anticipated gains from creating a strategic entente with them. In this scenario, Pakistan could fortify its defenses against India, but China would not use Pakistan to confine India's presence to South Asia. All empirical evidence suggests that India is keen to assert its presence on the larger Asian stage. China's attempts to foil this trajectory would only complicate its relations with India, not to mention causing problems for Russia.

The political stability and economic viability of Pakistan remains crucial to regional stability. The specter of Pakistan as a "failed state" creates a disturbing vision for not only India but also the larger region. A balkanized Pakistan may become a vortex of religious irredentism that would fuel Islamic fundamentalism in the already delicate regions of Central, western, and South Asia

A larger point bears mention here. On most yardsticks of measurement, India is a bigger and stronger country than Pakistan. Stoking the fires of Indo-Pak rivalry not only perpetuates an uneasy tension in South Asia but also diverts attention from a persistent problem faced by Pakistan. Fifty years after gaining independence, it is still locked in a perpetual conflict with India, underlining its belief in a "two-nation theory" that makes their peaceful coexistence inherently untenable. What would ultimately benefit Pakistan, in addition to robust economic growth, is nurturing a new identity for itself. Its anti-Indian and pro-Islamic identities have limited payoffs. Its leadership would be eminently better off by charting a pro-Pakistani identity, a notion that incorporates its Islamic moorings with the immutable geographical reality of being a South Asian state.

The issue of Kashmir is also germane to this discussion. Setting aside competing perspectives on the veracity of Pakistani claims to Kashmir, the objective reality is that India and Pakistan have to coexist as South Asian neighbors. While resolution of the Kashmir dispute remains an important element in Indo-Pak dialogue, that issue should not be allowed to eclipse exploration of other areas of convergence. In other words, given the relative nonnegotiability of each side on this emotional issue, an exclusive focus on Kashmir would condemn their relationship to the same fossilized mind-set that the nuclear non-proliferation issue has done to the Indo-US dialogue.

Despite the recent economic turmoil, the Asia-Pacific region will remain the locus of economic development in the coming decades. This makes it imperative for the United States to maintain and enhance its strategic relevance in the region. A dialogue with the major Asian powers, which at a minimum should involve Russia, Japan, China, and India, is an absolute necessity for the United States.

## CONVERGING ECONOMIC AND POLITICAL VECTORS

There is some recognition in both India and the United States that their overall economic and political vectors are intersecting. So far, in many respects, the United States has adopted a wait-and-see approach about the success of the Indian economic program. On the Indian side, this has resulted in a growing sense of frustration. They would prefer that the United States be deeply involved in this process rather than an interested bystander. Such hands-on cooperation would also translate into greater understanding and trust, elements that could prove vital to deepening and widening their bilateral relationship.

In this context, greater participation by US business interests in the Indian economy would be mutually helpful. Already apparent is the active participation in economic and political debates in India of the Indian-American community and the growing community of scholars in nongovernmental organizations. These emergent trends augur well for the growth of a common epistemic community that can communicate and engage in dialogue on issues such as technology transfer, regional security, and strategic cooperation. The role of Track II in introducing newer issues into the bilateral agenda has grown over the past decade. Its ability to offer policy-relevant recommendations should be recognized and nurtured by both governments.

## SUSTAINED DIVERGENCE IN PERSPECTIVES ON TECHNOLOGY

Another issue of critical import in the bilateral dialogue relates to control versus sharing of technology. Through much of the Cold War period, the United States perceived technology controls as a tool to influence the foreign and domestic policies of other countries. Though such controls were adopted in a multilateral framework, the United States has nevertheless sought to make access to advanced technology contingent upon the recipient state adhering to certain international agreements. At the same time, it recognized that sovereignty and equality of nations in the international system were heady watchwords for the entire spectrum of post-colonial states. As such, the United States preferred to pursue its unilateral interests through the multilateral framework, thereby according legitimacy to its efforts. On the other hand, India sought unrestricted access to technology for its legitimate developmental needs. By holding the United States accountable to its declared ideals in the multilateral arena, India was able to carve a place for itself as the leader of the newly-independent states.

US-Indian interactions have been understood by both sides as tests of resolve, always linked to larger principles and clothed in morality, hence not subject to negotiation. Technology has been important to both: for the United States to maintain its leadership, and for India to assert its arrival into the major league. Each has attempted to shape the debate on technology around clashing principles. The debate has involved establishing which principle, access to technology or verification and monitoring over uses of technology, is crucial for the maintenance of international systems. India has held that technology, as a common global resource, should not be dominated (owned) and doled out by a few, to the extent that some sections of the global community are systematically excluded from using it. For the United States, not only is technology subject to ownership laws, but its dual-use (civilian and military) nature mandates that its diffusion be controlled responsibly, in the interests of the entire international community.

Many problems in the US and Indian perspectives are rooted in their varied understandings of ownership, control, and classification of technology. We submit that these differences permeate their relationship in the security sphere as well as in technology-related interactions. Whether we assign cultural, structural, or institutional reasons for these differences, recognition of such differences is crucial for the success of any international attempts at building a viable post–Cold War system.

## THE IMPACT OF UNCERTAINTIES

There is little likelihood that India would be a security threat to the United States. But the lack of trust about India's intentions will continue to govern US policy unless some dramatic changes in Indian behavior become apparent. For instance, what is the guarantee that India will not use its growing capabilities against US interests, much as it has done through most of the Cold War period? Given its hegemonic ambitions, will it attempt to match the United States? Or will it collaborate with China and Russia to challenge US hegemony in Asia? Similar agonizing is visible in contemporary Indian thinking. Will the United States concede hegemony over Asia to its newfound friend China? Will it maintain its preference for efficient economies with authoritarian systems over inefficient economies with democratic systems? Even if the United States accepted French and Chinese (and Israeli) nuclear capabilities reluctantly, it did so eventually. Would a similar acceptance be forthcoming for India and Pakistan?

The continuous emphasis on worst-case scenarios and apprehension for the future have hobbled the US-India relationship. This mode of thinking could be interminably justified in the United States but is presenting some acutely disturbing lessons for India. The most common conclusion that the majority of Indians draw from US-China interaction is that India should force the issue. It should develop its capability without US support, and present the latter with a fait accompli.

However, it is possible to draw a better, less ominous lesson from the same interaction. Rules of international conduct on issues of technology and multilateralism are being re-written at the end of the Cold War. All those states, including China and India, that had found the Cold War rules unbearable now have the chance to get involved in rule making. This time they can shape changes rather than just submit to them.

In sum, Indo-US relations are poised on the cusp of significant possibilities. A proactive approach to the ambit of their common interests, conceived in a holistic framework, could lead to dramatic gains for both sides. On the other hand, an insistence on a case-by-case approach, with suspicion serving as the dominant psychological backdrop, is liable to produce substantially suboptimal outcomes whose implications extend far beyond the pale of their bilateral relationship.

At the end of the Cold War, and on the threshold of a new millennium, the US leadership is actively seeking a new paradigm that would impart fresh momentum to global cooperation and suffuse international institutions with optimism generated by the spirit of collective enterprise. India, emerging from centuries of colonial oppression and decades of painful national consolidation and restructuring, is anxious to a play a larger role on the regional and global stage. It hopes that the international community will take cognizance of the wisdom that its ancient past has bequeathed its contemporary policy, as well as the lessons gained in the effort to nurture and sustain a vibrant democracy in the face of divisive pressures and economic hardships. It would be a pity indeed if the world's greatest democracy, in its quest for a new paradigm of collective enterprise, were to choose to marginalize the support and cooperation of the world's largest democracy. The two countries would still cobble together a working relationship, even if this sad trend were to continue. But as one peers into the mists of the new millennium, one wonders if the "brave new world" would not be a better place if these two countries decided to lend their weight behind the effort to create cooperatively a better world.

# Contributors

**Kanti Bajpai** is Associate Professor in the School of International Studies, Jawaharlal Nehru University, New Delhi. His most recent publications include *Brasstacks and Beyond: Perception and Management of Crisis in SouthAsia* (1995), *Securing India: Strategic Thought and Practice* (1996) and *Jammu and Kashmir: An Agenda for the Future* (forthcoming, 1999). He is currently writing a book on India's grand strategy.

**Gary K. Bertsch** is the University Professor of Political Science ("for highest recognition of significant impact on the University of Georgia") and Director of the Center for International Trade and Security. His research focuses on the domestic and international politics of weapons trade and proliferation. He has served as Chairman of the Education Committee of the American Association for the Advancement of Slavic Studies and a member of the National Research Council's Committee on Dual-Use Technologies, Export Controls, Materials Protection and Accounting, 1995-97. He has published numerous articles in journals such as the *Washington Quarterly* and *Pacific Review*. In addition, he has authored or edited approximately 20 books, including: *Arms on the Market: Reducing the Risk of Proliferation from the Former Soviet Union* (Routledge, 1998), *Dangerous Weapons, Desperate States* (Routledge, 1999), *Crossroads and Conflict: Security and Foreign Policy in the Caucasus and Central Asia* (Routledge, 1999), and *International Cooperation on Nonproliferation Export Controls* (1994).

**P.R. Chari** is the Co-Director of the Institute of Peace and Conflict Studies in New Delhi. He has served as the Director of the Institute for Defence Studies and Analyses, New Delhi (1975–80), an International Fellow, Center for International Affairs, Harvard University (1983–84), Additional Secretary in the Ministry of Defense in India (1985–88), and Research Professor, Center for Policy Research (1992–96). He has published extensively on nuclear disarmament, non-proliferation and Indian defense issues. His co-authored or co-edited books include: *Indo-Pak Nuclear Stand Off: Role of the United States* (1995), *Brasstacks and Beyond: Perception and Management Crisis* (1995), *Nuclear Nonproliferation in India and Pakistan: South Asian Perspectives* (1996), and *India: Towards Millennium* (1998).

**Richard T. Cupitt** is Associate Director for Research and Washington liaison for the Center. Currently, he co-directs the Asian nonproliferation export control initiatives of the Center. He is an editor of two books on nonproliferation and export controls, and has published dozens of articles and book chapters on export controls, nonproliferation, international trade, and international conflict. He serves on the editorial board of The Nonproliferation Review, has been a member of the US delegation to the 3rd and 5th Asian Export Control Seminars, and has been a consultant or reviewer on export control projects for Science Applications International

Cooperation, Lawrence Livermore National laboratory, the US Office of Technology Assessment, and the Rumsfeld Commission on the ballistic missile threat to the United States.

**Aabha Dixit** is an independent analyst, currently based in the Netherlands. She was formerly a Research Associate at the Institute for Defense Studies and Analyses, New Delhi, and has had Visiting Fellowships at the University of Western Australia and the University of Illinois at Urbana-Champagne. She has contributed more than 1,000 articles to newspapers and journals in India and elsewhere, on issues of South, South West, and Central Asia, as well as Indo-US relations.

**Seema Gahlaut** is the Associate Director of the South Asia Program and a Senior Research Associate at the Center for International Trade and Security. In addition, she is also an Instructor in the Department of Political Science. Dr. Gahlaut's research focuses on Indian export control policy, Indian nuclear energy scenarios, and Indo-US technology transfer issues. She has authored *Indian Export Control Policy: An Overview* (occasional paper, CITS, Athens, July 1998), and "Removing the (Cob-)webs of Technology Controls: Assessing India's Relations with Multilateral Export Control Regimes," in Amitabh Mattoo, ed., *Indian Nuclear Deterrent: Pokharan II and Beyond* (1999).

**Suzette R. Grillot** currently serves as Founder and President of IntaLab: The International Affairs Laboratory for Research and Education, which is based in Oklahoma City, and as Visiting Professor of Political Science at the University of Oklahoma. Her research and teaching interests focus on international security issues. She is also involved in facilitating international awareness and activism at the community level. Dr. Grillot has presented her research at many national and international conferences, and her collaborative research has appeared in journals such as the *British Journal of Political Science* and *Political Psychology*. She is also co-editor of and contributor to the book *Arms on the Market: Reducing the Threat of Proliferation in the Former Soviet Union* (Routledge, 1998).

**Virginia I. Foran** is currently an Instructor in Political Science at the University of Mississippi and a doctoral candidate at the University of Maryland, College Park. From 1996-97, she was a Research Associate at the International Institute for Strategic Studies, London, England; from 1992-1997 she was Assistant Director then Research Director of the Nuclear Non-Proliferation Project, at the Carnegie Endowment for International Peace. She has published a number of articles on arms control and South Asia, including: "The Case of Indo-US High-Technology Cooperation," *Survival* (1998), "The Application of Incentives to Nuclear Nonproliferation," with Leonard Spector, in David Cortright ed., *The Price of Peace: Incentives and International Conflict* (1997), and "After the Cold War: Prospects for Nuclear Arms Control in South Asia," in Marianne van Leeuwen ed., *The Future of the International Non-proliferation Regime* (1995).

**Amitabh Mattoo** is Associate Professor at the School of International Studies, Jawaharlal Nehru University. A D.Phil in International Relations from the University of Oxford, Dr. Mattoo has been a Visiting Professor at the Joan B. Kroc Institute of International Peace Studies, University of Notre Dame. His publications include *India's Nuclear Deterrent: Pokhran II and Beyond* (1998), *India and the Bomb: Public Opinion and Nuclear Options* (1996), and journal articles in *Survival* and *Asian Survey*. He is a Review Editor for the journal *International Studies* (Sage) and columnist for *The Telegraph* (Calcutta).

**C. Raja Mohan** is currently the Strategic Affairs Editor of *The Hindu*, the leading English language daily in India. Dr. Mohan has also served as the Washington correspondent of the Hindu, and as Senior Fellow at the Institute for Defense Studies and Analyses, New Delhi. He has been a Jennings Randolph Peace Fellow at the United States Institute of Peace (1992–93). He has published extensively on India's nuclear, security, and foreign policies, as well as arms control and disarmament issues.

**Jyotika Saksena** is a research associate at the Center for International Trade and Security. A doctoral candidate in the Department of Political Science, her work involves examining issues of multilateral export controls, India's nuclear policy and Indo-U.S. defense cooperation. Other research interests include international trade and technology transfer. Ms Saksena has co-authored the article, "Feasible Deals on Glenn Sanctions," in *Asian Survey* (Spring 1999).

**Anupam Srivastava** is the Director for South Asia Program and Senior Research Associate at the Center for International Trade and Security. In addition, he is an Instructor in the Department of Political Science at the University of Georgia. Dr. Srivastava's research interests include India's space and missile policies, Indo-Pakistani and Indo-Russian strategic relations, and the emerging force-balance in southern Asia. He has served as a Research Associate at the Sam Nunn School of International Affairs, Georgia Institute of Technology, Associate Member of the Asian Development Research Institute, and Assistant Editor (in-charge Book Review section) for the *Hindustan Times*. He has published widely in journals and newspapers, including *The Bulletin of Atomic Scientists*, *Comparative Strategy*, *World Affairs*, *Defense News*, *The Hindu*, and the *Hindustan Times*.

**Milind Thakar** is a Research Associate at the Center and a doctoral candidate in Political Science. He is specializing in international and comparative political and economic issues, Indo-Pak relations and democratization. Mr. Thakar has co-authored the article, "Feasible Deals on Glenn Sanctions" in *Asian Survey* (Spring 1999).

# Index